Ethics for OCR Religious Studies

Copyright © Mark Coffey and Dennis Brown 2015

The rights of Mark Coffey and Dennis Brown to be identified as Authors of this Work have been asserted in accordance with the UK Copyright, Designs and Patents Act 1988.

First published in 2015 by Polity Press

Polity Press
65 Bridge Street
Cambridge CB2 1UR, UK

Polity Press
350 Main Street
Malden, MA 02148, USA

ISBN-13: 978-0-7456-6325-8(hb)
ISBN-13: 978-0-7456-6326-5(pb)

A catalogue record for this book is available from the British Library.

Typeset in 9.5 on 13 pt Utopia Regular
by Servis Filmsetting Ltd, Stockport, Cheshire
Printed and bound in the UK by Clays Ltd, St Ives PLC

The publisher has used its best endeavours to ensure that the URLs for external websites referred to in this book are correct and active at the time of going to press. However, the publisher has no responsibility for the websites and can make no guarantee that a site will remain live or that the content is or will remain appropriate.

Every effort has been made to trace all copyright holders, but if any have been inadvertently overlooked the publisher will be pleased to include any necessary credits in any subsequent reprint or edition.

For further information on Polity, visit our website: politybooks.com

Ethics for OCR Religious Studies

The Complete Resource for AS and A2

MARK COFFEY and DENNIS BROWN

polity

Contents

Acknowledgements

This book has been a labour of love for the authors and we could not have accomplished the finished product without the help of many people. We would like to thank everyone at Polity Press who has been involved in the project, especially Emma Hutchinson and Pascal Porcheron, who have worked tirelessly with us and have shown enthusiasm, support and patience in their editorial role at every stage. Thanks also to Sarah Lambert, Clare Ansell, Leigh Mueller and others who have shown their creative talents in producing this book.

Thanks are also due to Polity's anonymous readers for their helpful comments on various chapters in the early stages, as well as our 'Guinea-pigs' – sixth-form students at the Manchester Grammar School – who have endured various drafts of chapters during the last two years and who have played a valuable part in the book's evolution, providing us with honest and sometimes forthright feedback.

Mark Coffey would also like to thank various teachers along the way: John and Margaret Parry, inspiring sixth-form English and RS teachers who resisted the temptation to concentrate on exam technique and encouraged him to think critically and independently; Professor David Clough and Professor Nigel Biggar whose expertise and skill as thinkers, writers and teachers also trained and guided earlier attempts at learning to write on ethics. Thanks also go to Mark's parents and brother, Professor John Coffey, for their wisdom, kindness and friendship. In addition, we remember our dear young friend and late colleague at Manchester Grammar School, Matthew Bennett, whose quick wit and wisdom on ethics and life were among his many gifts that we miss.

The authors and publishers are grateful to all who gave permission to reproduce copyright material. While every attempt has been made to acknowledge all the sources we have drawn upon, we would like to apologise if any omissions have been made and would invite any such copyright holders to contact Polity Press, so that these may be rectified in future editions.

Foreword

Why should you study Ethics? You may well have thought about this already, but here are some reasons why we think you will enjoy and benefit from studying this subject.

The quick answer is that you are studying an Ethics specification for A Level. But why did you choose it? Perhaps it was a negative choice – you did not want to study Physics and you were not interested or suited to some other subjects and Ethics was the only one left to choose. Hopefully, it was a more positive reason – you will have noticed that ethics seems to appear in newspapers and on TV a lot – rape, theft, murder, war, abortion, environmental crises and medical dilemmas seem to be discussed very frequently. With all these issues, there always seem to be many different and differing opinions. Some people talk about rules to be obeyed; others talk about the consequences of our actions; still others talk about what their religion says.

All these different approaches can be very confusing. Whose opinion should we follow? Is there one correct answer to ethical questions? How are we to find out?

The twentieth-century Existentialist philosopher Albert Camus said that 'a man without ethics is like a wild beast loosed upon this world'. One of the aims of this book is to teach you how many people – some from the past and some from the present – have attempted and do attempt not to be 'wild beasts' in their dealings with other people. What Camus was trying to say was that a code of ethics is essential to allow a society to function properly. Without such a code of ethics, there would be no society and people would simply do what they wanted to, regardless of what anyone else thought. This would result in chaos and anarchy.

Ethics is important. This is why you should study it. Studying ethical theories like Utilitarianism, Natural Law and Kantianism will help you to discover and discuss the principles upon which people base the decisions they make from day to day on important issues like abortion, euthanasia, war, business and the environment. When you read what other people have said about these issues, you will gradually form your own views about the same issues. We hope that you will agree that it is important that everyone has a right to an opinion, as long as it is thought through and informed by rational argument.

As you work through this book, you will be challenged to think long and hard about difficult theories and issues. We do not apologise for this. We want to stretch you to think through these theories and issues. We hope, however, that by the end of your study of Ethics, you will also have enjoyed the journey as far as we have taken it in this book. Ethics, of course, is dynamic. There are no definitive, once-and-for-all answers in ethics. Because human nature and the world we live in are always changing, new situations and examples come to light and force us to go back to first principles again, and to re-think our position on any issue. This is both the joy and the challenge of ethics – no two cases are ever the same, so we have to keep thinking and making decisions with every new case. We hope that you will buy into this journey – we enjoy it and hope that you will too.

How to Use This Book

Obviously we want you to enjoy reading and learning as much about ethics as possible as we feel it is such an important topic, but we have, of course, designed this book so that it will help you not just to pass your exam, but to achieve the best grade possible. As you will have noticed, the chapters follow the structure of the AS and A2 Levels very carefully and each chapter is designed to be relatively self-contained and to cover the knowledge and the skills you will need to succeed in the Religious Ethics section of your A Level Religious Studies.

To this end we have highlighted important terms in the margins. They are also included in a comprehensive Glossary at the back of the book, which you should use for revision purposes when it comes to preparing for your exams. The list of Further Reading at the end of each chapter will direct you to specific sources of information on individual topics – pursuing these will be a terrific way to extend your knowledge and also to explore further the topics that interest you.

The chapter summaries outline the key points that you should know after studying each chapter and these can be used as revision checklists as you complete the work in each chapter. If you don't feel confident in everything outlined in the summary then you should read back through the chapter again to refresh your memory. At the end of each topic, some past paper and typical exam-style questions are included to help you revise the topic. You should attempt these under exam conditions, as it will really help you practise for your exams and also give you an indication of just how ready you are.

Each chapter also contains a number of exercises to get you thinking about the topic in question, as well as Discussion Questions for you to talk through with your fellow students and your teacher. These are especially important, as debating some of the issues in the book really is the best way to learn about them and to figure out your own opinions on the various ways of thinking about ethics.

Websites

There are a range of websites mentioned throughout the book, and, while you always need to proceed with caution when using sources from the web, it will provide a great resource to further your knowledge. You will also find more information linking directly to the chapters in the book available at www.politybooks.com/ethics.

Ethical Thinkers' Timeline

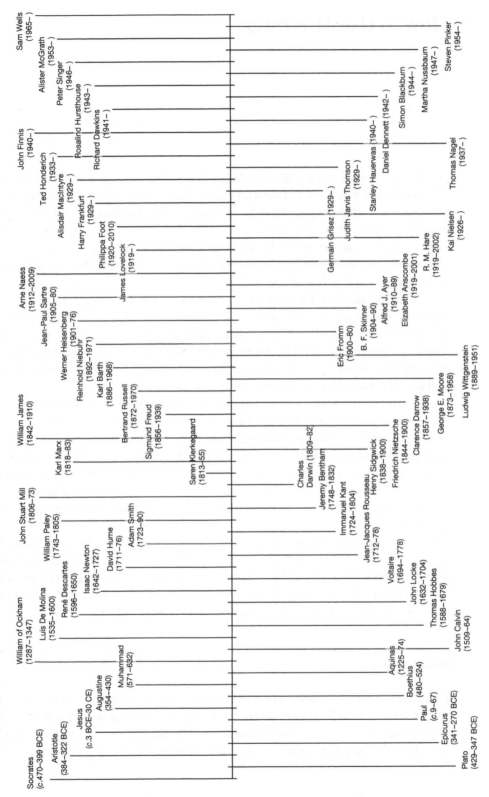

How to Write an A Level Essay

Honing your skills

Welcome to your course in Ethics for OCR Religious Studies. A Level is a step up from GCSEs and the essay-writing at the heart of it calls for a range of skills and techniques as well as fluency in your style. Mastering technical terms, providing examples and having a good grasp of the strengths and weaknesses of theories are all part of the mature essayist's work. In short, taking the mystery out of exam success is our aim in this chapter.

Planning lots of skeleton outlines to past paper questions will help you to take a broad question and focus it down to a relevant and well-crafted argument. Practice trains you to select examples, reasons and evidence. It also keeps you focused, assists with avoiding tangents or fallacies, and helps you to spot gaps in your revision. Timed essays in class will also train you to allocate minutes in proportion to the marks available and to work out how many paragraphs you can reasonably write in the 90 minutes available for planning and writing two essays.

This chapter will give you a good idea of what examiners are looking for in the answers of top candidates, and it should serve as a guide as you learn to research and plan your essays. We'll begin the chapter focusing on AS essay skills and then move on to cover what is distinctive about writing A2 essays. Remembering that irrelevancy and running out of time are two major reasons for underperformance, essay skills are at the heart of your success in this subject. Making lots of essay plans and structuring them in paragraphs will help to hone your skills as an essay writer. For example, take the AS question below:

> May 2012 (b) 'The ends justify the means.' Discuss. [10]

Then brainstorm some key ideas around it.

Brainstorm ideas and key points	Thinkers
— Instrumental not intrinsic right/wrong	Bentham Mill Singer
— Bentham's Quantitative Form – injustices when majority oppress minority's rights – higher values trumping lower ones	
— Consequences – unpredictable future	**Advice**
— Lack of time to research or expertise to judge every means to an end	Try to list examples of wrong/right moral decisions Utilitarianism leads to
— Higher pleasures – Mill's 'competent judges' elitist?	

Brainstorm ideas and key points

— Is the statement in the question above equally true of Act and Rule Utilitarianism?

— Would Act Utilitarianism be harmful for society if everyone adopted it?

— Worth considering some applied examples – favouring the interests of sentient over non-sentient foetuses/Persistent Vegetative State (PVS) patients?

— Intentions and motives ignored

— No Doctrine of Double Effect? No distinction between omission and commission?

+ New & improved – Rule and Preference Utilitarianism overcome above problems

+ A lowest common denominator ethic that people of all beliefs can agree upon

+ Flexible and informed by facts of particular circumstances

+ Ideal when tough-minded decisions are unavoidable – war, or medical budgets and cost–benefit analysis

Crafting your essay argument

Decide on your *thesis* (the broad argument you are going to advance taking into account any qualifications you might offer).

Weigh up the *extent* to which you agree with the statement above – is it true of all or some forms? Are you aware of other *perspectives* that could be taken?

Be clear on the counterargument and key reasons and examples *opposed* to your thesis + evaluation of strengths and weaknesses of these. Showing your awareness of this builds the credibility of your own position.

Then set out the reasoning of key thinkers and arguments *for* your thesis and evaluation of strengths and weaknesses of these.

Evaluate arguments and counterarguments and (if you have time) bring them into dialogue.

Summarise the reasons for your concluding judgement.

Dialogue not monologue

Aristotle commented that 'it is a mark of the educated mind to be able to entertain a thought without accepting it'. One of the lessons to learn as you move from GCSE/IGCSE to A Level is that arguments that oppose your own conclusion deserve a fair hearing, and their criticisms of your position require you to respond to them. Avoid setting up straw-men opponents that are easy to demolish. Seek to understand the weaknesses of your position and arrive at a well-reasoned and balanced conclusion.

A pincer movement

It is helpful to inform your revision by using a pincer movement between the *OCR Specification* on the one hand and *past paper mark schemes* and *Examiners' Reports* on the other.

Specification

Familiarise yourself with the assessment objectives

- AO1: Select and demonstrate clearly relevant knowledge and understanding through the use of evidence, examples and correct language and terminology appropriate to the course of study.

- AO2: Sustain a critical line of argument and justify a point of view.

in applying theories to ethical issues as you produce revision notes. Pay particular attention to making lists of the **Strengths** and **Weaknesses** of moral theories. This will help you go beyond parroting off bullet point lists and develop your analytical and evaluative skills. Make bullet point lists of key concepts, terms and thinkers.

ADVANCED SUBSIDIARY GCE
RELIGIOUS STUDIES
Religious Ethics
Duration: 1 hour 30 minutes
total number of marks for this paper is **70**

Map out time for planning and writing of each section of the exam

Familiarise yourself with the key words in questions and *allocate time in proportion to the marks available* (do not spend too long on AS section b which is only worth 10 marks!)

AS – 2 questions worth 35 marks

25 marks AO1 10 marks AO2

45 minutes per question, 5 minutes reading and planning, 40 minutes writing.

A2 – 2 questions worth 35 marks

Both AO2 evaluative questions

Examiners' Reports on AS Levels help you to see what keeps cropping up for praise and blame in student essays. Alongside *past paper mark schemes*, these take the mystery out of what sets a good essay apart from a bad one.

Common complaints in Examiners' Reports	What examiners want to see in top-grade essays
• Candidates assessing strengths and weaknesses in part (a) AO1 questions *or* giving information without evaluative analysis in part (b) AO2 questions.	• Close attention to the wording of questions and key words.
• Candidates spending too long on part (b) answers on their first question and rushing (a)/(b) on their second answer.	• Clear, practical examples and a sound ability to engage theory in practice.
• Pre-rehearsed answers that ignore the specific wording of the question. Irrelevance and poor timing are the key reasons students underperform (e.g. spending more time and ink on part (b) answers (10 marks) than part (a) (25 marks).	• Good grasp of concepts and distinctions. E.g. a clear understanding of philosophical grammar in distinguishing 'infer' from 'imply', 'refute' from 'deny', or 'a priori', 'a posteriori', etc.
	• A balance between breadth and depth guided by the terms of the question.
• Generalisations (e.g. all Catholics are pacifists) or lists of ideas without examples and explanations.	• Good use of specific cases and, where appropriate, biblical references.
• Incoherent or longwinded arguments that do not transition the essay thesis from paragraph to paragraph. Your essay should weave the threads of the argument together coherently.	• Clear logical structure and tightly argued paragraphs that do not waffle.
	• Clear analysis of strengths and weaknesses of rival positions in assessing their merits.
• Analysis of evaluative questions reserved for the concluding paragraph rather than strengths and weaknesses being interspersed throughout AO2 paragraphs.	• Critical analysis leading to a reasoned judgement in part (b) answers. This will involve an awareness of the distinctions between rival positions taken by key thinkers. This dialogue/debate may result in an either/or judgement between two rival positions or even a blend of them.
• Confusion or conflation of ideas belonging to two distinct thinkers, e.g. Bentham and Mill.	• Excellent engagement between ethical theory and practical issues.

Assessment objectives AO1 and AO2

You will notice that questions are broken down into two sections, (a) and (b). These are assessment objectives AO1 and AO2 respectively. *Ensure you stick to knowledge and understanding on AO1 answers and weave strengths and weaknesses throughout AO2 ones. Candidates who evaluate on AO1 and merely describe and explain in AO2 will be marked down.*

Assessment objective 1	Assessment objective 2
Demonstrate accurate and relevant knowledge and understanding through the use of evidence, sources, examples and lucid technical language and terminology. Show familiarity with a variety of scholarly views.	Critically evaluate and justify a point of view through the use of evidence and reasoned argument. This must be coherent and well-organised, clearly identifying strengths and weaknesses, and both accurate and fluent. An informed viewpoint and evidence of independent thinking will be rewarded.

Reading and planning your essay

Homework essays are time-consuming and labour-intensive. It is tempting to skim read in preparation or even to write them straight off without research and planning. But teachers and examiners can tell apart those students who have taken the time to read and plan their essays from those who have not done so. Reading builds your vocabulary and understanding of concepts. It sharpens your writing style and offers you a wider range of examples. If this all seems too much like hard work, there are lots of good online audio resources to listen to, some of which we highlight on the website that accompanies this book.

Characteristic features of good essay writing

There are many important elements of good essay writing that you will grow into from AS Level through to university essays. These include the following.

Ordering your thoughts in a logical sequence of ideas and reasons

- *A sentence* is a grammatical structure ending in a full stop.
- *A paragraph* is a collection of sentences grouped around one purpose or theme. Single-sentence or full-page paragraphs sound alarm bells when examiners scan essays. You should organise your argument into a step-by-step logical argument.
- To do this, it is best to brainstorm your essay into a series of steps and then to *shuffle your paragraphs* to find the most *logical order* to your essay. For example, you might begin with the weaker position or the one you disagree with, noting its strengths and the critical questions it raises for the position you wish to advance. Every view deserves a fair hearing in the court of your essay, so do not be too quick to dismiss opposing positions and to assert the strengths of your own view. A critically considered conclusion will carry more credibility.

- Remember that *key terms* in the question are often *contested* – where this is the case, do not be too quick to settle their meanings – let the rival definitions wrestle over their meaning and context. For example, the question of when 'life' begins or 'life' ends in the abortion and euthanasia debates hinges partly on what criteria we use to decide these life-and-death issues on.
- *Introduction.* Lead your reader by the hand. Unpack the question, set out your thesis point by point and think of essays as dialogues between ideas – not monologues or, worse still, rants. Be concise and clear about structure.
- *Links/transitions* between paragraphs. Avoid a repetitive style. Try to avoid the same stock phrases – style matters. (See the examples offered below.)
- *Evidence.* Your *general* argument needs *particular* examples both to illustrate it and to give the reasons grip. These can take the form of academic authorities who advance a position or demonstrations of how a theory proves to be more or less workable in practice. Balanced arguments can give you more credibility through your impartial handling of the evidence.
- *Include examples, case studies and quotes.* These illustrate your essay and develop a more engaging style. Examiners are human too – interest them in your work, and they will be better disposed to awarding you marks.
- *Quotations* are important. For each essay topic, learn five or so quotes that will enhance your style by showing a familiarity with primary sources.
- *Paragraphs*
  - *Signposts at the beginning*
  - Give the marker a clear sense of your structure as they scan your answer by stating your main argument in the opening sentence of your essay.
  - *Intermediate conclusions at the end*
  - Arguments can subtly go off the rails if they do not keep on course with the focus of the question. Recapping what your examples, evidence and reasons have established in a sub-conclusion (one or two sentences) allows you to shift the argument forward. You may even take a different course, persuading the reader that, though the initial position had its merits, it was mistaken, inadequate or needed revision. Sub-conclusions act like intermediate conclusions to establish shifts in the argument, like switches that move your train onto a new set of tracks.
- *Fluency with key words.* Be aware of key vocabulary from glossaries and indexes in your textbook and have a clear idea of trigger words in questions (see below).
- *Scholars, textual sources, statistics.* Be accurate and selective – let the reasoning drive the essay. Evidence and examples ought to make an essay's reasoning more persuasive and engaging. Read textbooks – they will make you more fluent with ideas.
- *Arguments and counterarguments.* These should form a dialogue in your essay. At times this can lead to a layering of a weakness identified, a response, then a further weakness that clinches the argument in favour of one side. If you were asked whether Utilitarianism is more practical than Virtue Ethics when applied to environmental ethics, for example, you could present strengths and weaknesses separately but also have a paragraph where some dialogue

and debate entered into the argument. This layering of reasons and responses creates a dialogue rather than a monologue, and builds more credibility for your evaluative conclusions.

- *Theory Summaries – the way to tame the abstract.* Top students bullet point the key elements of abstract theories in their revision notes and clearly define the meaning(s) of key concepts. They deliver these concisely and clearly in exam essays. Weaker students ramble because they have not read and short-noted enough to understand the theories fully. The timed conditions of the exam are not the place to wrestle with your understanding. Save yourself time by short-noting so that recall in the exam (once you've selected the relevant material and clearly identified the key words in the question) feels like writing out a pre-planned paragraph rather than on-your-feet thinking.

- *Conclusion.* Here's where you summarise your argument rather than embarking on a new one. Looking back, all paragraphs in the essay should lead logically to the conclusion.

- *If it is an AO2 evaluative question, come to a judgement.* It may seem like a novel idea, but if it's a homework essay, don't hand it in without first re-reading it! On this proof reading, check it for spelling and grammar errors. Then ask yourself whether your explanations are clear in their understanding of concepts and theories. Also try to be self-critical about whether you've relevantly addressed the question, reflected a range of perspectives, and structured a well-evidenced argument in the right sequence or order. If not, then re-edit it. It is tempting to think that it is your teacher's job to rewrite your essay for you, but this is like putting the oil randomly on a canvas and expecting your art teacher to make a painting of it! You are learning to be an INDEPENDENT thinker, so critical self-review is the way to mature as an essay writer.

Transitional phrases

As mentioned above, one element of becoming a good essay writer is to transition from one paragraph to the next in such a way as to lead your reader through the steps in your thought. This avoids repetition, makes your logic clearer and ought to make it more persuasive. Structure, substance and style all help to engage an examiner and makes their job easier, so it is likely they'll be more favourably disposed to your essay.

Whilst you do not need to have a formal stock of transitional phrases up your sleeve, you do need to work on the style and structure of your homework essays so that you mature as an essay writer, offering a logical progression from one paragraph to another. Below is a list of exemplar phrases that illustrate this process.

Introductions

The key terms of the question are contested by different moral theories.
My working hypothesis is that . . .

My thesis in this essay will be that the terms in the question . . .

At the outset of this essay, I wish to clarify the contested terms in the essay title.

Variant theories contest the terms in the essay title above . . .

A position presented

Philosopher X makes a case for . . .

It may be argued that . . .

I find the argument of X persuasive in terms of how . . .

It is instructive to examine one of the examples X cites in his work.

X's suggestion of . . . is a useful starting point for considering the . . .

Although this is a matter of debate, and is certainly unprovable, I would argue that . . .

A more radical approach to this issue is that of X, who argues that . . .

It is arguable, though unverifiable, that . . .

To illustrate this point, let me draw attention to . . .

Another possibility worth considering is that . . .

Of relevance, in this regard, is X's proposal that . . .

Thus it seems a "fair assumption" that . . .

This contention will be validated further by . . .

This view substantiates/supports the observations of X that . . .

One author defends his/her position

Commenting on . . . X asserts that . . .

Regardless of the individual criticisms that can be made of X's proposal, this theory undoubtedly has the advantage(s) of . . .

X presents us with another alternative when considering the . . .

Nevertheless, he is correct to point out that . . .

X recently reached similar conclusions, when he argued for . . .

X cogently defends the view that . . .

X, in support of this option . . .

X marshals considerable support for . . .

There is good reason to adopt X's reading.

Difficulties with a position / positions

X does not properly account for . . .

It may be objected to X's position that . . .

X's assumption that . . . does not hold up to criticism and is easily disproved.

Against such views, there is a strong voice of criticism from . . .

Not all arguments presented by X have survived scrutiny.

Several problems appear with this position.

That argument needs to be made cautiously, given the . . .

There is a significant problem with this argument.

Although X's approach is very welcome, it contains at least two awkward features.

. . .but this remains in the realm of conjecture

This dismissal, however, is too simplistic.

The argument is undermined by the fact that . . .

A more fruitful line of argument is . . .

This is a plausible idea, but it fails to explain why . . .

To rebut this position, it is worth examining X's writing.

It is worth noting, however, that her/his sceptical position is not shared by everyone.

A different position/contrasting view

While all of this may be true enough, an opposing position set out in B is that . . .

A has responded to B by marshalling good evidence to the contrary.

After evaluating the evidence, A argues that B was wrong when he insisted that . . .

From a different perspective, X maintains that . . .

On the other side of the issue, X contends that . . .

As for the . . . I am still more persuaded by the argument of X.

While this is a valiant effort, it does not ultimately succeed.

This is a plausible idea, but it fails to explain . . .

In contrast, an alternative argument is put forward by X . . .

The alternative view is spearheaded by X, who . . .

A second/third approach, however, has received substantial support, namely, that . . .

Authors' positions disputed/compared

A handful of scholars theorise that . . .

The hypothesis of A and B is that . . .

A and B suggest . . . but this is not clearly the case . . .

A criticises B for . . .

A thus concludes, in contrast to B, that . . .

A, in particular, provides a powerful rebuttal of B's charges at this point.

The critique of X, who says . . . fails to convince.

Against A, for example, B reasonably suggests that . . .

Conclusions/summaries

With X, I conclude that . . .

In conclusion, let me summarise briefly the results of my investigation.

The argument developed up to this point enables us to distinguish between . . .

The most striking observation(s) in my contrast and comparison here is/are . . .

It is also once again a reminder of the need for modesty in conclusions.

In concluding, let me recap the basic points I have tried to make.

In spite of the prevailing uncertainty, I believe there exists broad agreement among
critical scholars that . . .

I see no compelling reason to doubt . . .

Thus, although X's conclusion that . . . is possible, it is not the only valid conclusion
one could draw.

In summary, I have tried to make a case for . . .

Be aware of the OCR Exam Board's command words for AO1 and AO2 type questions

In each exam question there are precise terms that set out the task before you.

AO1	Demonstrate knowledge and understanding using evidence, examples and correct terms.
Analyse	Methodically dissect an idea into its component parts. Explain, compare and point out the complexity of different components of an issue, process, argument or proposition and consider to what degree they are supported by evidence, relevant, logically consistent or able to be tested empirically.
Compare and contrast	Set out the similarities and differences between two theories. Do justice to the relative strengths and weaknesses of each. Part of this process may involve counterarguments or a dialogue between two thinkers.
Define	Write down the precise meaning of the term and all that term implies, using examples where appropriate.
Describe	Identify and write a few sentences on each of the main factual elements of the required; if the 'trigger' word is modified by 'in detail', write as much factual information as possible on the precise term, activity or concept.
Examine	Write out, with some details or examples, the essential elements of the concept, theory or reason and establish the relationship or links between them; but if the 'trigger' word is modified by 'critically', see 'Analyse' above.
Explain	Demonstrate understanding by exploring reasons, usually with the use of examples.
Identify	Write a little about each specific, salient feature.
Illustrate	Provide examples to explain a statement.
Outline/summarise	Write a concise account of the main features, incidents or principles, omitting examples and detailed or peripheral information.

AO2 *Critically evaluate and justify a point of view through evidence and reasoned argument.*

Assess/evaluate	Appraise a specific statement by weighing up two or more opinions, or appraise a defined aspect through a review of its strengths and weaknesses, and conclude with a reasoned personal judgement.
Critically assess/Discuss how far/to what extent/the validity of	Elucidate the pros and cons of a particular view or issue by stating and explaining the evidence, and then reach a reasoned judgement about the accuracy, validity or truth of that view or issue. Assessing the relative strengths and weaknesses of rival positions and extremes at either end will make for a justified conclusion.

Note taking throughout your course

As you go along, keep bullet point short-notes on comparisons and contrasts, similarities and differences, between theories. You need to be conversant with these. Also write down questions you have regarding the material your teacher covers, or that you would ask of theories and thinkers. Bring these up in lessons. Much of evaluative essay writing involves the requirement to

Compare common ground between theories and
Contrast distinctive features/contested approaches to practical ethical issues to form evidence-based judgements

Evaluate strengths and weaknesses throughout the essay

Strengths		**Weaknesses**	
Reasons	+ evidence and examples	Reasons	+ evidence and examples
Similarities		**Differences**	
Reasons	+ evidence and examples	Reasons	+ evidence and examples

---

Exercise

Photocopy several opinion or editorial pieces from quality newspapers. Then. . .

(1) Ask yourself whether the writer has given a fair-minded assessment of alternative or opposing views rather than misrepresented them (the straw-man fallacy).
(2) Highlight key words and phrases from each paragraph to identify the skeletal outline of the argument.
(3) Critically evaluate whether you think other evidence or information about context or more specific examples/case studies are necessary to support the author's argument – are the conclusions overdrawn (more conclusions drawn out than reasons and evidence put in)?

Integrate theory and practice

Approach the course with the aim of integrating ethical theory and its practice or application. You'll be taught various ethical theories (Kantian, Utilitarian, Natural Law, Religious and Virtue Ethics). The top marks will be gained by candidates who can critically evaluate these theories throughout their essay (not simply in their concluding paragraph!). Consider how these strengths and weaknesses emerge when the theories are applied to the ethical issues of the course. Natural Law's Primary Precept of preserving life comes under scrutiny when a mother's life is endangered by continuing with an ectopic pregnancy that is likely to result in her death, or when she gives birth to an anencephalic infant who will die shortly after and has no self-awareness. How relevant is Divine Command Ethics in the abortion or euthanasia debate in a secular society or parliament? Will it take more than the instrumental reasoning of Utilitarianism to halt the environmental crisis (in other words, will our industrialised consumer society, which is energy-hungry, slow down just with 'if . . . then' logic, rather than a deeper moral motivation rooted in community, character or worship?). At the end of most chapters this textbook will evaluate strengths and weaknesses – of each theory in turn, and then as these are applied to issues. The skill of integrating your thinking, of pinpointing your evaluative judgements, is what will get you a top grade. This evidence of independent thinking will help you interpret an exam question and structure your essay. It goes further than trotting out pre-rehearsed paragraphs and it is ultimately what demonstrates the transition from GCSE- to University-level thinking.

Each theory has its strengths and weaknesses – for example:

Table 1 Ethical theories' strengths and weaknesses

Theory	*Strength*	*Weakness*
Kantian Ethics	Objective and universally true duties offer clear guidance.	Their unbending nature can lack compassion or attention to the importance of emotion in moral motivation.
Utilitarianism	Practical and able to calculate outcomes drawing on past data – an instrumental mindset which can make steely decisions in emotionally charged situations when demands outstrip supply.	Is grounding ethics in optimising choices or pleasure a solid foundation? Are all goods measurable by the single currency of pleasure/pain?
Natural Law	Assuming an objective moral order to the universe makes ethics realist and offers a clear account of how human nature best flourishes. Believes that humans naturally incline to do good even if this is apparent good, rather than real good, at times.	Is what is natural right? Is there such a moral order built into the universe, or are facts quite different from values? Is human nature fallen or selfish?

Be strategic about your planning and preparation

- In an AS exam of 1 hour, 30 minutes, you have to answer two questions each worth 45 marks. So allocate your time in proportion to the potential marks. How many paragraphs can you write in the minutes available? Plan the structure of your essay, listing examples, quotations from texts and scholars, key reasons, etc.
- Think about your style – be concise and target the question's focus in your sights.
- Make sure your information is accurate and relevant. Arrive at your concluding judgement(s) only after a balanced comparison of the strengths and weaknesses of theories.
- In preparing revision diagrams on topics, collect as many past paper questions together as possible (here it may even be worth looking up past papers from other exam boards to see if there could be a broader range of questions to test your knowledge).
- Work through mark schemes and level descriptors to see precisely what examiners were looking to reward in past exam questions.
- Mine books and web links for examples and case studies to illustrate your essays (though let the reasoning drive the essay, not the examples).

Mind mapping

Try setting out all of the angles from which you can think of questions coming at you. Look over the specification itself, research all of the past paper questions (and those

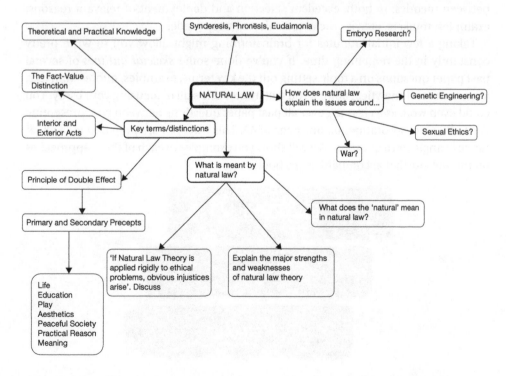

you can find from other exam boards). This will help you to select relevant content when you see the actual question. It will also offer some guarantee that you are ready to handle any question thrown at you. Mark Schemes and Examiners' Reports are invaluable in checking that you've covered the ground.

Why essays make you employable

Essay writing might seem like a real chore. Yet in developing transferable skills of persuasiveness, analysis and creative thinking, you are becoming more employable. As you read around theories and issues, you will find your fluency with ideas and your capacity to extract relevant data from your research growing with each essay.

Not losing the wood for the trees – seeing the big picture of your argument

To use an analogy, you can get lost in the woods of concepts and abstract arguments with no visible way out. Equally, you might feel the need to airlift your wayward argument out of the forest in the concluding paragraph as you realise that you have not relevantly addressed the terms of the question. Yet a safer way out of the forest may be to leave stores of food there: to have well-rehearsed key points ready to go once you've selected what's relevant to the question. This is truer of AO1 questions, as AO2 ones tend to require more evaluative engagement of theory and practice or contrast between theories. In both, excellent selection and deployment of relevant reasons, examples, thinkers, etc., is crucial to achieving a top grade.

Taking a few initial minutes for brainstorming might allow you to write pretty constantly in the remaining time. If you've done some *skeletal outlines* of several past paper questions on a topic setting out the key terms, examples, quotes, thinkers, arguments and analytical points, you will master this skill of focusing your essay. You could even work as a class to cover all past paper questions between you, presenting each other's essay outlines on one page of A4. This way, you are prepared for a wider range of angles on a question. We will show you examples of each of these approaches on the website that accompanies this book.

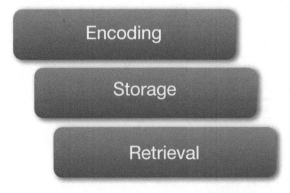

Encoding

Storage

Retrieval

Doing well in exams is a feat of memory – use bullet points, acronyms and mnemonics to help your recall become exam-proof.

Exams are not just about understanding theories and applying them. They are also timed tests of your recall. Under such pressure, you need to find a process or system for encoding the information that will make it easy to retrieve. Lists of key principles and concepts in theories, as well as evaluative lists of strengths and weaknesses, should be memorised. This is best done in a concise orderly way using mind maps or bullet points, or with the aid of acronyms and mnemonics.

Acronym	*Mnemonic*
An acronym is an abbreviation using the first letter of each word. For example AIDS is an acronym for Acquired Immuno-Deficiency Syndrome	A mnemonic is a short phrase that you use to help remember something. So 'Richard Of York Goes Battling In Vain' helps me to remember the colours of the rainbow – red, orange, yellow, green, blue, indigo, violet
Acronym generator: www.cs.uoregon.edu/Research/paracomp/anym/	Phonetic mnemonic generator: www.remarkablemarbles.com/memory/phonetic-mnemonic-generator

The following two websites may assist you in generating acronyms and mnemonics. We've included the grade descriptors for OCR Religious Ethics at AS and A2 Level to help you bear in mind how examiners will grade your work. When you receive back a marked essay, it is worth looking up your level and taking the time to see whether and how you could improve on your level next time.

Final note: as your teacher marks your essays, identify the level you are presently at and be clear about what you need to do to improve. The mark schemes below will be helpful.

AS levels of response mark scheme

Level	Mark/25	AO1	Mark/10	AO2
0	0	absent/no relevant material absent/ no argument	0	absent/no argument
1	1–5	almost completely ignores the question • little relevant material • some concepts inaccurate • shows little knowledge of technical terms.	1–2	very little argument or justification of viewpoint • little or no successful analysis • views asserted with no justification.
Communication: often unclear or disorganised; can be difficult to understand; spelling, punctuation and grammar may be inadequate				
2	6–10	a basic attempt to address the question • knowledge limited and partially accurate	3–4	a basic attempt to sustain an argument and justify a viewpoint • some analysis, but not successful

Level	Mark/25	AO1	Mark/10	AO2
		<ul><li>limited understanding</li><li>selection often inappropriate</li><li>might address the general topic rather than the question directly</li><li>limited use of technical terms.</li></ul>		<ul><li>views asserted with little justification.</li></ul>

Communication: some clarity and organisation; easy to follow in parts; spelling, punctuation and grammar may be inadequate

Level	Mark/25	AO1	Mark/10	AO2
3	11–15	satisfactory attempt to address the question<ul><li>some accurate knowledge</li><li>appropriate understanding</li><li>some successful selection of material</li><li>some accurate use of technical terms.</li></ul>	5–6	the argument is sustained and justified<ul><li>some successful analysis which may be implicit</li><li>views asserted but not fully justified.</li></ul>

Communication: some clarity and organisation; easy to follow in parts; spelling, punctuation and grammar may be inadequate

Level	Mark/25	AO1	Mark/10	AO2
4	16–20	a good attempt to address the question<ul><li>accurate knowledge</li><li>good understanding</li><li>good selection of material</li><li>technical terms mostly accurate.</li></ul>	7–8	a good attempt to sustain an argument<ul><li>some effective use of evidence</li><li>some successful and clear analysis</li><li>considers more than one viewpoint.</li></ul>

Communication: generally clear and organised; can be understood as a whole; spelling, punctuation and grammar good

Level	Mark/25	AO1	Mark/10	AO2
5	21–25	a very good/excellent attempt to address the question showing understanding and engagement with the material<ul><li>very high level of ability to select and deploy relevant information</li><li>accurate use of technical terms.</li></ul>	9–10	a very good/excellent attempt to sustain an argument<ul><li>comprehends the demands of the question</li><li>uses a range of evidence</li><li>shows understanding and critical analysis of different viewpoints.</li></ul>

Communication: answer is well constructed and organised; easily understood; spelling, punctuation and grammar very good

What's different about A2 Level essay writing as opposed to AS Level?

A2 level study is a progression from AS. Students ought to have matured their analytical and critical skills. The coherence with which they advance a thesis statement, through a series of arguments that are well illustrated with examples and substantiated using relevant evidence, will show greater maturity than in their AS year. Their fluency with technical terms and complex ideas together with the capacity to select and deploy evidence and argument should have come along. Critical analysis of the strengths and weaknesses of a variety of viewpoints and the ability to apply a wider range of theories to issues all require a greater competency as an essayist. Many of the groundwork principles remain the same such as:

- paying attention to the key terms in the question.
- planning and ordering your material into a paragraph structure.
- having signpost sentences at the start of paragraphs indicating the focus to the reader.
- including sub-conclusions at the end of paragraphs setting out how they relate to the question (this both ensures that you don't stray from the terms of the question and it clarifies the argument you have established).
- fluency and clarity of style including good transitional sentences so that the thread of the argument is clear.

It is worth remembering that readers often skim-read essays. In their initial assessment or first reading, so too may examiners. It is here that legibility, a clear structure, the use of key terms and the flagging up of thinkers and theories proves its worth even before a more careful reading of the quality of the analysis is done. First impressions count!

Beyond this, there are several fundamental differences at A2 Level that should impact on your essay writing:

(a) **Timing** – At AS level, candidates have 90 minutes to answer two questions, each with a part (a) (worth 25 marks) and a part (b) (worth 10 marks). This requires careful timekeeping and a clear distinction between assessment objectives 1 and 2.

At A2 level, you still have 90 minutes, but just two questions that integrate AO1 and AO2 in one answer. The shift is that the timing of your answer must be more heavily loaded to assessment objective 2 with its greater evaluative and synoptic elements.

(b) **Weighting of marks** – At AS level, 70% of the marks were focused on AO1, 30% on AO2. At A2 Level, 60% of the marks are AO1, 40% on AO2. So there is a greater weighting towards the higher-level skills of analysis, evaluation, and application.

(c) **Integration** – One question without a part (a) and (b) to guide your structure requires you to integrate knowledge and understanding, on the one hand, with analysis, evaluation, and application.

(d) **Synoptic** – The OCR specification says that 'Synoptic assessment tests the candidates. It encourages the development of a holistic understanding of the connections between different elements of the subject.' In addressing specified aspects of human experience (listed below), the A2 course is 'intrinsically synoptic'.

The A2 Synoptic themes as outlined in the OCR Specification.

	Concept of deity and relationship with humanity	*Authority and truth in religion*	*Experience and religion*	*The Human Condition*
Religious Ethics	Theological determinism	Meta-ethics – use of ethical language	Nature of and experiences of conscience	Applied ethical issues – sexual ethics, business and environment.
	Religious ideas of free will	Conscience as an authority	Application of religious ethics to applied ethical issues	Free will and determinism
	Applied ethical issues and teachings of religious ethics	Religious ethics		Implications of views for moral responsibility

In terms of exam technique then, you need to marshal a 'range of evidence' and show an understanding of 'different viewpoints'. So not losing the wood for the trees, and setting out a thesis statement and knowing your final position after initial brainstorming and planning may help. It takes practice to get good at a critical analysis of the strengths and weaknesses of rival positions. Rather than just set them out in isolation, you need to compare and contrast positions. The best candidates are sharp and concise in their style, and efficient in their delivery. They select and deploy relevant evidence and argument. You will improve this skill if you take the time to re-edit your homework essays before submitting them (as well as learning from and applying feedback from your teacher(s)). Take a look at the A2 mark scheme below to see what examiners are looking for in level 5 answers.

A2 levels of response mark scheme

Level	Mark/21	AO1	Mark/14	AO2
0	0	absent/no relevant material	0	absent/no argument
1	1–5	almost completely ignores the question • little relevant material • some concepts inaccurate • shows little knowledge of technical terms.	1–3	very little argument or justification of viewpoint • little or no successful analysis • views asserted with no justification.
		Communication: often unclear or disorganised; can be difficult to understand; spelling, punctuation and grammar may be inadequate		
2	6–9	a basic attempt to address the question • knowledge limited and partially accurate • limited understanding • might address the general topic rather than the question directly • selection often inappropriate • limited use of technical terms.	4–6	a basic attempt to sustain an argument and justify a viewpoint • some analysis, but not successful • views asserted but little justification.
		Communication: some clarity and organisation; easy to follow in parts; spelling, punctuation and grammar may be inadequate		
3	10–13	satisfactory attempt to address the question • some accurate knowledge • appropriate understanding • some successful selection of material • some accurate use of technical terms.	7–8	the argument is sustained and justified • some successful analysis which may be implicit • views asserted but not fully justified.
		Communication: some clarity and organisation; easy to follow in parts; spelling, punctuation and grammar may be inadequate		
4	14–17	a good attempt to address the question • accurate knowledge • good understanding • good selection of material • technical terms mostly accurate.	9–11	a good attempt at using evidence to sustain an argument holistically • some successful and clear analysis • some effective use of evidence • views analysed and developed.
		Communication: generally clear and organised; can be understood as a whole; spelling, punctuation and grammar good		

Level	Mark/21	AO1	Mark/14	AO2
5	18–21	a very good/excellent attempt to address the question showing understanding and engagement with the material • very high level of ability to select and deploy relevant information • accurate use of technical terms.	12–14	a very good/excellent attempt which uses a range of evidence to sustain an argument holistically • comprehends the demands of the question • uses a range of evidence • shows understanding and critical analysis of different viewpoints.

Communication: answer is well constructed and organised; easily understood; spelling, punctuation and grammar very good

Philosophy as the history of ideas

One distinctive feature of this textbook lies in its attention to the history of ideas. Ideas are not treated as though they float around in the abstract. They emerge from and give impetus to movements and periods of change. Just think of the influence of the ideas of Jesus, Muhammad or Marx 100 years on from the end of their earthly lives. Technology such as the printing press at the time of the Protestant Reformation was to distribute ideas across Europe at a pace that was unseen before. The advent of the modern state, accounting practices and the growth of Utilitarian thought is hardly coincidental. Attention to the history of ideas along with the analysis of primary texts is central to the study of Philosophy at university. But even in A Level study, it brings Moral Philosophy and Ethics to life if you can see how the biographies, times and ideas of key thinkers interact.

So keep in mind the current of ideas and a sense that thinkers are often moved to write in opposition to influential movements or writers of their day. Kant, for example, wrote that Hume awoke him from his 'dogmatic slumbers'. He was moved to justify his knowledge claims and to meet Hume's scepticism. So, as you read through the chapters, try to situate thinkers in their periods and enquire into the changing times in which ideas emerge. Often it is the artists, poets, engineers and inventors who innovate change; as Simon and Garfunkel sang, 'the words of the prophets are written on the subway walls'. The philosophers may not be the first to get there, but they do articulate new social, political, religious or cultural movements in language, and make these ideas more clearly understood. So refer back to the timeline on page **x** as you read through this book and seek to build up a mental picture of when key thinkers are writing and how their context may shape their ideas or account for what they're reacting to or how they innovate.

PART I

AS RELIGIOUS ETHICS

ETHICAL THEORIES

1 Key Debates in Ethics

As we begin to examine key debates in Moral Philosophy, it is useful to keep in mind three branches of the study of Moral Philosophy.

1 Practical or applied ethics

Practical ethics looks at the specifics of how ethical judgements and reasoning work out in real-life issues. It is here where the theories you are studying prove themselves or fall short as they are applied to issues such as abortion, euthanasia, business ethics and the environment.

2 Normative ethics

Normative ethics sets out standards or principles by which character or actions can be judged or evaluated. Ethical principles and criteria offer a means of judging how we ought to act (e.g. Kantian, Utilitarian, Virtue, Natural Law ethics). Normative ethical theories broadly divide between

deontological – ethics based on principles which are more fixed and absolute in determining behaviour, e.g. Kantian, Divine Command and Natural Law; and
teleological – ethics based on optimising outcomes or consequences, e.g. Utilitarianism and Situation Ethics.

3 Meta-ethics

Meta-ethics is the study of the meaning of moral terms (e.g. justice, goodness) and metaphysical questions (beyond scientific scope) such as 'Is morality objective?', 'Are there moral facts?' or 'Is there a relationship between morality and human happiness and flourishing?' It is *analysis* rather than action – the study of the meaning of the terms and concepts used in moral judgements. It is sometimes described as the epistemology (the justification of what we can be said to know) of ethics because the very meaning of terms such as 'good' and 'bad', 'right' and 'wrong' is so debatable. Meaning (semantics) and justification (epistemology) are inter-related in terms of critical debate and analysis. '*Meta*' is a Greek word meaning 'around' and deals with questions surrounding the meaning of ethical terms and the question of moral realism. It helps us see, for example, that a **relativist** and **absolutist** may both live by a strict moral code of honouring promises, telling the truth and campaigning for human rights, for example, but the relativist would see this as a matter of cultural or personal preference rather than a dutiful obedience of a moral law.

In this chapter we will introduce contrasting positions taken up in ethical debate. Whilst debates can be adversarial, it is better to see these as more of a spectrum with strongly held views at each end.

Objective		Subjective
Absolutist	As contrasted with	Relativist
Deontological		Teleological

Relativism:
Moral relativism goes further than merely observing the disagreements among people and in society about ethics. It goes on to suggest that moral claims are true or false relative to the standpoint of a society, community or person that holds them. For example, in Buddhist countries, meat-eating is more morally dubious than in the West. Facts are distinguished from values and this position is held to promote toleration as any claim to absolute and universal moral norms is likely to be false.

Absolutism:
The view that certain moral standards are unchanging and universal and ought never to be violated, even if it may at times be difficult to agree upon what these are or if making exceptions would avoid suffering. Moral absolutists would agree, for example, that slavery and cannibalism did not become wrong at a certain point in history – they were always so. Divine Command and Kantian Ethics are generally taken to fit this mould.

Class activity: choose two students to take the parts of Rick the Relativist and Alison the Absolutist

Rick the Relativist (RR) As I see it, tolerance is crucial to the smooth running of society given the variety of cultures and contradictory moral values people hold to. Absolutists disagree about what is just and society's values vary, so, pragmatically, to keep the peace, we need to live and let live. Morality is a matter of personal choices or tastes – it's not objective like science.

Alison the Absolutist (AA) Well, if no culture can be wrong or mistaken, then surely there's no such thing as contradictions in moral values. How can we speak of moral progress? Today we condemn the slave trade, which was part of Britain's history and wealth – is this just a matter of 21st-century tastes being different from those of the past – like 1950s cooking being considered bland in our era of TV chefs?

RR What's right is what the majority of people in a culture decide to be right. In a democratic society, lawmakers ought to follow this. If the majority of UK voters show themselves in surveys to be for euthanasia, it ought to be made legal.

AA So, in your view, reasoning about moral claims or values in an attempt to persuade people to change their minds is pointless? What we're actually doing is just trying to get them to share our feelings (Ya! Boo! Morality).

RR Well, morality is largely rooted in human emotions of praise and blame, but that's not to say it's pointless to argue. We ought to reason consistently and be informed in making our choices. Also, we can see negative consequences and preventable suffering following from certain actions (such as corruption, abuse of power, theft, indiscriminate violence, etc.). So there may be good reason to think over the facts in order to alter people's feelings or seek more informed decision-making about outcomes. This doesn't make morality objective and real like the world our senses perceive.

AA Imagine a relativist state in which the majority of citizens hated a minority and felt strongly that they ought to be discriminated against, keeping them down through poor education, inadequate housing, lack of employment opportunities, and even imprisonment at the slightest infringement of the law. There could be no such thing as an unjust law for such a state. Morality and laws would be relative to the culture and no law unjust. By your principle of morality by popular opinion, this would be fine.

RR Well, we could seek to persuade the citizens and political leaders in this country that its success will be more assured if advancement happens through merit and the playing field is kept fairly level. Denying one sector of the population access to the competition will only restrict the competitiveness of this country in the global marketplace.

AA Suppose that the majority of the country so hate the minority in question that your argument is in no way persuasive – they're prejudiced enough to think that they're not going to miss out on the talent this minority might have added. Your arguments fail to gain a grip on people because they don't believe in unjust laws (just unpopular or involuntary ones) that one has a duty to break in favour of a higher law that reason sets out. Morality cannot just be a matter of opinion – it is universal. You must agree that the Aztecs were immoral to consider human sacrifices acceptable.

RR The problem with you high-minded absolutists is that, in the name of justice, you end up creating inflexible laws and principles that look just in theory, but, when applied, can take little or no account of the complex circumstances of a case and cause a great deal of suffering. Backstreet abortions resulting in infertility, even death, for women who find themselves in countries where abortion is illegal, and the spread of AIDS through a refusal to back safe-sex education, are two examples that spring to mind. Furthermore, it is a thin line between being absolutely convinced you're right, and wanting to force others to accept your beliefs. Intolerance and persecution were common in the Middle Ages up to the religious wars of the seventeenth century. So, humbly accepting that we might be wrong is a virtue to the relativist. Be pragmatic – see what works. Moral codes or values change between cultures and, if there is an objective morality, it sure is hard to find agreement beyond some form of the golden rule of treating others as you would like to be treated or not doing to others what you wouldn't want to have done to yourself.

AA Relativists slip from noting cultural differences to making claims about the nature of morality itself. They contradict themselves here by holding to this one absolute – that there are no absolutes! There is still a lot of agreement beneath the surface. Cannibalistic tribes often imposed the death penalty for murder of anyone in the tribe, and James Rachels gives the example of Eskimo tribes in the past who sometimes practised infanticide on girls in order to secure the lives of male children who were to become the hunters and providers of meat (males would die in greater numbers given the risks attached to their work). So there may be more core values than you initially think. It can be misleading to exaggerate all moral differences – sustaining a culture requires that its infants be well cared for over a prolonged period, that taboos on incest and indiscriminate murder are strong.

Which of these two thinkers do you find yourself more inclined to agree with and why? Can you defend yourself against the challenges that the other throws at you?

Moral subjectivity vs moral objectivity

When we praise or condemn actions, on what basis do we make our moral judgements? Moral subjectivists believe that we do this on the basis of our culture, our personal emotions or the psychology with which evolutionary history has shaped us. They agree with the standard psychological view, beginning with Hume, that *we are motivated by our desires far more than by our reasons*. Reasons relate to beliefs, logic and sense experience, but *our motivation to act stems from desires*. For subjectivists, the very idea of being able to uncover moral 'facts' just seems odd. Having rejected a moral order arising from belief in God or human reason, the subjectivist sees no grounds for any 'objectivity' in ethics. This said, the subjectivist could still say that we all recognise that we generally make bad decisions when we lose our temper or when we have not investigated the facts behind a choice or the consequences of our actions. We can moderate our desires and seek to be as impartial as possible in order to bring about a better outcome (personal happiness, social welfare, etc.).

For a subjectivist, a sentence like 'You were wrong to call in sick to school on Monday when you were not unwell but just fancied a chill-out day to catch up after a wild weekend' means 'I personally disapprove of . . . '. For the subjectivist, there are no moral facts out there in the universe beyond human minds, or, as Hamlet puts it in Shakespeare's play, 'there is nothing either good or bad, but thinking makes it so'. Moral **subjectivism** is therefore 'non-realist' in seeing morality as depending on human feelings rather than in terms of God, or the objective reasoning of human minds like deductive logic or algebra. Yet morality need not be driven by the herd instinct – the individual subjectivist values personal freedom. For example, a resolute student can choose to opt out of the drinking, laddish culture of his rugby club.

By contrast, **objectivists** hold that there are moral facts. These are grounded in some objectively rational or divine foundation. Right and wrong are independent of our personal or cultural habits and inclinations. Slavery did not become wrong with the birth of the abolitionist movement to end its practice – it was always wrong by some higher moral law. Although it may be difficult to prove, in principle, objectivists claim that moral statements can be true or false.

Non-religious rationalists can also believe that objective moral facts can be known by properly working rational minds, just as logic can be. As James Rachels puts it, 'Because the moral law is the law of reason, rational beings are the embodiment of the moral law itself' (Rachels 1999). For Kant, human beings deserve respect as ends in themselves because they are rational and autonomous, not merely objects like pawns on a chessboard to move around at will. Reason can stand above the culture of time or place and give us a more impartial, objective standpoint from which to assess our ethics.

Relativism refers to judging the moral beliefs and behaviour of others by the standards relative to individuals or more commonly to cultures. Cultural relativists observe the many different cultures around the contemporary world and across time. Some have justified enslaving conquered peoples. Others have been cannibalistic, even eating the bodies of their deceased fathers, perhaps believing the spirits of the deceased were somehow absorbed in the act. Some have made human sacrifices to

Subjectivism: Subjectivists see morality in terms of personal preferences or tastes. They reject the idea that there are objective moral values that may be established by reason. They see moral values as subjective – as Hume saw it, human behaviour was more passional than rational.

Objectivism: For the objectivist, objects exist independently of a subject's perception of them. In the case of moral objectivism, the claim is that moral truths exist independently of culture or personal preferences.

> **Moral relativism vs moral absolutism – Mr Relativist and Dr Critic**
>
> **Mr Relativist (Mr R)** Everything in moral reasoning is a matter of taste and opinion. We invent ethical standards and they're subjective and relative to their time and culture. There are no absolutes out there to be discovered like new planets.
>
> **Dr Critic (Dr C)** So, let me get this right – the only absolute you hold to is that there are no absolutes?
>
> **Mr R** Well, perhaps that sounds like a paradox, but it's just the logic of relativism. That's not to stop me being passionate about causes like the environment, but destroying our planet affects other people and animals and, as I want my freedoms to be respected, I ought to live consistently and respect those of others.
>
> **Dr C** Well, I don't know how you're gonna take this. But I guess, if you're a relativist, you'll not condemn it. Last year, four mates and I each put £50 into a pot totalling £250. We then bought a 5-gallon pot of sulphuric acid and poured it into Lake Windermere. We each guessed how many fish would float to the surface after 5 minutes. The one nearest to the correct figure won the £250 minus the cost of the acid.
>
> **Mr R** That's appalling! I ought to report you to the police.
>
> **Dr C** I'm only kidding. But seriously, on what basis would you condemn my behaviour as a relativist? If you're a total relativist, then no one view is any better than another, so your condemnation amounts to 'most people don't share your opinion, so they will force you to take their view or face punishment'.
>
> *Discuss: how do you think Mr Relativist might respond?*

the gods, lived without clothes, or been polygamous or polyandrous. Even in today's globalised world, we may experience culture shock when visiting a country radically different from our own.

Louis Pojman, who taught at the US Military Academy, set out ethical relativism in terms of two key elements:

1. the Diversity Thesis – we observe differences between the values and behaviour of individuals and cultures (descriptive moral relativism);.
2. the Dependency Thesis – morality depends on the time, place, society, and culture, together with human nature and the human condition.

The second point here is sometimes termed 'meta-ethical moral relativism' and goes well beyond the merely descriptive observation of diversity to the claim that this is the foundation for all morality. Cultural relativists believe that moral codes of right and wrong are a social construct of our language, environment, habits, tradition, and culture.

Contemporary anthropologists who live with tribal groups have to learn to leave behind their cultural biases and presumptions of what is normal. Compared to their nineteenth-century predecessors, they may be less prone to making value judgements on behalf of the 'civilised world' about 'primitive' peoples, but human rights and feminist appraisals may still judge the culture being examined by liberal democratic standards. The absence of absolute standards by which to judge other cultures or individuals would reduce the personal subjectivist to merely expressing

QUICK QUESTION
In Tunisia, a man takes his ram to a fight (possibly to the death) with another ram on which bets will be placed. If this is wrong, why is this so?

their distaste for, say, the public nudity that seemed scandalous to Catholic and Protestant missionaries of centuries past in parts of Africa or Latin America. Practices such as female genital mutilation (FGM), child labour or sex tourism overlooked by local police would be hard for the moral subjectivist to condemn if the local culture considered these acceptable. They may still be able to condemn such practices on the grounds that freedom ought to be extended to all if those who enjoy it are to exercise their reasoning consistently.

When moral relativists express a preference for their moral code in their social context, it may be seen as a kind of social convention that urges one 'when in Rome, to do as the Romans do'. Yet cultural relativism may go further than this when it takes a normative form (takes the form of an 'ought' statement). There are varieties to the strength of such relativism, such as:

1. We ought to regard no one value system or moral code as better than another.
2. Any moral values ought to be tolerated as long as they cause no harm to the freedom of other individuals.

In a globalised world, it is easy for dominant cultures to insist that they are right. The cultural relativist warns us not to devalue what is strange to us, even if we happen to ascribe to the dominant cultural worldview. Yet, as we've seen, relativists vary greatly. The cultural relativist judging by the standards of liberal democracy will condemn such practices as execution for adultery or blasphemy in other countries.

Moral absolutists believe that, beyond the subjective appearance of things, there is an objective moral order of right and wrong. This can take a number of different forms, such as:

1. Divine Command Ethics (moral laws revealed by God).
2. Absolutes based on the claim that human reason can think impartially and universally to derive right and wrong rules as it would formulae for physics.
3. Universal human rights rooted in some essential view of human nature or just established as a kind of contract that is agreed upon. The Universal Declaration of Human Rights represents a turning-aside from relativism. It states that human beings are 'born free and equal' with 'inalienable rights', including the right not to be held as a slave (article 4) or tortured (article 5).

Absolutism does justice to a lot of our intuitions about morality, such as our sense of moral failure when lying or cheating, or our sense that there can be moral growth or regression. Post-Apartheid South Africa and a Free France liberated from Nazism, are generally seen not just as the result of change, but as progress in history.

Of course, the relativist would reply that, if our value system happened to be formed by the propaganda machine of the Third Reich, then, for us, that would make the final solution and genocide of Jews, gypsies, homosexuals and Jehovah's Witnesses morally acceptable, within the warped worldview of Nazism. Yet, for the absolutist, such a view is reprehensible because there are timeless moral values with which to make moral judgements. This is not to deny that certain moral absolutes, like saving life, can trump others, such as not lying. But the meta-ethical claim is that moral facts exist – in principle, absolutists can speak in terms of moral truth and falsehood.

QUICK QUESTION
Can the relativist ever see moral 'progress', as Martin Luther King did when he worked to see an end to racial segregation in America?

The character of moral absolutism is summed up neatly in the Stoic maxim 'Let justice be done though the heavens fall.' For the absolutist, moral principles are fixed and not relative to the circumstances (e.g. time or place) in which dilemmas arise. Doing what is 'good' may prove costly, for example when truth-telling gets you into trouble, or promise-keeping leaves you financially ruined. Absolutist laws have forced victims of rape to go through the pregnancy and birth against their will because abortion was prohibited. Lives have been lost as a result of the prohibition on blood transfusions among Jehovah's Witnesses, and due to a prohibition by the Catholic Church on the use of condoms to prevent the spread of HIV/AIDS. Problems may also arise when two absolutes conflict, for example the duty of compassion and that of promise-keeping. Imagine I promise to take an elderly and infirm person to the doctor and then come across a car accident where I provide first aid and call an ambulance, thus preventing me from fulfilling my promise.

Weaknesses of moral relativism

There's a *logical leap between pluralism and relativism or between the diversity thesis and the dependency thesis.* Observing the plurality of cultures and different moral codes need not lead to the conclusion that there can be no objective truth to morality. Such a prescriptive conclusion (you ought not to regard any moral values more highly than others) does not follow from the descriptive or factual premise (there exists a variety of moral values). Disagreement over what is objectively or universally true need not lead us to the conclusion that no such truth exists.

Do cultural relativists live consistently with their belief? Are cultural relativists from liberal democratic societies only able to describe the practice of genocide, imprisonment and execution without trial, the enslavement of citizens, discrimination against racial minorities and the oppression of women as 'wrong' by their *relative* standards? If this is the case, then how can we judge any society to be 'progressive' or 'backwards' morally? How can the relativist say that the repeal of the slave trade or Gandhi's fight for Indian independence, or the 1960s civil rights movement in the US represented progress and enlightened values in history in any real sense? To criticise or condemn either practices in our own society or those in another, which we find reprehensible, is to assume some *standard independent of culture.* This is precisely what the cultural relativist denies. Yet, in a globalised world, cultural relativists may still seek to impose their view on other states or to condemn the actions of corrupt and brutal regimes. Should a relativist return the asylum seeker who has fled female genital mutilation or execution for apostasy (converting from one religion to another) to their country of origin on the grounds that it is the norm there?

The law of non-contradiction asserts that two mutually exclusive and contradictory 'truths' cannot both be right. The law of non-contradiction says that 'opposite assertions cannot both be true at the same time'. To this, the moral subjectivist may respond by saying that moral statements are just emotional expressions like 'Boo to abortion!' or 'Hurrah for capital punishment!' This may be so, but, for their argument to be rational, a minimal requirement is for their sentences to be logically consistent. A logical problem results if the subjectivist asserts that two sentences making contradictory moral claims are equally true. The subjectivist may avoid this problem by seeing the language of their sentences as simply voicing emotional expressions or choices and tastes.

Practical reasoning from our experience may help us to see that beneath very different cultures, there are shared and stable values that work and sustain societies. Any stable society will need to value human life and the rule of law. To survive beyond a generation or two, a society must care for its young and set up constraints on indiscriminate and unchecked theft and murder that would result in anarchy. If lying and breaking promises are the norm, then communication and co-operation will also break down. Even if this is purely a practical contract between citizens set up for their own welfare, it could still call into question the views of extreme relativism.

Whilst relativists helpfully warn us against the dangers of dogmatic absolutists imposing their convictions on everybody, absolute neutrality is a myth. As Thomas Nagel put it, it is the 'view from nowhere' when in fact everybody lives somewhere. Indeed, *relativists hold to at least one absolute – that there are no absolutes.* Their one objective moral claim is that there are no objective moral facts. So when they are in charge, their values would oblige them to limit the freedoms of, and perhaps even silence, the moral absolutist. So how tolerant and liberal are relativists when the one absolute they hold to is threatened?

Subjectivism seems *a very weak basis for action* in society. Would moral subjectivists ever have championed the Universal Declaration of Human Rights, or the Geneva Convention which, among other things, enshrines the rights of prisoners of war?

Weaknesses in moral absolutism

The moral subjectivist is all too aware of *how wrong human judgements can be* and perhaps more likely to be reasoned with because of this. Whilst we may admire the conviction of pacifists willing to die for their belief in non-violence, the fanaticism of absolutists who show no compromise (e.g., in honour killings of daughters who become pregnant outside of marriage, or the execution of homosexuals) is chilling.

Absolutism can follow the letter of the law without grace or compassion. Its uncompromising adherence to *rules can become oppressive*. The pacifist's resolute refusal to use violence even in self-defence can endanger others unable to defend themselves (e.g., the very young, old or disabled) and who depend on her for safety. Given human moral failings, any moral system needs to make room for a second chance, and absolute moral rules give a sense of rules which, when broken, lead to judgementalism. Moral absolutism can lead to the psychology of legalism: to an adherence to the letter but not the spirit of the law. In his Sermon on the Mount, Jesus condemns the hypocrisy of legalism by criticizing those who condemn the act of adultery while themselves looking at women lustfully.

Cultural relativism indicates the undeniably *complex and varied situations and dilemmas* people confront. Particular circumstances can be unique and consequently misunderstood when looked at from a different culture, time or place. The moral absolutist insists on the universality of moral principles, yet many have become obsolete e.g. the biblical commandments in Leviticus which are now obsolete, such as stoning to death mediums or spiritists (Leviticus 20:27).

Is absolutism the same as objectivity, and relativism the same as subjectivity in ethics?

Whilst absolutism and objectivity tie in strongly together just as relativism and subjectivity do, they are not exactly the same. It is possible to be relativist in certain respects while holding to an objective view of ethics. Take the example of a religious believer who considers sex before marriage to be wrong according to God's revelation in the Bible, but respects the right of his son and his partner to live together without mentioning this because they regard this as the loving thing to do in this situation. There is often a *gap between* what is knowable through reason and science (*epistemology*) and what is actually the case (*ontology*). Bridging this gap is particularly difficult in Moral Philosophy when we see the world from a particular culture, language, place and time, making it nearly impossible to arrive at the impartial perspective of the objective knower. Without a perspective external to time and place, one may be an objectivist, but wisely steer clear of absolutism in practical ethics. The same problem arises when two moral demands conflict – say, when a situation requires either truth-telling or compassion, or when killing innocent civilians is wrong but inevitable when going to war to defeat an aggressive and corrupt state.

One could also adopt absolutism for its effectiveness while not being an objectivist. For example, Singapore has the death penalty for kidnapping and drug trafficking, and law and order are important in a densely populated country. Between 1994 and 1999 it executed 13.83 people/100,000 per year. One could be a moral subjectivist, but support the absolutism of such laws in deterring dangerous actions. It is also possible to arrive at an objective rule in ethics while being relativist. Take a rule like 'Everyone ought to follow the principles whose universal acceptance everyone could rationally will and no-one could reasonably reject.' This rule begins from an objective rational basis (that of impartiality), yet it could be applied in a whole variety of ways relative to the circumstances of time and place.

Colonial powers in the Americas, India and Africa were convinced that they were 'civilising' primitive peoples. Postcolonial and postmodern critiques of this view of history show how, at the heart of their '*objectivity*', was a vision of the world with rich and powerful white European males at its centre. This moral 'objectivity' secured power for the privileged few, and slavery became justified from this perspective. So claims to moral objectivity come into conflict with human self-interest.

There is often *a gap between* what is knowable through reason and science (*epistemology*) and what is actually the case (*ontology*). Bridging this gap is particularly difficult in Moral Philosophy when we see the world from a particular culture, language, place and time, making it nearly impossible to arrive at the impartial perspective of the objective knower. Without a perspective external to time and place, is objectivity possible or knowable?

What happens *when two objective demands conflict* – say, when a situation requires either truth-telling or compassion, or when killing innocent civilians is wrong but inevitable when going to war to defeat an aggressive and corrupt state? Kant understood the dangers of making exceptions to rules given the human capacity to rationalise ourselves out of our obligations when they threaten to become too costly. When obedience to rules increases human suffering, then they seem to be irrational.

Deontological vs teleological approaches to ethics

Deontological ethics focus on duty (from the Greek, '*deon*', meaning 'what is true', or 'duty'), motives, and the rightness or wrongness of actions or rules rather than their justification in terms of consequences. It views 'goodness' in terms of what is morally right in and of itself, as opposed to instrumentally good in terms of the outcome, consequence or end goal of an act.

Philosophers distinguish between act and rule deontological theories. Although we will cover these in more detail in the chapter on Kantian Ethics, in brief, *act-deontologists* judge the rightness of their actions on the basis of what any just and impartial person would do in the same particular set of circumstances. By contrast, *rule-deontologists* follow fixed principles or rules that apply regardless of their ability to deliver favourable outcomes in specific cases. Immanuel Kant's Categorical Imperative offers one example of rule-deontology. Its fixed principle of acting with Good Will and in terms of universalising the rule by which one acts applies whether or not it promotes pleasure or pain. Kant is well aware of the human tendency to make exceptions to rules, for example when the obligations of a promise prove costly.

It may be supposed that deontological thought is seldom seen in areas of public policy, but this is not the case. Examples of deontological thinking are common to medical codes of conduct in the UK and internationally, such as:

- doctor–patient confidentiality (assuming that what is revealed does not break the law of the country concerned);
- patients not to be discriminated against on the grounds of age, disease or

Deontological ethics: Deontological ethics are concerned with fulfilling our duty (*deon* in Greek means 'duty'), to obey the moral law, as opposed to justifying an action in terms of motives or consequences. Duty presupposes a fixed and universal law, and the spirit of this approach is captured in the phrase 'Let justice be done though the heavens fall.'

disability, creed, ethnic origin, gender, nationality, political affiliation, race, sexual orientation, social standing or any other factor.

> **Teleological ethics:**
> **Telos** is the Greek word meaning 'goal' or 'end', and teleological ethics refers to moral statements based upon consequences. Actions are justified in terms of the favourable outcomes they result in.

Furthermore, in the post-World War II Geneva Declaration (1948), the clause about a doctor not using his/her medical knowledge contrary to the laws of humanity was framed partly in response to cases such as that of the infamous Nazi doctor Mengele, known as the 'angel of death'. He oversaw a team of medical doctors whose torturous 'experiments' in the notorious 'Block 10' at Auschwitz concentration camp included many operations without anaesthetic, as a result of which nearly all 'patients' lost their lives painfully and within hours or days. The idea that doctors may at times be bound by their duty to a moral law that transcends those of their country is deontological.

Teleological ethics (from the Greek, '*telos*', meaning 'goal' or 'purpose') can, confusingly, be used in two distinct senses.

(a) Aristotle's ethics focuses on the purpose of actions and beings. In this sense of teleology, everything is aimed towards an end purpose. This may be because some divine being(s) designed them that way, or simply because living things by their nature, work towards certain goals (whether consciously or not).

(b) Teleology can more simply refer to acting on the basis of achieving certain consequences or outcomes.

So teleological theories agree that our actions are goal-orientated. For Eudaimonistic theories like Virtue Ethics (which use '*telos*' in the sense of (**a**)), that goal is human flourishing or happiness in seeking the virtuous life ('*eudaimonia*' means happiness in the sense of flourishing).

By contrast, others use '*telos*' in the sense of (**b**), in which that outcome is the maximisation of pleasure (Bentham), or preferences/ choices (Singer). Here, the end goal can justify the means and, rather than having intrinsic rights and wrongs, choices and actions are instrumental or useful in bringing about good outcomes. This gets complicated because Mill (a Utilitarian) also reads Aristotle and broadens out Bentham's idea of pleasure to be more eudaimonistic and to speak of happiness in its broader sense of human flourishing.

The philosopher Elizabeth Anscombe, who was heavily influenced by Aristotle, came up with the term 'consequentialism' to describe the second sense of teleology above (**b**). She was extremely critical of this position (and of Utilitarianism in general) for several reasons:

- It denied that there was any difference between actions that were intended and those that were foreseen but not intended.
- If right and wrong are to be decided purely by outcomes, then where does ends – means justification stop? Anscombe was appalled at the use of the atomic bomb on Nagasaki and Hiroshima on these grounds.
- Motives or intentions are vital to understanding human behaviour and responsibility, yet consequentialism gives little or no importance to them.
- If it is true that right and wrong are to be judged by the consequences of decisions, we don't need to be consistent in our choices or lives. Whilst consistency

isn't an intrinsic good, if everyone works purely on a consequentialist basis, ethics becomes more inconsistent and has few enduring or basic values and principles.

For the purposes of your exam, teleological ethics is best seen in the sense of (**b**), and Anscombe's criticisms are relevant to it.

Case study from James Rachels

In his *Elements of Moral Philosophy*, James Rachels explains that what on the surface appears to be a conflict over *values* is simply one over *practice*. He cites the case of Eskimos who practised infanticide, often on perfectly healthy baby girls. On the surface, this 'gendercide', which would result in prosecution in the West, was a radically different ethic. Yet where resources are scarce and male hunter-gatherers (who have a high casualty rate) vital to the survival of a family, parental preferences for boys were more understandable. Taken together with the fact that Eskimo children needed to be breast-fed for four years and that mothers struggled to carry more than one on their back as they were a nomadic people, the Eskimo practice may be less about values (they did respect life and, where couples were childless, adoption was also common in Eskimo families) and more about necessity. The nomadic practice of moving from summer grazing grounds to sheltered winter land 500 miles away took Eskimos through life-threatening conditions such as blizzards. Stopping to care for elderly or infirm relatives could mean the difference between life and death, so they brought about quick deaths by, for example, dropping an elderly straggler through a hole in the ice.

Do you agree with the relativist's claim that Eskimos have different values or with Rachels' that this is more a matter of practice than values, and that Eskimos still highly value human life?

Eskimo woman, c.1907

Discussion Questions

1. Would you think of yourself as more of a relativist than an absolutist – what are your reasons for leaning one way or the other?
2. Are there certain issues on which you would consider yourself relativist/absolutist?
3. If you accept certain absolutes (e.g. that genocide is always wrong), on what basis are your principles uncompromising?
4. Ought a relativist to think of the United Nations Universal Declaration on Human Rights as mistaken? Why/why not?
5. What problems might arise with the view (taken by the ancient Greek thinker Protagoras) that 'Man is the measure of all things', and all morality is constructed by humans?

Exercise

Read through the summary of the two stories below and answer the questions that follow them.

Fyodor Dostoyevsky

Woody Allen

Crime and Punishment

In Dostoyevsky's book, Raskolnikov is a murderer whose conscience needles away at him so that in the end he confesses his crime and acknowledges some higher law or moral order to which he is obligated. He plotted to murder an elderly pawnbroker and moneylender. In the event, he kills both the pawnbroker and her half-sister, fleeing with only a few stolen items. Through a series of coincidences, he gets away with his crime. Yet he is plagued by guilt and falls ill under the weight of it, betraying himself whenever the now public news of the murder comes up.

The detective Porfiry begins to suspect him and, over time, becomes convinced on psychological grounds and because of motive, of Raskolnikov's responsibility for the crime. But without circumstantial evidence or

Crimes and Misdemeanours

In Woody Allen's film, Judah Rosenthal rejects the advice of a rabbi to confess his adultery to his wife. Instead, he pays to have his mistress murdered when she threatens to confront his wife with details of their affair. In the movie's final scene, Judah meets Woody Allen's character (Cliff). After learning that Cliff is a film producer, he pitches a supposedly hypothetical story to him in which a guilt-stricken man who has had an affair seeks to cover it up by ordering the murder of his mistress. A drifter is prosecuted and the murderer's crisis of emotions and guilt at the death of his mistress give way to a happy life. While Cliff objects that such a guilty character will forever have to deal with the lingering guilt of his crimes and misdemeanours, Judah dismisses his naivety.

witnesses, he has no case. Then another suspect confesses to the crime under questioning and Raskolnikov realises he will get away with it. But, as he meets and falls in love with Sonya, he confesses his crime to her and she eventually persuades him to confess his crime and goes with him into penal servitude in Siberia. Here, he finds redemption and new hope.

Dostoyevsky wrote this novel in part to counter the radical ideology of Russian nihilism. This revolutionary movement sought to overturn the order of society with ideas influenced by rationalism and Benthamite Utilitarianism (so that the categories of good and evil were replaced with pleasure and pain). The character Raskolnikov begins by weighing the expendable death of one selfish pawnbroker and moneylender against the good he can do for others with her money. He ends up believing that his subjective moral judgements about the worth of individuals are accountable to the moral order established by the higher justice of God.

He leaves, relaxed and respected as a family and professional man once again in control of his life and untroubled by his crimes.

Woody Allen's film offers a very different take on the question of whether a respectable and outwardly law-abiding citizen could live with the knowledge that he had ordered someone's murder. As an agnostic, Woody Allen, like his character Judah Rosenthal, has an existential take on life. He conceives that it is psychologically possible for Judah to live on, forgetting his affair and the murder of his mistress and enjoying his life as a loving father and husband savouring the comforts and joys of his life. His pleasures outweigh his troubles and he can forget about the past and live contentedly as a moral subjectivist.

1. Why may it be easier for a nihilist or a relativist to live with the guilt of committing murder than for a moral absolutist?
2. Raskolnikov confesses his murders while Judah Rosenthal forgets about his and gets on with a happy and prosperous life. Imagine they met each other, Raskolnikov taking the moral standpoint of an objective, deontological thinker and Rosenthal that of a subjectivist/relativist thinker. How do you think the conversation would go?
3. Try (as a deontologist) to convince Judah Rosenthal's character that he should hand himself in to the police.

FURTHER READING

Julia Driver (2009) *Ethics, the Fundamentals*. Blackwell Publishing

Harry J. Gensler (1998) *Ethics: A Contemporary Introduction*. Routledge, chs. 1 and 2 on Relativism and Subjectivism

Norman Lillegard (2010) *The Moral Domain: Guided Readings in Philosophical and Literary Texts*. Oxford University Press

James Rachels (1999) *The Elements of Moral Philosophy*. McGraw-Hill, 7th edition

Peter Singer (ed.) (1993) *Companion to Ethics*. Blackwell

Noel Stewart (2009) *Ethics: An Introduction to Moral Philosophy*. Polity

OCR Past Paper Questions

JUNE 2009
    (a) Explain the concept of relativist morality.   *[25]*
    (b) 'Relativist ethics are unfair.' Discuss.   *[10]*

JANUARY 2010
    (a) Explain what is meant by moral absolutism.   *[25]*
    (b) 'Moral absolutism cannot be justified.' Discuss.   *[10]*

JUNE 2010
    (a) Explain the differences between absolute and relative morality.   *[25]*
    (b) 'Relativist theories give no convincing reason why people should be good.'
        Discuss.   *[10]*

MAY 2012
    (a) Explain the differences between deontological and teleological
        approaches to ethical decision-making.   *[25]*
    (b) 'The ends justify the means.' Discuss.   *[10]*

JANUARY 2013
    (a) Explain the concept of absolute morality.   *[25]*
    (b) 'Considering consequences is more important than following rules.' Discuss.   *[10]*

CHAPTER

2 Natural Law

LEARNING OUTCOMES

In this chapter, you will learn

- the origins of Aquinas' Natural Law in Aristotle's idea of purpose
- Aquinas' ideas of purpose and perfection
- the use of reason to discover Natural Law
- the Primary and Secondary Precepts
- to discuss these views critically and their strengths and weaknesses

Malala Yousafzai. When the Taliban occupied the Swat Valley in Pakistan and attempted to ban girls from attending school, through writing a blog on the BBC website, Malala became an activist campaigning for her right to an education. After threats intended to silence her, on 9 October 2012, a gunman asked her name, then fired three shots at her from his pistol. **The Taliban gunman had force, so why did they fear Malala speaking out? Article 26 of the UN Declaration of Human Rights states that everyone has the right to an education. Are rights invented or self-evidently true?**

Malala Yousafzai in 2014

Law and justice

Do you have a moral duty to disobey unjust laws?
What gives law its authority?

Whenever we ask questions like 'What gives laws their legitimacy?', 'Do we have a duty to disobey unjust laws?', or 'Is there an objective standard (e.g. human reason or God) by which we can judge good and evil?', we are drawn into an age-old discussion of Natural Law. In ancient Greece, the Stoics used the term 'logos' to mean the ordering principle of the universe. Ethics was objectively grounded in the very nature of reality. Natural law was a kind of universal moral gravity. Socrates had paid the ultimate price for his belief in the just rule of law – he had accepted the unjust death sentence of an Athenian court. Determined not to accept an offer from friends to bribe guards to secure his escape, he refused to undermine the rule of Athenian law which he had spent his life advocating, even when its unjust judgement went against him. For Socrates and Plato, politics was a form of social ethics. The laws and judgements of Athenian courts were just insofar as they conformed to the eternal form of justice. Their unjust judgement on his teacher and mentor Socrates was to trigger Plato's lifelong quest for the eternal and universal justice by which such travesties could themselves be judged.

Plato (429–347 BCE), whose name may result from the width (*platos*) of his shoulders, was from a noble family who had political and poetic ambitions for him. Instead, he opted for philosophy and became a devoted pupil of Socrates, whose unjust death sentence at the hands of the Athenian court in 399 caused him to leave Athens. He was motivated to seek the perfect form of justice and attempted to train philosopher-kings who could implement this. Socrates speaks in most of Plato's dialogues and it is hard to distinguish the thought of one from the other. Plato founded the Academy, a school of philosophy in Athens. This is seen as the first university and it sought unchanging truth, Mathematics being central to this quest as it offered knowledge unspoilt by the changing physical world. For this reason, Plato placed the command 'let no-one ignorant of geometry enter here' above the entrance to his Academy. His work the *Republic* has a claim to being the most important political text in history. It sees politics as a form of social ethics and advocates the making of virtuous citizens through education. For Plato, defining ethical concepts clearly has a practical bearing on our lives. The questions he raised and his influence on Christian, Jewish and Islamic thought, not to mention Western philosophy and politics, led Alfred North Whitehead to comment that European philosophy is 'a series of footnotes to Plato'.

Developing this tradition in his *Nicomachean Ethics* (*NE*), the Greek philosopher Aristotle distinguished between *legal* justice and *natural* justice, 'which everywhere has the same force and does not exist by people's thinking this or that'. The Roman lawyer Cicero saw Roman laws as legitimate not because they were set down or 'posited' by authorities like the senate or emperor, but because they were grounded in a universal 'natural law' by which not only Roman citizens, but all humanity, were bound. In *De Republica*, he writes,

'True law is right reason in agreement with nature. It is applied universally and is unchanging and everlasting . . . there will be no different laws in Rome and in Athens, or different laws now and in the future, but one eternal and unchangeable law will be valid for all nations and all times.'

Natural Law is also evident in Paul's statement in Romans 2:14–16:

> *When Gentiles, who do not have the Law, do by nature things required by the Law, they are a law for themselves, even though they do not have the Law, since they show the requirements of the Law are written on their hearts, their consciences bearing witness, and their thoughts now accusing, now excusing them.'*

What do you think Paul meant by the above statement?   N.B. Gentiles are non-Jews

Moving on from the first century to the eighteenth, the opening line of the American Declaration of Independence refers to 'the Laws of Nature and of Nature's God' in grounding inalienable human rights: 'We hold these truths to be self-evident, that all men are created equal, that they are endowed by their Creator with certain

unalienable Rights, that among these are Life, Liberty and the pursuit of Happiness.'
The idea of a universal moral law appeared to be 'self-evident' though this may have
owed much to the widely held belief in God.

Do you think this is a less 'self-evident' belief in today's world?

This belief in Natural Law and rights is a tradition that Martin Luther King drew on
in his 1962 'Letter from a Birmingham Jail' in arguing that:

> There are two types of laws: just and unjust. One has not only a legal but a moral
> responsibility to obey just laws. Conversely, one has a moral responsibility to disobey
> unjust laws. We should never forget that everything Adolf Hitler did in Germany was 'legal'.
> I submit that an individual who breaks a law that conscience tells him is unjust, and who
> willingly accepts the penalty of imprisonment in order to arouse the conscience of the
> community over his injustice, is in reality expressing the highest respect for law. . . . How
> does one determine whether a law is just or unjust? A just law is a man-made code that
> squares with the moral law or the law of God. An unjust law is a code that is out of harmony
> with the moral law. To put it in terms of St. Thomas Aquinas; an unjust law is a human law
> that is not rooted in eternal law and natural law.

Martin Luther King (1929-68) was an American clergyman and a leader in the African
American civil rights movement. He led protests against segregation on buses in Montgomery
in 1955 and confronted the brutal police of Birmingham, Alabama, with non-violent protests
to focus national attention on the injustices of racial discrimination and segregation. King was
an electrifying orator who said in his 'I have a dream' speech to over 250,000 in Washington
(1963), 'When the architects of our republic wrote the magnificent words of the Constitution
and the Declaration of Independence, they were signing a promissory note ... that all men -
yes, black men as well as white men - would be guaranteed the unalienable rights of life,
liberty, and the pursuit of happiness. It is obvious today that America has defaulted on this
promissory note insofar as her citizens of color are concerned ... But we refuse to believe that the bank of justice is
bankrupt.' In 1964, he received the Nobel Peace Prize and, in 1968, Congress was to pass the Civil Rights Act before
his assassination on 29 March of the same year.

**How might the language of MLK's words above be said to draw on an appeal to a moral law from which
national laws gained their legitimacy and authority? What is it that makes rights unalienable (they can't be
bought, sold or transferred), if it is not that they are 'endowed by the creator'?**

Understanding Aquinas' Natural Law theory – four types of law

Aquinas' response to the kinds of questions asked at the start of the chapter was to
distinguish between four types of law: eternal law, divine law, natural law and human
law. As we see below, he saw human laws as just, or actions rational, insofar as they
participate in the eternal law of the creator.

> *Eternal law* was the mind or reason of God. This could be seen only in terms of its effects
> in Natural Law and in 'moving all things to their due end' (*Summa Theologica* (*ST*)). The
> wisdom of God was reflected in his creation and sustaining of nature but could not be known
> directly by man.

Divine law was revealed in the laws and moral precepts of scripture, providing a corrective to the fallenness of man. Aquinas believed that human reason was not so impaired by the fall as to be unable to think rightly about ethics. The revelation of scripture and the worship of the Church supplemented our understanding of the divine purposes and motivated our moral life with an inspiring vision of divine perfection and holiness. Yet it was not exhaustive in directing our moral conduct or applying to all circumstances, and here, natural and human law both express and supplement divine law.

As Aquinas writes, 'the theologian considers sin principally as an offence against God, whereas the moral philosopher considers it as being contrary to reason' (*Summa Theologica*, Ia IIae, 71, 6, ad5).

Natural Law is innate to all of nature which is ordered by the divine lawmaker. Morality is reason thinking rightly in humans, who, by their innate knowledge and natural inclination, can discern primary goods which are worth pursuing for their own end. God has ordered nature with essences/inclinations suited towards their purpose or end goals. Innate to human minds is the synderesis rule (that good is to be done and evil avoided).

Human law. Aquinas was no anarchist. He sought to underpin respect for proper human law and authority that sought the common good. What begins in nature is, through custom and usefulness, established in human laws through practical reasoning and experienced judgement (*phronēsis*). There can be unjust laws that are not rooted in Natural Law. As he writes, 'if in any point it deflects from the law of nature, it is no longer a law but a perversion of law' (ST I–II, Q.95, A.II).

Exercises

1. The ancient Greek philosopher Protagoras wrote that 'man is the measure of all things'. In contrast, Aquinas wrote that a law bears the character of a measure and since measures should be accurate and certain and human reasoning is not certain, no law can arise out of human reason. Instead, it must be measured by its participation in the eternal law.
   Do you think laws against murder are based on objective moral rules or on the subjective thoughts of humans?

2. Aquinas claimed that slavery, though 'devised by human reason for the benefit of human life, did not alter 'the law of nature . . . except by addition'.
   What problems might arise from the fact that we think that slavery is immoral today and yet Aquinas accepted it within his system of Natural Law?

Aquinas' medieval synthesis of Aristotle and Augustine – what he learned from each

Aquinas saw Natural Law as 'nothing else than the rational creature's participation in the eternal law'. He *synthesised* the 'new' knowledge of Aristotle's system of thought with that of the Bible and Augustine at a time when many thought it incompatible. He saw faith and reason, philosophy and theology as a collaborative search for truth. Revelation had nothing to fear from the insights of reason. Fallen as it was, man's reason had not been so impaired as to make the ethical life impossible. In the two sections that follow, we shall explore what he learned from Aristotle and from Augustine.

Aristotle (384–322 BCE)
Aristotle's father was the physician to the king of Macedonia and, like many parents today, wanted his son to be a doctor too. From eighteen years of age, Aristotle studied at Plato's Academy in Athens. Through his connections, he became a personal tutor to a thirteen-year-old who would become Alexander the Great, and Aristotle was later to set up his own school, The Lyceum, in Athens in 334 BCE as he began to diverge from Plato and develop his own ideas. Following Plato's death, his nephew became head of his Academy, rather than Aristotle (perhaps because, as a non-citizen, the latter could not own property in Athens). Aristotle is seen as an early empiricist. He comes to base judgements more on sense perceptions than pure reason, studying biology and classifying types of objects in the natural world. Where Plato's Academy had focused on subject matters like Geometry or the harmonics of sound, Aristotle was more practical, performing dissections (his father may have given him some lessons in medicine, even surgical technique) and categorising knowledge in a more systematic way. In some ways a precursor to science, though his findings here – more than his method – are obsolete, his writings on ethics, rhetoric and politics remain influential today.

In the Early Middle Ages, Muslim scholars had translated or preserved Aristotle's ancient-Greek writings in Arabic/Aramaic. The recovery of forty-two books where there had previously been two caused controversy. When these works differed from the Church's teaching on a personal God, an immortal soul or creation, some censorship occured. In his *Summa Theologica* (1265–74), however, Aquinas sought to synthesise Aristotle with the Christian tradition.

From Aristotle, Aquinas learned that . . .

Nature is goal directed

As Aristotle writes, 'Nature makes nothing without a purpose' (in his treatise *On the Soul*). Drawing on Aristotle's teleology, Aquinas believed that God's eternal law had so devised the natural world and its creatures that they possessed a natural tendency to pursue the behaviour and goals appropriate to the natures he had given them. An acorn's purpose or end goal (***telos***) is to grow into an oak tree, and an oak tree flourishes with growth and produces more acorns. A 'good' eagle is one whose attributes (eyesight, talons, wing-span, strength) make it a supreme predator.

Aquinas' goal-orientated or teleological view of nature drew on Aristotle's account of the four causes.

For Aristotle, nature was directed towards an end – it was teleological (*telos* = goal/end). We need to pay attention to our nature or form, the second kind of cause. We are bodily, social and rational beings, so it follows that we should ask after the goals and habits that allow our potential to be fully actualised. Aristotle uses the word *kalon* meaning beautiful/good in respect of good acts or habits that allow us to realise fully our essential nature. Attending to our purpose or end goals relates to the third and fourth causes. The 'good life' (***eudaimonia*** refers to the good or flourishing life) is to be spent training our habits and desires (in some sense, the efficient cause of character growth in virtue) to the rational end of flourishing rather than stunting our development (final cause).

Telos:
The goal or end purpose of anything. All of nature is seen in Aristotle's thought as directed towards a final end – as goal-orientated.

1 Material cause (matter)	What is it made of? Marble
2 Formal cause (form)	What are its characteristics? Sculpted marble in human form.
3 Efficient cause (source)	What brought it about? Sculpted by Michelangelo
4 Final cause (purpose)	To depict the biblical king/ make money

Seeing the four cases in Michelangelo's *David*

Aristotle held a goal-orientated or teleological view of nature. The potential of every object or being in the material world was fulfilled when directed towards its proper purpose or end. The unmoved mover was the ultimate cause, everything else was moving arrowlike to its intended target.

Aristotle would agree with the warning that sometimes appears on TV – 'Do not try this at home on your own!'; how do you develop virtues like generosity or justice, humility or compassion on your own? We need families, communities, even states, to thrive in and fully express our natures.

For Aristotle, the supreme expression of the final cause of nature was the unmoved mover. As the highest conceivable good, God's being was fully actualised – perfectly fulfilled potential. In contrast to the divine, the natural world was constantly changing and full of potential – for example, infants have the potential to grow into adults. Nature is dynamic and Aristotle argued that nature's order, beauty and goodness were not due to mere chance. Nature was, in its essence and inclination, directed towards ends and purposes that fulfilled its potential. There was *logos* or a rational principle (for Aquinas this was the mind of God) ordering nature.

Humans possess a rational soul that can recognise God's law

The soul was the essence of a thing for Aristotle. Within it was contained the potentiality for growth or the actualisation of its essence. The essence of man was his rational soul. The rational soul was able to intuit the Natural Law. Thought and intellect are what set mankind apart as being capable of contemplation in art, maths and science, and as possessing the capacity to will goals and train their habits. Here Aristotle distinguished between the three kinds of soul shown in the table.

1 The soul of material things	2 The soul of animals	3 The soul of humans
Vegetative	Appetitive	Rational mind *(nous)*
(Potential for nutrition, growth and reproduction)	((1) + potential for sensation, movement, reproduction and training of offspring)	((1, 2) + potential for practical and theoretical reasoning and intellectual and moral virtues (the latter being the ordering of the will through habitual training to govern the appetites), and for worshipping God)

True happiness or flourishing (*eudaimonia*) is bound up with a virtuous life

Aquinas saw that we desire happiness and that it is often realised in the fulfilment of our true potential. The highest of goals 'is always desirable in itself, and never for the sake of something else' (*NE* 1.7). For Aristotle, true fulfilment of human potential (***eudaimonia***) came in the pursuit of excellence (***arêté***) in terms of moral and intellectual virtues. His *Nicomachean Ethics* was either edited by or dedicated to his son (Nicomachus), and drew together his notes from his school, the Lyceum. It taught the *interconnectedness of virtue and happiness*. The life well lived was dedicated to the fulfilment of the highest intellectual and moral virtues, for virtue is its own reward. In flourishing as a rational, social and moral being, it is our faculty of reason that most closely connects us with the divine, therefore 'We must . . . strain every nerve in order to live in accordance with the best thing in us' (*NE* 10.7). The paradox is that self-actualisation cannot be selfish. Our soul's good cannot be fulfilled with 'selfish' desire. The *polis* or peaceful and harmonious ordering of communities like the Greek citystate of Athens is fundamental to the thriving of each citizen. So politics is really a form of social ethics. Through experience and practice, as well as by working with wise teachers, we develop the practical wisdom (***phronēsis***) to make wise judgements in any given situation.

> ***Eudaimonia:***
> The good life – flourishing, fulfilment and happiness in a holistic sense – the flourishing of any form of life aimed at actualising its full potential

> ***Arêté:***
> Virtue, or any good characteristic or excellence. *Arêté* involves committed and purposeful training and practice usually under the tutelage of a master-practitioner.

Augustine (354–430 BCE)
Augustine became Bishop of Hippo and remains the single most influential Christian theologian in the West outside of the New Testament writers. His *Confessions* offer a spiritual autobiography of striking insight and honesty. After a fairly hedonistic lifestyle, in his late twenties, he lived with a woman by whom he had a son, and he admits in his *Confessions* to God that, 'I delayed from day to day the conversion to you . . . even while I sought for it. I thought that I would be miserable if I were kept from a woman's arms.' Such quotes are taken by many to advocate virginity and take a low view of sex, starting a long tradition of guilt associated with sexuality. Yet it may be that Augustine's relationship had been with a freed slave, in which case the law would have forbidden him, as a Roman Citizen, from marrying her.

   Augustine saw God as the source of all goodness and of no evil, but human nature, like the natural world, had a tendency to decay and to fall away from its eternal creator. Such is the corruption of the human will to obey divine commands that, without the assistance of God's grace, humankind would be powerless to fulfil them.

From Augustine, Aquinas learned that. . .

Human nature and reason are corrupted by the Fall

As is evident from his *Confessions*, Augustine is very aware of the fallenness of human nature which, without divine grace, is incapable of living up to its own standards let alone God's, or of earning its own salvation. He drew on St Paul who wrote that 'what I do is not the good I want to do; no, the evil I do not want to do – this I keep on doing' (Romans 7:19). Evil is a privation of good, a falling short of the flourishing life. The problem here is that our will is moved not only by reason, but also by our desires – by our loves. So, for Augustine, the moral life is not simply a question of knowing what makes for the flourishing life. It is also one of confession, divine grace and habitual training in virtue. We can see Augustine's influence in Aquinas' highlighting of *seven vices* (later termed deadly sins) – pride, greed, lust, envy, gluttony, anger and sloth, which corrupt the capacity of our reason to know the Natural Law.

Mankind's proper end is a harmonious relationship with his creator God

As Augustine famously put it, 'Thou hast made us for Thyself, O Lord, and our hearts are restless until they rest in Thee' (*Confessions*, ch. 1). For Augustine, the Fall has obscured humankind's vision of God. Despite this, reason and free will have not been lost. Here, the theological virtues of faith, hope and charity/love allow us to flourish fully in an ethical way in directing us to our ultimate end – *union with God given to us by his grace*. Aquinas sees that the cardinal virtues of temperance, wisdom, justice and courage will need to be transposed onto a higher level by the theological virtues of faith, hope and charity/love. As he puts it, 'Temperance is love keeping itself entire and incorrupt for God; fortitude is love bearing everything readily for God's sake; justice is love serving God only and therefore ruling all else well; prudence is love distinguishing between what helps it towards God and what might hinder it' (*On the morals of the Catholic Church*, XV). Moral virtues lead us to God as the source behind Natural Law and our ultimate end. As C. S. Lewis put it, 'The human mind has no more power of inventing a new value than of imagining a new primary colour, or, indeed, of creating a new sun and a new sky for it to move in' (Lewis, *The Abolition of Man*, Clarendon Press, 1943). Yet mankind's imperfect happiness and fulfilment in this life were an indication that our souls were created for another life beyond death. This should direct our reason to the heavenly and eternal beatific vision of God as the ultimate source and satisfaction of human desire.

Aquinas' *Summa Theologica* became a central text in European universities of the Middle Ages. Here we consider several key terms in his work.

Thomas Aquinas (1225–1274)

Thomas Aquinas, the most significant theologian/philosopher of the medieval period, was canonised (declared a saint by the Catholic Church) in 1323. Born in a castle to the Count of Aquino, his family were bitterly opposed to him becoming a Dominican friar (a monk devoted to study). They had ambitions for him to rise to a powerful position in the Church. His brothers are even said to have kidnapped him, keeping him for more than a year in the family castle. Having begun his studies aged five at the Abbey of Montecassino, he went to the University of Naples and then entered the Dominican Order. Nicknamed the 'dumb ox', perhaps because of his size and possibly his weight, his academic flair soon became evident. At his death aged no more than fifty, he had penned around 8 million words in commentaries and works of natural theology. His *Summa Theologica* was to synthesise the scientific reason of Aristotle (on whose works Aquinas had written commentaries) with Christian teaching on faith and scripture. He wanted to integrate revelation and human reason and see them as compatible. Many truths (including knowledge of the existence of God and the moral law) can be arrived at through human reason and logic, independent of revelation. Thomism (the name for his school of thought) still remains central to Roman Catholic theology and ethics.

The Synderesis Principle

The Synderesis Principle 'that good should be done and evil avoided' (*ST* II, I, 94 art. 2) is innately known by our conscience. According to Aquinas, this is our inner knowledge of and natural disposition towards doing good and avoiding evil – one that is innate – a natural disposition of humans to understand the first principles of morality. For Aquinas, all creation is ordered by God's eternal law and each part of it expresses its essential nature in its inclination towards the Natural Law. For example, a 'flourishing' eagle is an efficient predator. As rational creatures, human beings possess reason and free will. Reason directs us towards our proper ends and the actions that lead to them.

The distinction between real and apparent goods

Aquinas distinguishes between real goods (which direct us to the happiness or flourishing that results from fulfilling our essential natures in accordance with the precepts of the Natural Law), and apparent goods (where a lack of practical judgement or virtue misdirects our actions towards ends that we mistakenly take to be good). One example he offers is 'A fornicator seeks a pleasure which involves him in moral guilt' (*Summa Theologica*, 1a, 19, 9). What is sinful here is that the fornicator who engages in sexual intercourse with an unmarried woman pursues pleasure as an end in itself. For Aquinas, the proper end of sexual intercourse is reproduction and, should a pregnancy occur as a result of fornication, the father may avoid his responsibilities as a parent. Real goods direct us towards the proper ends that preserve and promote the flourishing of human nature.

Pleasure is not a primary good, and the pleasure paradox is that if we make it an end in itself, it recedes from us, as anyone who's eaten too much chocolate will know. Humans naturally incline towards courses of action in which 'good is to be done and pursued and evil to be avoided'; few intentionally and wholeheartedly pursue evil ends, yet we may choose a bad action under the appearance of a good one. Examples would be wilfully doing evil so that good may come of it (e.g. giving a terminally ill patient a lethal injection to end their suffering) yet breaking the Primary Precept of preserving life.

> **Primary Precepts:** Arrived at by observing the goals towards which human action tends to gravitate

Primary and Secondary Precepts and how they are derived

Primary Precepts concern the goals towards which human action gravitates (e.g. the preservation of life). These are absolute and universal principles that are self-evident and express natural human inclinations. Aquinas sees natural human inclinations as directing us to certain precepts:

> **Secondary Precepts:** These make Primary Precepts normative in terms of what ought to be done (e.g. provision of shelter, healthcare, protection for the vulnerable). Through practical knowledge, the primary goods come to be applied.

- to preserve life and health
- to live in an ordered society
- to worship God
- to learn and seek truth and educate offspring
- to reproduce.

Secondary Precepts are derived from Primary Precepts through practical reasoning and consider what ought to be done in a more specific way. Primary Precepts are descriptive of natural inclinations, whereas secondary ones are prescriptive, having the force of a duty or command. Primary Precepts are absolute and universal, whereas secondary ones can vary widely based on the circumstances of time or place. For example, how in practice, we educate or look after our health has varied greatly according to time and place. Examples of Secondary Precepts may be seen below:

Do not legalise euthanasia.
Education ought not to be denied to people on the grounds of wealth or gender.
Do not waste your opportunities to learn by being lazy.
Obey just laws and authorities.
Work for the common good of your community and society.

Phronēsis – practical reasoning and judgement

Phronēsis:
Practical judgement or wisdom generally built up through experience and observation, and seen in judgements that find the mean or middle course between deficiency and excess

To understand how these primary goods come to be applied, we need to grasp Aristotle's distinction between theoretical and practical knowledge. Theoretical knowledge is abstract and intellectual, but practical reason, wisdom or judgement (*phronēsis*) is necessary if we are to avoid being unduly swayed by our passions and do the right things for the right reasons at the right time. Such practical wisdom develops through virtuous habits that dispose us to act rationally; right reason must be married to right desire. Aquinas defines virtue as 'a good habit bearing on activity', so a combination of reason, virtuous inclination and conscience together help us to arrive at practical judgements in the specific cases. The virtues strengthen our practical rationality – for example, prudence and temperance inform our judgements and train us to desire the right things.

Motives matter – the distinction between exterior and interior acts

Aquinas makes another distinction between interior acts (intentions or motives) and exterior acts (actions). A kind act (e.g. giving alms for charity) may be motivated by a wholly selfish intent (for vainglory or to buy favour or obligation). As rational creatures, we are responsible for both our desires and our motives according to Aquinas. The intention that wills the act determines whether it is good or evil. Exterior acts can be evil in themselves, such as adultery or theft, but as Jesus identifies in the Sermon on the Mount, the rightness of a deed or act springs from the inner motive – 'he who looks at a woman lustfully has already committed adultery with her in his heart' (Matthew 5:28).

The Doctrine of Double Effect

In the *Summa Theologica*, Aquinas addresses the problem of killing in self-defence. In using force when faced with life-threatening violence, a person both upholds and goes against the Primary Precept of preserving life. Aquinas addresses such cases in which the harmful effects are part and parcel of the good effect, by paying attention to the motives involved. Four criteria are set down to establish this:

The act to be done must be good in itself or at least indifferent.
The good effect must not be obtained by means of the bad effect.

The bad effect must not be intended for itself, only permitted.

There must be a proportionately grave reason for permitting the bad effect.

We will look at this principle in more detail in the chapters on abortion and euthanasia.

Proportionalism – a revision of Natural Law, or consequentialism creeping into it?

The more absolute character of Natural Law can appear to lead to harsh and unbending decisions. Yet it has a long tradition of casuistry (taking general moral principles and considering how best to apply them to particular cases). A controversial example of this type of thinking is seen in **Proportionalism** (a view popularised by Bernard Hoose in a book of the same title and also by Richard McCormick). This position is seen as a kind of middle way between consequentialism and deontological ethics. In unavoidable circumstances where both good and evil will result from an action, the proportion between the two is weighed in choosing the lesser of two evils.

Some examples of Proportionalism may be seen in Just War theory, in which violence may be used to bring about peaceful ends, or in a case where the theft of food would prevent starvation from hunger (both of which Aquinas sanctions). Hoose extends this. In ectopic pregnancies, for example, the embryo mostly implants in the fallopian tube. If this ruptures, internal bleeding could result in the death of the mother, whilst lasering the embryo would destroy it without threatening her future fertility. Hoose argues for this as the lesser of two evils, a proportionate response. The treatment is being done with the primary intention of saving life but in full knowledge that it would go against the Primary Precept of preserving life (in terms of the embryo). Here certain goods of character, such as dignity, integrity or justice, are being served. For Proportionalists, this is not consequentialist reasoning but the application of Natural Law in practical reasoning to bring about a proportionate good as opposed to the cruel inflexibility of exceptionless laws. The Catholic Church has, however, condemned proportionalism as a form of consequentialism (see the encyclicals *Veritatis Splendor* (*The Splendour of Truth*, 1993, s. 75), and *Evangelium Vitae* (*The Gospel of Life*, 1995, art. 68).

Exercise

Write out the terms opposite on a series of cards. In 1 minute, describe or define them without mentioning the actual word on the card. See how many correct terms your fellow students can come up with.

The final cause
The efficient cause
The eternal law
Natural Law
Real and apparent goods
The Synderesis Principle
Phronēsis
Arêté
Eudaimonia
Interior and exterior acts
Primary Precepts
Secondary Precepts
The Doctrine of Double Effect
Proportionalism

Criticisms of Natural Law theory

Evolutionary science has led to a widespread rejection of final causes or purpose in nature

It may be argued that Aquinas' thirteenth-century belief in nature as purposive and goal-orientated becomes obsolete after Darwin. In *On the Origin of Species* (1859), Darwin argued that nature evolved in the competition for survival. Natural selection is the blind watchmaker – unsighted and uncaring. So whilst Aristotle's knowledge may have been new in Aquinas' day, the idea that we can see in nature that the essence of everything is ordered to a purpose or goal by the unmoved mover is by no means obvious in modern science.

The Fact–Value Gap

Natural Law attempts to move from the facts about the essential nature of the world to values about how we ought to live in it: from descriptions of the essential nature of things in the world to prescriptions about how we ought to act or behave. For David Hume, there is a gap between these two types of statement. We simply do not 'see' moral facts. The factual statement 'People lie' is different from the value judgement 'You ought to tell the truth.' As James Rachels puts it, 'It may be that sex does produce babies, but it does not follow that sex ought or ought not to be engaged in only for that purpose. Facts are one thing, values are another' (Rachels 2006, p. 52). Take the use of Natural Law theory to condemn homosexuality on the grounds that the natural order of sexual relations is heterosexual and open to reproduction. Can what is 'good' be identified as being 'natural' without begging the question 'Is what is natural good?' We may observe that 'the function of the eye is to see', but the statement that 'the function of human sexuality is reproduction' seems to make a moral judgement when it involves ruling out barrier methods of contraception as contrary to nature.

The list of basic human goods varies across time and cultures

The atheist philosopher Kai Nielsen dismisses Aquinas' out-dated view of a fixed or essential human nature. In his view, Natural Law theory is to be rejected along with medieval physics and cosmology. Science, history and anthropology dismiss the idea of a single human nature common to humankind across time and place. Aquinas saw homosexuality as unnatural, and yet it is observable in non-human animals.

Cultural anthropology shows us just how variable human values and goods turn out to be. The prohibition on usury (interest on loans) was praised in a feudal age when the aristocratic class rarely borrowed, but with the increasing wealth of financiers and industrialists, the prohibition on usury ended. Some recent Natural Law scholars have even added marriage as a basic good.

Its absolutism leads to negative consequences

Utilitarians believe that they can weigh basic goods against one another on the scales of pleasure and pain. While we may be tempted to find the foundations for human rights in Natural Law, morality seems far from rooted in self-evident natural principles that are universally agreeable. In particular, Natural Law's aversion to making moral decisions based on consequences (except in the **Doctrine of Double Effect**) makes decision-making in dilemmas very difficult to calculate. Utilitarians are far happier to weigh conflicting goods on the scales of pleasure and pain and steel themselves as they trade off compassion against promise-keeping, or preserving life against truth-telling, in achieving the best outcome. Modern citizens generally approach ethical theories from the angle 'What should I do in this dilemma?' rather than 'How do I pursue a flourishing and worthwhile life?'

The Principle of Double Effect and Proportionalism recognise the serious dangers of principles or rules that can lead to greater suffering. With the world population at 7 billion and rising fast, if every life has to be preserved, and not only abortion but also contraception are forbidden, this can lead to overpopulation, suffering and poverty. An absolutist view of the Primary Precept of life (its preservation and reproduction) can lead to policies that do little to address the spread of HIV/AIDS or the suffering of the dying. If the promotion of contraception rather than sexual abstinence were undertaken, the spread of HIV could be lessened. If euthanasia were legalised, many terminally ill patients could be granted an end to pain which is, in their view, unbearable and pointless. Of course such logic runs counter to the absolutism of the Primary Precepts.

Natural Law theory is too closely allied to the Roman Catholic Church

The Catholic Church's justification for viewing abortion, euthanasia, contraception and IVF as morally wrong, as well as the emphasis on marriage as a basic good, is rooted in Natural Law thinking. As Peter Singer comments, Natural Law is 'The semi-official philosophy of the Roman Catholic Church to this day' (*Practical Ethics*, p. 243). The papal encyclicals on the ethics of the sanctity of life – see *Humanae Vitae* (*Human Life*, 1968), *Veritatis Splendor* (*The Splendour of Truth*, 1993), and *Evangelium Vitae* (*The Gospel of Life*; 1995) – are all based on Natural Law principles. While some secular thinkers are drawn to it (e.g. the philosopher Jeffrey Stout at Princeton), others, such as Singer, are suspicious that it is a veiled attempt to present Church teachings as common sense.

A theological objection: the fallen reason of mankind is not free and it is optimistic to think that it naturally inclines to doing good and avoiding evil or that it only goes wrong when mistakenly aiming at apparent rather than real goods

Drawing on Augustine, the protestant theologians Karl Barth and Reinhold Niebuhr questioned the faith that Aquinas' Natural Law placed in the moral reasoning of fallen human beings. Aquinas believed that, despite the fall, mankind retained an innate tendency to do good and avoid evil (the *Synderesis* Principle) and morality was reason thinking rightly.

Niebuhr argued that it is not simply the virtue of love that was corrupted at the fall, but also human justice and free will. Human beings are creatures made in the image of God. Yet they are also sinners, as is taught in Calvin's doctrine of total depravity. Reason's powers to discern good from evil are corrupted by pride and self-interest.

Karl Barth saw Natural Law as man seeking autonomy or independence from God's commands. Barth's friend, the German theologian Dietrich Bonhoeffer, even argued that ethics, or knowledge of good and evil, began at the fall. He believed that ethics represented an attempt to become our own creators, separate from God, and to know right from wrong not in relation to God but autonomously from him. In this view, ethics ought to reconnect with God, and emphasise the need for divine grace through Christ's atoning death, the revelation of scripture, and the Holy Spirit's inner work in convincing the conscience and renewing the will.

Karl Barth (1886-1968)
Karl Barth was a Swiss-German theologian who wrote *The Barmen Declaration* (1934), the Confessing Church's rejection of Nazism and its attempt to control the state church. He refused to sign the oath of allegiance to Hitler and had to leave his German lectureship in Bonn to take up one in his native Switzerland (in Basel). He saw nineteenth-century liberal theology, biblical studies and philosophy of religion as accommodating God's mystery to natural reason and thereby taming and domesticating God. Modern man sought to 'bolt and bar himself against revelation'. Yet, for Barth, apart from God's revelation in Christ's incarnation and through scripture and his Spirit, God remained wholly other. He agreed with Kierkegaard about the 'infinite qualitative distinction between God and mankind'. That so many of his highly educated university teachers and peers should capitulate so easily to the Nazi regime revealed for Barth just how accommodated they were to the spirit of the age. Barth believed that any capacity he and his fellow-theologian Dietrich Bonhoeffer had to see the idolatry of the Nazi state and Hitler came through attention to the 'strange new world of scripture', which revealed the divine command and named the injustices of the day for what they were.

Exercise

Which of the six criticisms of Natural Law theory do you find the most serious challenges to the theory? Choose three and explain why you have chosen them.

Taking it further: the revival of Natural Law
John Finnis (1940–), Germain Grisez (1929–)

With all of the above objections, it might look as though Natural Law is indefensible today. Yet the work of several thinkers has led to a revival of this theory in a form that meets many of these criticisms. Aquinas' approach to Natural Law said 'This is your essential human nature – now be who you are.' This tends to produce an ethic that is conformist and heavy on 'Do not' precepts, focusing on laws not persons. By contrast,

Table 2 Natural Law theory: the pros and cons

Pros	Cons
• It has a long tradition over many cultures – Jewish, Greek, Roman, etc. It can also provide a basis for dialogue in a multicultural society. It points to what is common to human nature and seeks an orderly society and world.	• Evolutionary science has rejected final causes and goal-orientated purposes in nature.
• It is based on reason and does not require scriptural revelation or laws. Just by using practical reasoning and observation of what activities human nature inclines towards, most of the Primary Precepts are clear and the Secondary ones derivable.	• The fact–value gap. Natural Law is guilty of leaping from descriptions of the essential nature of things in the world (facts) to prescriptions about how they ought to act or behave (values).
• It offers a foundation for law that gives it legitimacy and can account for why certain actions are universally and intrinsically wrong, e.g. torture. This allows for moral judgements to transcend cultural differences. The UN Declaration of Human Rights expresses this universality and absolute nature of ethics.	• The list of basic goods varies across time and culture. • Is there a single morality or is ethics relative to time and place? Relativists could challenge the claim that there is a single morality from the study of history. Even Natural Law theory has evolved over time.
• It is morally realist and offers a basis for universal moral principles. If one assumes there to be a fixed human nature and eternal moral law built into the universe, then the fact–value distinction can be rejected.	• Natural Law theory is too closely allied to the Catholic Church. Why should secular minds accept traditional sources of moral authority? They claim that the idea of a fixed essence to human nature and morality is used to argue for arbitrary limits to human freedom.
• It offers a holistic account of character, intentions and actions as well as finding a natural harmony between community and co-operative practice over individualism.	• Protestant theologians have questioned Aquinas' belief in the natural inclination of human nature to do good and avoid evil. Is Natural Law too optimistic about the human capacity to act morally under its own reason and not solely by divine grace?

the new Natural Law theorists accept Hume's distinction between 'fact' and 'value' statements. They work inductively through practical reasoning, first identifying basic goods that make for human flourishing, then applying these to specific circumstances.

Princeton Law professor Robert George has also argued that the foundations of legal theory cannot simply rest on legal positivism (the view that law rests on the authority of society/its legislators rather than upon any necessary connection with morality). In his view, it is crucial to guarantee human rights with a more secure moral foundation than that they are currently agreed by the powers that be.

The philosopher John Finnis

Finnis usefully develops the idea of **phronēsis** in nine principles of practical reasoning to offer a clearer idea of how to move from Primary Precepts (what he calls basic goods) to Secondary Precepts.

1. *Good* is to be done and evil avoided in a purposeful and rational way. Have a life plan and pursue it with commitment of time, energy and resources.
2. Do not discount as of no value or *exaggerate* any of the basic human goods.
3. Be *impartial* in dealing with others and do not discount or exaggerate the value of other people's participation in human goods.
4. Avoid becoming fanatical about your own projects – keep a sense of *perspective* and be able to detach yourself from your immediate goals and see wider perspectives.
5. Be creative and committed, and think about the *consequences* of your actions.
6. Be *efficient* – do not waste opportunities or overlook foreseeable bad consequences of your choices. Material resources, time and energy are limited, so use them wisely.
7. Foster the *common* good of your community.
8. Do not justify going against any basic good by arguing that the *end* justifies the means.
9. Do not go against your *conscience*. For example, do not pursue apparent goods knowing them to be only the simulations of real goods even when they bring about real emotions or satisfactions.

Old Style Natural Law theory	Finnis—Grisez School of Natural Law theory
Logic is deductive. (from essential nature to action)	Logic is inductive. (from practical reason rather than human motives urges and inclincations)
Heavy on prohibitions	Develops practical rationality to deal better with dilemmas
Conformist and too rigid	A rich and flexible understanding of the human good that moves from facts to values through practical reasoning.

FURTHER READING

Peter Baron (2012) *Kant and Natural Law*. PushMe Press

John Finnis (1979) *Natural Law and Natural Rights*. Clarendon Press

Robert P. George (2009) *In Defence of Natural Law*. Oxford University Press

Stanley J. Grenz (1997) *The Moral Quest*. Apollos, IVP

James Rachels (2002) *The Elements of Moral Philosophy*. McGraw-Hill

Peter and Charlotte Vardy (2012) *Ethics Matters*. SCM Press, ch. 5

OCR Past Paper Questions

JANUARY 2001
  (a) Explain the theory of Natural Law.   *[25]*
  (b) 'If Natural Law theory is applied rigidly to ethical problems, obvious
      injustices arise.' Discuss.   *[10]*

JANUARY 2007
  (a) Explain how a follower of Natural Law might respond to issues raised
      by genetic engineering.   *[25]*
  (b) 'Genetic engineering is "playing God".' Discuss.   *[10]*

JUNE 2007
  (a) Explain the main strengths of Natural Law theory.   *[25]*
  (b) 'Natural Law theory is the best approach to moral decision-making.' Discuss.   *[10]*

JANUARY 2008
  (a) Explain how a follower of Natural Law might approach the issues
      surrounding embryo research.   *[25]*
  (b) 'Natural Law is the best approach to embryo research.' Discuss.   *[10]*

JANUARY 2010
  (a) Explain the strengths of Natural Law theory.   *[25]*
  (b) To what extent could a follower of Natural Law accept embryo research?   *[10]*

MAY 2011
  (a) Explain how a follower of Natural Law theory might approach the issues
      surrounding abortion.   *[25]*
  (b) 'Natural Law has no serious weaknesses.' Discuss.   *[10]*

JANUARY 2012
  (a) Explain how Natural Law theory can be used to decide the right moral action.   *[25]*
  (b) To what extent is Natural Law the best approach to ethical decision-making?   *[10]*

3 Utilitarianism

Introduction

The seeds of Utilitarian thought can be traced back to the ancient Greek thinker Epicurus (341–270 BCE), who emphasised moderation in balancing pleasure and pain, or the Chinese philosopher Mo Tzu (420 BCE), who judged actions on the basis of their utility (useful consequences). Modern Utilitarianism grew up in a time of political upheaval under thinkers like Hume, Hutcheson and Sidgwick, and most notably with the ideas of Jeremy Bentham (1748-1832) and John Stuart Mill (1806-73). Bentham had much to say on subjects as diverse as prison reform, religion, poor relief, international law and animal welfare. A visionary far ahead of his time, he advocated universal voting rights and the decriminalisation of homosexuality. Philosopher Francis Hutcheson was to advocate 'applying a mathematical calculation to moral subjects', a phrase which indicates the altogether more empirical and non-utopian view of ethics in which Utilitarians supplied practical judgements in the real world of politics and dilemmas. Utilitarian ideas come to prominence in the late eighteenth and nineteenth centuries with the birth of the modern states like France and America. As James Rachels puts it:

> the revolutions of 1848 showed the continuing power of the new ideas of 'liberty, equality, fraternity'; in America, a new country with a new kind of constitution was born, and its bloody civil war put an end, finally, to slavery in Western civilisation; and all the while, the industrial revolution was bringing about nothing less than a total restructuring of society.
>
> (Rachels 2002, p. 39)

Jeremy Bentham (1748–1832)

Bentham's father was a prosperous lawyer who had ambitions for him to become Lord Chancellor. He studied Latin from three years of age and was found reading a history of England from his father's desk as a toddler. Rather than practising law, he looked at ways to improve upon it. After his father's death in 1792, his independent means allowed him to write between ten and twenty sheets a day for forty years, setting out his philosophical system and critiquing the laws of the day. University College London set up The Bentham Project in the 1960s to produce a scholarly edition of his works and correspondence, and they're now nearly done! He wrote on poor relief, international law, the decriminalisation of homosexuality, animal welfare and universal suffrage. His thought was to shape public policy making in the decision-making of modern states.

Bentham's 'Auto-Icon' at UCL

The frontispiece of Thomas Hobbes' Leviathan, 1651. The body which possesses sovereign authority has the king as its head and is made up of individual citizens, whose bodies blur together in the social contract. Together, they balance Church and state power (bottom right and left). As Hobbes puts it, 'A multitude of men are made up of one person, when they are by one man, or one person, represented; so that it be done with the consent of that multitude in particular.'

Principle of Utility: A phrase first used by Jeremy Bentham in his *Introduction to the Principles and Morals of Legislation*, to refer to the principle that should govern society and bring the greatest amount of happiness to the greatest number of people. Bentham was a social reformer and wished that all members of society could achieve as much happiness (and avoid as much pain) as possible during their lives. This is the fundamental idea behind Utilitarianism.

It is far from coincidental that it was in this context that Utilitarian logic took hold. It offered a theory geared to the greatest good of the greatest number (the **Principle of Utility**), in which the interests of each were to count equally, and where, regardless of the diversity of people and opinions, there was a means for settling policy based upon outcomes that optimised choice or pleasure. The religious wars and the English Civil War of the seventeenth century gave greater momentum towards concentrating power in the hands of the state and settling disputes on a more secular basis. As Thomas Hobbes (1588–1679) had remarked in his political treatise *Leviathan*, without the governance of the state, the natural state of mankind is no utopia, but a 'warre of every man against every man' in which 'the life of man [is] solitary, poore, nasty, brutish, and short'. The laws of just states brought about order, but where they reflected the status quo of social hierarchies like the aristocracy or Church, Utilitarians called for a radical rethink. They were practical and political reformers, Bentham pressing for changes in the penal system and Mill (as an MP) presenting the 1868 Bill before Parliament calling for the vote for women. The influence of Utilitarianism grew with the rise of the social sciences (e.g., economics and sociology) and the policy decisions arising from this for growing nation states.

Classic Benthamite Utilitarianism

Hedonic Calculus: This is also known as the Felicific Calculus. It refers to Bentham's quantitative method of determining what will provide the greatest good for the greatest number, and is therefore the moral thing to do. Its seven elements help an individual to add up the pros and cons of the possible consequences of an action.

Supportive as Jeremy Bentham was of the American Revolution and, initially at least, of the French Revolution, he dismissed the intuitive belief of each in the natural rights of man as 'nonsense on stilts'. For Bentham, natural rights were a fiction. Rejecting religion, intuition or abstract rules as a secure basis for ethics, Bentham founded ethics on a principle of psychology. In two clear senses, he followed Hume. Firstly, he agreed that facts were different from values – you could not infer a moral 'ought' from a factual 'is'. Secondly, he saw human beings as being motivated chiefly by desires, not reasons. As he wrote, 'Nature has placed mankind under the governance of two sovereign masters, pain and pleasure. It is for them alone to point out what we ought to do, as well as to determine what we shall do' (Bentham 'The Principles of Morals and Legislation' 2005 [1781]). Controversially, Bentham believed pleasure to be a 'simple and unitary concept' – even offering 'fifty-eight synonyms for pleasure' (MacIntyre, *A Short History of Ethics*, Routledge, 1971). For Bentham, goods such as knowledge, beauty and justice were all comparable in terms of pleasure and could be weighed on the same set of scales. As he wrote, 'Prejudice apart, the game of push-pin is of equal value with the arts and sciences of music and poetry.' Bentham was well aware of the criticism that this approach reduces all kinds of goods we value to the one set of scales – pleasure and pain. His response was to devise the 'Felicific' or **'Hedonic Calculus'** that brought a mathematical precision to optimising pleasure. The acronym FEDPPIC can help you to recall this.

Fecundity	How fertile will one pleasure be in producing others? An intense hit of an addictive drug may well be pleasurable but is almost certain to lead to pain (addiction, emotional and physical abuse).
Extent	When considering public policy, widening the view – how many are affected?
Duration	How long will the pleasure/pain go on for? The acquisition of knowledge (language, expertise) may be hard work at first, but learning how to read Shakespeare may lead to a lifetime of pleasure.
Purity	Some pleasures come at the expense of other people, or are ill-gotten (through cheating, exploiting).

Propinquity	How close or remote is a pleasure?
Intensity	The Epicureans advocated moderation in all things, and although we may be drawn to intense pleasures, this factor needs to be weighed against others. We cannot spend our lives bungee jumping, and intense drug-fuelled pleasures are short-lived.
Certainty	How guaranteed or predictable is the pleasure we aim at?

Bentham's independent wealth and legal training gave him the means and freedom to pursue his desire for reform in British law and politics. He famously designed a prison to increase efficiency in the surveillance of inmates. Known as the Panopticon, its guard could instantaneously look into all of the individual prisoners' cells from his central viewing platform without them knowing whether they were being watched or not. Julia Driver notes that 'in Port Arthur, Australia, where a model prison incorporating some panopticon features was built, prisoners would later complain that the psychological punishment was worse than the physical punishment' (Driver, *Ethics: The Fundamentals*, Wiley-Blackwell, 2006, p. 43). Bentham certainly considered the detail of prison reform down to the size of prison beds and his penal reform advocated the moderation of sentences to the optimal level for both deterrence and reform (too short and the pain may not be sufficient to deter, too long and an inmate may become institutionalised and reform may no longer be the object). Bentham would have favoured today's diminishing of sentences for good behaviour if this aided reform and prison order. Driver even infers that he might have agreed with the idea of the surveillance state if it could be shown to reduce crime. Utility or usefulness in achieving optimal consequences was the key. Bentham was unsentimental about conventional norms, bequeathing his body for medical research. This curious 'Auto-Icon' (today with a wax replacement for his own head) is still on view in University College London. Utilitarianism sought societal change through a practical-minded blend of political, legal and ethical reforms.

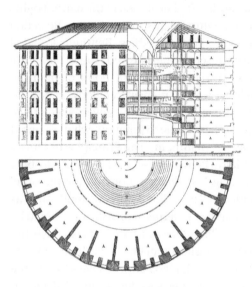

The Panopticon, Bentham's design for an institutional building

Classic Utilitarianism's emphasis on sentience (the ability to feel pleasure and pain) and on equality (each person's interests to count equally and none to count for more than one) was to have ramifications across many areas of practical ethics, including abortion, euthanasia, animal welfare and universal suffrage. Bentham anticipated many future reforms in the following passage:

The day may come when the rest of the animal creation may acquire those rights which never could have been withheld from them but by the hand of tyranny. The French have already discovered that the blackness of the skin is no reason why a human being should be abandoned without redress to the caprice of the tormentor. It may one day come to be recognised that the number of the legs, the villosity of the skin, or the termination of the os sacrum are reasons equally insufficient for abandoning a sensitive being to the same fate. What else is it that should trace the insuperable line? Is it the faculty of reason, or perhaps the faculty of discourse? But a full grown horse or dog is beyond comparison a more rational, as well as more conversable animal, than an infant of a day or a week or even a month, old. But suppose they were otherwise, what would it avail? The question is not, Can they reason? Nor Can they talk? But Can they suffer?

(Bentham, The Principles of Morals and Legislation *2005 [1781]*)

We've seen that, for Bentham, Utilitarian moral judgements were based upon three central ideas:

1. *Consequences matter* – good intentions can have disastrous outcomes, and agents who act selfishly can still bring about good ends. So not only are motives difficult to see rationally, conversely, outcomes are easier to model, make predictions about, and they deliver practically in a way that an ethics focused on the character of the agent rather than the outcome of an action fails to do.
2. *Minimising pain and maximising pleasure are and ought to be the sole goal of our actions* – though we may on the surface aim at knowledge, leisure, friendship, fame or wealth, these are just forms of pleasure for different tastes. As Bentham puts it, 'Prejudice apart, the game of push-pin is of equal value with the arts and sciences of music and poetry. If the game of push-pin furnish more pleasure, it is more valuable' (Bentham, *The Rationale of Reward*, 1830).
3. *Actions should aim at the greatest good of the greatest number* and each individual's interests are to count equally. Private happiness should be guided by public interest for Bentham, for, as MacIntyre puts it, 'society is nothing but a collection of individuals' (MacIntyre 1971, p. 232).

Each of these was to cause problems for classic quantitative Utilitarianism, which John Stuart Mill sought to remedy.

Exercise

Ask your teacher to bring in a chocolate bar as an object lesson. Then attempt to persuade them that it is in their interests to give you each a share of the chocolate bar to eat, by using each element of Bentham's Hedonic Calculus.

John Stuart Mill's qualitative Utilitarianism

John Stuart Mill recognised that not all pleasures and pains could be weighed quantitatively on the scales of the Hedonic Calculus. Here he was beginning to address problems that emerged from the three central tenets of classic Utilitarianism. If we are obliged in our every action to seek the greatest good of the greatest number, any luxury or personal enjoyment could be a cause of guilt. Because omitting to minimise the pain of others can be as bad in terms of consequences as deliberately causing pain, burn-out seems inevitable and some immediate questions arise:

J. S. Mill (1806–1873)

J. S. Mill was Britain's greatest nineteenth-century philosopher. A child prodigy, he spoke several languages before his teens and yet burnt out in his twenties, recovering from his depression through his love of the Romantic poets, especially Wordsworth. Politically liberal and empirical in his method, he believed in extending individual freedom through law and rational policies for social improvement that gave people freedom to pursue their own goals. His father's aim of educating a Utilitarian who could implement social change succeeded in his son John. In assessing human rights or social and political policies on the basis of their general usefulness to all, each individual's interests to count equally, Mill was progressive, naturalist and radical. In 1865 he became the MP for Westminster and championed equality for women, compulsory education, birth control and land reform in Ireland. With his wife Harriet Taylor, whom he admired as an intellectual equal, he wrote *The Subjugation of Women,* which remains an important text in the development of feminist thought.

---

1. Is pleasure the only good or is it just a by-product of other goods?
2. If we seek the optimisation of pleasure and the minimisation of pain for the greatest number, can this result in outcomes in which the interests of the majority are unjust towards those of the few?

John Stuart Mill's father, James Mill, was a disciple of Bentham's teaching. He home-schooled his sensitive young son rigorously in Greek, arithmetic and history, aiming to accelerate his intellectual development in order to achieve the greatest good of the greatest number. Yet, at twenty, Mill had a nervous breakdown, largely resulting from this hot-house life which stunted his social and emotional growth. In his recovery, the burdens and failures of Benthamite Utilitarianism became all too evident to Mill in three particular senses.

1. Aligning personal happiness with seeking the good of the greatest number proved elusive. If all of the reforms that Bentham and Mill's father dreamt of were to be achieved, would this fulfil his personal happiness? Mill was to rediscover his *joie de vivre* in the poetry of Wordsworth and Coleridge and in his friendship with Harriet Taylor, a married woman whom he met when he was aged twenty-four and whom, after a close personal friendship that raised Victorian eyebrows, he married a year after the death of her husband, in 1852. Mill could not live as the 'mere calculating machine' of felicity that his father educated him to be. As he wrote in his autobiography, 'the habit of analysis has a tendency to wear away the feelings . . . Analytic habits [are] a perpetual worm at the root of the passions and the virtues.' Odd as Mill's home-schooling was, there was something in it which

was symptomatic of a fault line that ran through Utilitarianism's focus on *acts* rather than *agents* (the character of the people behind them). Virtue Ethics places more value on motives, character and personal flourishing as bound up with that of the thriving of wider society. Bentham's calculations of felicity see society as individual units whose total happiness can be aggregated. That the theory should fail before its second generation on this front should serve to highlight the significance of our sympathy for our fellow human being as well as the dispositions of character that strengthen this. Life is not lived in abstract case studies, but in interpersonal ties and attachments. Mill saw the wider value to society of special relationships like family life, which were the seed bed of virtues like loyalty, empathy, kindness and obligation.

2. Bentham's quantitative and unitary idea of pleasure/pain proved inadequate. A pleasure pursued as an end in itself (like seeking pleasure by gorging oneself on chocolate) could be empty, whereas another pleasure (like gaining a love and understanding of a subject for itself by trying to get a good exam grade in it) could creep up on one 'by not making it the direct end'. As Mill wrote, 'Those only are happy (I thought) who have their minds fixed on some object other than their own happiness; on the happiness of others, on the improvement of mankind, even on some art or pursuit, followed not as a means, but as itself an ideal end.' (J. S. Mill, *Autobiography*, ed. Jack Stillinger, Oxford University Press, 1969). Mill was to reject the idea of pleasure as a simple concept as Bentham's quantitative Utilitarianism conceived it to be. Instead, he was to distinguish between *higher* (intellectual) and *lower* pleasures (of the body). As he wrote, 'Human beings have faculties more elevated than the animal appetites . . . It is better to be a human being dissatisfied than a pig satisfied; better to be Socrates dissatisfied than a fool satisfied. And if the fool, or the pig, are of a different opinion, it is because they only know their own side of the question' (Mill, *Utilitarianism*, ed. Roger Crisp, Oxford University Press, 1998, pp. 56-7). For Mill, Bentham's quantitative view of pleasure was open to injustices. In opposition to intuitive or common sense morality, it would seem to offer little ground on which to condemn a situation in which ten sadistic guards torture one masochist (who enjoys pain). More seriously, it could lead to the will of a majority oppressing a minority (as was the case with Nazi anti-Semitism, or when a racist majority in an economically depressed area scapegoats members of immigrant communities there). Mill responded by distinguishing pleasures and pains qualitatively. He argued for the somewhat elitist idea that the most competent judges (those who had experienced both pleasures of the mind or intellect and more bodily pleasures) would favour the former over the latter. Bentham may have rated push-pin higher than poetry, but Mill did not. Perhaps on the same basis, he would have elevated opera over football.

3. Where Bentham has a hedonic view of happiness as the overall balance of pleasure and pain in society (as a collection of individual units), Mill's thinking becomes more eudaimonic. Pleasure as an intrinsic good is not just the sum total of pleasures and pains, but the good or flourishing life, which gives a greater place to virtue, relationships and other higher goods of the mind. The influence of the Romantic movement (Wordsworth and Coleridge in particular) and

Aristotle's account of *eudaimonia* all serve to shape a more holistic view of happiness in Mill than Bentham offered: 'Virtue, according to the Utilitarian doctrine, is not naturally and originally part of the end, but it is capable of becoming so; and in those who love it disinterestedly it has become so, and is desired and cherished, not as a means to happiness, but as a part of their happiness' (Mill, *Utilitarianism*, pp. 35–6). Mill therefore recognised that people valued virtue as well as happiness as an 'authentic fact'.

The Hedonic paradox

In his book 'The Methods of Ethics' (1874), philosopher Henry Sidgwick (1838–1900) noted the paradox that, if aimed at directly, pleasure vanishes. The disappointment or despair a recreational drug user might experience at the ever lessening effect of their substance abuse realises this paradox. Strangely, pleasure results indirectly. In his autobiography, Mill writes:

> But I now thought that this end [one's happiness] was only to be attained by not making it the direct end. Those only are happy (I thought) who have their minds fixed on some object other than their own happiness . . . Aiming thus at something else, they find happiness along the way . . . Ask yourself whether you are happy, and you cease to be so. (Mill *Autobiography*, 1909, p. 94)

So Mill's more eudaimonic version of Utilitarianism is influenced by Aristotle here in seeing pleasure as more holistic and not as an end in itself.

Act and Rule Utilitarianism

Act Utilitarians treat each situation on its merits, rather than entering into it with a commitment to generalised rules or principles, other than to act so as to produce the greatest good of the greatest number in the pursuit of pleasure and avoidance of pain. Bentham's Hedonic Calculus offered a ready reckoner to evaluate the likely outcome of one's decisions in particular circumstances. Act Utilitarians like David Lyons (*Forms and Limits of Utilitarianism*, 1965) argue that Rule Utilitarianism collapses into **Act Utilitarianism**. When exceptions to rules require that sub-rules be devised, or when they become burdensome or even cruel (e.g. when an estimated thirty women died each year prior to 1967 due to the ban on abortion), utility is not served. Rules have to be judged by their usefulness in maximising the greatest good of the greatest number. In contrast, Rule Utilitarians argue that a higher utility is achieved when the population as a whole follow laws and customs aimed at maximising the general happiness and minimising their pain, rather than if everyone does their own calculation on an act-by-act basis. The individual therefore has to have strong reasons to break the law or bend rules that facilitate the greater good. Making exceptions for ourselves for selfish reasons breaks the Utilitarian principle that each individual's interests are to count equally.

Act Utilitarianism: This is Bentham's version of Utilitarianism, which operates by taking each situation on its own merits, wishing only to achieve the greatest good for the greatest number of people involved. There are no general rules, only the situation that applies to the individual.

Rule Utilitarianism:
This is (arguably) Mill's version of Utilitarianism. The greatest good for the greatest number is achieved when everyone follows laws and customs that aim to maximise the happiness of everyone, not just some individuals.

Rule Utilitarianism seeks to follow those principles and rules that would maximise aggregate utility if universalised. After all, if Act Utilitarianism were to be universalised, this could have negative consequences. If each moral agent acted within the bounds of their own knowledge without a sense of the general rule or pattern of expected behaviour, the likely result would be far more disorder, unpredictability and less co-operation. This is not to say that all rules have to be absolute (without exceptions and qualifications). J. L. Austin defines Rule Utilitarianism in the principle 'Our rules would be fashioned on utility; our conduct on our rules' (quoted in J. L. Mackie, *Ethics, Inventing Right and Wrong*, Penguin Books, 1977, p. 136). That is to say that the total sum of happiness or preferences is better achieved if everyone follows rules rather than if they seek to calculate the best course of action at the time of each and every action they take. Consider the two cases below.

1. Traffic laws. Stopping at a red light in a sleepy rural area when there is no traffic around can be a pain; if speeding to make it in time for a crucial interview would secure employment, then weighing the risks of breaking the speed limit against providing for one's children may make it seem worthwhile. But, overall, the aggregate safety and minimisation of pain is best achieved if everyone in the UK keeps to the Highway Code. Rules have developed as more traffic has taken to the roads to optimise the safe flow of traffic. Mill uses the example of sailors improving their calculations and course by using an Almanac rather than navigating by the stars. By analogy, rules and laws are the accumulated wisdom of past experience and collectively prove their worth by avoiding much suffering and conflict.

   If it was down to the individual to weigh up each act on the basis of its usefulness in terms of the greatest good of the greatest number, can you think of other cases where this could lead to injustices or risks and conflicts?

2. Imagine a fictional scenario in a racist town in which, as a result of one person's act of terrorism, there are riots and mob violence. Police round up a suspect who is a petty criminal and fits the profile. Would it be easier for an Act than a Rule Utilitarian to be tempted to imprison this individual even if they knew them to be innocent in respect of the terrorism charges, in order to preserve public order?

   Why may a Rule Utilitarian object more strenuously than an Act Utilitarian to this scenario?

Strong and Weak Rule Utilitarianism

Another distinction may be made regarding the importance attached to rules. Strong Rule Utilitarians emphasise the utility of rules to the extent that they should be held to even where they cause inconvenience, or even harm, in particular cases. There has to be an overwhelming reason to break them. Emergency vehicles like ambulances and fire engines may speed in built-up areas, for example, but a strong weight is attached to rules. By contrast, Weak Rule Utilitarians give more of a role to individual autonomy in moral decision-making. Rules ought to be adhered to, especially in cases where it is difficult to predict outcomes, or where we lack adequate information and have to take account of the general good. But there is more willingness to modify or bend them when they cause harm (for example, as when, in 2010, the Director of Public Prosecutions formally declared that he would not pursue cases of UK citizens assisting in a suicide by transporting a relative to the Dignitas clinic in Switzerland, as juries would not convict relatives acting on compassionate grounds and it was therefore a waste of taxpayers' money). The usefulness of rules and laws in minimising pain and maximising welfare would make reform rather than revolt an important goal of Rule Utilitarians. As an MP, John Stuart Mill campaigned for parliamentary reform, labour unions, proportional representation and equal political rights for women.

On Liberty – the importance of individual freedom in Mill's thought

We can liken the distinction between Act and Rule Utilitarianism to the respective approaches of the *judge* and the *legislator*. The judge adheres strictly to the application of legal statutes *to particular cases* (for Act Utilitarians in terms of the Hedonic Calculus), whereas the legislator seeks, by logically inferring from the evidence of present practice, the *principles* by which to enact future just laws. For Mill, one of these was *the Harm Principle,* which gave greater weight to the interests of the individual. Law should not override the liberty of the individual unless they caused harm to others. In this sense, Mill's work *On Liberty* (1859) addressed some of the concerns about the 'tyranny of the majority' raised by Bentham's work. No longer could 'the greatest good of the greatest number' mean the curtailment of individual freedom purely on the wishes of the majority. Mill's idea of aggregate happiness (the greatest good of the greatest number, each individual's interests to count equally) recognises that, where individuals have liberty and thrive, the general happiness is increased. Losing the individual's happiness in the pursuit of the general happiness is to miss the point that 'each person's happiness is a good to that person, and the general happiness, therefore, a good to the aggregate of all persons' (as Mill argues in chapter 4 of *Utilitarianism*). He described a society in which everyone's sole duty was to live for the

The Statue of Liberty in New York Harbour has welcomed many generations of US immigrants with its symbolic promise of freedom. Political philosophers debate negative and positive versions of freedom and Mill saw that freedom can mean radically different things to different people.

good of others as 'liberticide' (the killing of freedom). Instead, everyone ought to have the freedom to pursue happiness in their own way whilst respecting the freedom of others. So respect for the individual's freedom is crucial – to the extent that they pose no harm or threat to society, the law should not curb their liberties. As he writes, 'If all mankind minus one, were of one opinion, and only one person were of the contrary opinion, mankind would be no more justified in silencing that one person, than he, if he had the power, would be justified in silencing mankind' (*On Liberty*, p. 33).

Was Mill an Act or a Rule Utilitarian?

Michael Sandel points out that Mill saw Kant's test of whether he could universalise the principle behind his actions as 'making a consequentialist argument after all' (2009). For Mill, rules (even universal ones like the **Categorical Imperative**)

Mill vs Kant

were good insofar as they were useful in maximising welfare. Sandel shows that Mill misunderstood Kant's thinking at this point. Kant's purpose in universalising the principles behind actions was to scrutinise motives and distinguish those who acted out of Good Will from those that acted out of self-interest in making exceptions to rules; unlike Mill, his aim was not to optimise outcomes. Mill's position is neatly illustrated in Zac Brown's cartoon.

Alasdair MacIntyre calls Mill an 'inconsistent utilitarian' (*After Virtue*, University of Notre Dame Press, 2007) and Roger Crisp concludes that 'Mill's utilitarianism focuses on actions and is an act, not a rule utilitarianism' (*Mill on Utilitarianism*, Routledge, 1997). In opposition to the intuitivists, Mill saw observation and experience as the best predictors of consequences and the most objective measure of ethics. During the 'whole past duration of the human species', writes Mill, 'mankind have been learning by experience the tendencies of actions'. In this way, the rules and customs of conventional morality (e.g. 'Do not steal', 'Honour promises' or 'Do not murder') are like the 'landmarks and direction posts' that guide travellers who would, if left to their own devices (like the single-level Act Utilitarian who ignores rules and relies on his/her own sense of direction at every turn), often take a wrong turn or lose their bearings. Landmarks, like rules, gain authority by reliably getting us to our end goal or destination. In this way, training children with an ingrained respect for customary moral rules of thumb such as 'Violence never solves problems' or 'It's wrong to steal' is important. But when two such principles conflict – like 'It's wrong to lie' and 'Always act to protect those you love from strangers who intend them harm and ask you their whereabouts' – then R. M. Hare argued that the Act Utilitarian needed to switch from a *conventional* to a *critical* level of ethical reasoning and consider consequences in this particular case. Here Mill would argue (opposing Kant's view) that you should lie to an axe-wielding killer who is after your friend's location, so he's no worshipper of rules. For Mill, the **Principle of Utility** provides us with the ultimate standard by which to judge 'all human conduct'. Customary rules and beliefs are to be judged and improved by using this standard as we see the consequences that follow from them. The terminology distinguishing Act and Rule Utilitarianism is later than Mill, and in setting out his basis for defending rights in Utilitarianism, Mill offers 'no other reason than general utility'. As he states:

> justice is a name for certain moral requirements, which, regarded collectively, stand higher in the scale of social utility, and are therefore of more paramount obligation, than any others; though particular cases may occur in which some other social duty is so important, as to overrule any one of the general maxims of justice. Thus, to save a life, it may not only be allowable, but a duty, to steal, or take by force, the necessary food or medicine, or to kidnap, and compel to officiate, the only qualified medical practitioner.
>
> Mill, *Utilitarianism*, chapter 5, 1863

Debate: rules are meant to be broken

Mill believes that, in individual cases, it is crucial for the Act Utilitarian to avoid egoism and act impartially for the general good. His Utilitarianism is multilevel, working at the level of customary morality because conventional laws and rules often serve to maximise the Principle of Utility. So you'd have to have a very good reason to make an exception for yourself in a particular dilemma. Roger Crisp does not see Mill as a Rule Utilitarian but as a thinker who says 'Do not perform any action by which, if people performed it generally, welfare would not be maximised.' Take the following cases in terms of road traffic or tax law. Which would you consider defensible?

1. A cyclist jumps red lights and crosses traffic at their own risk (they reason that according to Mill's Harm Principle, they are most likely to be the one harmed, not motorists).
2. A driver breaking the speed limit to get his injured son (whose life is in danger and where time is critical) to the hospital faster than an ambulance can do the round trip.
3. A police car speeding in a residential area to catch a suspected murderer thought to be fleeing the scene of a crime at high speed in a fast car.
4. A builder who receives payments by cash and only declares part of his profits to the government for taxation purposes.
5. A wealthy investor who exploits tax loopholes and evades tax by offshoring his/her investments, which would have added to tax revenue for education and the NHS.

QUICK QUESTION
If emergency services can jump red lights, should individuals do so if they judge that getting to a hospital on time might save a life?

QUICK QUESTION

Free market economists would argue that we only need the present generation to be concerned about the planet they leave to their grandchildren to get them to value and act upon sustainability issues. Do you agree?

Preference Utilitarianism:

This is the version of Utilitarianism proposed by Peter Singer. It aims to maximise the choices made or preferences shown by individuals. The interests of all sentient beings (not just humans) need to be taken into account when ethical decisions are made. It focuses on minimising pain rather than maximising happiness. The theory is sometimes known as Negative Utilitarianism.

Discussion Questions

1. Bentham wrote that 'The community is a fictitious body, composed of the individual persons who are considered as constituting, as it were, its members. The interest of the community then is, what? – the sum of the interests of the several members who compose it.' Yet Mill emphasised the usefulness of rules and general happiness rather than calculating individual acts or individual private happiness. How does this deal with the criticism of Benthamite or Classic Utilitarianism that there is not enough time, before every action, to weigh up the consequences of every individual's decision to bring about the greatest happiness?

2. What objections might be raised against Mill's distinction between higher and lower pleasures and his idea of 'competent judges' who, having experience of both, can reliably tell us which are preferable?

3. If our actions are to be judged in terms of their usefulness in bringing about the greatest good of the greatest number, then whether it is right to tell the truth or to lie is dependent upon consequences. What does this do to one's personal integrity (Bernard Williams' objection) '– see page 57'?

4. If actions are to be judged by their consequences and not their motives, is Peter Singer right to hold you responsible for the preventable deaths of infants and children in the developing world who could be saved by money you currently spend on luxuries '(see page 48)'?

5. Singer argues that: 'If it is in our power to prevent something bad from happening, without thereby sacrificing anything of comparable moral importance, we ought, morally, to do it.' Do you think of it as your duty to help starving children or victims of natural disasters when aid can save lives, or is this a charitable act which is praiseworthy, but whose omission is not equivalent to murder if you fail to do it?

6. As Utilitarianism judges actions in terms of their consequences, a great deal of weight must be attached to the assessment of potential risks and rewards in its calculations. How is this both a strength and a weakness in Utilitarian thought?

7. Tim Mulgan's book *Future People* adopts a Rule Utilitarian approach to advocate intergenerational justice in which we balance our own needs against those of our descendants. He argues that Act Consequentialism does not require us to consider the interests of *future people* who cannot feel pleasure and pain now. Perhaps if we do not know what future generations will think or desire, we cannot wrong them. What weight ought we to give to the interests of future generations when we think about our present needs as opposed to the environmental sustainability of our economy or our present-day use of nuclear energy and natural resources?

Negative Preference Utilitarianism and Peter Singer

Mill has been viewed as an elitist who elevated intellectual pleasures over lower bodily pleasures. Yet Peter Singer's **Preference Utilitarianism** moves away from judging which choices should count (push-pin and the pleasures of pigs and fools were no match for poetry in Mill's estimation). Instead, it seeks to maximise the choices or preferences of individuals. For example, Singer is a libertarian in respect of patient choice in terms of euthanasia or abortion. Pleasure and pain take many forms, but consistency requires that we consider the interests of all sentient beings, including those caught in absolute poverty and dying of preventable diseases as well as of animals. Furthermore, as a *Negative Utilitarian*, Singer prioritises the minimising of unnecessary suffering over the maximising of pleasure. So vegetarianism and strong regulatory control of animal experimentation in medical science are logical conclusions from the desire to minimise the unnecessary suffering of animals. Equally, before wealthy westerners optimise their pleasures by pursuing more afflu-ent lifestyles, they ought to prioritise the welfare of those in absolute poverty and dying of preventable diseases in the poorest countries in the world.

Australian academic and activist Peter Singer (1946–)
Peter Singer is the Princeton Professor of Bioethics. His book *Animal Liberation* (Vintage Press, 1995) – known as 'the Bible of the Animal Liberation Movement' – has sold over 500,000 copies and his *Practical Ethics* (1993) is Cambridge University Press' most profitable philosophy text to date. On animal welfare, abortion, euthanasia, ecology, global trade and Bush's war against terror, Singer is motivated to reduce the suffering of sentient beings. He gives 20 per cent of his income to charity and does not eat or wear any animal products. He has sat in a cage to draw attention to the plight of battery hens, and has been physically assaulted and vehemently condemned by disabled rights protesters angered by his comparisons between the capacities of intellectually disabled humans and non-human animals, and by his advocacy of voluntary euthanasia and infanticide. He has been arrested for attempting to photograph confined sows on a pig farm partly owned by Australia's prime minister, and stood as a Green candidate for the Australian Senate. When he arrived in Princeton (where he has inspired students to start a chapter of UNICEF), proctors (university police) had to escort him around campus out of fear he would be attacked. Provocative and rigorously logical in his Preference Utilitarianism, he wants philosophers 'back on the job' of reaching beyond the academy and changing the way we think and act in the world. This aim to be relevant and effect change in animal welfare and the injustices in the global community towards the poor and the environment gives him a reasonable claim to being the most influential living philosopher.

Singer studied at Oxford under the moral philosopher R. M. Hare. Hare made a distinction between reasoning at the intuitive/ *conventional* and at the deeper *critical* level. As James Rachels (*The Legacy of Socrates: Essays in Moral Philosophy*, Columbia University Press, 2007) puts it, "When we operate on the intuitive level, we act according to 'prima facie' (as they appear at first sight) moral rules, fitted to the hurly-burly circumstances of everyday life; when we operate on the critical level, we formulate those prima facie rules and decide what to do when they conflict"(See Rachels' website, jamesrachels.org, for a review of Tim Mulgan's book *Future People*). Peter Singer accepts the value of an intuitive, common-sense ethic in which general rules or principles count since "we could be calculating in less than ideal circumstances. We could be hurried or flustered. We might feel angry or hurt, or competitive . . . Or we might just not be good at thinking about such complicated issues as the likely consequences of a difficult choice' (Singer 2011) Yet in the many more complex cases in which rules fail to maximise welfare, a critical level of reasoning is needed. So in books like *Rethinking Life and Death,* Singer argues that 5 old commandments are in urgent need of a Copernican revolution (for example, 'Be fruitful and multiply' is replaced with 'Bring children into the world only if they are wanted'). Singer is the most prominent Utilitarian philosopher at work today. In *A Darwinian Left: Politics, Evolution, and Cooperation* (Yale University Press, 2000), he argues that it is time for the left wing of politics to see that Homo Sapiens are evolved social beings with the capacities for both competition and co-operation. Such insights should move beyond an anthropocentric speciesism that sets a 'gulf between humans and other animals' who can also feel emotional and physical pain. In *The Expanding Circle* (1982), he argues that our kin-altruism can and should extend impartially in a multiracial society for example, or when we find structures and channels that encourage co-operation and help us to see altruism in terms of self-fulfilment rather than self-sacrifice.

A recent development

> Non-Religious Ethics is at a very early stage. We cannot yet predict whether, as in Mathematics, we will all reach agreement. Since we cannot know how Ethics will develop, it is not irrational to have high hopes.
> (Derek Parfit, *Reasons and Persons*, Oxford Paperbacks, 1984, p. 454)

In his book *On What Matters* (Oxford University Press, 2011), philosopher Derek Parfit seeks to reconcile consequentialist and Kantian Ethics, arguing that they are 'climbing the same mountain on different sides'. Continuing Mill's attempt to reconcile cost–benefit consequentialism with Kant's duties and principles, he brings these two together in the formula: 'An act is wrong just when such acts are disallowed by the principles that are optimific, uniquely universally willable, and not rationally rejectable.' Parfit thinks that reason can lead us to objectivity in ethics and that this can strengthen the argument that 'we rich people [should] give up some of our luxuries, ceasing to overheat the Earth's atmosphere, and taking care of this planet . . . so that it continues to support intelligent life'. Virtue theorists would say that morality cannot be reduced to a single tidy formula, and those in the tradition of Hume, like Simon Blackburn, would argue that human actions are more passional than rational, and that formulas are unlikely to revolutionise behaviour. He sees recent studies of human decision-making in cognitive science and evolutionary psychology as supporting the view that moral judgements are emotional attitudes of disapproval/approval rather than reasoned formulas. Nevertheless, it could be that Mill had anticipated some integration of the insights of Utilitarian and Kantian thought that Parfit has clarified. Parfit seeks to defend a secular form of objectivity in ethics in contrast to that of nihilists and subjectivists. His 2011 book reflects an increasing sense among philosophers that, to the extent that human behaviour is rationally motivated, we should have the good sense to see good arguments triumph over bad ones and not simply shrug our shoulders and dismiss moral judgements as expressions of emotions.

Strengths of Utilitarianism

Utilitarianism emerged with the growth of the nation state and it proved practical on three counts:

1. It found pragmatic *solutions to allocating scarce resources when massive demands were made.* The practical reasoning of Utilitarianism was *agreeable on secular grounds* and it sought to act impartially and *think globally* (*One World* is a title of a book by Singer along these lines). Its simple and unitary goal of maximising pleasure (Bentham/Mill) or preferences (Singer) offered a means of finding common ground in the public policy of diverse societies. Whatever disagreements of belief or culture exist, people can agree to the minimal requirement of minimising pain and maximising the greatest good (pleasure/preferences) of the greatest number. Consequentialist logic takes a hard-headed empirical look at dilemmas and moves away from abstract beliefs to find the optimal trade-off between conflicting preferences. Singer seeks to persuade consumers of meat for example, that intensive factory farming of chickens, pigs or cattle makes their lives more of a burden than a benefit to them and that paying more at the supermarket to prevent this is worth it for the sake of justice. So where the process of finding common ground proves difficult, Utilitarians aim to inform our decisions on the basis of all available evidence and to help us reflect on the likely consequences of choices. As Singer writes, 'Ethics is practical or it is not ethics.'

   Utilitarianism has been from its inception, and is today, *reformist.* It questions the rationality of abstract and (as it often turns out) arbitrary rules, and brings a particular kind of clarity in banging heads together to work out solutions in a 'lowest common denominator'-type way. Bentham worked on prison reform, Mill on the right for women to vote – to name just two campaigns. Singer was arrested for trying to photograph confined sows on a pig farm partly owned by the Australian prime minister and sat in a cage to draw attention to the plight of battery hens. He's campaigned on animal welfare and been on the receiving end of an assault, and angrily protests for his views on abortion, euthanasia and infanticide. Utilitarians do not content themselves with theorising – they are, and always have been, practical in their ethics.

2. Negative Utilitarianism's *emphasis on the priority of reducing unnecessary pain and suffering* clarifies what should be centre-stage in practical ethics. Famous contemporary Utilitarians like Peter Singer (*The Life You Can Save*, Picador, 2010) (www.thelifeyoucansave.com) and Toby Ord (www.givingwhatwecan.org) are putting their money where their mouth is and giving generously, reducing their global footprint and living as vegetarians whilst wearing non-animal products. They have encouraged thousands of people to give substantial percentages of their income to alleviating absolute poverty, thereby reducing the preventable deaths that so often result from it. Their conviction that, in investing their energies in an effort to reduce preventable suffering, 'the ethical life is not self-sacrifice, but self-fulfilment' (Singer, *How Are We to Live?*, Opus, 1995) seems to be an urgent and persuasive message.

3. Rather than begin with a whole raft of abstract metaphysical beliefs, *Utilitarian thought is empirical and informed by the human and natural sciences* such as psychology, social anthropology and neuro-biology. Utilitarians observe human psychology and the evolutionary traits of human behaviour rather than beginning with a fixed view of human nature, as Aristotle did. They work with the grain of both human self-interest and co-operation. Such an approach is informed and adaptable. Its solutions should prove workable and well evidenced.

Weaknesses of Utilitarianism

1. Ultimately, consequentialism must come back to *at least one non-consequential starting point.* In answer to the question 'What is a good outcome?', the answer 'pleasure' simply raises further questions, such as: What makes pleasure good as an end in itself? Is pleasure amorphous (taking one basic form that can be assessed quantitatively: 8 points for a Sky Dive, 5 for a good meal, 28 for getting into university, 40 for meeting the love of your life) or polymorphous (taking different forms that are not comparable, e.g. beauty, truth, goodness, justice, knowledge, family, friendship, and higher (aesthetic and intellectual) and lower (bodily) pleasures)?

2. Utilitarianism *moves from the 'is'*, or supposedly factual, observation that everyone seeks their own pleasure *to the 'ought'* statement of saying that they 'ought' to seek pleasure (albeit one in which individuals curb their private self-interest in favour of maximising pleasure for the greatest number). G. E. Moore's *Open Question Argument* applies here – if it makes sense to ask the question 'Sure this action maximises pleasure, but is it right?', then the definition commits the Naturalistic Fallacy: that because, by nature, people pursue pleasure and avoid pain, they ought to do so. If pleasure was an adequate definition of goodness, we would be asking a circular question like 'She's an unmarried woman, but is she a spinster?' John Stuart Mill regarded the general observation that each person desires their own happiness to be *a proof of Utilitarianism.* Yet an egoist could see their own happiness as subjectively good, without it logically following that they ought to will the general happiness. What the third great Utilitarian thinker, Henry Sidgwick, argued, in his book *The Methods of Ethics*, is that an egoist who sees their personal happiness as an objective good cannot logically argue that their happiness is 'more objectively desirable or more good than a similar happiness of any other person', so they must then agree with the Utilitarian that universal happiness is 'the real end of Reason, the absolutely Good'.

3. It is difficult to predict the future except by modelling it on past outcomes. Calculating consequences on models that assume the future will resemble the past can be risky. Should past generations whose nuclear power plants provided short-term energy while creating long-term leakage and danger be held accountable for the consequences they failed to predict? If predicting consequences is so crucial, surely the practical ethics of Utilitarianism cannot be left to ordinary people and belongs to highly specialised expert bureaucrats, making it elitist

rather than democratic as Bentham and Mill supposed it to be. And if we put all of our moral eggs in one basket (predicting good future outcomes for the greatest number), and it should turn out that our predictions were erroneous, then the basis of our decision-making turns out to be faulty. Take an Act-Utilitarian justification for the use of monkeys or apes in scientific experiments in which the medical benefits of a proposed drug treatment have been inflated and turn out to be non-existent. Here the deontologist may console themselves, in the event of a tragic outcome, that at least they stuck to what they believed to be right.

4. It has no *backward-looking reasons*. Some moral considerations have to do with the past, such as keeping promises. If I judge the rightness of an action purely on the basis of consequences, then this trivialises the breaking of promises in individual cases in which the utility of keeping them is low. An example of this might be returning a kindness done in the past.

5. The Harvard philosopher Robert Nozick presents an attack on **hedonism**, or the view that pleasure = goodness or an intrinsic good. As he writes:

> Suppose there were an experience machine that would give you any experience you desired. Superduper neuropsychologists could stimulate your brain so that you would think and feel you were writing a great novel, or making a friend, or reading an interesting book. All the time you would be floating in a tank, with electrodes attached to your brain. Should you plug into this machine for life, pre-programming your life experiences? Of course, while in the tank you won't know that you're there; you'll think that it is all actually happening. Would you plug in?
>
> (Nozick, *Anarchy, State and Utopia*, Basic Books, 1974)

If, as John Stuart Mill wrote, 'The utilitarian doctrine is that happiness is desirable, and the only thing desirable, as an end; all other things being desirable as a means to that end', then the answer may well be 'Yes!' Yet this would seem to be a shallow substitute for real life, a virtual world in no way comparable to what non-Utilitarians take to be the intrinsic goods of friendship, knowledge, beauty, etc.

6. A further problem is that pleasure is polymorphous – it takes many different forms. Where many systems of morality treat 'goods' of life, such as knowledge, beauty, truth, justice, life and health, etc., as separate and incommensurate (not able to be converted into comparable points on a scale), *Utilitarianism lumps every good onto the same set of scales and weighs them together.* Yet there's no guarantee that these goods are combinable in a simple exchange mechanism without losing something of their intrinsic worth. Your father's health is worth 10 points of a total 100 while you studying for a degree in engineering is worth 20, and you getting the limited family funding for a degree rather than your younger sister (who wanted to study fine art) is 30 on the scale. Sure, Utilitarianism can deliver policies on how to allocate scarce health resources when there is massive and conflicting demand, but, as Alasdair MacIntyre argues, 'the use of a conceptual fiction in a good cause does not make it any less of a fiction' (MacIntyre, *After Virtue*, University of Notre Dame Press, 2007).

7. Utilitarianism has a 'breathtaking systematisation' to its 'thin language, with 'too few feelings and thoughts to match the world as it really is' (a phrase used by

Hedonism: The term comes from *'hedone'*, the Greek word for 'happiness'. Hedonism is an ancient school of thought, allegedly founded by Aristippus of Cyrene, a pupil of Socrates, which argues that happiness is the highest good. In most forms of Hedonism, happiness is interpreted as 'pleasure'.

Charles Taylor in *Sources of the Self*, Harvard University Press, 1992). It is happy to take a free ride on the intuitive, conventional morality which says 'if society follows principles and instils virtues whilst thinking morality objectively real, it will fare better on the whole'. Yet, at a critical level, pleasure and pain or people's preferences are the only intrinsic goods, and conventional morality is naively mistaken. So Utilitarianism is parasitic upon conventional morality, whilst at the same time accelerating its decline. The over-emphasis on impartial reasoning underestimates the power of compassion and devalues the special relationships with family and friends in which this empathy grows. Bernard Williams has argued that the impartial thinker that Utilitarianism idealises distances us from the interpersonal world of empathy, competition and loyalties that is so valuable to us. Indeed it is in the soil of personal relationships that virtue grows and **egoism** is weeded out.

> **Egoism:**
> The belief that individuals have a moral duty to optimise the good consequences for themselves

Robert Solomon comments that American soldiers fighting in Cambodia in the 1960s who were not college-educated 'typically remained sensitive to and repulsed by the war crimes that had by then become a daily feature' of the war whereas college-educated recruits 'were able to rationalise these handily, using familiar Utilitarian arguments, cutting themselves off quite effectively not only from the guilt and shame but from the human tragedies they caused and witnessed': Solomon, 'Peter Singer's Expanding Circle' in *Singer and his Critics*, Wiley-Blackwell, 1999

8. *Utilitarianism is too morally demanding*. Philosophers distinguish *obligatory* from *supererogatory* actions. The former are required but the latter are above and beyond the call of duty, though all the more praiseworthy for that. As a consequentialist, Peter Singer believes that we are *responsible for omissions as well as commissions* – for what we fail to do as well as what we do. Furthermore, our responsibilities do not just relate to those close to us – to ignore a child dying on the other side of the world from a preventable disease which our disposable income could prevent or cure is no better than walking past a drowning child in a shallow pond on the way to our work. So, whilst a Utilitarian might feel obliged to give away as much of their disposable income to those living in absolute poverty as they possibly can, many would judge this to be morally praiseworthy, but not obligatory. Indeed, feeling guilty about every luxury purchase you make and every personal pleasure that does not pursue the greatest good of the greatest number could make for the very life that led to Mill's mental breakdown.

Discussion Questions

Imagine a case in which a surgeon finds himself with four patients on his ward, all of whom will die without a transplant in the next few weeks. One needs a new heart, another a new pair of lungs, another a liver, and a final one, a pancreas. A young homeless man with no traceable records or next of kin arrives on the ward unconscious, having fallen off a bicycle. It is touch and go whether the surgeon could save his life anyway and it looks like no-one will miss him, whereas four loving families visit their loved ones on the ward every day. The hospital is in a remote area and the surgeon on night duty is very skilful. He could extract all of the vital organs that night and transplant them the next day with the help of unsuspecting fellow surgeons who could be told that 'multiple donors had become available'.

1. What would an Act Utilitarian/a Rule Utilitarian do in the above situation?
2. Would they justify their action on the same basis?

FURTHER READING

Jeremy Bentham (2005 [1781]) *An Introduction to the Principles of Morals and Legislation*. Adamant Media Corporation

Krister Bykvist (2007) *Utilitarianism: A Guide for the Perplexed*. Continuum

John Stuart Mill (1998) *Utilitarianism*, ed. Roger Crisp. Oxford University Press

Peter Singer (2011) *Practical Ethics*. Cambridge University Press

J. J. C. Smart and Bernard Williams (1973) *Utilitarianism For and Against* Cambridge University Press

OCR Past Paper Questions

JANUARY 2009
  (a) Explain how Bentham's version of Utilitarianism can be used to decide on the right course of action.   *[25]*

JUNE 2010
  (a) Explain the main strengths of Mill's Utilitarianism.   *[25]*
  (b) 'Utilitarianism can lead to wrong moral decisions.' Discuss.   *[10]*

MAY 2011
  (a) Explain the Preference Utilitarianism of Peter Singer.   *[25]*
  (b) To what extent is Preference Utilitarianism the best form of Utilitarianism?   *[10]*

JANUARY 2012
  (a) Explain the main differences between the Utilitarianism of Bentham and that of Mill.   *[25]*
  (b) 'Mill's Utilitarianism is superior in every way to the Utilitarianism of Bentham.' Discuss.   *[10]*

JANUARY 2013
  (a) Explain how Mill's Utilitarianism might be used to decide the right course of action.   *[25]*

MAY 2013
  (a) 'Utilitarianism is not a good guide for resolving ethical dilemmas.' Discuss.   *[10]*
  (b) Explain the main principles of the classical forms of Utilitarianism.   *[25]*

CHAPTER

4 Kantian Ethics

LEARNING OUTCOMES

In this chapter, you will learn

- the difference between the Categorical and Hypothetical Imperatives
- the various formulations of the Categorical Imperative
- Kant's understanding of the universalisation of maxims
- Kant's theory of duty
- Kant's ideas of the moral law, Good Will and the *summum bonum*
- to discuss these theories critically and their strengths and weaknesses

Life and works

Immanuel Kant was born on 22 April 1724 in Königsberg, at that time the capital city of the province of East Prussia. It was a busy commercial city, with an important military port, and its own well-respected university. Kant was born into a working-class family; his father made saddles and harnesses, and his mother was the daughter of a harness-maker. The family were Pietist and Kant attended a Pietist school, the Collegium Fridericianum, until he was fifteen. Pietism was an evangelical branch of the Lutheran Church which emphasised the importance of Christian piety, a strong moral conscience and control of the passions. His mother, who died when he was thirteen, encouraged his intellect and imagination and taught him about nature and the starry heavens. His mother's religion was one of prayer, Bible study, quiet humility, and living out the golden rule in kindness to others. He judged her faith 'genuine' and 'not in the least enthusiastic' (fundamentalist), though he did rebel against the more zealous Pietism that sought to reform the mainstream German Lutheranism of his day. While at school, Kant reacted strongly against the Pietism of his youth and this may partially account for his later emphasis on rationality and autonomy. For Kant, religion ought to operate as 'religion within the boundaries of mere reason' (the title of one of his books, published in 1793). He turned to the Latin classics, which formed an important part of the school's curriculum. Later, Kant attended the University of Königsberg (known as the Albertina), where he quickly became fascinated by Philosophy, which was a compulsory first-year subject, studying Logic, Metaphysics, Ethics and Natural Law.

Immanuel Kant (1724–1804)
Immanuel Kant was a German philosopher at the heart of a movement known as the Enlightenment. He reacted against the evangelical Lutheran Pietism of his schooling, with its emphasis on religious devotion and biblical literalism. He valued reason independent of revelation or emotion, though he did imbibe his parents' values (they were harness-makers) of 'hard work, honesty . . . and independence'. Despite shaping modern Western philosophy, Kant never travelled any great distance from the Prussian port city of Königsberg. A bachelor, he kept to a strict routine of walks and early bedtimes for the sake of his health. From 1755 to 1770, he was a Privatdozent (a lecturer funded by collecting fees from those who attended his lectures). He was a popular lecturer and, as his career matured, his philosophical writings sold well.

Context of Kant's ethics

In order to understand Kant's ethical thinking, we need to consider the intellectual context in which his thoughts developed. Kant wrote towards the end of the formative years of the 'European Enlightenment', sometimes called the 'Age of Reason'. Kant was one of the last, and probably the greatest, thinkers of the Enlightenment.

The Enlightenment developed radical ideas about the rights of the individual and democracy which led to the French and American Revolutions. Two key themes of the Enlightenment were a focus on the individual and on **reason**. Significant figures in the Enlightenment included:

> **Reason:**
> The ability to work out correct ethical decisions, with which every human is born. This is a key concept in Kantian Ethics.

- *Isaac Newton and John Locke*, who emphasised the importance of rational and scientific explanations for natural phenomena. Newton's universal laws of motion were to shape Kant's desire to uncover similar laws in Moral Philosophy.
- *David Hume and Voltaire*, who showed scepticism about inherited tradition and authorities in politics, religion and the universities.
- *Jean-Jacques Rousseau and Thomas Paine*, who put forward revolutionary ideas opposing the status quo and emphasised reason and autonomy rather than the **heteronomy** (law of the other) of monarchy, Church and aristocracy.
- *Francis Hutcheson and Thomas Reid*, who proposed a moderate, 'common-sense' approach to developing society's values.

Newton's influence

Kant saw in Newton an example of how reason had transformed physics and astronomy. Newton's mind had not only brought order to our perception of the natural world, he had offered a new vision or model of seeing in which universal laws were discoverable in nature under the light of reason. As the poet Alexander Pope (1688–1744) wrote, 'Nature, and Nature's laws lay hid in the Night. God said, Let Newton be! and all was Light.' Kant saw the moral law as knowable by a priori reasoning about maxims that would be universalisable in a manner analogous to the laws of nature. His mother was well educated and taught him about nature (bears and wolves lived around Königsberg) and the stars. For his tombstone, Kant's friends selected the quotation 'Two things fill the mind with ever new and increasing admiration and awe, the more often and steadily we reflect upon them: the starry heavens above me and the moral law within me.' Though his mother died when he was thirteen, he says of her: 'I will never forget my mother, for she implanted and nurtured in me the first germ of goodness; she opened my heart to the impressions of nature; she awakened and furthered my concepts, and her doctrines have had a continual and beneficial influence in my life.'

Isaac Newton, (1643–1727)

The influence of Jean-Jacques Rousseau on Kant's ethics

Kant's belief that humans are responsible for their actions and could do otherwise than they do is not provable – he terms it instead a postulate of practical reasoning (without freedom, we cannot reasonably be held responsible). Some scholars think he gets this first from Rousseau, who wrote *The Social Contract* (which argues that political freedom is possible only when a people are governed by their collective general will, not by external authorities such as the monarchy or the Church). Rousseau gives Kant an anti-elitist respect for the common man.

Jean-Jacques Rousseau (1712–78)
A political philosopher whose *Social Contract* (1762) saw liberty and equality as promoting a spirit of fraternity – a kind of commonwealth of ends. It includes the famous phrase 'man is born free; and everywhere he is in chains', which expressed the *Zeitgeist* of the French Revolution and many revolutionary movements since then. Kant initially supported the French Revolution but soon became troubled by the bloodshed and injustices. Nonetheless, he supported republican government and saw that historical progress often came about through violent and unjust actions such as war. Kant's emphasis on freedom and reason draws on Rousseau's republicanism and reputation as a liberator who supported individual freedom.

To research:
Find out more about the Enlightenment and how it affected philosophy, politics, literature and culture.

Kant's emphasis on the universalisability of ethics draws on both Newton and Rousseau. Kant wished to universalise moral judgements in a manner analogous to Newton's three universal laws. Yet his Kingdom of Ends is, in some senses, an extension of Rousseau's social contract.

Kant's works on morality

Kant wrote several books on morality. The main ones are:

- *Groundwork of the Metaphysics of Morals* published in 1785
- *Critique of Practical Reason* published in 1788
- *The Metaphysics of Morals* published in 1797

Deontology vs teleology

> **Deontology:**
> The idea, central to Kant's ethics, that there should be universally applicable rules, which are true without exception and not dependent upon the consequences of actions

The term '**deontology**' comes from the Greek word '*deon*', which means 'duty'. Examples of deontological ethics include that of natural law, divine command ethics, and Kantian ethics. This differs from 'teleological' ways of thinking and decision-making. In the latter, we look at the world around us, searching for evidence of how things are. This evidence is gathered from our five senses, so we see, or hear, or touch things, and learn from doing this that things exist. For example, if we want to know whether it is sunny today, we would look out of the window to check. If we wanted to know the temperature at which water boils, we would heat some water up and measure the temperature when it started to bubble. In teleological thinking, therefore, we 'know' things by experiencing them.

For Kant, this teleological way of learning was fraught with difficulties. We know that sometimes we get things wrong, because we can be mistaken about what we have seen or heard. Think of a trial in a criminal court; sometimes two witnesses will give conflicting evidence about what they have seen. This leads to conflict and might have serious consequences for the defendant. It is quite common to read about 'miscarriages of justice', when someone has been convicted wrongly, based on faulty evidence provided by a witness.

In his book *The Critique of Pure Reason* (1781), Kant argues for the existence of a priori knowledge. This is a kind of knowledge that does not depend on our experience of the world. He links a priori knowledge with our ability to reason, to think rationally and logically. The purpose of the *Critique* was to examine whether human reason is capable of achieving a priori knowledge, and, if so, how and to what extent. He wanted to avoid the pitfalls of teleological thinking, so that our knowledge of the world, and our moral decision-making, would be on a firm basis and could not be faulted. He makes the distinction between a priori and a posteriori knowledge. A priori knowledge is the knowledge we gain from our ability to reason, and a posteriori knowledge is what we learn through our experience of the world.

Kant believed that the ability to reason is innate in human beings, and is a distinctive and necessary characteristic of being a human. It exists more or less equally in every person. Humans' ability to reason and think objectively (not merely from one's own point of view, or one's preferences and wishes) is one of the important things that sets them apart from all other creatures. According to Kant, humans have an intrinsic dignity because of their ability to reason. This ability thus has a unifying function: because all humans have the ability to reason, they should all come to the same conclusion about any moral problem, as there is only one correct answer – i.e. the rational conclusion.

For example, if one person argues rationally and logically to a particular conclusion – say, that telling the truth is the correct thing to do – then all other people, going through the argument and thinking rationally, will come to the same conclusion. The important thing here is that reason dictates that their answers are the same. Kant says that this principle holds for all moral problems. If I reach the conclusion that a particular action is correct (using my powers of reason), then all rational people would arrive at the same conclusion.

We may put this principle in a slightly different way. Kant believed that human beings are made up of two different aspects. Their desires, urges, and appetites link them to the beasts, but their capacity to reason objectively according to the moral law, made them more like the angels and God. He makes a distinction between the 'phenomenal' world and the 'noumenal' world. The phenomenal world is that of the physical, instinctive (non-rational) self, while the noumenal world is that of the higher, rational being. As will be clear, if a person is to be a moral being, he/she must act in accordance with this higher, rational, noumenal self. This is because the noumenal self is objective and rational. Acting according to the rational, noumenal self is to have freedom and autonomy; acting according to the phenomenal self is to be a slave to base instincts, and therefore against reason. This is to lower oneself to the status of a creature, to be non-human. Paradoxically, when human reason conforms to the moral law, it is free (self-willed) and autonomous (self-governing). When it is controlled by desires/passions or by external rulers such as kings, it is dictated to by another law external to itself (heteronomy – *hetero* = different/other, *nomos* = law).

This conclusion about the rational, noumenal self leads Kant to say that:

- all moral laws must be universal – they must be obeyed by all people at all times
- the way to decide which laws are moral is to apply reason to them
- if reason is universal, then any law based on reason will be universal and therefore applicable to everyone.

In the *Groundwork of the Metaphysics of Morals*, Kant sketches what these moral rules are and how they are created by reason.

The Good Will

Kant's aim in the *Groundwork of the Metaphysics of Morals* was to give an overview of Moral Philosophy, so that people could develop a clear understanding of how they should make moral decisions. He begins the *Groundwork* with these words: '*It is impossible to conceive of anything in the world, or even out of it, which can be called good without qualification, except a Good Will*' (Kant, *Groundwork*, Cambridge Texts in the History of Philosophy, ed. Mary Gregor, Cambridge University Press, 1997, p. 7).

As he is a deontologist, Kant says that the moral law, if it is to be unconditionally and universally obeyed, must be unconditionally and universally good. This good must be good in itself and the highest good. He calls this the *summum bonum*. He clarifies what he means by excluding some possibilities. The highest good cannot

Kant's emphasis on the Good Will

Clumsy with his hands, Kant was not cut out to follow his father into the harness-making business, but he did learn from him the importance of hard work and truth telling. He records an incident from his childhood in which his father became involved in a heated labour dispute between the saddle-makers' and the harness-makers' guilds. He notes that his parents conducted themselves among other ill-tempered and self-interested people with forbearance, love and honesty towards their opponents and this incident had a lasting effect on him.

In some sense, Kant's view of reason possesses intellectual virtues such as integrity, truth-telling, honest and fair dealing and consistency of word and deed. So the **Good Will** sets motives centre-stage in moral reasoning. This is hard to measure but important to value, and Kant's three formulations of the Categorical Imperative can be seen as an extension of the Good Will into principles of practical reason.

The Good Will: Kant's term for acting in accordance with the moral law and out of a motive of duty rather than for pleasure or to achieve a desired outcome. The Good Will is intrinsically good. Unlike other goods such as pleasure, wealth, or health, the Good Will cannot be used for bad purposes; the Good Will is good without exception, an honourable motive even if the consequences do not turn out as hoped.

be anything that depends on the results or consequences it produces, because this would be teleological, not deontological. Many factors other than reason, and therefore outside of our control, might influence the results. The Good Will comes about when a person acts rationally and gets rid of his inclinations or wishes (as these would be contrary to rational decision-making). Kant also dispenses with the 'talents of the mind' like intelligence, wit and judgement. He rules out various 'qualities of temperament' like courage, perseverance and resolution. Eliminated also are the 'gifts of fortune' – power, wealth and honour, as well as the motive of happiness. None of these can produce the Good Will. He does not say that any of these characteristics are necessarily wrong. They may be admirable qualities for any individual to possess, but they are not a reliable guide to the intrinsic rightness of moral behaviour. Each of these characteristics is rejected by Kant because it is capable of making a situation morally worse. The Good Will must, for Kant, be intrinsically good, or 'good without qualification', i.e. it cannot be capable of reducing the moral worth of a situation.

Exercise

Make a list of each of the characteristics Kant rejects above, and then give an example of how they might make a situation morally worse. For example, an 'intelligent' blackmailer is more likely to succeed in extorting money from his victim.

The concept of the Good Will must assume that people are free to make rational and unconditioned moral choices. Without this prerequisite, there can, for Kant, be no morality, as morality assumes that an individual has the real ability to choose freely to do the right thing, or the wrong thing. If individuals do not have this freedom of decision-making, then they are not moral agents, just mere automatons.

Kant has shown by this point that it is not the consequences of an action that make it right, and that individuals must be able to make free decisions. What is of paramount importance for Kant in terms of the Good Will is having the right intention. The person's motive for performing any moral action is of the utmost importance, not the consequences. He says: 'A good will is not good because of what it effects or accomplishes . . . It is good through its willing alone – that is, good in itself.' For example, if someone avoids running a child over with her car, and the car then crashes into a house, that person would not be thought of as acting wrongly. Although there were unfortunate consequences to her action, her motive for saving the child was correct. We would think of that person as being brave and doing 'the right' thing. Her action was motivated for the right reason – to save the life of the child. The fact that she put her own life in danger did not occur to her; the fact that she might be praised as a brave person afterwards did not occur to her; she wanted to stop the child from being run over. For Kant, this would be an example of the Good Will in action.

Duty

Kant says that acting according to the Good Will, i.e. unselfishly, is the same as acting according to 'duty'. He gives an example to illustrate what he means by duty.

> It certainly accords with duty that a grocer should not overcharge his inexperienced customer; and where there is much competition a sensible shop-keeper refrains from so doing and keeps to a fixed and general price for everybody so that a child can buy from him just as well as anyone else. Thus people are served honestly; but this is not nearly enough to justify us in believing that the shopkeeper has acted in this way from duty or from principles of fair dealing; his interest required him to do so. We cannot assume him to have in addition an immediate inclination towards his customers, leading him, as it were out of love, to give no man preference over another in the matter of price. Thus the action was neither from duty nor from immediate inclination, but solely from purposes of self-interest.
>
> (I. Kant, *Groundwork to the Metaphysics of Morals*, ed. Mary Gregor, Cambridge University Press 1997 p. 63)

Kant is here explaining that the grocer is not acting according to duty. He is merely acting according to his own selfish interests. Keeping prices the same for all customers is good for business; if he charged different people different prices, he would get a bad reputation and would not be trusted by customers, and could easily find himself out of business. It might be that the grocer is honest by inclination, but this, says Kant, is not the Good Will in action. The grocer may gain pleasure from treating customers honestly, but he is not due any praise for something that comes naturally to him. It is merely a coincidence that his action is the same as the Good Will, but he has a selfish motive in performing it – to do what he enjoys. It may be that he would treat his customers differently if his circumstances changed – if perhaps he no longer enjoyed treating them fairly, or his business was in financial trouble, etc. So this is not an example of the Good Will.

If a person is to do the Good Will, they must be acting in accord with duty. This means that in disregard of personal motive they do things because it is their duty, rather than because they will gain something for themselves from it, whether it is personal pleasure, a sense of importance, praise from others, or whatever other reason. Shedding all personal motives allows those acting from the Good Will to act in accordance with reason, so that the noumenal self is in control; the good person's only motive in doing the right thing is their awareness that they are doing it out of their sense of duty and for no other reason. They act morally because it is the right thing to do.

QUICK QUESTION
Why ought the grocer to be honest? Out of duty, self-interest (he's after customer loyalty and repeat business) or inclination that results from training in virtue?

The Categorical Imperative

According to Kant, being a moral person has to do with acting according to duty. This duty is universal, because reason is universal. This means that acting morally (according to the Good Will) is something 'good-in-itself', rather than merely instrumentally good, or good because of the consequences it brings. It is at this point that Kant introduces the principle of the **Categorical Imperative**.

An imperative is a command, something that you ought to do. There are two kinds of imperative: the hypothetical, and the categorical.

A hypothetical imperative takes the form 'If x, then y'. For example, 'If you want to achieve an A* grade in your RS A Level, then you must work very hard.' Here, the result (gaining an A* grade) is dependent upon the means (working very hard). If, however, you do not want to gain an A* grade in RS, the command is not relevant for you. Of course, for Kant, it is clear that the hypothetical imperative is not the imperative of morality. 'Working very hard' is not seen as a good thing in itself, it is merely a means to an end, and it is not universally applicable. He rejects the hypothetical imperative because it is only an instrumental good, not an intrinsic good.

A categorical imperative takes the form 'Do x' (or 'Do not do x'). For example, 'Tell the truth' and 'Respect your teachers' are examples of categorical imperatives. The Categorical Imperative is a command which is 'good-in-itself'. It is universal, as it applies to everyone; it is unconditional, as it is not dependent upon circumstances or situations. The Categorical Imperative would be followed by any rational person; it is an end in itself, not a means to an end. For Kant, the Categorical Imperative is the 'imperative of morality'. Moral duties are followed for the sake of duty alone, not because of any ancillary gain. As Pater Vardy notes, 'Categorical imperatives are arrived at through practical reason and they are understood as a basis for action' (Vardy, *The Puzzle of Ethics*, 1996, p. 68).

Kant wrote about the Categorical Imperative in different books, over a number of years and using different wording. He expresses the Categorical Imperative in three major formulations. In each, he is attempting to establish a test for showing whether our maxims can become universal moral principles. He does this because he wants our moral thinking to be as certain as the rules underlying mathematics and logic. To establish universally binding moral principles would mean for Kant that everyone must obey them, and that they will be acting in accordance with reason and moral rules will be incapable of contradiction.

'So act that the maxim of your will could always hold at the same time as a principle establishing universal law'

Kant gives four examples to explain how the Categorical Imperative works.

Suicide

A person feels so full of despair about his quality of life that he contemplates committing suicide. He still has his powers of reason, however, and asks himself whether committing suicide would be contrary to his duty to himself. Could his maxim count as a universal law of nature? His maxim is: 'From self-love I make it my principle to shorten my life when continuing it would lead to more evil than pleasure.' Kant says that we can see immediately that this would lead to a contradiction – life is a fundamental principle in nature, so any action that would take it away would be against nature. Therefore, Kant argues that suicide is always morally wrong.

Borrowing money

A man needs to borrow money, but knows that he will not be able to pay it back. He also knows that no one will lend him money unless they think he will repay it. Should he ask to borrow money and lie about his intention and ability to pay it back? His maxim would be: 'When I believe myself to be in need of money I shall borrow it and promise to repay it, even though I know this will never happen.' Kant asks again what would happen if this became a universal law. It is clear that this could never become a universal law as, if everyone made promises that they had no intention of keeping, the whole institution of promise-keeping would be meaningless. No one would believe anyone who promised to do anything, and, in Kant's words, 'would laugh at all such expressions of vain pretences'.

Talent

Another person has a talent that could be useful in a number of different contexts. However, this person has a comfortable life and he prefers to give himself over to pleasurable pursuits rather than cultivating his talent. He still asks himself whether this could be a universal law, so that everyone should live for pleasure and neglect their natural gifts. He concludes that it *is* consistent with reason and duty for all people to do this, and devote their lives to 'idleness, amusement, procreation – in a word, to enjoyment'. However, Kant says, this person cannot possibly *will* that this should become a universal law, because, as a rational being, he necessarily wills that all the capacities in him should be developed, because they serve him and are given to him for all sorts of possible purposes.

Selfishness

Everything is going well in life for someone, but he sees that other people have to struggle to survive. He could help them without much difficulty or hardship to himself. Should he do this? He considers the maxim: 'Let each person be as happy as heaven wills or as he can make himself; I shall take nothing from him nor even envy him; only I do not care to contribute anything to his welfare or to his assistance in need.' According to Kant, this maxim could be applied universally, because there is nothing logically inconsistent in it. However, for Kant, we could not possibly *will* that this ought to become a universal law. This is because it might backfire on us, as, if we needed help at some point in our lives, no-one would help us.

These four examples show that Kant understands the Categorical Imperative in two different ways. First, he understands the morality of actions as being decided by whether they are self-contradictory according to reason and logic. The first two scenarios are examples of what Kant calls *contradictions in the law of nature*. These are rules that do not make logical sense – they contradict themselves if applied to all people. Examples of such a contradiction would be 'Open the door but do not open the door', or 'Hold this but do not hold it.' These commands simply do not make sense. For Kant, committing suicide and failure to keep promises are self-contradictory if they are applied to all people all the time.

The final two scenarios are different; they are not logically self-contradictory, but what Kant calls *contradictions in the will*. No rational person would wish these laws to be universally applicable, because they are unacceptable. They are unacceptable because no one could possibly want to have a situation where they were in need but no one would help them. Holding that people should be selfish is counter to what we would want if we needed help ourselves. In this case, the contradiction lies in making universal a rule that might later be used against us.

'Act in such a way that you always treat humanity, whether in your own person or in the person of any other, never simply as a means, but always at the same time as an end'

This is known as the 'formula of the end in itself'. Kant argues that it is always morally wrong to treat people as a means to an end. They should be treated as 'ends in themselves', as having their own needs, desires and rights. It would be wrong, then, to become friends with someone simply because you could gain some benefit from that friendship. In this case, you would be treating them as a means to an end. All human beings, according to Kant, merely by being human, have certain rights, one of which is to be treated as equal to ourselves. Kant is here stating the important principle of the equality of every human being, irrespective of race, colour, class, gender, age or social status.

This principle runs counter to the Utilitarian principle of 'the greatest good of the greatest number'. If a law were enacted, or a decision made, that would benefit the majority of people in a community but where a minority were thereby disadvantaged, Kant would object to it on the basis of this second formulation of the Categorical Imperative.

Exercise

Find out about the Bakun Dam in Indonesia, which was instigated to produce hydro-electric power to benefit hundreds of thousands of people, but which required the flooding of a significant area which was home to 10,000 tribespeople and many indigenous animal and plant species. What would Kant have said about this plan?

'Act as if you were, through your maxims, a law-making member of a kingdom of ends'

Kant here describes a possible community where all the members have similar ideas about what is good. They make laws on the basis of making rational decisions which are consistent with the laws of logic. The laws made by this community will be accepted by everyone in it and, if there were any disputes, these would be resolved by using rational arguments. Kant was not enough of an idealist to believe that this could actually happen in practice, but he said that it was important to attempt to make it happen, as most humans are rational and want to live in harmony with others.

Strengths of Kant's ethics

1. Kant's system is logical and based on the use of the innate ability of all humans to reason.
2. Every human being, just by being human, has the ability to make valid and objective moral decisions.
3. The Categorical Imperative provides a clear and unambiguous method for testing the validity of proposed moral actions.
4. The Categorical Imperative produces moral rules that apply to everyone at all times, thus simplifying moral decision-making.
5. Kant says that the moral value of an action is based on the nature of the action itself, not on any of its potential consequences.
6. Kant's system does away with any special pleading or vested interests, as it is based not on feelings or emotions but on reason. Bias towards family members or national interests, therefore, is avoided.
7. Kant sees all humans as having value and dignity as they have the innate ability to reason. This means that things like paedophilia or the subjugation of women are automatically outlawed. In putting reason before desires, he emphasises the dignity of man compared with beasts.
8. All people should be treated equally, so that the view of a poor person is just as important as that of a rich one.
9. Kant's ethics is independent of any external authority, like God. It works simply on the basis that all people have the ability to reason.
10. It ensures that each individual takes part in moral decision-making by ensuring they are autonomous and free to make rational decisions.

Weaknesses of Kant's ethics

Conflicts of duty

The Existentialist philosopher Jean-Paul Sartre gives the example of a student of his during World War II who was faced with the dilemma of either going to war against the Nazis by joining the Free French fighters, or looking after his aged mother. Sartre writes:

> The Kantian ethic says, never regard another as a means, but always as an end. Very well; if I [the student] remain with my mother, I shall be regarding her as the end and not as a means; but by the same token I am in danger of treating as means those who are fighting on my behalf; and the converse is also true, that if I go to the aid of the combatants I shall be treating them as the end at the risk of treating my mother as a means.

Jean Paul Sartre (1905–80)
Sartre defined French Existentialist philosophy. He was a playwright, novelist and political theorist. In 1980, 50,000 people turned up at the funeral of a philosopher of radical freedom whose work had inspired students in the 1968 student uprising in Paris. He served as a meteorologist for the French Army in 1939 and was captured and imprisoned in 1940. On his release, he considered joining the Resistance but, being unable to decide between the Gaullists and the Communists, instead devoted his time to writing his diaries, *Being and Nothingness*, and his first play. He turned down a Nobel Prize for Literature in 1964, but he is perhaps most remembered for his 1945 lecture 'Existentialism and Humanism' which marked him out as a writer who brought optimism and hope to a post-war generation.

The problem for Sartre in this example, and the problem for many non-Kantians, concerns how helpful Kant's Categorical Imperative actually is when there is a conflict of duty. The conflict for Sartre's student is between the principles of 'caring for your mother' and 'fighting for justice'. Both principles are worthy, and both are universalisable, but the student cannot enact both at the same time.

The conflict of duties raises a significant problem for Kant's theory. To take a different example, if it is always wrong to tell a lie, and always right to keep promises, what should I do if I have to tell a lie in order to keep a promise? Consider what might happen if you have promised your friend that you will hide him from a potential murderer. Do you lie to the murderer when he turns up at your door asking for your

'Immanuel Kant – ruining date night since 1785'

friend? More recent followers of Kant agree that he did not give enough thought to this kind of situation, where principles could be in conflict with each other. Modern Kantians say that, because his theory does not help in this situation, we should probably make an exception to the general rule to overcome this difficulty.

Universalisability

The English-born philosopher Alasdair MacIntyre has noted that it is possible to use Kant's idea of **universalisability** to justify anything: 'All I need to do is to characterise the proposed action in such a way that the maxim will permit me to do what I want while prohibiting others from doing what would nullify the action if universalised' (*A*

Short History of Ethics, Routledge Classics, 2002, p. 126).

For example, consider the maxim: 'All people called Mark, living in Manchester and having a cat called Troy, should be given free access to concerts at the Bridgewater Hall.' This maxim could be universalised – it would not be self-contradictory – but it is clearly so specific as to apply to only one person. This is not what Kant had in mind with the principle of universalisability, and is therefore a problem for his ethical system. Some way needs to be found that limits the ability to universalise any maxim but allows valid principles to be formed, which can logically and coherently apply to all people.

Universalisability: Refers to Kant's first version of the Categorical Imperative: what would happen if everyone were to do what is proposed? If a maxim is universalisable, without contradiction, it is the moral thing to do.

Abstract nature

One of the real strengths of Kant's ethical theory is that it is powerfully argued, carefully presented and thoroughly abstract. The three formulations of the Categorical Imperative, for example, are very precisely and unambiguously stated. The level of abstraction, however, is also seen as a weakness of the theory. As we have seen above, Kant has concentrated on stating his theory in an abstract way but sometimes does not think through how the theory would actually work in practical situations. Many critics would say that the whole point of an ethical theory is to help with solving practical difficulties and dilemmas in real-life situations. If this is true, Kant's theory fails to deliver. Another way of putting this is that Kant's theory tells us the right *type* of action to do, but does not tell us *what* to do in particular situations.

Lack of humanity

Kant argued that people should perform moral actions because they have the *right intention*. People will be acting morally if they *intend* to do some good, by which he meant doing their duty. In the real world of practical morality, however, most people do not act from 'duty', but because they want to help someone else, perhaps because they feel sorry for them, or because an injustice has been done, or because they want to make things better for the person. That is, they act morally because of the *end* or *result* of their potential action, not because it is their duty to do it. People act out of emotion and a feeling for humanity, not out of (abstract) duty.

Hegel argued that Kant placed too low a value on the place of community in the moral life. The state is not just the total of individuals but an organic culture involving language, social practices and values. Its strength of wanting to universalise maxims can become a weakness if it totally ignores the special relationships that provide the very roots of our morality in terms of kinship-altruism or loyalties and duties that obligate us to, say, care for our children (or parents in later life).

Consequences

Almost all people perform any action, including moral actions, only after thinking about the consequences of that action. For example, in deciding whether I should help the old lady across the road, I would weigh up the pros and cons: Is it a dangerous

> **Exercise**
>
> Watch the film trailer for *The Remains of the Day* and consider the dutiful butler played by Anthony Hopkins. How does his unquestioning duty to his employer lead him to neglect other duties (to his own flourishing by not falling in love, to the protection of Jewish workers, and to his country in not questioning his Lordship's pact with the Nazis)? Is Kant's own strict and abstemious life after severe ill-health and as a bachelor shaping his moral austerity?

place to cross? Might she fall on the way across? Will she reward me for helping? Will my friends laugh at me? . . . etc., etc. In a more serious example, would having an abortion be a 'good' thing for the pregnant fifteen-year-old? This would normally be approached by looking at the possible consequences, not by considering whether she would be acting according to duty – that is, according to a principle without thinking about what would happen if . . .?. Kant's theory goes against the way that human beings think and normally operate.

Freedom

In 1947, the English philosopher H. J. Paton in *The Categorical Imperative* (Hutchinson 1947), raised a serious objection to Kant's theory. Kant's ethical theory is founded on two ideas: (1) our innate ability to reason, with which we can build non-contradictory and universalisable principles; and (2) our freedom to agree to do our duty. Paton says: 'we have no independent insight into the alleged necessity for presupposing freedom. Kant is indeed ingenious and, I think, sound in suggesting that freedom . . . is a necessary presupposition of all thinking. This may serve as a defence of the presupposition . . . but it is not sufficient to justify this presupposition' (p. 244).

Many people in the world do not possess the freedom to make valid moral decisions, even if they have the rationality to do so. Thousands of people live under political regimes that take away the freedom of individuals to make decisions which disagree with the government. Many women live in societies where they are limited in doing what they want to do, in terms of either education, dress or personal ambition and freedom. Kant's theory does not recognise the severe limitations for many people on the practical possibilities of acting in accordance with his theory. For these people, Kant's theory is of little value.

On the other hand, the German philosopher Jürgen Habermas (1929–) argues that, in modern societies, nearly all reasoning is instrumental. This is to say that we nearly always think in terms of hypothetical imperatives – 'we think about how to achieve certain ends, while the ends in themselves are not subject to rational assessment (instrumental reason). Thus "reason" may tell me to build divided highways to enhance rapid movement of traffic, but it is not clear how it could tell me that a social organisation requiring such rapid movement is itself "reasonable"' (Norman Lillegard, *The Moral Domain*, Oxford University Press, 2010). So, according to Habermas, Kant provides a much-needed corrective in our times. The dominance of economic growth or technological progress is accepted as reasonable and policies are instruments in delivering these ends. Kant shows us a freer form of reasoning whereby we can stand back and question the dominance of such instrumental reasoning and ask what ends we ought to be pursuing. Is the accumulation of wealth the primary end goal of society? Is what we currently take to be reasonable growth environmentally sustainable? Are the elites who set the terms of the debate really thinking universally or more short-term and out of self-interest? Here, as impractical as Kant's Categorical way of thinking may appear, it could yet help us to recover our freedom to think outside of the acceptance that the way things are is the way they ought to be and always will be. We are given grounds to critique the worst aspects of instrumental reasoning in public life.

Limiting human characteristics

Following on from the previous criticism, another important point to make concerns the narrow focus of Kant's theory. He argues that the ability to reason is the sole characteristic that should be considered in making moral rules. In this, he was following in a lofty tradition reaching back to Plato, Aristotle and Descartes. Many philosophers, however, have taken issue with this view and argued that reason is not the most important human capability. The Scottish philosopher David Hume (much admired by Kant), for instance, said that reason should be less important than the emotions, needs and desires of an individual. He famously said: 'reason is and ought only to be the slave of the passions, and can never pretend to any other office than to serve and obey them'.

Many people, then, use other human characteristics to establish ways of acting morally. Virtue ethicists, for instance, look at a range of characteristics that humans have – courage, honesty, sense of justice, practical wisdom, understanding, among others (see ch. 13). A further point, made by Alasdair MacIntyre in *After Virtue: A Study in Moral Theory* (2007), is that Kant not only uses only one human characteristic to determine his moral theory, but also assumes that this ability to reason is set at birth and does not develop as a person goes through life. Virtue ethicists, like Aristotle, argue that humans begin life as *potentially* good persons; they only become *actual* good persons by putting into practice the moral and intellectual virtues. People have to practise doing good things if they are eventually to become morally fulfilled people. Our ability to make the 'right' decisions in moral dilemmas, that is to say, is not innately part of our character; we have to develop this ability, through the practice of a number of qualities of mind and character. Just as a good musician needs to practise their instrument, often for years, before they become proficient, so a person who wants to be proficient at making moral decisions needs to practise using their qualities, throughout their lifetime. Kant was wrong, therefore, to assume that: (1) reason is the only relevant characteristic in making moral decisions; and (2) it is present and fully developed from the moment of birth, without the need for development.

Discussion Questions

1. Think of an example of a country where an individual's freedom to act morally is impossible or severely limited. What would Kant say about their moral duty in such cases?

2. Whilst a world where people break all their promises or always lie to avoid taxes would fail to work, what if this only happened rarely or infrequently? In cases where people did so, it would lower the general level of trust and increase the costs to honest citizens, but, as in our own world, a lack of universal goodness does not cause society to collapse. What would Kant say to this pragmatic defence?

3. One example of a Hypothetical Imperative is 'If you want to be successful in life, be generous to your friends', and one of a Categorical Imperative is 'Always tell the truth and never lie! This is your duty.' Think of one more example of each.

4. Would it be a contradiction of the will to say 'Look out for yourself and disregard the needs of others, and will that others leave you alone when you are in need'? How would Kant respond to this objection?

5. In his lectures on ethics, Kant comments on people as having the dignity of beings as ends in themselves. He writes, 'Everything has either a price or a dignity. If it has a price, something else can be put in its place as an equivalent; if it is exalted above all price and so admits of no equivalent, then it has a dignity.' Would this give Kant grounds to argue that prostitution (even where consent is given) ought to be made illegal?

6. Although Kant emphasises the law-like quality of the Categorical Imperative, he argues that only when we are not governed by heteronomy (ruled by another law, such as happiness, virtuous inclination or consequences) are we autonomous or truly free-thinking individuals. How does reason make us free according to Kant?

7. Kant seems to set up emotion as an obstacle to fulfilling the moral law. But could I feel that an action were both my duty and a privilege and source of happiness or fulfilment (such as caring for an elderly parent or, as a soldier, fighting for my country?) What would Kant say for and against this?

8. How, in Habermas' view, can Kant's Categorical Imperative prove more relevant to our times than ever?

Amendments to Kant's theory

The twentieth-century British intuitivist philosopher W. D. Ross was a critic of Kantian Ethics. He thought that, in boiling ethics down to universal rules or to the one motive of the Good Will, Kant had oversimplified the moral life. Kant mistakenly supposed the moral life to be a 'contest between one element which alone has worth [i.e. the Good Will] and a multitude of others which have none; the truth is rather that it is a struggle between the multiplicity of desires having various degrees of worth' (*Foundations of Ethics*, 1939, 206). Kant's idea that moral rules have 'absolute authority admitting of no exception' (*Foundations of Ethics*, 313) also neglects our intuition that a wide range of sometimes conflicting duties need to be taken into account. In his books *The Right and the Good* (1930), *Foundations of Ethics* (1939) and *Kant's Ethical Theory* (1954), Ross proposed that a better way of responding to the problem of conflicting duties is to explore 'prima facie' duties, which allow us to make exceptions. Prima facie means 'at first sight', and a **prima facie duty** is one that is conditional and allowing of exception. This kind of duty can always be overridden by a different duty if the occasion arises. So, for instance, the command to 'Always tell the truth' is a prima facie duty, which may take second place to a more important duty, such as 'Always keep your promises', if the situation demands this. If it is normally our duty to 'tell the truth', this should be the way we operate unless there is a more important and compelling duty in a particular instance.

Ross lists seven prima facie duties:

> **Prima facie duty:** W. D. Ross' attempt to clarify a difficulty with Kant's theory. When there is a conflict of duty, Ross suggests that they are put in order of importance.

1.	Duties of fidelity or promise-keeping	I act in accordance with a promise I made previously
2.	Duties of reparation for harm done	I act to make amends for something I did wrong previously
3.	Duties of gratitude	I act to repay a debt of some kind
4.	Duties of justice	I act in order to gain an equal distribution of pleasure and happiness
5.	Duties of beneficence	I act so that others will benefit, particularly in terms of virtue, intelligence or pleasure
6.	Duties of self-improvement	I act in order to improve my own intelligence or virtue
7.	Duties of non-maleficence	I refrain from doing anyone else any harm

The first three of these duties have to do with past events; the others look to the future. Ross stresses the personal character of our duties, which all have to do with other individuals. He was also aware that this list was not complete or definitive. Ross anticipates that a person will use these seven duties in any order depending upon the situation. If someone regularly gives money to a charity for homeless people, for example, then the duty of beneficence would be appropriate, as they would be acting for the benefit of someone other than themselves.

Ross' idea of prima facie duties is not without difficulties and has not been accepted by all modern Kantian scholars. There are two important sticking points with his list of duties:

How do we know what a prima facie duty actually is?

Ross places emphasis on the role of intelligence in his list of duties, but why should we agree with this? Ross was an academic philosopher, who spent his time discussing issues and matters which were of little or no concern to people outside the university. Why should we not come up with a different list of prima facie duties, using (for example) developing musical ability, or driving a car, or knowing how to behave at a dinner party? His list can be considered to be rather arbitrary, and different people could come up with a quite different list of duties.

What happens when there is a conflict of interest?

Ross says little about what should happen when there is a conflict of interest. Surely, however, any moral system must be judged by whether it can successfully navigate through conflicting moral rules. Ross does not provide any guidance about how to prioritise his seven duties. He says that we would intuitively 'know' which rule to prioritise in a given situation, as we apply reason in specific circumstances. This is not very helpful, though, as different individuals could disagree and Ross's system would be useless.

Discussion Questions

1. Work through Ross' list of seven duties, giving an example for each one.
2. Ross is trying to deal with an issue that in his view, Kant leaves unresolved – what to do when duties conflict. In your view, do moral intuitions solve this problem? Is intuition something Kant would have accepted in his moral universe – is it a type of reasoning or quite apart from it?
3. Is Kant right to give greater moral respect to the dutiful worker who is tempted to steal from their employer but resists from a sense of duty to the moral law, than to one who is by nature honest and works to the very best of their ability out of loyalty to their boss and a sense of pride gained from their work?

Exercise

Read the following paragraph and then discuss whether you agree with the list of moral rules presented. Give reasons for agreeing or disagreeing.

One example of a philosopher who has produced a competing list of moral rules is the contemporary American philosopher Bernard Gert. Gert says in his book *Common Morality: Deciding What to Do* (2004) that morality can be summed up in a list of moral rules, and that each rule in his list is rationally accepted by everyone. He does not mean that all people will accept all the rules all the time, but that, if people were rational, they would accept his list of rules. His list is as follows: Do not kill; Do not cause pain; Do not disable; Do not deprive people of freedom; Do not deprive people of pleasure; Do not deceive; Keep your promises; Do not cheat; Obey the law; Do your duty.

FURTHER READING

Roger Scruton (2001) *Kant: A Very Short Introduction*. Oxford University Press

Sally Sedgwick (2008) *Kant's Groundwork of the Metaphysics of Morals: An Introduction*. Cambridge University Press

Roger J. Sullivan (1994) *An Introduction to Kant's Ethics*. Cambridge University Press

Jennifer K. Uleman (2010) *An Introduction to Kant's Moral Philosophy*. Cambridge University Press

OCR Past Paper Questions

JUNE 2009

    (a) Explain the strengths of Kant's theory of ethics.   *[25]*

    (b) 'Kant's theory of ethics is not a useful approach to abortion.' Discuss.   *[10]*

JUNE 2010

    (a) Explain how a follower of Kant's ethics might approach issues surrounding
the right to a child.   *[25]*

    (b) 'The right to a child is an absolute right.' Discuss.   *[10]*

JANUARY 2011

    (a) Explain Kant's argument for using the Categorical Imperative.   *[25]*

    (b) 'The universalisation of maxims by Kant cannot be defended.' Discuss.   *[10]*

MAY 2011

    (a) Explain the differences between the Hypothetical and Categorical Imperatives.   *[25]*

    (b) How useful is Kant's theory when considering embryo research?   *[10]*

MAY 2013

    (a) Explain, with examples, the importance Kant placed upon doing one's duty.   *[25]*

    (b) To what extent is doing one's duty the most important part of ethics?   *[10]*

Christian Ethics

This chapter focuses on Christian ethics in particular, rather than that of world religions in general in order to go into greater depth and because, in Western thought, Christian ethics remains important, and secular ethical theories have drawn on it or reacted against it. Nonetheless, similar beliefs and critical issues arise within other forms of classical theism, such as Judaism, Islam and the ethics of other world faiths.

This chapter focuses on several key areas of debate in religious ethics. Questions that arise include:

1. What sources of authority ought Christian ethics to depend on (from scripture, reason, tradition, leaders, conscience or experience)?
2. How do morality and the divine will relate to each other? The Euthyphro Dilemma. Can you be good without God and can morality be known by reason quite apart from religious faith? How do religious and secular ethics relate to each other?
3. Is Christian ethics relativist or absolutist? Is religious ethics too legalistic or inflexible to take account of consequences and the dilemmas posed by special circumstances?
4. Is it possible to discover a 'biblical' position on modern ethical issues?

The sources and character of Christian ethics

Given the estimated approximately 2.1 billion adherents of global Christianity, along-side its 2000-year history, Christian ethics is understandably diverse, with three main traditions (Orthodox, Catholic and Protestant).

The Pope is seen as inheriting the authority invested by Jesus in his disciple Peter. Roman Catholic moral teaching would draw on papal encyclicals (letters from the Pope to Catholic bishops worldwide, setting out the official and absolute teaching of the Church), Church councils, the Bible and the tradition of Natural Law. Collectively, the authoritative teaching of the Church is referred to as the *magisterium*.

Protestant denominations (of which there are thousands, with the Anglican, Baptist, Methodist, Presbyterian and Pentecostal denominations being some of the better-known examples) would place central importance on the Bible and the Holy Spirit who inspired it and guides its readers, and give a greater role to the individual conscience. As well as denominational differences, a spectrum from fundamentalist to liberal readings of the Bible causes controversy over interpretations (e.g. over abortion or homosexuality) within many denominations. So Christians disagree over the weight of authority to give to:

- biblical commands, values and virtue
- the traditions of the Church councils and key thinkers
- Church leaders
- religious experience (e.g. prayer, worship, baptism, communion)
- the Guidance of the Holy Spirit to the individual conscience
- reason and science

Long before 'Ethics' arose as a specialist field in universities, as distinct from theology or Church life, God and morality were an inseparable part of a worldview and way of life. Seventeenth-century Europe had seen wars of religion between Protestants and Catholics, so it seemed only reasonable to find a secular basis for ethics to ensure a peaceful and tolerant basis for society. 'The Enlightenment' or the 'Age of Reason' and the birth of modern science also began to question and doubt the authority of the Bible. With the birth of modern states like France and the United States, it was thought that, in order to avoid conflict over disputes of faith, religion had to be kept private and out of public life or state laws. This was not to deny that Church worship and communities provided rich soil for character formation and positive values like justice or compassion, but religious beliefs themselves were taken to be incidental to the content of ethics. Further to this, the growing complexity of the modern world, in terms of medical ethics or modern warfare, made it harder to find straight rules or quotes from the Bible to settle complex dilemmas. As broad principles are applied to the specifics of a situation, disagreement between people of good will can be frequent and seemingly irresolvable. At the heart of this debate is an age-old question about whether we're better off accessing ethics through reason rather than faith. It first arises in one of Plato's early dialogues and has come to be known as **The Euthyphro Dilemma**.

The philosopher Anthony Flew has claimed that whether one can grasp the point

The Euthyphro Dilemma:
From a dialogue between Socrates and Euthyphro related by Plato – does God command an action because it is right, or is it right because God commands it?

and the force of this dilemma is a good test for one's aptitude as a philosopher. So test yourself.

The Euthyphro Dilemma

Plato's Euthyphro Dilemma is set out in a dialogue in which Socrates questions the young Euthyphro when the two of them are on their way to court. Socrates is up for a pre-trial hearing, accused of corrupting the youth of Athens and questioning the gods. The irony in this dialogue is that, in one sense, Socrates is guilty of both of the charges he is accused of – attacking the gods of Athens and corrupting the minds of the young. At the heart of the whole dialogue is a search for what true justice looks like.

Euthyphro is at court, to Socrates' amazement, to begin prosecuting his father for murder (a religious crime in Athenian law). The murdered man had been hired by Euthyphro to help on the family farm, but, in a drunken rage, he had slit the throat of another servant. Euthyphro's father had then bound the murderer and thrown him into a ditch before sending for the official responsible for dealing with such crimes. Tragically, he'd died before this official arrived. Euthyphro was convinced that he was acting justly in obeying the divinely ordained law and prosecuting his own father. To him, it was the only pious or holy thing to do. Flattering him, Socrates asks for instruction about what is pious or holy, and the young Euthyphro says that what is pious or just is what is agreeable to the gods (though the gods of ancient Athens do not always agree). Socrates then asks

1. Is something good because the gods ordain it?

2. Or do the gods ordain it because it is good?

This throws Euthyphro onto 'the horns of a dilemma' as it presents two stark choices, each with significant downsides. Euthyphro departs disgruntled.

Socrates (c.470–399 BCE)
Socrates had been a stonecutter and a soldier before becoming a philosopher (for which, Plato insists, he took no fee). Judged to be the wisest of all men by the oracle of Delphi, whose declarations came in the form of riddles, his wisdom lay in knowing that he did not know. Socratic method interrogates claims, raising counterexamples and refining statements in dialogue, always aware of its fallibility while searching for true knowledge.

A magnetic personality, Socrates attracted young and radical disciples. He was a principled man who, as a soldier, refused an order to be party to the death of an innocent man. Being seen as a 'gadfly' or troublesome critic of Athenian political elites, as well as making some unfortunate associations with enemies of the state, resulted in his being accused of impiety and corrupting the youth of Athens and sentenced to death by the drinking of hemlock. His legacy is filtered through the dialogues of Plato in which he features prominently and it is difficult to distinguish the distinctive qualities of each thinker.

Option (1) is a form of the **Divine Command Theory** (also known as theological voluntarism because it is based purely upon God's will). The worst exponent of this view was William of Ockham (1288-1348). Ockham held that, as God was free and sovereign, he could (hypothetically) have decreed actions that we now think of as evil to be good (Ockham gives the examples of theft and adultery). It would then be our duty to perform them. As Peter Singer puts it, 'if the gods had happened to approve of torture and disapprove of helping our neighbours, torture would be good and helping our neighbours bad' (*Practical Ethics*, 1999, p. 3). That God could have commanded us to murder and enslave people, but did not, was for Ockham all the more reason to praise him. But his mistake was to define God's being in terms of his all-powerful freedom rather than in terms of his love or justice. This makes his judgements appear arbitrary. And if there is no standard of moral behaviour independent of God, then on what basis can his actions or character be praised? It may be prudent to praise dictators if your life is in their hands, but this does not make them moral – indeed, you may have a moral duty to resist them.

Option (2) is no less difficult for the polytheist/theist because, as John Arthur (*Morality and Moral Consequences*, 2005, p. 20) expresses it, 'If God approves kindness because it is a virtue and hates the Nazis because they were evil, then it seems that God discovers morality rather than inventing it.' Reason can access justice by a higher standard than God, a standard to which he is accountable. This appears to place God under a higher moral law and to separate ethics from religion as an area of knowledge that is accessible to reason quite apart from faith.

Classic monotheists today seek to avoid the horns of this dilemma by offering a third option – that of divine essentialism. They do this by suggesting that moral perfection is essential to the divine nature. They begin by distinguishing Plato's and Socrates' concern about the gods of ancient Greece – who were fickle, prone to warring with each other, and got up to lots of mischief with humans – from the God of classic monotheism, who is morally perfect – i.e. all-loving and just. God is not subject to a higher moral law external to himself. The god acts consistently with his nature. Plato developed an elaborate metaphysical world of 'the Good' that lay beyond our world in the perfect, eternal world of forms. In this, he found a basis for virtuous characteristics like Truth, Justice or Courage. Yet theists object that moral goodness cannot exist in abstract ideas like 'wisdom' or 'justice' as virtue only exists in personal beings.

> **Divine Command Theory:**
> The idea that morals derive from God (or the gods); there is no standard of moral behaviour that is independent of God

William of Ockham – is he responsible for giving Divine Command Theory a bad name?
Ockham was a radical Franciscan whose defence of poverty against Pope John XXII led to his excommunication. Following this, he advocated the separation of Church and state.

Divine Command Theory and its critics

Problems in the language and meaning of equating 'God' with 'Good'

G. E. Moore, (1873-1958)

The 'Open Question Argument' of G. E. Moore (1873-1958) teases out the circular reasoning of the theist that the Euthyphro Dilemma has suggested. Suppose I ask 'I know she's a spinster, but is person X female?' – that would be a closed question because, as a spinster, she is by necessity female; it could not be any other way. This can be deduced from the concept of being a spinster. Not so with goodness and God, reasoned Moore; 'Is something good because God commands it?' remains an open question. So Moore believed that this established that God was not the same as good. Indeed, one could reply 'No – after all, many gods of the past have been wicked.' So the open question 'What does it mean to call God good?' requires a meaning to the word 'good' other than 'godly'. Otherwise, in ordinary language, the question is empty of meaning.

God = Good?

Another way of putting this (termed 'The Emptiness Problem') is put forward in the book *Ethics Without God* (Prometheus Books, 1990) by Kai Nielsen (1926–). If we're saying the same thing twice in the different words 'God' and 'good', then one of them is redundant. So 'God's actions are good' would be a trivial statement meaning 'God's actions are God's actions.' If true, this would make the statement 'God commands me to do X but I ought not to do it', meaningless. In order to know that what God wills is good; we would have to judge independently that it is good. We would need some criterion to help us identify the goodness of God. Religion and ethics are, in Nielsen's view, logically independent of each other and we must look somewhere other than in God for the foundations of our morality.

In her book *Philosophers Without Gods, Meditations on Atheism and the Secular Life* (Oxford University Press, 2010), Louise Antony (1962–) argues that religious believers do not really believe in Divine Command Theory, as can be seen from their reading of certain biblical texts. She cites the troubling passage in Genesis 22:2, where God commands Abraham to sacrifice his son Isaac – 'Then God said, "Take your son, your only son, whom you love – Isaac – and go to the region of Moriah. Sacrifice him there as a burnt offering on a mountain I will show you.", She argues that most religious believers (both conservative and liberal) are at pains to interpret these texts as not commanding child sacrifice because these acts are wrong and God is good. This shows that they do not follow Divine Command Theory as they judge surface readings of scripture to be mistaken on some separate basis.

This text is read by some commentators as setting apart the goodness of God and his people from the child sacrifices of their pagan neighbours. In Jeremiah 19:5, God says of one of Israel's neighbours, 'They have built the high places of Baal to burn their sons in the fire as offerings to Baal – something I did not command or mention, nor did it enter my mind.' Both Jewish and Christian theologians make the point that the commandments cannot be properly understood outside of God's covenantal relationship with Israel over time. The covenants with Noah (Genesis 9), with Abraham (Genesis 15) and with Moses on Sinai (Exodus 19/20) all express a partnership in which God's essential nature is shown to be just, loving, and faithful. So this is not an unqualified obedience of divine commands but

The Giving of the Law on Mount Sinai to Moses is the classic example of Divine Command Ethics. It is given within the context of a covenantal relationship and God rescuing his people from slavery in Egypt. The character of the lawgiver and the law are inseparable.

one proven through the course of 'salvation history'. Seen out of context as a set of rules to be obeyed, the commandments look arbitrary. Indeed in Genesis 18, Abraham appeals to the essential goodness of the divine nature to rule out indiscriminate judgement by God on the city of Sodom. As he says, 'to kill the righteous with the wicked, treating the righteous and the wicked alike. Far be it from you! Will not the Judge of all the earth do right?' He can appeal to the character of a God whose just and loving nature is known in the experience of his forefathers, Isaac and Jacob.

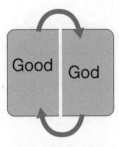

QUICK QUESTION

*The Euthyphro
Dilemma*

*Do you lean towards
A or B?*

(A) Goodness can be
known by reason and
experience, which are
a more secure basis
for morality than faith
in God and the divine
law.

(B) We may come
across goodness
before we come
across God, but the
moral law lies not
above God, but is
essential to his nature
(Essentialism).

In a secular age, Reason and experience come first and we judge God by them. Yet, for Aquinas, nothing we can discover by reason can contradict what is disclosed by revelation. Here philosopher J. P. Moreland (1948–) makes the point that it is indeed possible to 'come across' morality before you 'come across' God, but that this does not rule out God being the final cause of goodness. So, for Aquinas, 'Nothing will be called good except in so far as it has a certain likeness of the divine goodness' (*Summa Contra Gentiles*, bk 1, ch. 40); behind human law is Natural Law, then divine and eternal law.

Strengths of Divine Command Theory

1. Rooting morality in a creator who has ordered the universe according to his eternal laws accounts for a widely held sense of the impartiality and objectivity of moral standards. The Utilitarian Henry Sidgwick talked of the point of view of the universe, but it does not have one – God (if he exists) may offer a reason behind this intuition. Our sense of moral responsibility and guilt may suggest a moral order innate within us which, to some, further hints at a moral mind and order behind the universe. Moral laws or commands require a lawgiver.

   The force of duties and obligations that the moral objectivity of theism provides was given up long after European thought had stopped believing in God. With its departure came a sense of loss, for, as the character Ivan in Dostoyevsky's novel *The Brothers Karamazov* says, 'Without God, everything is permitted.' Religion can be a powerful motivator to serve one's fellow human beings.

2. Kant observes that, though our experience is sense-based and of the phenomenal world, for morality to work we have to posit the existence of a noumenal realm beyond the senses. God and the afterlife were necessary to rational morality because we could never square happiness and virtue in just this life. The *summum bonum* or perfect moral standard was unachievable in this lifetime and often doing good was costly, even involving death. So moral absolutism is possible, but difficult without God and the afterlife.

3. Although many secular philosophers (e.g. Singer, Rachels and Timmons) teach that Divine Command Ethics is uniformly of the kind William of Ockham proposed, and that it is now obsolete, both statements are untrue. As we have seen, many major contemporary philosophers and theologians (e.g. A. Plantinga, W. Lane-Craig, J. P. Moreland, R. Adams) defend it in a revised form.

4. It is easy to dismiss Divine Command Ethics, but, given the worldwide numbers of religious believers who hold to moral objectivity because of the created order of the universe, this is a widely held view. The sociologist Peter Berger (*The Desecularisation of the* World, Wm B. Eerdmans Publishing, 1999) assesses that a large percentage of Jews, Muslims and Christians see morality as governed by the divine will. For them, the religious form of life integrates moral norms with practices like prayer and worship and they seek to follow God's will and commands. We may want to be perfectly free, but it seems odd to our moral intuitions that we

should create rather than discover moral norms, finding them in a transcendent source.

Weaknesses of Divine Command Theory

1. *Is morality human or divine?* As sociobiologist E. O.Wilson puts it, centuries of debate leave us with two options. Either morality has a supernatural source outside of human minds, or it is invented by human minds as a result of their experience and can be explained in biological and cultural terms (it arises through kin-altruism and as game theorists argue, in laws or co-operative rules which offer a better strategy for group success). We have scientific evidence of how morality might have developed from our evolutionary past, so it is, more reasonable to see morality as a human invention.
2. Kai Nielsen's book *Ethics Without God* (1990). To construct a moral argument for God's existence or assert that he is worthy of praise, an external standard of judgement is needed. We cannot praise God's actions purely on the basis that he wills them. For the Divine Command theorist simply to assert that 'goodness is what God ordains and God ordains it because it is good' is circular.
3. *The 'no reasons' or 'evil command' objection.* Richard Dawkins has argued that only religion makes good people do evil things (e.g. the Crusades/the Spanish Inquisition/terrorism in the name of God). If there is no reason to condemn genocide or slavery other than the divine will, then, it is argued, there is no independent or rational check on what religious adherents might believe God to have revealed to them. This is sadly not an academic matter, as religious wars have been launched on the belief that they were the divine will. For Bertrand Russell, religion was the enemy of moral progress in creating wars and preventing a rational education free from tribal identities, intolerance and anti-scientific mythology.
4. *The autonomy objection.* The Enlightenment of the eighteenth century championed the independence of reason from any arbitrary authority, for example monarchy or God. To assert that morality is fixed by divine commands is to limit human freedom. Imagine a conflict between one's conscience and what is thought to be a genuine command of God. Which gets the upper hand in judging the right action? To the secular mind, what gives humankind its self-governing dignity is the capacity to reason and act autonomously according to one's own will. In this view, an analogy of God's will determining 'right' and 'wrong' as well as our conscience would be a dictator implanting a chip in our brain to make our thoughts conform to his will. Were we to somehow get wise to this, we would regard God as immoral.
5. *The pluralism objection.* With so many religions offering conflicting accounts of the revealed commands of God in their scriptures, which is the correct one? Even within one tradition, disputes exist over what a command should mean in practice or whether it was valid then, but obsolete now.

Is Christian ethics relativist or absolutist?

There is a story from the first century BCE of two leading Rabbis who interpreted the law very differently. It is said that a Gentile came to each of them asking them to teach him the whole Torah in the time he could stand on one foot. Rabbi Shamma drove him away with his measuring stick. By contrast, Rabbi Hillel converted the Gentile by telling him: 'That which is hateful to you, do not do to your neighbour. That is the whole Torah; the rest is commentary.'

In the Sermon on the Mount, Jesus also opposes the harsh legalism of his day, suggesting that the spirit of the law is more to do with the true motives that lie behind actions than mere lip service obedience to the law. It is on this basis that more relativist interpretations of Christian ethics arise, one famous version being **Situation Ethics**.

> **Situation Ethics:** A radical Christian-based Utilitarian moral theory, developed by Joseph Fletcher. The only absolute moral principle is to do 'the most loving thing in any situation'.

Situation Ethics

In 1966, the Episcopalian priest Joseph Fletcher (who later became a professor of social ethics) wrote an 'explosive book' entitled *Situation Ethics: The New Morality*. In his controversial work, Fletcher set out 'act agapism' as a kind of Christian parallel to Act Utilitarianism in which love applies directly to situational judgements and not to rules. The morality of actions is to be judged on their consequences rather than on obedience to divine commands. Situationism's 'pragmatic–empirical temper' sees conscience as a verb instead of a noun, as the reason making moral judgements prior to a contextual decision rather than some mysterious inner faculty or external source (such as the Holy Spirit) which passes judgement after the event.

Fletcher's radical approach offered a third way between the *legalism* of rigid laws and absolute rules that often did more harm than good, on the one hand, and an irresponsible rejection of any moral law in *antinomianism* (*nomos* = 'law' in Greek) with its ad hoc approach threatening inconsistency and even moral anarchy, on the other. *Situationism* charted a middle course of 'principled relativism'. Fletcher spoke of the one law of *agape* ('selfless love'), drawing on the wisdom (*sophia*) of the Church and culture, and applying these in the *kairos* or moment of decision. Love decided 'then and there', using moral principles as 'rules of thumb'. His was a radically contextual ethic which worked empirically and inductively from the facts and circumstances of a particular case, building upon a minimal number of principles (four) and propositions (six).

These are:

Four working principles

Pragmatism
Drawing on the American pragmatists James, Dewey and Peirce, the focus of ethics should be on what works – that is, what brings about goodness, flourishing, or beneficial consequences. This is not about establishing universal rules or norms, but, in the specific context of a decision, to consider the *summum bonum* or highest good,

which is the serving of love. Concrete rather than abstract decisions are informed by the facts of the situation and the likely consequences resulting from it.

Relativism

Absolute rules that prohibit ('Never do x'), or prescribe ('Always do y') are absent from Situation Ethics. Instead, all ethical judgements are relative to agapeic love. Yet, as Fletcher writes, Christian situationism 'relativizes the absolute, it does not absolutize the relative!' Fletcher sets out three polarities which are in tension in Christian ethics – law and love, authority and experience, and fixity and freedom. Seeing these in 'fruitful tension' and approaching moral decisions in humility is the way forward. The 'why' remains the same, whereas the 'what' and the 'how' may change depending on the circumstances.

Positivism

Following Hume, Fletcher acknowledges that the gap between facts and values means that 'We cannot verify moral choices. They may be vindicated, but not validated.' As in Anselm's phrase 'I do not seek to understand in order that I may believe, but I believe in order that I may understand' (*Credo ut intelligam*), he considers value judgements in ethics to be a decision we commit to living by rather than a statement to be proven. The leap of faith Fletcher proposes is to regard love (*agape*) as an axiomatic value. Here he takes 1 John 1:4's 'God is love' to be defined in terms of God's love in Christ and our love as a response to this ('We love because he first loved us.' – 1 John 4:19). Such faith commitments are the essence of Christian ethics for Fletcher. Unlike natural theology's claim that reason underpins its beliefs, Fletcher sees such commitments as voluntary.

Personalism

We ought to put people, as opposed to objects, rules, authorities or tradition, at the heart of our value system. This draws on Martin Buber's distinction between I–it relationships (which can result in the use of people as objects or a means to an end) and I–thou relationships that are characterised by reverence and respect. As we are made in the image of a personal God, we should remember that 'things are to be used; people are to be loved'. For Fletcher, the Holy Spirit is present wherever love is at work in those of any faith or none. He quotes William Temple's statement that 'the atheist who is moved by love is moved by the spirit of God'.

Six propositions

1. Only love is intrinsically good. It is the 'regulative principle of Christian ethics' typified in the sacrificial and selfless death of Christ on the cross. To be known as Christ's disciple is to love one's neighbour, for, as Augustine says, 'in order to know whether a man is a good man one does not ask what he believes or what he hopes but how he loves' (quoted in Fletcher, *Situation Ethics*, Westminster John Knob Press, 1966, p. 63).
2. Love is the only ruling norm of Christian decision-making. Fletcher takes the collision between Jesus and the Pharisees to be over legalism – in particular, whether the love of God and one's neighbour are to govern the interpretation of all

other laws. Jesus' disciples pluck grain on the Sabbath and fail to observe certain fast days, and he frequently touches those who are diseased and ritually unclean. Love governs his reading of the law. As Augustine put it, 'Love with care and then what you will, do' (p. 79).

3. Love and justice are the same, because justice is love distributed. Prudence and practical wisdom (*phronēsis*) are valued in the virtue tradition and Fletcher gives the example of a field commander who has to decide whether a platoon or company or even a regiment is expendable. Love is rational, not purely emotive – at times it carefully calculates the outcomes and distributions of good. Agapeic love is not 'one-to-one' but 'multi-lateral' in its love of all neighbours, and 'optimific' in a manner that sounds very much like Utilitarianism with its equal consideration of interests. Fletcher would respond by asserting that the agapeic calculus (the greatest amount of neighbour welfare for the largest number of neighbours possible) goes further than the Hedonic Calculus in its obligations to serve others. Furthermore, he argues that where laws are unjust (e.g. in the segregation laws), civil disobedience can be a duty of justice understood agapeically.

4. Love wills the neighbour's good whether we like him or not. Love should not be sentimentalised because *agape* is not *eros* (intimate or romantic love) or *phileo* (friendship) – forms of love in which we are attracted by our emotions and a reciprocity or benefit we gain from the relationship. *Agape* is benevolent in that it seeks to love its enemies and to will them good and not evil. Love can be hard-headed (as when 'a nurse in a military hospital deliberately makes wounded soldiers hate her enough to motivate them to get them on their feet again' or when a priest turns away beggars, for, as the *Didaché* (4:5) says, 'Do not be one who opens his hands to receive, or closes them when it is time to give').

5. Only the end justifies the means – this end is love. Legalism is prone to sticking to principles and rules out of a mistaken sense of duty far removed from the original intention behind the law. When nurses lie to schizophrenics to keep them calm for treatment or when Bonhoeffer rejected his pacifism to take part in the plot to assassinate Hitler, the end of love justified the means undertaken. Bonhoeffer happily takes on the Jesuitical maxim 'Finis sanctificat media' ('the end justifies or sanctifies the means'). Jesus legitimised King David taking the showbread from the temple in desperate circumstances (Matthew 12:4), unlawful as this was. Fletcher gives the example of a Romanian Jewish doctor who saved the lives of 3,000 pregnant Jewish women prisoners admitted to a concentration camp by aborting their embryos. Regardless of our view of abortion, the end of saving 3,000 lives justified this means.

6. Love's decisions are made situationally not prescriptively – it decides there and then. Law may offer security and limit the room for error that trusting human freedom over decisions might introduce. It may be that, as we do not know the future, decisions like Captain Scott's to stretcher an injured man from the South Pole, which may have cost him his life and that of his team, was the right one at the time. Equally, the choice of the seaman in charge of a lifeboat overloaded with seven crew and thirty-two passengers in 1941 to throw most of the males into the sea off Newfoundland resulted in his conviction for murder. As Fletcher writes, 'Situation ethics says it was bravely sinful, it was a good thing.' The universals of Situationism

are love for God's sake and for one's neighbours. The '*kairos* factors' of the when, the where, the which, the how are down to the particulars of the dilemma.

The moral life – we are what we habitually do, or how to survive in a crisis

Fletcher sets out a case of sacrificial adultery in which a World War II German prisoner of war can only bring about her release from a Ukrainian prison camp by becoming pregnant by a Russian guard (pp. 164ff.). She takes this course of action as she urgently wishes to be reunited with her family and to bring up her three children (plus her newborn, Dietrich, who is loved more than the rest because he brought about her freedom). Fletcher asks us to consider whether Mrs Bergmeier has done the right thing. He relates that, after Dietrich's christening, she asks the same question of her Lutheran pastor.

It is said that extreme cases make bad law, and one criticism of Situation Ethics is that Fletcher's examples build a moral system around exceptional cases that do not properly characterise the moral life. Virtue ethicists would remind us that the moral life has far more to do with trained habits of practice and inclinations of character and will than with intermittent and extreme dilemmas. In another example, Fletcher asserts that an unmarried couple 'living together' who love each other are more pleasing to God than a couple whose marriage is characterised by conflict and mutual disdain. Offensive and unorthodox in 1966, such a view appeared to move too easily with the spirit of the age.

Strengths of Situation Ethics

1. Situation Ethics pays attention to the exceptional nature of dilemmas rather than being legalistic and inflexible.
2. In placing agapeic love at the heart of its ethic, it claims to restore the spirit of the law that Jesus spoke of in the Sermon on the Mount.
3. It is practical and realistic. It is a Christianised form of Act Utilitarianism that takes a realistic account of the fallen, broken and complex world, in which the right thing to do may not be obvious from pre-determined rules.
4. More comfortable with individual and subjective intuitions about identifying the loving thing to do than was Natural Law or Divine Command Ethics, it appealed to the liberalising spirit of the late 1960s in which Fletcher was writing.

Weaknesses of Situation Ethics

Ethicist Neil Messer judges that 'Fletcher's Situationism has not worn well and many Christian ethicists now regard it as little more than a historical curiosity . . . as a theological theory of ethics, it looks distinctly thin' (*Christian Ethics*, SCM, 2006, p. 81). Fletcher sees himself as part of a long tradition of writers and theologians who fought legalism in their day with an emphasis on love and realism (including St Paul (cf. 1 Corinthians 6:12), the author of 1 John, Augustine, Abelard, Aquinas, Luther, Leo Tolstoy, Emil Brunner, Paul Tillich, Reinhold Niebuhr and Paul Ramsey). He quotes, with approval, Augustine's famous maxim: 'Love with care, and then what you will, do' (p. 79). But one cannot help but see a very selective reading of these thinkers which interprets them as Situationists ahead of their time. In 1952, Pope Pius XII rejected Situation Ethics as opposing concrete circumstances to Natural Law and God's revealed will in scripture. He condemned it as altogether too individualistic and subjective.

Other common criticisms of Situation Ethics

1. *It sets people or love against rules*, thus failing to see that rules are essential to protect rights and limit harms done to people. Society requires extensive legislation to protect the vulnerable and it is naive to see laws or rules as legalistic because they can become inflexible in particular cases when (as Rule Utilitarians accept) they deliver better outcomes on an aggregated basis. Rules co-ordinate actions consistently and coherently (as in traffic laws), maintain trust (as in doctor–patient confidentiality) and reduce self-deception (because they guard individuals against self-interest or their limited perspective, and remind them of their duties).

   A contemporary of Fletcher's, Paul Ramsey, argued that rules often assist us in adjudicating between contradictory courses of action grounded in love. Ramsey's solution (in *Deeds and Rules in Christian Ethics*, 1967) was to reject Fletcher's *act agapeism* and propose a *rule agapeism* which entailed 'rules of practice' that operated in areas of human activity or institutions. Thus, the institution of marriage ought to embody love as a rule of practice. There should be a presumption against separation and divorce unless the burden of proof against this was overwhelmingly met (e.g. in persistent abuse or unfaithfulness). Similarly, in the rules governing the practice of a Just War, genocide and torture were ruled intrinsically immoral, but other actions were judged in terms of the proportional weighting of good and evil outcomes. Ramsey disapproved of the US policy of targeting cities in the Soviet Union with nuclear weapons, for example, arguing that they should be directed only against military targets.

   One example of how difficult it is for well-intentioned people to agree about the loving thing to do can be seen in Fletcher's statement that 'On a vast scale of "agapeic calculus" President Truman made his decision about the A-bombs on Hiroshima and Nagasaki.' By contrast, the pacifist and founder of the Catholic worker movement, Dorothy Day, wrote of this event:

   > Mr. Truman was jubilant. President Truman. True man; what a strange name, come to think of it. We refer to Jesus Christ as true God and true Man. He [Truman] went from table to table on the cruiser which was bringing him home from the Big Three conference, telling the great news; 'jubilant' the newspapers said. Jubilate Deo. We have killed 318,000 Japanese.

   > (Day, *The Catholic Worker*, September 1945, 1: www.catholicworker.org/dorothyday/daytext.cfm?TextID=554)

   Without rules or principles, is it possible for love to elicit from the context the right outcome?

2. Situation Ethics too readily slips into the antinomianism (being anti-law) it claims to avoid. If rules are never prescriptive, but simply to inform our judgements, individuals come to regard them as negotiable – as Kant would see it,

given human nature, exceptions to rules quickly become the rule. This was why Pope Pius XII judged Situation Ethics to be 'an individualistic and subjective appeal to the concrete circumstances of actions to justify decisions in opposition to the Natural Law or God's revealed will'.

3. What may be needed is to revise the application or formulation of a rule rather than to abandon it. Rules caution us against treating our situation as unique because we look at it from a self-centred viewpoint. We ought to universalise all of our actions in like situations rather than justifying our breaking of rules on the basis of the uniqueness of our situation. New Testament ethics emphasises the *koinonia* or community, in which love is expressed through mutual obligations, duties of care and service. Situationism is in danger of morphing into the individualism of the age.

4. Fletcher's 'middle way' between legalism and antinomianism sounds eminently reasonable but ignores the long tradition of what medieval thought referred to as casuistry. This may have got a bad press as a way of finding loopholes while seeming to honour rules, but the Christian tradition has provided resources for applying and interpreting rules in the context of situations. One such example is the idea of proportionality in Aquinas' Just War theory. Here he argues that the force should be proportional to the evil remedied. As he writes, 'though proceeding from a good intention, an act may be rendered unlawful, if it be out of proportion to the end'. Another example might be the Doctrine of Double Effect in which the primary intention of any action is beneficent or therapeutic, but foreseeable harmful effects may result. So rules need not be applied without regard to consequences, but motives remain important in justifying any exceptions to them.

5. Moral rules can prohibit actions that are intrinsically and absolutely wrong (for example, the prohibition on bestiality in Leviticus 20:16), or indiscriminate violence towards the innocent or genocide. To regard the rightness or wrongness of every action as dependent upon its context may relativise the absolute wrongness of some actions and thereby undermine the morally educative nature of law.

6. As with consequentialist ethics more generally, we cannot be sure of the outcome of our actions, so to put all of our eggs in this basket, so to speak, is risky. What if (in the case of sacrificial adultery above), the war's end would have resulted in the mother's release two months later? Situationism presupposes human capacities of intuition and discernment in a manner that fails to reckon with human weakness. The Christian doctrine of the Fall (with which Bonhoeffer begins his ethics) must take into account our finitude in calculating, predicting and controlling consequences, as well as the universal effects of sin.

Is it possible to discover a 'biblical' position on modern ethical issues?

Is it possible to get at agreed moral principles from an ancient biblical text? The library of sixty-six books in the canon of Protestant scripture (seventy-three in the Catholic) emerges from a range of social and historical contexts. As Christian ethicists discuss biblical interpretation, the question arises of how to bridge the gap between a revelation received in a pre-scientific world with an agrarian economy based on kinship loyalties under the rule of a king or regional superpower, and the modern context in which the values and principles in the text are to be applied. We typically read the Hebrew or Greek of the original text in translation and from the vantage point of a scientific age and democratic society in an age of global capitalism. Additionally, new technologies such as genetic engineering and nuclear weaponry raise complex dilemmas and challenges. Synthesising or drawing together themes and principles from the whole of scripture (what Reformation theologians referred to as *tota scriptura*), requires a careful reading of the various types of literature in the Bible (e.g. law, narrative history, gospel, letters, wisdom).

Applying an ancient text to modern-day ethical issues is not simply about finding proof texts upon which to hang an ethical stance. It is more of a process of crossing a wide river while retaining consistent principles:

1. Understand the text in its historical context – what did the text mean to the original author(s) and biblical readers and listeners?
2. Measure the width of the river to cross (differences in language, culture, history, situation – agrarian, pre-science/technology, covenant, worldview, etc.)
3. Bridge this with theological principles (e.g. covenant, values, virtues, salvation history, authorial intent, Israel, the Church's use in tradition, allegory, typology, etc.)
4. Relate to contemporary context – theologian Karl Barth urged Christians to read both the Bible and the newspapers, but to interpret the newspapers from the Bible.

Scholars like Charles H. Cosgrove and Richard B. Hays emphasise the importance of finding analogies between biblical values and principles that speak to modern-day contexts. Values such as concern for the sanctity of human life, justice for the marginalised, and the proper stewardship of creation can guide normative ethics in modern contexts despite originating in vastly different ones. These scholars also focus on key theological themes such as creation, fall, community, the cross and new creation. Hayes cites Jesus' fruit test: 'A good tree cannot bear bad fruit, nor can a bad tree bear good fruit . . . you will know them by their fruits' (Matthew 7:18,20), concluding that the value of Christian biblical interpretation in ethics 'will be tested by their capacity to produce persons and communities whose character is commensurate with Jesus Christ and thereby pleasing to God' (Hays, *Moral Visions* 1997, p. 7). Ethical truth claims must be embodied if they are to be persuasive. As Aristotle set out in *The Art of Rhetoric*, *logos* (reason) and *pathos* (emotional persuasion) are never as powerful as *ethos* (the habits of a life well lived and consistent with the claims it makes).

Discussion Questions

1. Given that there are quite different traditions of ethics among Roman Catholics and Protestants, do you think there can be any single thing called 'Christian ethics'?
2. In your view, do the strengths of Divine Command Theory outweigh its weaknesses?
3. 'It is impossible to use the Bible as a viable source of Christian ethics because it is full of contradictions.' Do you agree?

FURTHER READING

John Arthur (2005) *Morality and Moral Controversies*. Pearson, 7th edition

Michael Banner (2009) *Christian Ethics: A Brief History*. Wiley-Blackwell

Malcolm Brown (2010) *Tensions in Christian Ethics*. SPCK

Robin Gill (2011) *The Cambridge Companion to Christian Ethics*. Cambridge University Press

Richard Hays (1997) *Moral Vision of the New Testament: A Contemporary Introduction to New Testament Ethics*. Continuum

D. Stephen Long (2010) *Christian Ethics: A Very Short Introduction*. Oxford University Press

Neil Messer (2006) *Christian Ethics*, SCM Study Guide. SCM

Sam Wells and Ben Quash (2010) *Introducing Christian Ethics*. Wiley-Blackwell

OCR Past Paper Questions

JANUARY 2009
    (a) Explain the ethical teachings of the religion you have studied.   *[25]*
    (b) 'Some religious ethics are too rigid for moral decision-making.' Discuss.   *[10]*

JANUARY 2010
    (a) Explain how the ethics of the religion you have studied might be applied
        to abortion.   *[25]*
    (b) 'Religious ethics fail to consider consequences.' Discuss.   *[10]*

JANUARY 2011
    (a) Explain how the followers of the ethics of the religion you have studied
        make ethical decisions.   *[25]*
    (b) 'Morality and religion are separate.' Discuss.   *[10]*

APPLIED ETHICS

6 Abortion

LEARNING OUTCOMES

In this chapter, you will learn about

- the concept of the 'Sanctity of Life' and how it applies to abortion
- the concept of personhood as applied to abortion
- the right to life as applied to abortion and the rights of all those involved
- the issues of infertility and the right to a child
- the status of the embryo
- the debate over whether a child is a gift or a right
- the application and the different approaches of the ethical theories (Natural Law, Kantian Ethics, Utilitarianism, Christian ethics) to abortion and the right to a child
- evaluating these issues critically and assessing their strengths and weaknesses

Abortion: definition, key terms and history

Natural abortion	Commonly referred to as a 'miscarriage', this is where the body rejects the pregnancy, usually because there is something wrong with the developing foetus
Medical abortion	Abortion is achieved by taking a pill (mifepristone) and inserting a tablet (prostaglandin) into the vagina 36-48 hours later. No surgery is involved
Surgical abortion	Abortion is achieved by suction methods (from the 7th to the 15th week of pregnancy), or by putting surgical instruments into the womb and removing the foetus (later than 15 weeks)
Therapeutic abortion	Where an abortion is carried out in order to protect the life or health of the mother, e.g. in the case of an ectopic pregnancy
Conception	The beginning of life, when the sperm and egg join together

Zygote	The fertilised ovum when it is between 0 and 5 days old
Pre-embryo (blastocyte)	The fertilised ovum, a group of multiplying cells between 5 and 14 days after conception
Embryo	The name given to the multiplying cells between 14 days and 8 weeks after conception
Foetus	The developing organism from 8 weeks after conception onward
Sentience	Having the ability of being aware
Viability	When the foetus is considered physically capable of living outside the womb (often with medical assistance)
Quickening	The moment at which the mother can first feel the foetus move, commonly at between 16 and 20 weeks of gestation
Potential	This relates to the ability of the foetus to become a human being
Ensoulment	In traditional Christian thought, the point at which a foetus gains a soul. According to Aquinas (based on Aristotle), this was 40 days for boys and 90 days for girls
Consciousness	Awareness of self, a key component of personhood
Birth	The point at which a foetus becomes a baby
Personhood	The distinguishing characteristics that make up an individual person
Quality of life (QoL)	A key term in the abortion debate, in deciding whether a foetus has a 'life' distinct from the mother
Sanctity of Life (SoL)	This is a key term in the debates over abortion and euthanasia. In the abortion debate, it argues that abortion is morally wrong because the foetus has the same 'God-given' status as all (born) humans.

Abortion is one of the most complex and emotional ethical issues to be discussed and has, as we shall see, an interesting and controversial history. An abortion is the expulsion of a foetus from the womb. In most ethical discussions, this is taken to mean the *deliberate* expulsion of the foetus, by a surgical or medical procedure. However, the majority of **abortions occur naturally**, i.e. without the intervention of anyone; this is known as a miscarriage. In these cases, the pregnant woman may not even know that she has been pregnant.

Natural abortion: Commonly referred to as a 'miscarriage', this is where the body rejects the pregnancy, usually because there is something wrong with the developing foetus

Abortion is sometimes thought to be a fairly modern phenomenon, but it was widely practised in the ancient world, not just in primitive societies, but in cosmopolitan and developed civilisations like Egypt, Greece and Rome. The earliest known written reference to abortion is contained in the Ebers Papyrus, an Egyptian medical compendium dating from about 1550 BCE.

Abortion was widely accepted in the Greek and Roman world. Early Greek philosophers argued that a foetus was not properly alive (i.e. was not human) until 40 days after **conception** for a male and about 80 days for a female (the difference was probably based on observation of aborted foetuses). Before this time, the foetus was thought to have a vegetable or animal soul. In the third century BCE, Aristotle wrote: 'when couples have children in excess, let abortion be procured before sense and life have begun; what may or may not be legally done in these cases depends upon the question of life and sensation' (*Politics* 7.16).

There are references to abortion in common Greek culture. One such reference occurs in Aristophanes' comic play *Lysistrata*, when a leading character, Calonice, refers to a young woman as 'well-cropped, and trimmed, and spruced with penny-royal'. Pennyroyal is a common herb of the mint family, but is very dangerous for pregnant women as it can trigger a miscarriage. In the play, it is deliberately used as an abortifacient (i.e. a substance which will bring about an abortion).

The Hippocratic Oath contains a prohibition on the use of pessaries to bring about abortion. Instead, Hippocrates advocates vigorous exercise to induce a miscarriage.

Abortions were usually performed by trained midwives. Plato, in the *Theaetetus*, mentions a midwife's ability to bring about an abortion in the early stages of pregnancy (*Theaet*. 149d).

In the second century BCE, the famous physician Soranus advocated abortion in cases involving health complications or emotional immaturity of the mother. He lists a number of safe methods for aborting a foetus and advises against the use of sharp instruments in the procedure.

The earliest Roman law code, the *Twelve Tablets*, dates from *c*.450 BCE. The philosopher Cicero (106–43 BCE) commented that one of its laws required that all significantly deformed children should be killed shortly after birth. It also allowed Roman fathers to kill any newborn female infants. Cicero himself, however, was a critic of the law on abortion, but he attacked it not on moral grounds, but because it cheated the father of his hopes, the family line, the family inheritance, the Roman state and the human race in general (Cicero, *In Defence of Cluentius*, 32). When the influence of Christianity began to change attitudes in the third century CE, abortion was banned because it infringed on parental rights.

Early Christian theologians were generally against abortion. One of the earliest Christian writings outside the New Testament, the *Didaché* (*c*.150 CE), says: 'Do not murder a child by abortion or kill a newborn infant. [2.2] . . . The Way of Death is filled with people who are . . . murderers of children and abortionists of God's creatures [5:1–2]'.

St Jerome (342–420 CE) talked about the everlasting consequences of practising abortion: 'Some, when they learn that they are with child through sin, practise abortion by the use of drugs. Frequently they themselves die and are brought before the rulers of the lower world guilty of three crimes: suicide, adultery against Christ and murder of an unborn child' (Letter 22:13).

St Augustine, in the fifth century, also believed that abortion was murder. However, his beliefs on earlier-stage abortion were similar to Aristotle's. He was ambivalent about whether aborted foetuses would be resurrected in the next life, because, although they were not fully formed persons, it might be unloving if God did not recognise their potential. During the Middle Ages and the Renaissance, abortion was tolerated as there were few laws against it.

At the beginning of the feminist movement in the latter part of the nineteenth

Conception:
The beginning of life, when the sperm and egg join together

century, feminist writers like the American Elizabeth Cady Stanton argued strongly against abortion on the grounds that it was used as a tool by men to exploit women and avoid their responsibilities in supporting a family.

In nineteenth-century Britain, despite the increased availability of contraception, there were still many unwanted pregnancies. Various means of inducing miscarriages were discreetly advertised in newspapers, and 'back-street' abortions were common.

In 1938, the *Rex* vs *Bourne* case allowed an abortion to an underage girl who had been raped, on the grounds of 'mental and physical wreck'.

In 1967, the Abortion Act was passed in Great Britain. It clarified existing law on a number of points and made abortion legal in Britain, and freely available on the National Health Service. Abortion was allowed on certain grounds:

- To save the woman's life
- To prevent grave permanent injury to the woman's physical health
- Under 28 weeks to avoid injury to the physical or mental health of the woman
- Under 28 weeks to avoid injury to the physical or mental health of the existing child(ren)
- If the child was likely to be severely physically or mentally handicapped

The Act required that the procedure must be certified by two doctors before being performed. The Act was amended by the Human Fertilisation and Embryology Act 1990, which allowed abortion up to full term for disability of the foetus. In May 2008, there was a debate in parliament about whether the limit should be reduced from 24 to either 22 or 20 weeks, but no changes have currently been made.

In 1973, in the landmark case of *Roe* vs *Wade*, the United States Supreme Court ruled that women had a constitutional right to have an abortion, at any time before viability, without interference from government. This decision was to have a major effect on legislation around the world, not just in the USA.

Medical abortion:
Abortion is achieved by taking a pill (mifepristone) and inserting a tablet (prostaglandin) into the vagina 36-48 hours later. No surgery is involved.

Therapeutic abortion:
Where an abortion is carried out in order to protect the life or health of the mother, e.g. in the case of an ectopic pregnancy

Pre-embryo (blastocyte):
The fertilised ovum, a group of multiplying cells between 5 and 14 days after conception

Abortion case studies: legal controversies

In May 2007, a woman from Levenshulme, Manchester, who, in early 2006, had an illegal late-term abortion at 7 months, was convicted of *child destruction* under the Infant Life (Preservation) Act 1929. The case is believed to be the first of its kind in Britain ('Baby destruction woman sentenced', *BBC News*, 24 May 2007).

In July 2013, the Irish parliament voted to allow abortion in limited circumstances. This authorised a termination when doctors believed that a woman was at risk of taking her own life. The decision followed the case of an Indian woman, Savita Halappanavar, who died in hospital after she was refused an abortion in 2012. The debate revealed deep splits in the predominantly Roman Catholic country. For opponents of the decision, it was not just a religious but a human rights issue as they believed that in any pregnancy the mother and foetus have equal rights to life. Others argued that the bill was too limited as it did not allow for terminations in cases of rape or incest, or when there was a foetal abnormality. Nor did it allow for termination when the foetus could not survive outside the womb. Before this law was changed, it was estimated that at least eleven Irish women each day travelled to England or Wales to have an abortion.

In July 2013, lawmakers in Texas passed a contested bill to limit abortions to no later than 20 weeks of pregnancy. The bill would also shut down most of the abortion clinics

Embryo:
The name given to the multiplying cells between 14 days and 8 weeks after conception

Zygote: The fertilised ovum when it is between 0 and 5 days old

Foetus: The developing organism from 8 weeks after conception onward

Surgical abortion: Abortion is achieved by suction methods (from the 7th to the15th week of pregnancy), or by putting surgical instruments into the womb and removing the foetus (later than 15 weeks)

Birth: The point at which a foetus becomes a baby

in the state, leaving only six 'surgical centres' where abortions may be performed. This would mean that many women seeking an abortion would have to travel hundreds of miles to have the procedure carried out. Supporters of the bill argue that this will protect the health of the women and their foetuses. A number of other states have passed similar abortion bills, but most of these are tied up in legal objections. The Texas Medical Association, Texas Hospital Association and the American College of Obstetrics and Gynaecology all oppose the bill. It might take several years to decide whether or not it will become law.

Abortion statistics

It's helpful at the outset to be aware of case studies and informed by statistics before considering moral theories in respect of abortion. Here are some statistics about abortion in England and Wales for 2011 (Source: https://www.gov.uk/government/uploads/system/uploads/attachment_data/file/127785/Commentary1.pdf).
In 2011, for women resident in England and Wales:

- The total number of abortions was 189,931, 0.2 % more than in 2010 (189,574) and 7.7% more than in 2001 (176,364).
- The age-standardised abortion rate was 17.5 per 1,000 resident women aged 15–44, the same as in 2010, but 2.3% higher than in 2001 (17.1) and more than double the rate of 8.0 recorded in 1970.
- The abortion rate was, at 33 per 1,000, for women aged 20, the same as in 2010 and in 2001.
- The under-16 abortion rate was 3.4 per 1,000 women, and the under-18 rate was 15.0 per 1,000 women, both lower than in 2010 (3.9 and 16.5 per 1,000 women respectively) and in the year 2001 (3.7 and 18.0 per 1,000 women respectively).
- 96% of abortions were funded by the NHS. Over half (61%) took place in the independent sector under NHS contract, up from 59% in 2010 and 2% in 1981.
- 91% of abortions were carried out at under 13 weeks gestation; 78% were at under 10 weeks, compared to 77% in 2010 and 58% in 2001.
- Medical abortions accounted for 47% of the total, up from 43% in 2010 and 13% in 2001.
- 2,307 abortions (1%) were carried out under ground E (risk that the child would be born handicapped).

Non-residents:

- In 2011, there were 6,151 abortions for non-residents carried out in hospitals and clinics in England and Wales (6,535 in 2010). The 2011 total is the lowest in any year since 1969.

Additional information from other areas of the world:

- The estimated number of abortions worldwide in 2008 was 43.8 million, a decrease from 1995 (45.6 million)
- The highest rate of abortions occurred in Latin America (32% of all pregnancies); the lowest in Oceania (17%).
- In Europe, there is a wide discrepancy between western Europe (12 abortions per 1,000 women) and eastern Europe (43 per 1,000).
- Nearly half of all abortions worldwide are unsafe, and nearly all unsafe abortions take place in the developing world (56% of all abortions in the developing world are unsafe, compared with just 6% in the developed world).

Rights in the abortion debate

The issue of rights is an important part of the debate when considering whether abortion is morally justified. The supposed rights of the foetus and the (potential) mother are the most important ones, but it is sometimes forgotten that the (potential) father may have certain rights too. The man provides half the genetic material which will make up any baby born from the fertilised egg, so it is possible to argue that, just as the woman providing the egg (containing one half of the genetic material) has certain rights concerning what happens in and to her body, so should the man. This right would apply to the man whether the pregnancy was intentional or not, or whether donor sperm was used. In any discussion between a couple about whether or not to have an abortion, it should be a joint decision, not just one that the woman makes on her own. If a pregnancy occurs as a result of casual sex, however, the man's moral rights become less clear. This is because he may not know that his sperm have caused a pregnancy, or he may not wish to be involved in making a decision (many men appear to think, erroneously, that it is a woman's responsibility to 'take precautions' during sex). In many cases, therefore, the man abrogates his rights, i.e. he gives up any rights he may have to being a decision-maker in deciding whether having an abortion is an acceptable thing to do.

> ### Exercise
>
> Go on the internet and search for 'safe and unsafe abortion statistics' on the WHO website (www.who.int). You should be able to access a pdf summary of global levels of safe and unsafe abortion from 1995 to 2008.
>   How do you account for the changes outlined in this summary? What factors might have influenced the changes? What reasons can you give for the differences between different parts of the world?

It is widely accepted that a woman has important rights in the decision to have an abortion. Much of the recent ethical discussion on this stems from the influential 1978 article by the American feminist philosopher Judith Jarvis Thomson, 'A Defense of Abortion'. She argues that a woman has a right to decide what happens to her own body. She uses the hypothetical example of a woman who is kidnapped and wakes up to find that she is attached by various tubes to a famous violinist. The violinist has potentially fatal kidney failure. Only the woman can help to cure it. If he is attached to her continuously for nine months, he will be cured. Unplugging the violinist will kill him. She will therefore have to give up some of her rights for nine months. She will not be able to do some of the things that she might like to do, her body will undergo various changes and she will suffer pain in the process. All of this will be necessary in order to save the violinist, and all of it has happened against her will and her wishes. Thompson's question is: Does the woman have a moral obligation to remain plugged in to the violinist for nine months? She argues, from this highly unlikely scenario, that the woman has no moral obligation to keep the violinist alive, but has a right to unplug herself. Her right to do to what she wishes with her body overrides any right the 'violinist' may have to life.

Thomson says:

> A great deal turns for women on whether abortion is or is not available. If abortion rights are denied, then a constraint is imposed on women's freedom to act in a way that is of great importance to them, both for its own sake and for the sake of the achievement of equality; and if the constraint is imposed on the ground that the foetus has a right to life from the moment of conception, then it is imposed on a ground that neither reason nor the rest of morality requires women to accept, or even to give any weight at all.

(Thomson, 'A Defense of Abortion', *Philosophy and Public Affairs* 1:1 (1971), pp. 130–50)

Exercise

Do you think Thomson's analogy of a 'violinist' is a good one? For example, are there more differences than similarities between being kidnapped and connected to an adult violinist and being a consenting adult who finds herself unwillingly pregnant after the couple's contraception fails? Does this analogy only work in respect of cases of conception following rape or could it equally apply to the above example?

Those who accept Thomson's argument that abortion can be a morally justifiable decision have been called 'pro-choice', i.e. they are in favour of abortion and think that the choice to have one should be the woman's, because her rights outweigh those, if any, of the foetus. Those who argue against this view are generally called 'pro-life', and hold the view that the rights of the foetus override those of the woman.

Other arguments in favour of the rights of the woman include the following.

Thomson, followed by others, argues that a woman owns her own body, just as a person owns their house or property. She therefore has a right to abort a foetus at any time, just as a house-owner has a right to do what she wants in her own home, such as changing the layout of rooms.

A woman has a right to self-defence. A pregnancy puts great strains on a woman's body and she has the right to dispose of a foetus in order to protect her body.

Exercise

Look up the famous *Roe* vs *Wade* case from 1973, when the US Supreme Court ruled that a woman had a constitutional right to have an abortion. What were the key arguments used? Do you agree with them?

It is argued that a woman has right to privacy. If a woman falls unexpectedly pregnant, she has the right to abort the foetus as she has not 'invited' it into her body. As Christine Overall argues in *Human Reproduction: Principles, Practices and Policies* (1993), making her keep the foetus inside her until birth would be like forcing her to give up one of her internal organs against her will; nothing can justify such an intrusion on the woman's privacy.

Another pro-choice argument links to the feminist view that to deny an abortion to a woman is to deny her equal rights to a man. The American comedian Rob Delaney puts it in this way:

> I don't know how to look at those who'd restrict or deny access to contraception and abortion and not see misogyny. Not sexism; that's a gender neutral word. Misogyny is the hatred, dislike or mistrust of women. It is an ugly word and it represents an ugly thing.
>
> And Good God, is it lazy. And disingenuous. And it is the warm and welcoming home to the idea that a pregnant woman who doesn't want to take her pregnancy to term should not have access to a safe and legal abortion.

(*Guardian*, 3 July 2013)

A final pro-choice argument focuses on the safety of the woman. There are many countries (and US states) where abortion is illegal. Pregnant women who wish to have an abortion either have to travel considerable distances to have the procedure carried out, or are forced to have it performed illegally. In such circumstances, procedures can go wrong because they are not performed by properly qualified people. Women can suffer pain and damage to their bodies, or even die because of post-operative complications. In the article just quoted above, Rob Delaney defends a woman's right to an abortion, saying: 'I support a woman's right to a safe, legal abortion because centuries of history shows us that women are going to get abortions whether they're safe and legal or not. And when they're not safe and legal, these women will often die terribly or be damaged irreparably.'

The question of whether a foetus has any rights is a complex one. The answer depends on whether the foetus is considered to be a person. There are two main issues that need to be considered here:

1. **personhood**
2. **sanctity of human life**

Personhood

The most important questions in the abortion discussion are: When does life begin?; and When does the foetus become a (human) 'person'? In one sense, these are very simple questions to answer: life begins when the sperm enters the ovum and the cell begins to split and multiply. This is the moment of 'conception', the first indication that a new life has begun. Although this may seem like an indubitable 'fact', there is no absolutely clear method of establishing when conception occurs. The stage of pregnancy is determined by the first day of the woman's last menstrual period. Most women have a 28-day menstrual cycle, ovulating around day 14, so fertilisation could occur around that time. Even this short summary shows that calculations concerning conception cannot be confirmed accurately and are somewhat vague. The exact date or time of conception, therefore, cannot be known, so to say that life begins at conception (which most pro-lifers do) can only be a theoretical or philosophical position to take, not an actual, factual, one.

One of the possible relevant ways this may relate to the abortion debate concerns the 'abortion pill' RU486. This is an artificial steroid (mifepristone) which blocks

Quality of life (QoL): A key term in the abortion debate, in deciding whether a foetus has a 'life' distinct from the mother

Personhood: The distinguishing characteristics that make up an individual person

Sanctity of life (SoL): Another important term in the abortion debate, arguing that abortion is morally wrong because the foetus has the same 'God-given' status as all (born) humans

progesterone, a hormone needed for pregnancy to be successful. The abortion pill may be used up to about 9 weeks after conception, and is claimed to have certain advantages, as it:

- does not require surgery or hospitalisation
- is more economical than traditional abortion
- is quicker for women – they do not have to travel potentially long distances to abortion clinics
- is intended to put women in control of the abortion.

Exercise

Rank the following issues from most [1] to least [10] significant in deciding your view on the issue of abortion. State any further issues that you consider to be important in deciding your own point of view.

[_] Whether or not the foetus can feel pain.
[_] Whether or not the pregnancy/birth of a child is wanted by the prospective parents.
[_] Whether or not the physical and mental health of the pregnant woman or her existing children will be put at greater risk by the continuation of the pregnancy than by its termination.
[_] The quality and stability of the relationship between the potential parents.
[_] Whether or not the argument from potentiality (the foetus seen as is a potential human life) works.
[_] Whether or not around 200,000 abortions in England and Wales each year is too many and if so, whether MPs should reduce the limit to below 24 weeks to lower this figure.
[_] Whether life begins at conception, viability (the ability of the foetus to survive outside the uterus), birth or some other point.
[_] Whether or not pre-natal tests show signs of foetal abnormality.
[_] Whether or not abortion (within limits or on demand up to birth) is an integral part of a woman's sovereignty over her own body.
[_] Whether or not life begins at conception and 'personhood' is a status held by the foetus from this point.

However, as Lord David Alton argued in 'The Dangers of RU486' in 2010, there are significant health risks associated with taking this drug, including very prolonged and serious bleeding and even death (www.davidalton.net/2010/12/23/the-dangers-of-ru486-2).

For most people who discuss the morality of abortion, the key debate concerns the point at which the foetus becomes a 'person'. There is very little agreement on this, because of the difficulty in defining what is meant by a 'person'.

Exercise

Before reading further, jot down what you think are the essential characteristics of being a 'person'.

Sanctity of life

Many Christians believe, on the basis of their interpretation of biblical passages, that all life is sacred and that this applies to the unborn foetus. According to this view, abortion at any stage is unambiguously wrong and against the will of God. Each and every conception is sacred to God, regardless of whether the foetus produced is healthy or not.

According to these Christians, the Bible clearly teaches that human life is precious to God and that abortion is equivalent to murder. They point to passages such as Genesis 9:6 and Exodus 20:13, which prohibit murder. Human beings have a unique position in the created world: only humans have souls; only humans have a special relationship with God; only humans are made in the image and likeness of God (Genesis 1:26).

In the US, the pro-choice vs pro-life debate has been more public and crucial in election campaigns than in the UK. Here a man protests outside an abortion clinic and advice centre.

Jeremiah 1:5 and Psalm 139:13 talk of God's establishment of a relationship with individuals from the moment of conception. This is taken to mean that the soul must be present from this moment too, so to perform an abortion on a foetus is to take away what God has created, which is clearly a sin.

Central to this view on abortion is the importance of the Incarnation. The Incarnation has revealed both the true nature of God as creator and saviour of humankind, and what it is to be truly human. Christ was 'conceived by the Holy Spirit and born of the Virgin Mary' (Matthew 1:20). Jesus was fully human as well as fully divine. He shared our humanity and was made like us in every way (Hebrews 2:14, 17). Therefore, according to this view, the life of every human being must also have begun at conception. Abortion is therefore wrong.

Other Christians, who interpret the Bible more liberally, will point to other guiding principles which may apply to abortion. It is important to note that the Bible does not talk of preserving human life *at all costs*. Hebrews 9:27, for instance, 'inasmuch as it is appointed for men to die once and after this comes judgment', reminds people that death is a natural part of every person's existence. Capital punishment was used and justified by reference to the command of God in relation to certain crimes (e.g. Genesis 9:6; John 8:3–11).

Christian views on abortion

What the Churches say

The Roman Catholic Church has always argued strenuously against abortion. Catholics believe that all human life is sacred from the moment of conception until the moment of death. Taking an innocent life, whether born or unborn, is morally unacceptable:

> Human life is sacred because from its beginning it involves the creative action of God and it remains forever in a special relationship with the Creator, who is its sole end. God alone is the Lord of life from its beginning until its end: no one can under any circumstance claim for himself the right directly to destroy an innocent human being.
>
> (Papal encyclical: *Donum vitae* (*The Gift of Life*, 1987), 5)

> The unborn human being's right to live is one of the inalienable human rights.
>
> (Pope John Paul II, 1985)

Ensoulment:
In traditional Christian thought, the point at which a foetus gains a soul. According to Aquinas (based on Aristotle), this was 40 days for boys and 90 days for girls.

Roman Catholics base their views on abortion on the idea of **ensoulment**, which St Thomas Aquinas took from Aristotle (384–322 BCE). Aristotle taught that a foetus originally has a vegetable soul, which later in pregnancy becomes an animal soul. Later still, this becomes 'animated' with a human soul. This 'ensoulment' takes place at 40 days gestation for males and at 90 days for female foetuses. The difference in timing probably had to do with Aristotle's observations of aborted foetuses and the assumption that boys tend to develop more quickly than girls in early life. For Aristotle, then, abortions were acceptable up to the point of ensoulment, when the foetus became human. Aquinas accepted this view and declared that abortion from the time of ensoulment was immoral. He was ambiguous, however, on the question of whether abortions could morally be performed before ensoulment.

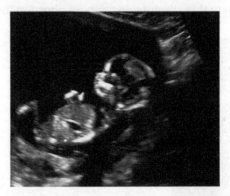

3D imaging of pre-natal life has confirmed the intuitions of many pro-lifers that this is not simply a collection of cells, but an individual life distinct from that of the mother. Other studies cited by pro-choicers claim that the pre-natal infant lacks sentience (the capacity to feel pain) until as late as 24 weeks.

The Church of England is strongly opposed in principle to abortion, but recognises that there can be 'strictly limited' conditions (e.g. where the mother's life is threatened by continuing the pregnancy) in which having an abortion may be morally preferable to any other available alternative. The Church believes that all human life, including the foetus, is created by God in his own image, and is therefore to be nurtured, supported and protected. The mother needs support and understanding and her wishes should be fully recognised. It believes that the abortion law should be more strictly applied so that the number of abortions will be 'drastically reduced', and that 'every support' should be given to pregnant women who are in difficult circumstances. (Summarised from www.churchofengland.org/media/45673/abortion.pdf.)

Natural Law and abortion

The Natural Law tradition is clear and unambiguous on the question of abortion. One of the Primary Precepts is to protect and preserve innocent life. It is clear that a foetus has life and is also innocent. To abort a foetus, therefore, is immoral and against the will of God. In this sense, prohibiting abortion is a Secondary Precept, flowing from the Primary Precept.

Natural Law adherents believe in the Sanctity of Life (SoL). Since all life is God-given, and human life is more important than other life on earth, humans are in a special position in the created world and have a special connection with God. They are sacred. For anyone to perform an abortion, therefore, would be not just a sin against that person, but a sin against God himself.

The first of Aquinas' Primary Precepts is the protection and preservation of human life as absolute. As life begins at conception in official Catholic teaching, abortion is always wrong, no matter what the circumstances. It would be immoral for a fourteen-year-old who is pregnant because of rape to have an abortion, just as it would be immoral for a woman who already has six children to have an abortion.

The only exception to this absolute position on abortion involves the Doctrine of

The Protestant Reformer John Calvin remarked that, just as it was more violent an act to attack a person in their house, so it was more reprehensible to abort the unborn child from the womb. The reproduction and preservation of life is among the five basic goods in Aquinas' list.

Double Effect (DDE). This is where a doctor acts with good intent, but where bad or unfortunate consequences result. According to this doctrine, it is morally permissible to perform an act that has both a good effect and a bad effect if all of the following conditions are met:

1. The act to be done must be good in itself or at least indifferent
2. The good effect must not be obtained by means of the bad effect
3. The bad effect must not be intended for itself, but only permitted
4. There must be a proportionately grave reason for permitting the bad effect

The most important element here is the *intention* in the mind of the doctor in judging the moral correctness of her action because of the Roman Catholic teaching that it is never permissible to 'intend' the death of an 'innocent person'. A foetus would count as an 'innocent person'. Take the example of a woman who has an ectopic pregnancy (i.e. where the fertilised egg implants outside the womb, usually in the Fallopian tubes). There are around 11,000 cases of this each year in the UK. The DDE would work in this example if the doctor saw that, if the pregnancy were to continue, it could bring about the death of the woman. The foetus would have to be terminated if the woman was to live. The doctor's intention is good (to save the mother's life) but the consequences are bad (the death of the foetus). For some, but not all, interpreters of the Roman Catholic Natural Law tradition, this would be acceptable, because the *intention* of the doctor is to save the mother's life, not to kill the foetus. So if the intention is to preserve life, but a secondary effect is foreseeable, this may be considered morally permissible under Natural Law theory. Writing on the question of whether it is lawful to kill a man in self-defence, Aquinas himself comments that

> the act of self-defence may have two effects, one is the saving of one's life, the other is the slaying of the aggressor. Therefore this act, since one's intention is to save one's life, is not unlawful, seeing that it is natural to everything to keep itself in '"being"' as far as possible. And yet, though proceeding from a good intention, an act may be rendered unlawful if it be out of proportion to the end.
>
> (*Summa Theologica*, Part II, Q.64, Art. 7)

Exercise

Discuss how the Doctrine of Double Effect (DDE) might work in the example of a pregnant woman who is diagnosed with cancer and needs chemotherapy urgently.

Modern Natural Law theorists Germain Grisez and Joseph Boyle argue that the concept of personhood is central in the discussion of abortion. There is no difference, they say, between being bodily alive and being a person. This would apply to the 'body' – the foetus – in the womb. It has a DNA which is distinct from that of its parents and its *telos* (just as an acorn's is to develop into an oak tree) is to grow to full term, to be born, and to learn and grow into adulthood. For them, it would be immoral to kill an able-bodied person, so it would be immoral to abort a foetus. Having a bodily life, like having friends and an appreciation of beauty, is a 'good in itself', and the foetus' life cannot be taken away arbitrarily. Abortion goes against the basic good of life and should therefore be forbidden.

Utilitarian views

Classical Utilitarianism, as espoused by Bentham and Mill, was a teleological system for making ethical decisions. This meant that there are no universal, absolutely correct, answers to ethical problems like abortion. Decisions had to be made on the basis of the available evidence and with respect, not to rules, but to the likely consequences of an action. For most Utilitarians, therefore, abortion would not be universally and absolutely wrong. The end justifies the means. Individual decisions would have to be made on the likely consequences for the individuals concerned. Regardless of whether it was thought that the foetus was a 'person', all the relevant people involved would have to be considered in making the decision. The key question to ask would be: what action will bring about the greatest happiness for the greatest number of people involved?

Jeremy Bentham developed his Hedonic Calculus to help make moral decisions. Many of the seven elements of this calculus could be useful in making a decision about abortion. Take the case of a fourteen-year-old girl who becomes pregnant as a result of rape. The seven points of the calculus are: Fecundity, Extent, Duration, Purity, Propinquity, Intensity, Certainty.

In this example, the girl, her parents, friends and other relevant 'sentient' persons would have to be considered. It would also have to be considered whether, or to what extent, the foetus had sentience. After 14 days' gestation, the 'primitive streak' appears, and with it the basic capacity to register pain. This is when sentience begins to develop, and this development continues until the moment of birth. It is very likely, though, that the foetus' views would not count as highly as those of the other relevant people in this example.

> **Exercise**
>
> Discuss each element in the Hedonic Calculus to decide whether the girl should have an abortion. Remember that you are trying to decide on the 'greatest good for the greatest number', where 'good' means 'pleasure and the avoidance of pain'.

For John Stuart Mill, Bentham's quantitative measurement of pleasure was not acceptable, and he developed his own qualitative measurement, using the distinction between 'higher' and 'lower' pleasures. It is very unlikely that the foetus can experience any higher pleasures, so those of the adults involved would take precedence in the decision. Although Mill did not ever write about the pros and cons of abortion, he would probably have argued that, in this case, it would be morally justifiable.

The Preference Utilitarian Peter Singer argues that the idea of the sanctity of human life is outdated, unscientific and irrelevant, even harmful to understanding the ethics of abortion and ought to be ignored (*Writings on an Ethical Life*, Ecco

(Harper Collins) 2000, pp. 319–29). Singer believes that the right to life depends upon an individual's capacity to hold preferences, and these are linked to his/her capacity to experience pleasure and pain. He rejects the argument from **potentiality**, believing the life of the foetus to have no intrinsic value as it does not possess self-awareness or desires of any kind. For Singer, our intuitions about issues like abortion and euthanasia stem from a society which, for well over 1,000 years, has been dominated by the Christian religion and its doctrine of the sanctity of human life. Prior to this, and not altogether banished from our moral intuitions, in Greek and Roman society new-born infants who were disabled were typically terminated. In *Practical Ethics*, Singer proposes a 'replaceability argument' which extends beyond terminating a foetus to killing a disabled infant on the grounds that 'The loss of happy life for the first infant is outweighed by the gain of a happier life for the second.' The total sum of happiness (for the parents and for the infant who 'replaces' the loss of the earlier disabled newborn) is greater, and this justifies the killing of the first. Singer has been accused of being fearless in driving the logic of Utilitarianism off the cliff of reason. Consider the following extract from *Practical Ethics*:

> Prenatal diagnosis still cannot detect all major disabilities. Some disabilities, in fact, are not present before birth; they may be the result of extremely pre-mature birth, or of something going wrong in the birth process itself. At present parents can choose to keep or destroy their disabled offspring only if the disability happens to be detected during pregnancy. There is no logical basis for restricting parents' choice to these particular disabilities. If disabled newborn infants were not regarded as having a right to life until, say, a week or a month after birth it would allow parents, in consultation with their doctors, to choose on the basis of far greater knowledge of the infant's condition than is possible before birth . . . killing a disabled infant is not morally equivalent to killing a person. Very often it is not wrong at all.

(Cambridge University Press, 2nd edn, 1989, p. 190)

Potential:
This relates to the ability of the foetus to become a human being

Discussion Question

If you agree that foetuses are not persons and that terminating them is not wrong, what moral differences do you consider Singer to have overlooked in wishing to grant parents the right to terminate after birth in cases of disability?

In *Rethinking Life and Death* (Oxford University Press, 1995) and *Unsanctifying Human Life* (Blackwell, 2001), Singer argues that a Copernican Revolution in ethics is called for – one in which we reconceive the notion of personhood along the lines of Bentham's statement: 'The question is not, Can they reason? nor, Can they talk? but, *Can they suffer?*' **Sentience**, together with self-awareness and desires or preferences for the future, elevate the interests and status of animals, particularly higher primates, and diminish the intrinsic value of foetuses. In the abortion debate, this also prioritises the interests of the women having unwanted pregnancies, and those of their existing children. As Singer writes, 'Those who regard the interests of women as overriding the merely potential interests of the foetus are taking their stand on a morally impregnable position' (*How Are We to Live?* Prometheus Books, 1993, p. 16).

Sentience:
Having the ability of being aware

Most pro-abortion campaigners argue against the idea that a foetus is a human being and therefore has a right to life. Singer says that human development is a gradual process and there is no one moment at which a foetus becomes 'human'. However, he argues with the premise that it is always wrong to kill a human being. Whether or not a foetus is 'human' is not the main point. Arguments for or against abortion should be made on the basis of a calculation that compares the preferences of the mother with the preferences of the foetus. According to Utilitarianism, an essential characteristic of being human is to have the capacity to experience pain and pleasure, to seek for some things (like satisfaction) and avoid others (like suffering). While the mother has this capacity, Utilitarians tend to hold that the foetus does not. This is not to say that Singer would wish to limit the freedoms of those parents whose belief in the sanctity of life (in his view mistaken) would mean that they chose to carry even severely disabled children to birth. He notes the disproportionate share of resources such children will take up, but his Preference Utilitarianism would protect the liberty of such parents to exercise their choice. More importantly, from his perspective, the law ought not to limit the choices of parents, as Mill's Harm Principle can have no bearing on foetuses that cannot feel pain and are not yet persons.

> **Consciousness:**
> Awareness of self, a key component of personhood

> **Viability:**
> When the foetus is considered physically capable of living outside the womb (often with medical assistance)

Does the foetus feel pain?

Disagreements abound over when the foetus can feel pain and the relative significance of neurobiological developments at 7, 18 and 26 weeks' gestation. Disputes centre on what can be inferred from developmental changes. 4D ultrasonic images of foetal development have led some to suggest that foetuses feel pain and that abortion law and clinical practice should establish measures to prevent this.

A 2006 *British Medical Journal* report concluded that, by 26 weeks' gestation, the neuroanatomical system for pain can be considered complete. It stated that 'A developed neuroanatomical system is necessary but not sufficient for pain experience.' On the basis of this evidence, any requirement to use pain-reducing drugs for the sake of the foetus before an abortion, which could put the pregnant woman's health at risk, was deemed unnecessary.

The British Medical Association's view on this question is that it remains a debatable point. Some argue that foetuses can feel pain at 10 weeks, others that this potential arises only at 26 weeks. The Association suggests that further research is needed and that lawmakers and clinicians should continue to be informed by the latest evidence available. They do, however, suggest that 'Even if there is no incontrovertible evidence that fetuses feel pain the use of pain relief, when carrying out invasive procedures, may help to relieve the anxiety of the parents and of health professionals.'

Kantian views

The starting point for Kant's ethics is the ability of every human being to work out the correct decision by using their powers of *reason*. This ability to reason is innate in every human being, so, if people are using their reason correctly, they will all come to the same decision about any moral issue. This innate ability to reason is what gives every human being an intrinsic value. It could never be correct to use another human as a means to an end. He also believes that every individual has a *duty* to do the morally correct thing. The test he applies to determine whether any potential action is the morally correct one is the *Categorical Imperative*. There are three main formulations of this, but the most widely used one is the *Universal Law* – the correct moral decision is the one that could rationally become applicable by *everyone*. As he says, 'the universal imperative of duty can also go as follows: act as if the maxim of your action were to become by your will a universal law of nature'.

The consequences of any action are not relevant to a Kantian; any consequences are purely incidental to the reasoned decision made according to the Categorical Imperative.

Kant's maxim on abortion might be: 'I plan to abort the foetus so that it will make my life happier.'

Using this first formulation of the Categorical Imperative, it would quickly become clear that this maxim could not be universalised. If we tried to make this maxim a Universal law, it would be contradictory. The desire for self-preservation, here reduced to the desire to lead an 'agreeable life', would result in the loss of life – for the foetus. This is irrational and therefore immoral. In the example above, abortion would be wrong because the maxim concerns a *hypothetical* imperative, not a *Categorical* Imperative. To put it in a slightly different way, the maxim states: 'If I have an abortion, then I will have a happier life.' This is clearly an 'if . . . then' clause and, according to Kant, this cannot be the 'imperative of morality'. Using this maxim with the first version of the Categorical Imperative therefore leads to an anti-abortion conclusion.

Part of the problem here results from Kant's sharp contrast between the duties we owe to material objects or animals, on the one hand, and those we owe rational beings, on the other. Could parents and society have duties to the foetus in virtue of its potential rationality or could the foetus be conferred rights on this basis? Kant's divide between rational beings as ends in themselves and animals/things as means to an end seems unsatisfactory. In 'A Kantian Approach to Abortion' (1989), R. M. Hare asks us to imagine a time switch allowing us to travel back and speak with our mother as she considers terminating the pregnancy that will result in our birth. If, for the sake of the argument, we take for granted that we enjoy a happy and normal adult life, and that our mother's life is not at risk in giving birth, then we would will her not to have an abortion. If we prescribe this for ourselves, rational consistency requires us to universalise this maxim or principle in all comparable cases. Of course, the foetus is in no position to give or withhold consent. But Hare is trying to bridge the gap between animals and humans in Kant's thinking by use of universal prescriptions. As he puts it in the above essay, 'I have argued that most people [would] prefer not to have been killed when they were foetuses; and that this gives us a general reason for having a principle that we ought not to kill foetuses' (p. 3). The problem here is that, while foetuses are not merely biomass that can be removed like a tumour or appendix, in the view of many, neither are they junior members of the Kingdom of Ends. Here the Kingdom or Commonwealth of Ends formulation might be extended. It could incorporate those in a coma, the mentally disabled, Alzheimer's patients whose rationality is not fully functioning, and even the foetus as one who will, if carried to full term, enter the world of autonomous rationality and law-making. By joining together Good Will and the formula of humanity, some Kantians attempt to extend Kant's thinking to the foetus.

Infertility and the right to a child

Infertility is described as 'a disease of the reproductive system defined by the failure to achieve a clinical pregnancy after 12 months or more of regular unprotected sexual intercourse' (World Health Organization). One in every four couples in the developing world is affected by infertility (2012 figures). There has been little change since 1990. In Britain, the figure is one in six couples.

Infertility is a complex subject to study. First, there is difficulty in accumulating accurate and up-to-date figures. Different countries and organisations use different methods for collecting and summarising the figures, and many couples do not wish to admit or talk about their difficulties in conceiving. Second, there is a variety of different methods of assisting couples to become pregnant. Many of these raise significant ethical issues.

Table 3 Fertility treatments

Method	Description
Fertility drugs	A number of drugs can be used to stimulate egg production and make the uterus more receptive to embryo implantation
Artificial insemination	Sperm are prepared ('washed') and inserted directly into the uterus to increase chances of conception
Donor sperm	Sperm from a man other than the partner
Donor eggs	Eggs are obtained from another woman and fertilised by the intended father
Donor embryos	Embryos are donated by couples who have successfully undergone IVF and have spare embryos
In Vitro Fertilisation (IVF)	A process starting with stimulation of ovaries to produce many eggs; these are fertilised by sperm in a lab. One or two embryos are implanted in the uterus, and spares frozen for future use.
Intracytoplasmic Sperm Injection (ICSI)	A single healthy sperm is chosen and injected directly into an egg. Once it develops, it is transferred into the uterus.
Surrogacy	A woman carries a foetus for another woman
Reproductive surgery	Sometimes used to correct abnormalities, remove scarring or clear blockages from either partner
Gamete Intrafallopian Transfer (GIFT)	The woman's eggs are harvested, mixed with partner's sperm and placed directly inside the Fallopian tubes
Zygote Intrafallopian Transfer (ZIFT)	Similar to IVF, but the embryo is placed in the Fallopian tube, not the uterus

Ethical questions surrounding infertility and infertility treatments

The first IVF baby was Louise Joy Brown, born in July 1978. Since then, about 5 million babies have been born by IVF, 200,000 of whom have been born in Britain. Various ethical issues have surrounded this technology:

- Should doctors be using this technology to create human beings? Is this not tampering with God's creation?
- Is IVF not a slippery slope to dangerous kinds of genetic engineering?
- Is infertility really a health issue? Is it not just a state of affairs, like dwarfism or colour of skin?
- Should treatments for infertility be funded on the NHS?
- In IVF treatment, what should be done with 'spare' fertilised embryos – should they be given away to other couples, frozen for future use, used for research, destroyed?

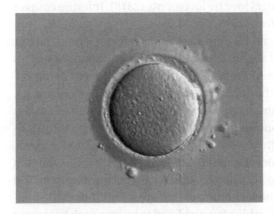

An Ovum. In Vitro Fertilisation refers to the fertilisation of the ovum by sperm outside of the womb. Around 5 million couples who were assisted in their fertility or sought to conceive healthy infants through pre-implantation genetic diagnosis have been grateful for this technology.

- What is the moral status of a sperm donor in relation to any child born?
- What is the moral status of an egg donor in relation to any child born?
- Should children born from donor sperm or eggs have the right to know the donors?
- Should surrogacy be allowed? If so, what is the moral status of the surrogate mother? Should surrogate mothers be paid for the service they provide? Should the surrogate have the right to abort the foetus?
- If fertility treatments are allowed, what should the lower and upper age limits be? (See the case of Rajo Devi Lohan, who gave birth for the first time after IVF at the age of seventy.)
- With a current success rate of only 32 per cent, shouldn't IVF treatment on the NHS be withdrawn in favour of treatment for other diseases or illnesses where there would be a higher success rate? Does IVF constitute 'value for money'?

Christian views on infertility

The Catechism of the *Roman Catholic Church* is very clear about the morality of fertility issues. It recognises that infertile couples suffer because of this (paragraph 2374), and says that research that aims to reduce human sterility is to be encouraged as long as it is placed 'at the service of the human person, of his inalienable rights, and his true and integral good according to the design and will of God' (2375). It is against any technique, like sperm or egg donation or surrogacy, that separates conception from the proper relationship between husband and wife (2376). IVF techniques are also morally unacceptable because they necessarily involve people other than just the married couple. This establishes a 'domination of technology over the origin and destiny of the human person' which is contrary to the dignity and equality of the relationship between parents and children (2377). Having a child is a gift, the 'supreme gift of marriage', not like acquiring a piece of property. Roman Catholics do not have a 'right to a child'; only the child possesses genuine rights, one of which is the right to be the fruit of a specific act of conjugal love by its parents (2378). Infertile couples may find happiness by adopting children (2379).

The *Church of England* agrees that children are a gift from God, not a right. All life, including that of the embryo, is sacred and must be treated with profound respect. In the 1984 report 'Human Fertilisation and Embryology' the Church declared that IVF was acceptable in all forms, including the donation of eggs and sperm by third parties, and that experimenting on 'spare' embryos was acceptable up to the limit of 14 days after conception. This limit was appropriate because, after this time, when the primitive streak appears, it is possible for the foetus to split into two and produce twins. This means that, up to that stage of development, the foetus is not really a human being. All people, including those who are infertile, deserve the love and care of God and should be able to have access to the technologies that are relevant to their situation. The exception is that of surrogacy, which is considered to be immoral: because it involves a third party in a major way (not just donation of eggs or sperm), it can create huge legal and moral problems for all concerned, including the child, and because it strikes at the heart of the family.

Natural Law on infertility

One of the Primary Precepts is reproduction. It is fundamental to human nature to reproduce. When a couple cannot fulfil this precept, they must turn to the Secondary Precepts, which are deontological, general principles that cannot be overridden, that must be obeyed and that can have no exceptions. Such a precept is 'Do not kill', so the destruction of embryos during IVF treatment is absolutely wrong according to Natural Law. This is because it would be morally wrong to break one precept (by killing) in order to fulfil another (reproduction). Further, Natural Law sees the use of a third party (egg, sperm or embryo donors, surrogacy) as an attack on the sanctity of marriage, which is the God-given (and therefore natural) place to produce children, rather than a laboratory. In *Dignitas Personae* (*On the Dignity of the* Person; 2008), the Catholic Church officially criticised IVF, pre-natal diagnosis, selective reduction and embryo donation. The basis of such opposition may be expressed in borrowing a phrase from the Nicene Creed – 'begotten, not made' – to mean that children should result from 'a specific act of the conjugal union' or be 'generated through an act which expresses the reciprocal love between a man and a woman' and not a 'technical action'. The prospect of therapeutic and enhancement techniques developing together in IVF research concerns Natural Law thinkers who see greater commodification of human life in reproductive choices as contrary to the Natural Law.

Utilitarian views on infertility

Utilitarians are consequentialists and look at the probable outcomes of actions rather than the nature of or motive behind the action itself. They look for what will bring about the 'greatest good for the greatest number' in society. In terms of producing a happy society as well as flourishing individuals, Classical Utilitarianism would have no objection in principle to using reproductive technologies. Bentham's Hedonic Calculus might be used to show how this could work: the pleasure felt by the parents and family of an IVF child would be intense and long-lasting, and would probably outweigh the uncertainty of becoming pregnant, the long wait that might be involved and the improbability of having another child by the same method. Although IVF is expensive, the resulting family life is long-lasting and this also benefits social welfare. Even if IVF is funded by the NHS, this is a short-term deficit and is far outweighed by the benefit to society. Most Utilitarians would have no difficulty with 'spare' embryos, as these could be used by other couples in their attempts to have a child.

For the *Preference Utilitarian* Peter Singer, the idea of 'autonomy' is important in respect to infertility treatments. Wherever possible, he says, individuals should have the liberty to choose certain goods, where the 'good' in this case would be a child. Among the choices available for infertile couples trying to have a child, this choice ought to be accommodated as far as possible. They should be able to use the relevant technology to enable them to fulfil their wish to have a child. Writing in the *Guardian* in 2009, Singer recognised that 'A better objection to IVF is that in a world with millions of orphaned or unwanted children, adoption is a more ethical way of having a child. If that is the argument, however, why should we single out couples who use IVF?' (he cites a case of an Arkansas couple who have 18 children). Whilst the 5 million IVF babies that have now been born do add to the global population, Singer sees the widespread acceptance of IVF technology in the face of religious opposition as further evidence that a Copernican Revolution in our ethics is underway.

Kantian views on infertility

Kant was a deontologist and believed that, by using our reason and seeking to do the 'Good Will', the correct answer to any moral problem could be reached. The second formulation of the Categorical Imperative – 'Act in such a way that you always treat humanity, whether in your own person or in the person of any other, never simply as a means, always at the same time as an end' – is appropriate in the case of fertility treatments. Donor sperm, eggs and embryos, as well as surrogacy, would be treating the donors and surrogate as means to the end of a couple becoming pregnant, not as ends in themselves. Approaching donors or a surrogate shows that the couple are driven by the overwhelming emotional need to have a child and not by reason. Also, their desire for a child reduces the child to a 'thing' – a means to their fulfilment and happiness, not an end in itself.

The fact is that Kant's contemporary interpreters are divided as to how to read Kant. For some, his call to treat 'humanity' as an end in itself does not apply to embryos, but specifically to persons capable of reason. So it is permissible to experiment on embryos or to use pre-implantation genetic diagnosis in IVF. Other interpreters widen the formula of humanity as Michael Novak does in arguing that: 'To use stem cells obtained by killing living human beings in their embryonic stage is still using them as a means.' In the US and UK, the process of IVF deliberately produces an excess of embryos (in 2008, there were half a million frozen spare embryos in the US). By now, some of these might have been donated to help other couples looking to conceive, or used in experiments aimed at assisting reproductive technology, but most will have been destroyed. So the application of Kant's idea that humanity should never be treated as a means to an end rests on the question of whether foetuses count as human persons and this divides Kantian scholars.

Discussion Questions

1. Does a woman have a right to refuse a Caesarean section birth when her foetus is in distress just because she does not want scars on her body?
2. Is it ever right to abort one of twins?
3. Under what circumstances, if any, should a surrogate mother have a right to abort?
4. Does the father (natural or donor) have any rights regarding abortion?
5. Would it be better to have no legislation on abortion?
6. Should a foetus be given anaesthesia before being aborted?
7. Should a foetus be given Last Rights before being aborted?

FURTHER READING

Robert M. Baird and Stuart E. Rosenbaum (eds.) (2008) *The Ethics of Abortion: Pro-Life vs Pro-Choice*. Prometheus Books, 3rd edition

Jonathan Glover (1991) *Causing Death and Saving Lives*. Penguin

Christopher Kaczor (2011) *The Ethics of Abortion: Women's Rights, Human Life and the Question of Justice*. Routledge

John Wyatt (2009) *Matters of Life and Death*. IVP Press, 2nd edition

OCR Past Paper Questions

JANUARY 2010
  (a) Explain how the ethics of the religion you have studied might be
      applied to abortion.   [25]
  (b) 'Religious ethics fail to consider consequences.' Discuss.   [10]

JANUARY 2011
  (a) Explain how a moral relativist might approach the issues raised by abortion.   [25]
  (b) 'A relativist approach to the issues raised by abortion leads to wrong
      moral choices.' Discuss.   [10]

JUNE 2011
  (a) Explain how a follower of Natural Law theory might approach the
      issues surrounding abortion.   [25]
  (b) 'Natural Law has no serious weaknesses.' Discuss.   [10]

JANUARY 2012
  (a) Explain how the concepts of personhood might influence ethical concepts
      of abortion.   [25]
  (b) 'The right to life is the most important issue when considering abortion.'
      Discuss.   [10]

MAY 2013
  (a) Explain how a follower of the religion you have studied might approach
      the issues of infertility.   [25]
  (b) 'The right to a child is not an absolute right.' Discuss.   [10]

7 Euthanasia

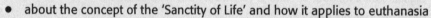

Introduction: definitions

The term '**euthanasia**' (or 'mercy killing') comes from the Greek word *'eu'* meaning 'good' and *'thanatos'* meaning 'death', so it means 'to die well'. Essentially, euthanasia means to bring about the death of a person who no longer wants to live, but is not in a position to end their life by themselves. Usually, such a person is suffering from an incurable or degenerative disease. Key to the definition of euthanasia is the idea that bringing about the death of the person is for his or her benefit. However, as we shall see, there are exceptions to this brief definition.

The first recorded use of the word 'euthanasia' was by the Roman historian Suetonius in his *De Vita Caesarum – Divus Augustus* (*The Lives of the Caesars – The Divine Augustus*), ch. 99, to describe the death of Augustus Caesar. However, Augustus' death, while termed 'a euthanasia', was not brought about by the actions of any other person – rather, it was meant literally as 'an easy death'. The term was first used in a medical context by the English philosopher and statesman Francis Bacon in the early seventeenth century, to refer to an easy, painless, happy death, during which it was a 'physician's responsibility to alleviate the "physical sufferings" of the body'.

Euthanasia:
Bringing about the death of a person in a painless and gentle way for their benefit. Sometimes called 'mercy killing'.

A brief history of euthanasia

Suicide:
A person takes his/her own life voluntarily and intentionally

Euthanasia was widely practised in the ancient world. The Stoic philosopher Epictetus thought that both euthanasia and **suicide** were acceptable options for individuals who no longer believed that they had any quality of life. Plato, in the early dialogues the *Apology* and the *Crito*, has Socrates say that death is nothing bad, is nothing fearful, is preferable to incurable disease, and will be a great gain for an afflicted individual.

The physician Hippocrates lived around the same time as Plato, but almost nothing is known about him, except that he was of small stature. The 'Hippocratic Oath', which all doctors promise to uphold, was formulated many centuries after his death. His writings, on all aspects of medicine, only exist in fragments, and many later books on medicine were ascribed to Hippocrates. Over the centuries, Hippocrates has acquired the reputation of being the epitome of the ideal physician and is referred to as 'the father of medicine'. It is not known what he actually thought about euthanasia. He is quoted as having said 'I will give no deadly medicine to anyone if asked, nor suggest any such counsel.'

The early Christian Church was opposed to the killing of humans in every context. Infanticide was forbidden, on the grounds that every human being, regardless of his/her quality of life, contained an immortal soul given by God. Suicide was forbidden because one's life was given by God, and only God had the right to take it away. Also, in the medieval period, Natural Law argued against euthanasia because this went against the Primary Precept of self-preservation.

In more recent times, during and after the Enlightenment, many philosophers tentatively moved away from Christian moral norms and argued that the religious foundation of doctrines concerning euthanasia were no longer justified. Philosophers such as Immanuel Kant and Wilhelm Friedrich Hegel argued that human reason and individual conscience should be used as the primary source of moral decision-making.

SoL:
Sanctity of (human) Life: the belief that human life is made in God's image and is therefore sacred.

Both Kant and Hegel believed that moral truths are known through the use of reason alone. Though they tackled euthanasia from a different angle from that of Christian thinkers, they ended up agreeing with religious views, arguing that suicide and euthanasia were immoral. A notable exception to this way of thinking was the great Scottish philosopher David Hume, who argued strongly that any individual has the right to end their life when he or she pleases. Hume mercilessly criticised the theological arguments on the **Sanctity of Life (SoL)**.

In the nineteenth century, a much more secular approach to morality became popular, mainly thanks to the writings of Utilitarian philosophers like Jeremy Bentham and John Stuart Mill. Bentham and Mill formulated a deceptively simple question: does providing a painless death for people who are dying in pain increase or decrease human happiness? As the main aim of the Principle of Utility was to increase the amount or quality of human happiness and avoid pain, the Utilitarians argued in favour of euthanasia and suicide as being morally correct.

Mill said that an individual is sovereign over his own body and mind; where his own interests are concerned, there is no other authority. Therefore, if a person wants to die quickly rather than linger in pain, that is purely a personal matter, and the government should not interfere. In fact, Bentham actually requested euthanasia at the end of his life.

Several significant movements and developments progressed the discussion during the twentieth century. In 1920, German authors Alfred Hoche and Karl Binding published the book *Permitting the Destruction of Life Not Worthy of Life*. They argued that patients who ask for 'death assistance' should, under very carefully controlled conditions, be able to obtain it from a physician. This book paved the way for the programme of involuntary euthanasia under the Nazi regime. Beginning in 1939, Hitler initiated a widespread programme for the 'mercy killing' of the sick and disabled. Using the code name 'Aktion T4', this enforced euthanasia programme focused on newborn and very young children, but it quickly expanded to include older disabled children and adults. Ultimately, this was further extended to include any and all people who did not meet the Nazi definition of 'human', and led to the enforced death of millions of Jews and other non-Aryan peoples.

Other landmarks in the history of euthanasia include the following.

In 1935, the Euthanasia Society of England was formed to promote euthanasia.

In 1942, Switzerland passed a law allowing terminally ill people to take their own lives. In 2000, three foreigners committed suicide in Zurich. In 2001, the number of death tourists travelling to Zurich rose to thirty-eight, plus twenty more in Bern. Most of the deaths occurred in an apartment rented by Dignitas, an organisation which promotes an individual's right to choose to die and campaigns for this right to be made legal in other countries. The number of people who travel to Switzerland is increasing year on year.

In 1995, Australia's Northern Territory approved a euthanasia bill. This came into effect in 1996 but was quickly overturned by the Australian Parliament in 1997.

In 1998, the US state of Oregon legalised **assisted suicide**. Oregon remained the only US state to support any form of euthanasia until 2008, when the state of Washington also legalised assisted suicide.

In 1999, retired pathologist and advocate of **physician-assisted suicide** Dr Jack Kevorkian was sentenced to a 10- to 25-year prison term for second degree murder and giving a lethal injection to Thomas Youk, whose death was shown on CBS News' *60 Minutes* programme.

In 2000, the Netherlands legalised euthanasia, after tacitly accepting it for many years previously. Belgium followed suit in 2002.

Assisted suicide:
A deliberate act that causes death, undertaken by one person with the primary intention of ending the life of another person, in order to relieve the second person's suffering

Physician-assisted suicide:
A qualified doctor prescribes a drug which assists a person to take their own life

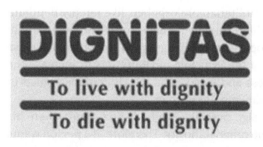

Rising numbers of UK citizens travelling to the Swiss Dignitas Clinic have brought media pressure to bear on the Director of Public Prosecutions and parliamentary legislators to alter the law – or its interpretation – on assisted dying.

Case study: Jack Kevorkian (1928–2011) – Dr Death, Jack the Dripper

> My aim in helping the patient was not to cause death. My aim was to end suffering. It's got to be decriminalized.

Kevorkian worked for many years as a pathologist, but gained worldwide fame in the 1990s for his claim to have assisted at least 130 terminally or chronically ill patients to end their lives. These included people suffering from diseases such as cancer, arthritis, heart disease, emphysema and multiple sclerosis. He developed a 'suicide machine', which he called a 'Thanatron', to help people take their own lives. The first client to use this machine was Janet Adkins, a 53-year-old who suffered from Alzheimer's disease. (The machine was put up for auction in 2011, but withdrawn after it failed to reach the reserve price.) He was imprisoned in 1999 for second degree murder, after sending a videotape of himself euthanising a terminally ill man to the CBS *60 Minutes* programme.

Kevorkian was prophetic in calling for the creation of euthanasia clinics, which now exist in Switzerland. In 2009, the film *You Don't Know Jack*, was made, starring Al Pacino as Kevorkian. Kevorkian died in 2011 from a long-standing kidney complaint and pneumonia. Among his supporters, he was seen as a pioneering reformer, even a liberator from their suffering. Yet some of those who came to him for assisted dying were misdiagnosed and were not terminally ill. Had they been properly treated, they may well not have wanted to die. In the end, the courts deemed that he had progressed from assisted suicide to **active euthanasia**.

Active euthanasia: Someone (e.g. a relative or a doctor) brings about another person's death for the second person's benefit, at their request

Exercise

As you begin to consider the issue, list in descending order of importance, what you consider to be the most (1) and least (7) important issues in the euthanasia debate. You may exclude options but justify why these do not influence your judgement.

[_] Financial costs to the taxpayer of the treatment of a growing population of elderly patients.

[_] The quality of life a patient has – whether they consider their life to be a burden or a benefit to themselves.

[_] The Sanctity of Life – a commitment to the giftedness of life which no human being has the right to end.

[_] Whether doctor–patient trust is harmed by legalising euthanasia.

[_] The ability to implement an effective euthanasia policy that gives a choice to patients who are terminally ill, in pain, and looking for death with dignity.

[_] Ensuring that regulation of euthanasia can prevent unscrupulous doctors or next of kin from putting pressure on others who do not want to be a burden but would rather live.

[_] Avoidance of elderly people being made to feel a burden to their next of kin and sensing that the 'honourable' course of action is to seek physician-assisted suicide.

Ethical issues in euthanasia

Quality of Life (QoL)

One of the major ethical issues in the euthanasia debate concerns the 'quality' of a person's life, particularly at the end of their life. Decisions have to be made not only about the quantity of life a person has left to live, but also about its quality. We live in a society where we are used to people living long lives, and technology is capable of helping people to live longer, but, when they become irreversibly ill, the question has to be raised whether it is appropriate to keep them alive at all costs. Should those who suffer from severe dementia, debilitating physical illnesses and psychological conditions be kept alive until 'nature takes its course'? Or, given also that there is an ever-increasing number of people in the world and only a limited amount of resources, should individuals and medical professionals take a different approach and look to the quality of a person's life and take action to end a person's life when its quality diminishes to a point where it is considered to be not worth living any more?

The term **Quality of Life (QoL)** refers to a person's total wellbeing, including physical, emotional and social aspects of a person's life. In this sense, QoL is not uniquely an ethical term. In ethical and medical contexts, the term 'Health-Related Quality of Life (HRQoL)' is sometimes used. This focuses the debate on how an individual's wellbeing may be affected by *disease*, *disability* or a *disorder*. In the UK, however, and in most books and discussions on euthanasia, QoL is used in this more specific sense.

The way that QoL is assessed is generally by means of a concept called **Quality Adjusted Life Years (QALY)**. This was set out by the National Institute for Health and Care Excellence (NICE). NICE uses an internationally recognised method of calculating an individual's QoL, considering factors such as the level of pain the person is in, their mobility and their general psychological state. They then look at available drugs to treat the person's condition and decide whether a certain drug will bring good value for money in the treatment of a patient. For example, one drug or treatment may help the patient live longer, but may also have serious side effects. A different drug or treatment may not help the patient to live longer, but may give them a better QoL for the time they are alive. The QALY method helps doctors to measure all the relevant factors so that they can compare different treatments for the same and different conditions. A QALY, therefore, gives an idea of how many extra months or years of life of a reasonable quality a person might gain as a result of treatment. Obviously, this is particularly important when considering treatments for chronic conditions, like cancer or Alzheimer's.

Once the doctors have used the QALY measurement to compare how much someone's life can be extended and/or improved with different treatments, they consider cost-effectiveness – that is, how much the drug or treatment costs per QALY. This is the cost of using the drugs to provide a year of the best quality of life available. Cost-effectiveness is expressed as '£ per QALY'. Each drug is considered on a case-by-case basis. Currently, if a treatment costs more than £20,000–30,000 per QALY, it would not be considered cost-effective. Although this appears to be simply a mathematical calculation for doctors to make, there will clearly be a personal response from the

Quality of Life (QoL):
Quality of Life: a key concept in deciding whether euthanasia is morally justified

Quality Adjusted Life Years (QALY):
A method used by physicians to calculate the Quality of Life of a patient to estimate the number of valuable months or years a patient may live

doctors and the patient and these will render any decision much more difficult to make and implement.

There are several ethical problems connected to the QoL:

Physician aid in dying:
A qualified doctor administers lethal medicine in order to assist a person who wishes to commit suicide

- The question about QoL can appear to assume that an individual life can be quantified. This is particularly evident when the QALY system is used to determine the value of a person's remaining life. Many people would disagree with this kind of assessment.
- The decision about the value of a person's life is put in the hands of a doctor – this gives a great deal of power to that doctor: is this ethically justifiable?
- If such power is given to a doctor, this may change the nature of the doctor–patient relationship. People may not have confidence in their GP or specialist, and this might affect their treatment or state of mind.

Sanctity of Life (SoL)

Most Christians are against euthanasia because they believe in the sanctity of human life. They argue that all life was created by God and that humans are made in the image of God. Life, therefore, is a gift from God and this makes humans unique among everything created by God. In Genesis 2:7, God breathes the breath of life into Adam. This implies that there is a special bond between God and humankind, something that is different from the rest of creation. The gift of life is precious, as it reflects something of the nature of God and that humans are made in God's image (Genesis 1:27). As Genesis 9:6 and Exodus 20:13 show, to take away someone's life is to commit murder, and, in a way, this takes away some part of God the creator.

As John Wyatt argues (2009, ch. 10), the idea that humans are made in the image of God has certain implications:

- it means that humans are dependent on God for their lives, because God is in control of every individual's life. See Job 10:8–12, 34:14f., and, especially, Jeremiah 10:23: 'A man's life is not his own; it is not for man to direct his steps.'
- it means that humans are in a relationship with God. Human beings live in relationship with other people (the poet John Donne said 'No man is an island') but they are also in a relationship with God.
- it means that each human life has a unique dignity. Because humans were created by God, this dignity is intrinsic, whether at the beginning or end of life, whether in health or illness. Life is received as an entrusted gift, not a possession.
- it means that all human beings are equal, so women are equal to men, adults to children, healthy to sick, race to race, powerful to weak. This is because all humans are made of the same Godlike material. Proverbs 22:2 says: 'Rich and poor have this in common: the Lord is the maker of them all.'

These points are claimed to be sufficient reason to argue against euthanasia. In just the same way that murder is wrong because it cuts short the life of a human being, so euthanasia is wrong, even if the person's life is cut short by as little as a day. It is still the equivalent of murder.

The Sanctity of Life argument has clear implications for decisions about euthanasia:

- patients in a **Persistent Vegetative State**, although seriously incapacitated, are still living human beings, and they continue to have an intrinsic value and should be treated the same as anyone else. It would obviously be wrong to treat their lives as worthless and to conclude that they 'would be better off dead' – we ought to care even – perhaps especially – when we cannot cure.
- patients who are old or sick, and who are near the end of earthly life, have the same value as any other human being.
- people who have mental or physical handicaps have the same value as any other human being.

There are many arguments that disagree with the idea that life is sacred. These arguments tend to take the view that all humans have *autonomy* – that is, human beings have the power to make real decisions on their own, specifically about whether they wish to continue to live or to die. The term comes from the Greek words *'auto'* (self) and *'nomos'* (law). Autonomy, therefore, has to do with a person allowing himself to determine what happens to him. Such a person has the freedom to define the parameters that frame his or her life and can make real choices about the way their life is lived. So a person could freely choose to live a religious life, or not; to go into politics, or not; to live by a certain set of rules, or not; and so on. If that person uses her autonomy to choose to die at a time they want and in a way she wants, she would do so on the basis of her autonomy. For this person, then, euthanasia is a valid, freely chosen option at the end of her life. It is a tool for achieving the goal that she has chosen.

Stanley Hauerwas and narrative theology on death and dying

Theological ethicist Stanley Hauerwas has written several books and articles on medicine and care of the sick and dying. He thinks that, with the death of God, secular thought has shifted the burden of suffering from theodicy (justifying God in light of the problem of suffering) to anthropodicy (limiting or ending all evil and suffering that we humanly can). He is a narrative theologian and argues that every philosophy or way of life is 'storied' – it has a perspective and attitude to life. In facing death, modernity's perspective is to put its trust in being able to control the chaos of life rationally and in medical science. As modern people, we hope that 'we can get out of life alive' or take control of death so we can at all costs avoid dependency on others. Yet the fly in the ointment is, as Hauerwas puts it, that 'Sickness challenges our most cherished presumption that we are in control of our existence' (1990). We are mortal, and in Hauerwas' phrase, medicine at the end of life is not just biomedical science operating on faulty mechanisms/organisms, but 'a tragic moral art'. It needs a virtuous community to sustain it – who will have the hope of resurrection to give them the patience to be present in the face of suffering; in recognising that 'we are our bodies', subject to ageing and dying, this leads Christians to see their story in light of that of a God who died in the agony of crucifixion. Hauerwas argues that modernity's story of being able to tame and control nature makes it harder to face death than in pre-modern societies. Modern people want a quick and painless death. Yet, as writer Michael Ignatieff comments:

> As secular people . . . we no longer share a vision of the good death. Most other cultures, including many primitive ones whom we have subjugated to our reason and our technology, enfold their members in the art of dying as in the art of living. But we have left these awesome tasks of culture to private choice. Some of us face our deaths with a rosary, some with a curse, some in company, some alone. Some die bravely, to give courage to the living, while others die with no other audience than their lonely selves.
>
> ('The Needs of Strangers', Chatto & Windus, 1984, quoted in Hauerwas 1990, p. 99)

Both the UK and US are increasingly elderly societies. In Hauerwas' view, modern culture is more individualistic than intergenerational. So if we view our lives in terms of time rather than as belonging to a wider story, the temptation is to increase longevity as far as possible. We lack what MacIntyre calls 'the unity of a narrative which links birth to life to death as a narrative beginning to middle to end' (1986).

Doctrine of Double Effect

Doctrine of Double Effect: Where a doctor acts with good intentions (e.g. giving a drug to help a patient's condition) but where bad consequences arise (the drug harms the patient)

The **Doctrine of Double Effect** (DDE) is where a doctor acts with good intentions (e.g. giving a drug to help a patient's condition) but where bad consequences arise (the drug harms or kills the patient). Some doctors sedate patients deliberately in order to keep them unconscious so that they do not suffer pain. The idea of the DDE was developed by Roman Catholic moral theologians in the sixteenth and seventeenth centuries.

According to this doctrine, it is morally permissible to perform an act that has both a good effect and a bad effect if all of the following conditions are met:

1. The act to be done must be good in itself or at least indifferent
2. The good effect must not be obtained by means of the bad effect
3. The bad effect must not be intended for itself, only permitted
4. There must be a proportionately grave reason for permitting the bad effect

The most important element here is the *intention* in the mind of the doctor in judging the moral correctness of his/her action, because of the Roman Catholic teaching that it is never permissible to 'intend' the death of an 'innocent person'. An innocent person is one who has not forfeited the right to life by the way he or she behaves, e.g. by threatening or taking the lives of others. The DDE is not, then, an example of assisted suicide, which is defined as 'a deliberate act that causes death, undertaken by one person with the primary intention of ending the life of another person, in order to relieve the second person's suffering'.

Those who wish to legalise euthanasia claim that the DDE is really a covert way of practising euthanasia. Those who do not wish to see euthanasia legalised counter this claim by saying that the mere fact that some doctors use the DDE in this way does not make it morally right.

Exercise

Consider how the DDE works in the following example.

A patient has an aggressive form of cancer. The doctors who treat the patient know that her chances of survival beyond one year are virtually nil, but they agree with the patient that treatment will be given to extend her life as long as possible. They use chemotherapy drugs to treat the cancer, knowing that these will have painful side effects. These drugs eventually stop working and the cancer spreads. After a time, the patient refuses any more chemotherapy, is transferred to a hospice, where she is treated with increasing amounts of morphine, which have the effect of keeping her in deep sedation until she eventually dies from the cancer.

DNR status

A 'Do Not Resuscitate' order means that a doctor does not have to try to restart a patient's heart if it stops. It can be thought of as a form of **passive euthanasia**. The purpose of a DNR order is to stop unnecessary suffering for the patient. If a patient signs a DNR order, he is signalling to the doctor that, if his heart stops, then CPR (Cardio-Pulmonary Resuscitation) should not be attempted. This supersedes the default position which assumes that every patient with a severe heart problem consents to CPR, chest compressions, defibrillation, lung ventilation and injection of drugs and other similar treatments. DNR is a legal order which affects CPR only; it does not affect other medical treatments. Some doctors have suggested that the term 'DNR' should be replaced with 'AND' (Allow Natural Death), arguing that 'not resuscitating' is a negative action, whereas 'allowing death' is a more positive action. A DNR order is written evidence enabling a patient's wishes to be respected even after they can no longer express those wishes. This makes it more straightforward for the medical team managing the patient's care. A DNR is a type of advance directive.

A potential problem with DNR orders arises when there is insufficient discussion between the patient and the medical experts about what the patient wants. In 2011, it was reported (*Daily Telegraph*, 15 October) that DNR orders were routinely being made in elderly patients' notes without the knowledge of the patient or their relatives. An investigation into the practices at 100 English hospitals revealed that elderly patients were being left to die just because they were old and frail. One charity called this 'euthanasia by the back door'. The hospital involved subsequently made improvements to their practices concerning DNRs.

Other ethical problems with DNRs include the following.

- A patient may request that CPR be attempted, even if the doctors think there is a very remote chance that it would do any good. The medical team would have to respect this choice, but would wish to have an honest discussion with the patient beforehand.
- Doctors might decide that they will not inform a patient of a DNR order. For instance, if the patient is approaching death, or is not mentally competent, informing the patient would be of no value, or cause great upset. In this case, notes must be kept explaining the reasons why the patient was not informed.

Passive euthanasia: A person (usually a doctor) allows another person to die painlessly by withdrawing treatment, which indirectly brings about that person's death

Involuntary euthanasia: A decision is made to end the life of a person, either without their knowledge or against their wishes

Non-voluntary euthanasia: A decision is made to end the life of a person who is not in a position to make that decision themselves

- In an age when health authorities are forced to cut costs, it may be tempting to use DNRs as one method of keeping costs down. If a patient has a DNR order in his file, doctors do not have to spend valuable time in attempting to resuscitate a patient who will probably die anyway. In the *Guardian* in 2011, it was reported that: 'In an era when nearly seven in 10 people die in hospital – and most have "do not resuscitate" orders – there is increasing pressure for more mentally competent adult patients to help plan towards the end of their lives' (www.guardian.co.uk/society/2011/aug/26/do-not-resuscitate-medical-patient).
- Abuses of the British Medical Association (BMA) guidelines have been documented and cases have been found where a DNR order had been placed in a patient's file without their consent, or where junior doctors had written the order but not consulted with more senior medical staff.

Advance directives or living wills

Advance directive: Also called a 'living will', in which a person states their wishes about dying before they become incapable of doing so

An **advance directive**, formerly called a living will, is a way for an adult to make a statement about what they wish to happen to them if their medical or mental state deteriorates to such an extent that they can no longer function as they would wish to. A patient can refuse future life-prolonging treatment, in case he becomes unconscious, loses his mental capacity or cannot communicate his wishes. This would mean that he wishes to die rather than live in what he thinks of as an 'undignified' way, with no quality of life.

The BMA's guidance on advance directives is contained in *Withholding and Withdrawing Life-Prolonging Medical Treatment*. This gives medical professionals advice on the ethical, legal and clinical issues, and sets out safeguards for decision-making. It indicates how human rights legislation applies in this area. It also seeks to provide a coherent and comprehensive set of principles that apply to all decisions to withhold or withdraw life-prolonging treatment.

Advance directives are legally binding – although there are certain criteria to be met – and are covered by the Mental Capacity Act of 2005. The patient has to be very specific about the circumstances in which he does not want to be treated and which treatments he wishes to refuse and show that he is aware that such refusal of treatment will put his life at risk. His written statement has to be witnessed. The main benefit of an advance directive is that it puts the patient in control of what happens to him in certain situations or circumstances. By writing such a document, he can direct the medical staff as to how he wishes to be treated in these cases.

One ethical issue here is that, if the patient has written an advance directive some time previous to the occasion when it is needed, he may have changed his mind but not got around to updating the document. Medical staff would not necessarily know this and would have to treat him according to the wishes expressed in the document.

Case study: Terry Pratchett (1948–2015)

Terry Pratchett was a best-selling British author whose many children's novels, especially his Discworld series, and other books sold approximately 60 million copies around the world. In 2007, Pratchett was diagnosed with posterior cortical atrophy, a rare form of Alzheimer's disease. (See the announcement at www.pjsmprints.com/news/embuggerance.html). After that, he continued to write, but also spent his time campaigning for a cure to Alzheimer's disease. In 2012, Pratchett's controversial documentary, about a 71-year-old man suffering from Motor Neurone Disease, who travelled to Switzerland for assisted suicide, won an award at the Grierson British Documentary Awards, for best Documentary on a Contemporary Theme.

Pratchett also joined the organisation 'Dignity in Dying', a campaigning organisation with over 25,000 members in Britain, including many celebrities. They want to see greater choice regarding where individuals die, who is present and the care they receive in their final stages of life. As their website says, they campaign for change in the law on assisted dying for terminally ill, mentally competent adults: 'We do this by lobbying decision-makers, educating legal and healthcare professionals and empowering terminally ill people, and their loved ones, who are suffering under the current system to have their voices heard.'

Their partner charity, Compassion in Dying, undertakes research on end-of-life care, provides free advance directives and works to educate and empower people around their existing rights at the end of life. (See www.dignityindying.org.uk/about.html)

Pratchett said:

> I endorse the work of Dignity in Dying because I believe passionately that any individual should have the right to choose, as far as it is possible, the time and the conditions of their death. Over the last hundred years we have learned to be extremely good at living. But sooner or later, and so often now it is later, everybody dies. I think its time we learned to be as good at dying as we are at living.
>
> (www.dignityindying.org.uk/about-us/patrons.html)

Christian views on euthanasia

In the discussion of euthanasia, as with other issues in this course, religious views have had an important historical and contemporary influence on the debate. Here, we will look at Christian views, in which much of the justification for firmly held beliefs emanates from the Bible. In general, Christians are against euthanasia, mostly because of the Bible's statements on the Sanctity of Life. The most often-quoted passages, which are all used to argue against euthanasia, are listed briefly below.

- *Genesis 1:26–7* 'Let us make humans in our image'. Human beings were made in the image and likeness of God. This is taken to mean that human life is sacred and it is implied that, because God created life, only God has the right to take it away.
- *Exodus 20:13* The sixth commandment says simply, 'You shall not commit

murder.' To perform any kind of euthanasia is taken to be equivalent to murder, and is therefore forbidden. Matthew 19:18 makes the same point.

- *Job 1:21* 'The Lord gave and the Lord has taken away.' The book of Job discusses the nature of suffering and justice. Job is afflicted with a great deal of suffering – the death of his wife and children, the ruin of his livestock and livelihood. Job, however, remains faithful to God and accepts that God is in control of the entire universe and that his suffering must have a purpose. By implication, therefore, for humans to perform euthanasia is wrong.
- *Psalm 31:15* 'My times are in your hand.' The Psalmist is talking to God and accepts that God knows everything and has a plan for each individual. Humans should not try to play God.
- *Ecclesiastes 3:1–2* 'To everything there is a season, and a time to every purpose under the heaven: A time to be born, and a time to die; a time to plant, and a time to pluck up that which is planted.'
- *Ecclesiastes 7:17* 'Do not be too wicked, and do not be a fool: why should you die before your time?'
- *Ecclesiastes 8:8* 'No man has power over the wind to contain it; so no one has power over the day of his death.'
- *1 Corinthians 3:16* 'You yourselves are God's temple.' St Paul reminds the Christian community in Corinth that they should abstain from immorality, and says that, because God created them, they should not do anything that would detract from their sacred origin.

Exercise

Look up the following biblical verses and work out what they have to contribute to the debate on euthanasia:

Numbers 16:22; 27:16
Ecclesiastes 3:21
Proverbs 31:6
Hebrews 9:27; 12:23
James 2:26

There are also some biblical passages which are used by those who wish to argue in favour of euthanasia from a Christian perspective:

- *Judges 9:50–5* The armour bearer of the Judge Abimelech assisted his master in dying. Abimelech had been waging war against the city of Thebez, but, when he was besieging a strong tower in the city, a woman from the city threw down a piece of a millstone which hit Abimelech on the head. To avoid the indignity of dying at the hands of a woman (!), Abimelech asked his armour bearer to thrust him through with his sword. The armour bearer did so.
- *I Samuel 31:4* Saul, Israel's first king, had been defeated in battle and was mortally wounded. This was a sign to him that he had sinned against God and that God was no longer protecting him. He asked his armour bearer to kill him. In this

incident, the armour bearer refused to do what Saul asked, so Saul committed suicide.

- In *II Samuel 17:23*, King Ahitophel committed suicide by hanging after putting his affairs in order.
- In *I Kings 16:18*, Zimri was defeated in battle, retreated to his palace and committed suicide by setting it on fire.
- In *Matthew 27:5*, Judas Iscariot hanged himself because of the guilt he felt after betraying Jesus to the authorities. (NB: the account of what happened to Judas in Acts 1:18–20 is somewhat different.)

Some Christians use these passages to argue in favour of euthanasia, though Christian opponents will argue that none of these accounts is approved of by the biblical writers.

Other Christians will also take the teaching of Jesus on love as a general principle which they then use to justify euthanasia as the 'most loving thing' in a particular situation. For them, euthanasia may be the most compassionate response to the suffering of a family member or close friend.

The Church of England's position

The 2012 Falconer Commission on assisted dying called for a change in the law to allow terminally ill patients to end their own lives at home with the assistance of a doctor. The Church of England responded that there were several flaws in the Commission's report. The response reiterated the Church's continuing strong opposition to any change in the law or medical practice to make assisted suicide permissible or socially acceptable. Authored by the Bishop of Carlisle, the Right Reverend James Newcome, the response acknowledged that the issues were complex, but argued for the intrinsic value of human life, a value that underpins much of human rights legislation, criminal law and social cohesion. If this principle were to be disposed of, there would be nothing wrong with such things as infanticide or capital punishment, or not giving money on Red Nose Day to alleviate the suffering of children in this country and abroad. The Church continued to encourage the view that suffering must be met with compassion, commitment to high-quality services and effective medication.

In February 2102, the then Archbishop of Canterbury, Rowan Williams, argued that allowing assisted dying would put both vulnerable patients and doctors under threat. Drawing parallels with the growth of abortion, he warned that any change in the law would create a situation in which life would be 'legally declared not to be worth living'. He said that 'every life in every imaginable situation is infinitely precious in the sight of God'. In his view, a compassionate society will invest in high-quality **palliative care** rather than lethal doses of poison.

> **Palliative care:** Caring for a person with an incurable disease so that they maintain some QoL and are not in pain in the final stage of their life

The Roman Catholic Church's position

Euthanasia is a grave violation of the law of God, since it is the deliberate and morally unacceptable killing of a human person . . . True compassion leads to sharing another's pain; it does not kill the person whose suffering we cannot bear.
Pope John Paul II, papal encyclical *Evangelium Vitae* (*The Gospel of Life*, 1995)

The Roman Catholic Church regards euthanasia as morally wrong. It has always taught the absolute and unchanging value of the commandment 'You shall not kill', as euthanasia is a form of, and morally equivalent to, murder. Any law that might be passed allowing any form of euthanasia would be unjust and against the will of God.

The Roman Catholic Church believes in the intrinsic value of human life. The value of a human life does not depend on whether people are happy, bring happiness to others or are socially useful, in terms of the work they do or any other part of living in society. The mere fact that someone lives a healthy and happy life does not make them more valuable than someone who lives a life of suffering and illness: both hold the same value in the eyes of God, because they are both human, made in the image of God. A person who is dying should trust in the all-encompassing love of God and should die with dignity by letting themselves be loved unconditionally by God and their fellow humans.

If an individual has an illness that involves suffering and pain, then there are many effective pain-killers, which are perfectly legitimate to use, unless they are the cause of death. For example, if a patient is given enough morphine to remove the pain he is in, but it also directly causes his death, this is not morally acceptable.

The Roman Catholic Church teaches that human beings have free will, but their freedom does not extend to ending their own lives. Only God has the right to give and take life, so euthanasia and suicide are both unacceptable.

The *Catechism of the Catholic Church* clarifies when medical treatment can be refused or stopped: 'Discontinuing medical procedures that are burdensome, dangerous, extraordinary, or disproportionate to the expected outcome can be legitimate; it is the refusal of "over-zealous" treatment. Here one does not will to cause death; one's inability to impede it is merely accepted.'

Since it is morally wrong to commit suicide it is also morally wrong to help someone commit suicide.

Case study: Dame Cicely Saunders (1918–2005)

Many people see the hospice movement as a viable alternative to euthanasia because of the emphasis on compassion and care for the dying person and their family.

(You matter because you are you, and you matter to the last moment of your life.)

Credited with founding the modern hospice movement, Cicely Saunders was the leading figure in the campaign to establish hospices around the world. She became a nurse, then a doctor, and specialised in developing ways to control pain. She believed hospices were a positive alternative to euthanasia.

She founded St Christopher's Hospice, established to relieve the physical and emotional suffering of the dying. She won an international reputation for her work and influenced the way in which people in many countries thought about the process of dying. She believed that the last days of a person's life could be understood positively and be happy.

Dame Cicely was guided by her Christian faith and strongly opposed euthanasia. She had a clear view of the role of hospices. She saw dying as an opportunity to say 'thank you' and 'sorry' to family and friends. According to her, death was 'as natural as being born', just a stage in a person's life. The process of death should be life-affirming and free of pain.

Due to her pioneering work, there are about 220 hospices in the United Kingdom and more than 8,000 around the world. Each year, about 60,000 people are admitted to hospices in the UK, with nearly half returning home again, and some 120,000 patients living at home are supported by hospice care, more than half of those dying from cancer.

Cicely's work on the development of the hospice movement was recognised with many awards: she was made a DBE in 1980, and awarded the Order of Merit in 1989 (one of only a handful of women to receive this), and an honorary doctorate of medicine (the first woman to receive this in nearly a century). She won the highly acclaimed Templeton Prize in 1981, and in 2001 she was awarded the financially most valuable humanitarian award – the Conrad N. Hilton Humanitarian Prize, worth £700,000 – for her life's work caring for the dying.

Cicely Saunders died peacefully at St Christopher's Hospice in 2005.

Natural Law and euthanasia

The essential principle in Natural Law is that God has created everything for a purpose. This purpose can be discerned by humans when they use their reason and they can make judgements about how to act in particular cases. The most important of the *Primary Precepts* formulated by St Thomas Aquinas was the *preservation of life*. Natural Law is not consequentialist; it is deontological, which means that we should look at the nature of the act itself, not its possible consequences.

How do these views relate to euthanasia?

- Natural Law adherents believe in the Sanctity of Life (SoL). Since all life is God-given, and human life is more important than other life on earth, humans are in a special position in the created world and have a special connection with God. They are sacred. For anyone to take their own life, or help to take the life of anyone else, therefore, would be a sin not just against that person, but against God himself.
- The Primary Precept of the preservation of life clearly goes against any form of euthanasia. It does not matter whether the person is in great pain, or in a **PVS**, or being tortured, or whether there are millions of people involved. The principle of the preservation of life is virtually absolute. Omitting to fight off an inevitable death aggressively is justifiable. Deliberative killing (a sin of commission) is not.
- However, if a patient wants to stop having treatment for an illness, he/she may do so, according to Natural Law. This is because the proposed treatment may go beyond what is reasonable or necessary for existence. Such a treatment would be taking *extraordinary means* to preserve her life.
- The *Doctrine of Double Effect* (DDE) has been used to argue in favour of euthanasia in cases where treatment with effective powerful drugs to preserve someone's life has the unfortunate and unintended side effect of shortening the patient's life. This outcome is allowed under Natural Law as long as the death of the patient is *foreseen* but not *intended*.
- Modern Natural Law theorists Germain Grisez and Joseph Boyle argue that the concept of *personhood* is central in the euthanasia discussion. According to them, there is no difference between being bodily alive and being a person. For them, someone in a PVS is still a person. It would be immoral to kill an able-

> **Persistent Vegetative State (PVS):**
> Most of a person's brain functions are absent, but the body may still function (i.e. heartbeat, breathing)

bodied person, so it would be immoral to let a PVS patient die. A PVS patient still retains his essential 'humanness'. Having a bodily life, like having friends and an appreciation of beauty, are 'goods in themselves', and these cannot be taken away arbitrarily. Euthanasia goes against the basic good of life and should therefore be forbidden.

Proportionalism (associated with thinkers like Bernard Hoose and Daniel Maguire) is a controversial revision of Natural Law that began in the late 1960s and was condemned by Pope John Paul II in two encyclicals (1993, 1995). Proportionalists still hold to the sanctity of human persons and consider intrinsic evils to be wrong. But, in taking a holistic view of principles, acts, intentions and consequences, they grant that there can be proportionally good reasons to make exceptions to well-established Secondary Precepts. In weighing goods or values against evils or disvalues, the likely consequences are considered. It is claimed that the roots of this view can be found in Aquinas' Just War theory, which incorporated 'proportional force' in warfare to justify killing in self-defence and when intended to bring about a greater good. Some proportionalists extend this logic to euthanasia in terminal cases. Daniel Maguire, for example, takes the revisionist view that, while euthanasia has been regarded as an intrinsically evil act in Natural Law, it is the lesser of two evils. Furthermore, as death is a pre-moral evil (one that, though it causes suffering, is not immoral), shortening the dying process is not an intrinsic evil. Life is a basic good, not an absolute one to be prolonged. When it has become burdensome to the point that it is agonising pain or biological life, but not personhood, that persists, it may be permissible to end it. The same could be true when a patient is in a persistent vegetative or semi-conscious state. When artificial feeding offers no benefit, medicine can become cruel in extending it. Given the arsenal of medical technology with which death can be fought off, in terminal cases we find ourselves in a grey area between the futility of extending biological life and bringing life to a close for a good death. For Maguire, there is proportional reason to choose the lesser of two 'pre-moral' evils – extended terminal decline, or deliberately shortened death.

> ### Discussion Questions
>
> Can you think of an example of euthanasia or physician-assisted dying which would satisfy all of the three conditions (see below) for an action to be permissible under the Doctrine of Double Effect?
>
> 1. The action is morally neutral or good.
> 2. The bad effect must not be the means by which the good effect is brought about.
> 3. The motive for the actions must be the bringing about of the good effect only.

Voluntary euthanasia: A person states their wish to die and a doctor brings this about

Utilitarian views

In general, almost all Utilitarians would argue that **voluntary euthanasia** is morally acceptable. This is because they believe that, while individuals have rights, these are not absolute. For Bentham and Mill, the 'greatest happiness principle' is the most important moral principle. Individuals ought to seek the greatest amount or quality of happiness that they can, as long as their happiness does not create unhappiness for the majority of people involved. Both philosophers are also consequentialists, in that they look at the consequences, or possible consequences, of actions to determine whether an individual action is morally correct.

In tandem with these beliefs in the 'greatest happiness principle' and consequentialism, Mill has an additional principle: the principle of Rights. In chapter 5 of his book *Utilitarianism* (1863), Mill says: 'To have a right, then, is, I conceive, to have something which society ought to defend me in the possession of. If the objector goes on to ask why it ought, I can give him no further reason than general utility.'

Mill is arguing here that every individual has certain rights as a human being. These rights cannot be absolute, therefore, because there will always be other people to consider in any action. As they have rights too, an individual must temper his rights if there is a conflict between what he wants to do and the general 'happiness'.

How do these views relate to euthanasia? A number of points may be made.

- Utilitarians do not generally take into consideration the Sanctity of Life (SoL). Most Utilitarians are not theistic, so the supposed sanctity of someone's life is of no relevance to them.

- Utilitarians are interested more in the quality of life (QoL), as they aim to increase the quality of an individual's happiness throughout their life. If someone is suffering because of a painful disease and they want to end their life, Utilitarians would see no moral difficulty with this. The person (and his family and friends) would clearly be unhappy with their current situation, and this could be brought to an end by euthanasia.

- For Utilitarians, a person's freedom to make decisions and his autonomy to carry out those decisions are very important to creating a 'happy' individual and a 'happy' society. It would be important, therefore, to allow a person to have a right to die when they choose to die, and a right to die in a way and at a time they wish to die.

- Another increasingly important argument for Utilitarians concerns the fact that many more people are living for longer and that medical and healthcare resources are not keeping pace. There may be a situation where a lack of resources to look after older people becomes a significant factor in deciding, on Utilitarian grounds, whether assisted suicide or voluntary euthanasia become more acceptable in society. It may be thought that the limited resources (of money, medicines and healthcare staff) could be better used for the benefit of the majority of people (i.e. younger people), rather than caring for older people, who are of little benefit to society.

- Preference Utilitarians, like Peter Singer, would also agree with these points. Singer believes that all humans have rights, including the right to decide when to die. So, if a person has an irreversible condition which is causing either physical or mental suffering, they have the right to choose to die. This is because for them to continue to live in this painful condition would reduce the happiness of not only the individual, but also of everyone they know. The main principle here, for Singer, is that the individual should have the autonomy to decide what happens to them, particularly at the end of their life. Singer's consequentialist logic has little time for distinctions frequently made by Roman Catholic Natural Law thinkers such as:

- Ordinary and Extraordinary means (making a distinction between treatments that preserve life and extend death)
- Omission and Commission (on the one hand omitting to use more aggressive methods to feed the patient, or to use drugs that would extend life, but on the other avoiding the use of non-therapeutic drugs like potassium chloride that would end life deliberately)
- The Doctrine of Double Effect (e.g. increasing the dosage of morphine to levels that effectively anaesthetise a patient and foreseeably hasten death but with the primary intention of alleviating pain)

He sees these as an attempt to allow passive euthanasia or mercy killing without the motive or intention breaking faith with the *synderesis* rule that good ought to be done and evil avoided. In his view, it's more honest not to cloak 'consequentialist views in the robe of an absolutist ethic'. He rejects the slippery slope argument that a liberalisation of the law allowing physician-assisted suicide would lead to the kind of compulsory or pressured euthanasia programme undertaken in Nazi Germany. He sees Holland as a working example of a country where euthanasia is legal within strict guidelines and carried out by the medical profession. In his view, the Sanctity of Life doctrine causes much more 'harm to those whose misery is needlessly prolonged' (*Practical Ethics*, Cambridge University Press, 1993).

Kantian views

The starting point for Kant's ethics is the ability of every human being to work out the correct decision by using their powers of *reason*. This ability to reason is innate in every human being, so, if people are using their reason correctly, they will all come to the same decision about any moral issue. This innate ability to reason is what gives every human being an intrinsic value. It could never be correct to use another human as a means to an end. He also believes that every individual has a *duty* to do the morally correct thing. The test he applies to determine whether any potential action is the morally correct one is the *Categorical Imperative*. There are three main formulations of this, but the one most widely used is the *Universal Law* – the correct moral decision is the one that could rationally become applicable to *everyone*. As he says, 'the universal imperative of duty can also go as follows: act as if the maxim of your action were to become by your will a universal law of nature'.

How does this apply to euthanasia?

- In the *Groundwork to the Metaphysics of Morals* (1785), Kant discussed the morality of suicide. He asks whether suicide can be consistent with the universal law of nature. His answer is 'no' because, if everyone were to commit suicide when they were in this state, they would be using themselves as a means to an end, and this would be going against the universal law of nature. It would also be to deny the intrinsic value of every human being. Just as this is wrong for suicide, it would also be wrong in all cases of euthanasia. It might be possible to formulate a maxim which allowed for people who wanted to die to pass Kant's test, however he warns against making maxims 'over-particular', for this would make the idea of a 'maxim' too specific, and this goes against the idea of a 'maxim' as a general rule.

- The second formulation of the Categorical Imperative – *'Always treat human beings as an end in themselves, never as a means to an end'* – would also argue against euthanasia. Euthanasia necessarily involves using a second person (a doctor, family member) to prescribe or administer the medicine which will end the life of an individual. This means that the dying person is using the other as a means to their death, not as an end in themselves.

Exercise

Read the quotation below from Jasper Conran and write a response to it:

> It seems extraordinary to me that as a nation we operate on a moral double standard. If our pets are hopelessly ill we have them put down to save them from pain and call that humane. If however our nearest and dearest are terminally ill and writhing in an agony that drugs cannot help any more, we allow the law to insist that we do nothing.
>
> (www.dignityindying.org.uk/about-us/patrons.html)

FURTHER READING

Jonathan Glover (1991) *Causing Death and Saving Lives*. Penguin

Stanley Hauerwas (1990) *Naming the Silence: God, Medicine and the Problem of Suffering*. Continuum Press

Richard Huxtable (2012) *Euthanasia: All that Matters*. Hodder & Stoughton

Alasdair MacIntyre (1986) 'The Virtues, the Unity of a Human Life and the Concept of a Tradition' in Stanley Hauerwas, *Why Narrative? Readings in Narrative Theology*. Wipf and Stock Publishers pp. 91–110

Gail Tulloch (2010) *Euthanasia – Choice and Death*. Edinburgh University Press

John Wyatt (2009) *Matters of Life and Death*. IVP Press, 2nd edition

OCR Past Paper Questions

JANUARY 2009

   (b) 'Utilitarianism is the best approach to euthanasia.' Discuss.   *[10]*

JUNE 2009

   (a) Explain why a follower of religious ethics might object to euthanasia.   *[25]*

   (b) 'Human dignity does not matter to a follower of religious ethics.' Discuss.   *[10]*

JANUARY 2011

   (b) To what extent is Utilitarianism a useful method of making decisions about euthanasia?   *[10]*

MAY 2012

   (a) Explain the moral issues surrounding euthanasia.   *[25]*

   (b) To what extent is the quality of life the least important factor when considering euthanasia?   *[10]*

MAY 2013

   (a) Explain how the concept of the 'Quality of Life' might be applied to euthanasia.   *[25]*

   (b) The 'Sanctity of Life' is the most important issue when considering euthanasia. Disscuss   *[10]*

Genetic Engineering

With the discovery of the double helix structure of DNA in 1953 by two Cambridge scientists (Francis Crick and James Watson, who went on to win the 1962 Nobel Prize for medicine), to the unlocking of the Human Genome with its 20,000–30,000 genes in 2000, a whole new world of possibilities has opened up in **genetic engineering**. With them come acute and challenging ethical dilemmas and responsibilities. The content of genes is made up of DNA molecules (the building blocks of protein synthesis), and Crick and Watson's model explained how DNA replicated and encoded hereditary information. The prospect of engineering plants, animals and even humans was to emerge out of these developments and has been greeted as perfecting nature. Yet scientific breakthroughs open up technological possibilities that lawmakers and regulators struggle to keep pace with. 'Playing God' without divine omniscience carries risks and raises dilemmas and questions.

> **Genetic engineering:** The deliberate introduction of changes to the genetic structure of cells

Discussion Questions

Dilemmas raised by genetic engineering

1. If competitive sport can presently catch drug cheats, what will happen when genetic enhancement technology is present at the embryonic stage and cannot be detected in blood or urine samples? A synthetic gene can presently strengthen muscle growth, speed up repair and limit deterioration in mice. EPO is a performance enhancer and banned substance that stimulates red blood cell production in the kidneys. Scientists have tested the insertion of a copy of the gene that produces EPO on baboons. Lance

Armstrong Mark II may have undetectable genetic enhancement allowing him to produce higher-than-normal levels of EPO. Should we just create two separate leagues or Olympics for 'Naturals' and 'Genetically Enhanced Athletes'? What about the gene pool of the future? Would this tear up any notion of Olympic values and fair play?

2. Gene therapy and enhancement are funded by the pharmaceutical companies for use by the healthcare consumers of the developed world. Does this mean that a 'Gen-rich' elite will pull away from the 'Naturals'? Is this free market economics or should it be regulated?

3. Will genetic information be collected yet remain confidential? Could it be used to deny medical insurance, a mortgage or access to jobs that require long-term training?

4. Can the future consequences of genetic engineering (of plants, animals and humans) to the environment or to the human gene pool be adequately tested and predicted to balance reward against risk?

Genetically Modified Organisms (GMOs)

The genetic engineering of plants

GMO: Genetically Modified Organism: Genes are altered in plants, bacteria or other substances to enhance the organism being changed. GMOs are widely used in scientific research.

For thousands of years, humans have bred crops to deliver higher yields and better flavour, and to extend their growing season. Taking a plant cutting could be considered a form of **cloning**, and horticulturalists have engineered plants selectively for centuries. As today's consumers seek cheaper, healthier, longer-lasting food, such demands stimulate the research and development of genetically modified crops. Currently, 800 million people suffer from malnutrition due to lack of food. With a global population at 7 billion and projected (on UN forecasts) to rise to 8.9 billion by 2050, feeding such increased numbers may require all the help the genetic revolution can offer. In some ways this may be analogous to the agricultural revolution (c.1500–1850) that supplied a growing urban population and was able to support unprecedented population growth. Additionally, as wealth increases in many developing countries, plant food is replaced with animal food in diets. Currently, around half of the grain produced in Europe, North America and Russia is used in animal food, but, in time, more crops will be needed to feed animals to supply our meat.

The pros of GM or transgenic crops

As the genes that accelerate growth, that extend shelf life by slowing down the enzyme responsible for breaking down the plant cell walls, that strengthen resistance to pests or herbicides, or that yield more starch are isolated, genetic modification seems the way forward. The precision of modern plant science allows these genes to be isolated and transferred. By this means, crop yields can be boosted, flavours and nutrition improved, flower growth accelerated and shape manipulated. Beyond this, drugs and vaccines can be produced in GM plants, and allergens and toxicants eliminated from them. There is even the technology to put genes from other plants or from bacteria or animals into crop plants. One example of this is golden rice, which has been genetically modified to produce beta-carotene for humans. It is taken up in the bloodstream to provide vitamin A (deficiency of which leads to around 2 million deaths per year and is a major cause of blindness). So there's a humanitarian case for the extension of GM crops, for example in introducing beta-carotene into bananas (in Uganda, plantain is a staple). Equally, GM crops make increased crop yields and profits possible for developing-world farmers. Seeds may be more expensive, but bigger crops that are more resistant to pests more than make up for this.

In November 2011, the *Telegraph* reported on work done at the University of Central China to develop Human Serum Albumin (HSA), the most abundant protein in human blood. This carries hormones and minerals around the body and mops up harmful toxins as well as helping to regulate blood pressure. Genetically modified rice has been developed to the point at which 10 per cent of the soluble protein produced in rice seeds is HSA. Human genes are inserted into rice via bacteria, turning them into bioreactor 'factories' that safely and economically produce proteins identical to those found in humans. In the UK 1.6 million pints of blood are needed each year and just 4 per cent of the population are eligible to donate. A global supply of 500 tonnes of HSA is needed every year and is presently sourced from blood donations. Potentially lifesaving solutions to medical shortages of this kind will emerge only with more GM research, so, in many people's opinion, it should be pursued vigorously.

The cons of GM crops

Chief among the ethical issues regarding GM crops are concerns over the future consequences, transparency over information, and consumer protection. Headlines such as 'Bionic Bread' (over GM bakers' yeast) and 'Frankenstein food' indicate a good deal of public unease and fear over GM foods. Agro-giant Monsanto's decision to grow GM and non-GM soya together raised alarms about cross-contamination and misleading food labelling. GM crops may also spread to non-GM crops over many miles as seed is distributed via bird droppings. Equally, according to Genewatch, 80 per cent of GM crops are produced by five multinational corporations. This leads to fears over future reductions in genetic diversity (e.g. in rice) along with monopolies or increased commercial control of crops. It can also lead to dependent relationships between corporations and farmers due to package deals that involve fertilisers, herbicides and seeds, which farmers buy into.

This desire for openness and to allow consumers to make informed decisions is the focus of public bodies such as the *Consumers' Association* or the *Advisory Committee on Novel Foods and Processes*. They seek clear labeling of GM food and testing methods to check this together with the strict separation of GM crops from non-GM crops. Public confidence in food safety has been hit by outbreaks of BSE ('Mad Cow Disease') and cases of infection with *E.coli* as well as the presence of horsemeat rather than beef in some UK supermarket products. Nonetheless, the scientific assessment of risk in the UK and Europe is subject to rigorous testing and controls.

Single-issue pressure groups can be guilty of using emotive language that brings more heat than light to the debate when food remains a basic need with tight regulation. Nevertheless, they do keep consumers informed and vigilant of risks. Take the prospect of isolating a gene that enabled fish to live in very cold water and inserting it into crops to minimise frost damage. Vegetarians could be eating animal by-products if uninformed about such a development in the food labelling. Or consider the prospect of introducing a new gene from a GM plant to another living organism with consequences that were not anticipated. Crops resistant to insects in the US, for example, can cause insect populations to decline, and, with them, farmyard birds such as skylarks.

The genetic engineering of animals

Humans have selectively bred cattle, sheep, dogs and pigeons (as Darwin did) for centuries. With genetic engineering however, the hope is that changes can be precisely targeted and efficient. Already some New Zealand cows have been engineered to produce milk for those who are allergic to it (which includes 3 per cent of children). Applying a technique known as RNA interference, extra genetic material has been added to 'Daisy' the cow's DNA to switch off the allergenic protein betalactoglobulin. Making this a commercial success by breeding a herd from Daisy as well as building public confidence in the milk are future challenges for the scientists who engineered her. In April 2011, the *Telegraph* reported that Chinese scientists had introduced human genes to 300 dairy cows to produce milk with the same properties as human breast milk. Where formula milk is criticised for being an inferior substitute, this GM milk contains high quantities of key nutrients that boost the immune system of babies. In a similar way, pigs have been engineered to produce higher levels of Omega-3 and (in the case of Enviropig™), to reduce the amount of phosphorus produced in their manure. There has also been a good deal of research into the genetic engineering of pigs' organs (e.g. kidney, liver, heart) for transplantation into humans (xenotransplantation). Fears have been expressed that 'swine flu' or other species-specific viruses could cross over from the genes of pigs to humans by this means, but, in their favour, these organs could be engineered to suit the recipient, addressing the acute shortage of transplant organs and suitable donors given the body's rejection of non-matching tissue.

"Okay—is there anybody ELSE whose homework ate their dog?"

The distinction between *animal rights* (where animals are taken to be psychological and social beings which deserve consideration of their own interests regardless of their value to humans) and *animal welfare* (that seeks the humane treatment of animals but considers rights to belong solely to humans) is important. If certain animals (e.g. dolphins, higher primates) have intrinsic rights, then they cannot be used for food, clothing, entertainment or medical experiment. The term 'Speciesist' is used by Peter Singer to indicate how we privilege the interests of *Homo sapiens* and regard those of animals only insofar as they impact our own interests. Where animals are deliberately infected with cancer or other diseased cells in order to advance medical research, they are treated as a means to an end. Peter Singer (author of *Animal Liberation*, Pimlico Press, 2nd edition, 1995) is unconvinced that most animal experiments are justified in terms of the medical advances they yield.

The genetic engineering of humans

Human genetic engineering presents ethical dilemmas and questions that can extend to future generations. Here it is important to distinguish between:

1. *Somatic cell gene therapy* which is restricted to a patient's own body and not passed on to the next generation. This type of treatment can offer a cure for diabetes by controlling insulin production. It involves the injection of packaged cells or replacement, corrected genes via vectors (viruses which transfer the gene of interest in their genetic material).
2. *Germ line gene therapy* refers to altering the DNA of sperm or eggs (the reproductive cells) in order to eliminate the genes that transmit a hereditary disease (e.g. haemophilia). As these changes enter the human gene pool, the risks are far greater. The gene is inserted into the germ line (sperm, eggs, embryos) so that when the modified individual reproduces in adulthood, all offspring will have the inserted gene instead of the original defective one.
3. *Enhancement* as opposed to therapeutic genetic engineering seeks to manipulate genes in order to improve certain human characteristics, such as height, strength and intelligence.

The obvious argument against germ line **gene therapy** is the prudential one that, until future risks can be quantified, the safest course of action is to postpone experiments

> **Gene therapy:**
> The use of genes to treat or prevent disease. In the future, this technique may allow doctors to treat a disorder by inserting a gene into a patient's cells instead of using drugs or surgery.

Exercise

1. *Class debate*
   Divide up the class and, over one lesson or homework, prepare a debate using the arguments around the motion:
   'This house believes that the potential risks outweigh the promised rewards of enhancement (as opposed to therapeutic genetic engineering)'
   Use the following list of potential risks and rewards to help inform your argument.

Risks of genetic enhancement	*Rewards of genetic enhancement*
Eliminating one/several faulty gene/s may start us down a *slippery slope* towards genetic enhancement of characteristics like height, intelligence, etc. Already 'gendercide', the aborting of female offspring due to a preference for male children (e.g. in China with its one-child policy) illustrates how subjective choices can be. Another more precipitous slope is towards *eugenics*. Thousands of sterilisations of 'undesirables' have been funded by various governments without the victims' consent and Nazi racist eugenics programmes demonstrated how new technologies have the capacity to be used against humanity to select and breed out 'undesirables' and further the dystopian vision of an Aryan-type super-race.	Surely identifying very specific and often single genes for Down's syndrome, cystic fibrosis, sickle-cell anemia, Huntingdon's chorea, Tay-Sachs and certain types of cancer would transform many people's lives and reduce a lot of suffering in the world. Furthermore, there is strong government regulation of genetic research laboratories in developed countries and a great deal of ethical and media scrutiny, so the prospect of a slippery slope to eugenics is just *scaremongering*. The UNESCO Universal Declaration on the Human Genome (1997, Article 11) states, 'Practices which are contrary to human dignity, such as reproductive cloning of human beings, shall not be permitted.'
In our rush to accelerate the foreseeable benefits, will we discover *irreversible (and unforeseen)* consequences to germ-line gene therapy among generations who did not give their consent? A germ-line error that is a recessive mutation could only become apparent in future generations, by which time the error has spread.	*The 'technological imperative'* (if we have the technology, we ought to use it) is too strong to hold back. There could be enormous health and economic benefits, increases in the length and quality of lives. Given our fear of death, the investment and desire to apply the technology will be hard to hold back.
Will a 'gen-rich' elite pull away from the 'Naturals' as Aldous Huxley imagined in his novel Brave New World? When practised by enough wealthy individuals, does genetic enhancement become a form of eugenics? How will the parents of disabled children born 'naturally' because their parents disagreed with genetic screening be regarded in a perfectionist society seeking to eliminate such 'errors' from the gene pool?	In genetic engineering, we have the *capacity to make responsible choices*. We can use gene screening to enhance the prospects for our children, to develop future medical cures, and to diagnose and predict propensity to disease. To reject this technology on the grounds of danger has been compared to rejecting nuclear technology in both energy and weapons, but the risks are smaller and the rewards potentially greater.
In order to assess adequately the risks with germ-line gene therapy, research on embryos may well need to go well beyond the 14-day period it is presently regulated for.	There are *cases in which germ-line gene therapy offers the only hope of finding a cure*. Indeed, if germ-line gene therapy is legalised, then the damage to the germ line of some patients can be prevented.

Risks of genetic enhancement	Rewards of genetic enhancement
For those who hold to the *intrinsic value of the embryo* because of the sanctity of human life, this is unacceptable. If it took 227 sheep to clone Dolly, thousands or millions of embryos may be needed to perfect gene therapies and this could further dehumanise people into genetic material.	Should germ-line gene therapy introduce unforeseen genetic faults, these may themselves be remediable. *The rewards may well outweigh any risks in the long term.* The prospect of predicting and treating diseases and extending lives is surely one the public would welcome.
Globally, *genetically caused disease accounts for a smaller proportion of suffering than deaths from malaria or malnutrition.* Advances are largely to benefit health and longevity of the wealthy developed nations. This is especially true for genetic enhancement as opposed to therapy.	At present, embryos are needed in cloning, but in the future, tissue cloning may allow matching organs to be grown for future transplantation. The *rewards in terms of future possibilities are too great to pass up for the sake of those who weigh the risks too heavily* by always considering the worst-case scenario.
Environment, health, lifestyle and hard work can be as significant for outcomes as genes. There's a *danger in reducing human life to genetic determinism* and this is made worse by setting so much stock by genetic engineering.	If cures for types of cancer and the eradication of many diseases including hereditary ones are possible, it is clear that there are also *risks in doing nothing* when much future suffering could be eliminated. Also, epigenetics pays close attention to the role of interaction between genes and environmental factors.
Future possibilities include somatic cell genetic engineering that develops *biochemical weapons* that target racial markers and spread deadly viruses.	If 'rogue' uses of genetic engineering are developed, there is a legitimate justification for developing this *technology to defend* against them.
Genetic testing for health or life insurance, mortgages and even employment could become commonplace and break confidentiality. If it did, people with genes that had even a small possibility of leading to a life-threatening condition (e.g. a propensity to cancer or heart disease) would be heavily disadvantaged. The fact that genetic information can be extracted from skin, saliva, a blood spot or hair also means that it could be *secured without a person's consent.* Currently in UK law, employers using such testing need to inform the Human Genetics Commission (see www.hgc.gov.uk).	DNA fingerprinting and genetics in medicine offer the *prospect of making our lives safer, healthier and longer lasting.* Every new technology has its pros and cons. Society would have to regulate to prevent discrimination and the application of GE creating a culture of winners and losers. But if it could fight crime or help people find their fathers (through paternity testing), this is further evidence of the benefits.

2. After reading through the relevant sections in this chapter, list one beneficial application and one concern that could be raised for the following:

	Beneficial use or application of this technology	*One concern or fear with this technology*
Genetically modified crops		
Genetically engineered livestock		
Human embryo research		
Human stem cell research		
Designer babies		
Saviour siblings		
Genetic enhancement of humans		
Cloning of human beings		

3. The slippery slope argument. Some slopes are more slippery than others.

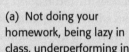 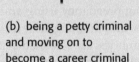

(a) Not doing your homework, being lazy in class, underperforming in your AS/A2 exam

(b) being a petty criminal and moving on to become a career criminal

(c) Taking cocaine and becoming a drug addict.

Do you think that genetic engineering of humans will inevitably move us from gene therapy to gene enhancement? Are there steps on the slope that we might stop on and introduce regulation before we end up with state or privately chosen eugenics?

IVF/IVM

In Vitro Fertilisation is a technique that collects and screens viable eggs, either directly from a woman's ovaries (**IVM**) or (in **IVF**) after drug treatment that causes 'super-ovulation'. Research into the reasons for increased infertility (in part due to sexually transmitted diseases and couples attempting to conceive later in life) is ongoing. The Latin 'In Vitro' literally means 'in the glass' and refers to the process of fertilisation being carried out in test tubes/petridishes. In cases where there are no viable sperm or eggs, donor ones may be used ('DI' refers to Donor insemination using sperm or eggs). Whilst this technique was originally developed to aid fertility, the capacity to screen fertilised embryos for abnormalities, or even, in the future, to correct these defects in germ-line gene therapy raises new ethical dilemmas. Experiments on the spare embryos created during the process of IVF can also help to improve IVF success rates, but this too raises key questions about the value and status of the human embryo. As we consider the ethics of **PGD**, stem cell research, designer babies and cloning, identify which of five views you most align with.

IVF: In-Vitro Fertilization: A medical process whereby eggs are removed from a woman's ovaries and mixed with sperm, and the fertilised eggs are implanted into the woman's womb. It is used for couples who have fertility problems.

The moral status of the embryo

In his book *Christian Ethics* (SCM, 2006), Neil Messer sets out five positions on the moral status of the human embryo:

1. The embryo is a human individual with developmental potential.
2. The embryo is no more than a piece of human tissue.
3. The embryo is somewhere between human tissue and a potential person.
4. We do not know the status of the embryo.
5. The question 'Is the embryo a person?' is the wrong question to ask.

> **Discussion Question**
>
> Which of the above statements do you agree most with and why? What do they tell you about the nature of human embryo research?

Pre-implantation Genetic Diagnosis (PGD) and screening

Watch the trailer to the film *Gattaca* to begin to open up some of the ethical questions around PGD and 'designer babies'.

At present, screening during pregnancy using amniocentesis or ultrasound can detect a range of abnormalities. In combining these techniques with Pre-Implantation Genetic Diagnosis (in which embryos are screened in IVF labs prior to implantation), conditions such as Sickle Cell Anaemia, Cystic Fibrosis, Spina Bifida and Down's syndrome can be detected. Yet geneticist Lee Silver envisages a time when a woman will produce around 100 embryos, whose genetic profiling will eliminate such birth defects, together with standardised selection for enhanced characteristics like intelligence and height (should they be isolatable). A whole new field of bioinformatics, which applies computer technology to the human genome, may be able to identify genes for conditions such as Huntingdon's Chorea, obesity, diabetes, heart disease, asthma or Tay-Sachs Disease.

We already know that the genes BRCA1 or BRCA2 predispose a woman to breast cancer. Yet this has begun to open up new moral minefields. The BRCA1 gene was discovered in the US while BRCA2 was discovered in the UK. Both were patented for use under licence in diagnostic tests, but, in the case of BRCA1, this was initially

PGD: Pre-Implantation Genetic Diagnosis: A treatment to assist some couples to have a child, whereby genetic material (DNA or chromosomes) that occurs within each cell is tested for a known genetic or chromosome abnormality, such as those linked with Sickle Cell Anaemia or Huntington's Disease

for profit (after much pressure, the company that developed it relented and made it free) while in BRCA2's case, it was licensed for free. Such controversies over the commercial funding of genetic research and the licensing of patents on human genes are here to stay.

A poster from the 1921 International Congress on Eugenics

Embryo selection is, in the view of geneticist Lee Silver, the future for healthcare consumers who value the overriding significance of personal freedom. Silver argues that American society is practically one of abortion on demand (for any reason at all). So it is not a big leap to freedom of choice over embryo selection. If the old eugenics was enforced by oppressive governments, the new eugenics will be by choice. As the technology of embryo selection develops, Silver thinks that the small numbers who presently use it will expand year on year. He seeks to allay fears in explaining that the genotype is not the same as the phenotype – genes and environment interact. So while the selected genes look to prevent any detectable disability or disease or even to enhance certain characteristics, there is, as it's put in *Gattaca*, 'No gene for the human spirit.' Hard work and loving parenting remain the basis for a child developing into a healthy adult. Geneticists are sometimes portrayed in the popular imagination as being able to determine human nature in the laboratory. Yet the epigenetic revolution has brought a new and humbling sense of the complex interaction of genes, diet, exercise, environment, etc., in deciding how our 20,000–30,000 genes express themselves in our 50 to 70 trillion cells. Nature and nurture, the genotype and the phenotype, are significant. This is a growth area and something of a biomedical revolution in the making.

The ethics of stem cell research

Stem cell research involves taking cells from an embryo five days after its formation (the blastocyst stage). These are *totipotent* (having the capacity to become any cell type in the body). As the embryonic stem cells continue to divide, they become *pluripotent* (having the capacity to develop into most, but no longer all, of the types of cells in the human body). Totipotent and pluripotent stem cells can differentiate into dopamine-producing neurons to help a patient with Parkinson's Disease or assist a diabetes sufferer in producing insulin. The ethical dilemma they pose is that the embryo must be destroyed in the process. Recently, scientists at Kyoto University in Japan have developed a method of deriving pluripotent stem cells from adult tissue. Induced pluripotent cells (iPSCs) are created by inserting a cell from a patient into an egg that has had its own nucleus removed and replaced by this cell. It is then stimulated electrically or chemically to begin its division to create a pluripotent stem cell that will be genetically identical to the patient who provided the nucleus of the egg. This prevents the immune system of the patient attacking tissue foreign to itself. It also avoids the destruction of the human embryo and means that these cells are taken with consent. They do, however, retain some of the memory of the tissue from which they were taken and so may not be as effective as embryonic stem cells.

If the embryo is regarded as a potential life, then experimenting on the hundreds of thousands of surplus embryos created for IVF is problematic. If embryos are just cells, then not using ones that would otherwise be disposed of could be regarded as wasteful. Embyronic stem cells are obtained either from the thousands of spare ones resulting from IVF treatments, or (more controversially) from foetal tissue obtained from terminated pregnancies. Both adult and embryonic stem cell research are currently funded in the US. Embryonic stem cell research in the UK is licensed by the Human Fertilisation and Embryology Authority (HFEA). Its potential benefits include advances in the treatment of infertility, our understanding of the causes of miscarriages or congenital diseases, more effective techniques of contraception, methods for detecting the presence of gene or chromosome abnormalities, and increased knowledge about the development of embryos.

Yet, back in 2000, Pope John Paul II advised that the direction genetic medicine ought to take is to 'make use of stem cells taken from adults [in order to] respect the dignity of each and every human being, even at the embryonic stage'. In 2001, President George W. Bush restricted federal funding for using embryonic stem cells in research, but this ban was lifted in 2009 by President Obama. Many ethical concerns remain about the use of embryonic stem cells, given the belief that they are genetically unique individuals. The search for an alternative led researchers to the creation of human stem cells that 'reprogramme' adult stem cells (rather than using embryonic ones), so that they become versatile or induced pluripotent cells (iPSCs). Since 2002, US government funding for non-embryonic stem cell research has grown from under $200 million to $504 million in 2012. Obtaining adult iPSCs is cheaper and often easier than collecting embryonic ones, and it involves consent from the patient. New techniques from Israel, recently featured in *Nature*, can create iPSCs in a week. Adult stem cell research offers new possibilities in regenerative medicine – for example, the study of how a disease will progress in extracted cells, outside a patient's body, in order to inform treatment. Cells in the pancreas could be reprogrammed to allow type 1 diabetes sufferers to produce more beta-cells which create insulin. The main use of adult stem cells is in drug screening to target the best medication for a particular patient's condition by seeing how their body will respond to a variety of treatments. Drug treatment can be fine-tuned using iPSCs to study the disease in a petri-dish.

Regimes used to treat a heart condition can then remove harmful aspects of a drug while retaining its helpful qualities.

Designer babies

Case study of a deaf child

Sharon Duchesneau and Candy McCullough caused controversy when, in 2002, they deliberately sought to have a deaf child through IVF involving the donation of sperm from a friend with hereditary deafness in his family. As a part of the 'deaf pride' movement, this lesbian couple regarded deafness as a 'special blessing'. Some ethicists questioned the justice of the couple in seeking to deprive their child deliberately of a sense, and thus giving it a diminished capacity to flourish. In the parents' view, belonging to the deaf community is not a disability but the chance to share in a culture and community in which they had found identity. Should societies respect patient autonomy and offer an unregulated free market choice to parents over the genetics of their children? (*BBC News*, 'Health').
What issues does this case raise?

Cloning

Cloning:
Making a group of genetically identical cells from a single cell

The word 'clone' comes from the Greek *'klon'* meaning 'cutting' or 'twig'. It refers to asexual **reproduction** from one ancestor. Clones are genetically identical to their parent. In 1996, Dolly the Sheep was cloned by a team of scientists from *The Roslin Institute* in Edinburgh University, led by Ian Wilmut. After 276 attempts, Dolly was cloned by collecting the nucleus from a cell taken from the udder of an adult sheep. The nucleus from an egg cell was extracted and that nucleus implanted in its place. Dolly developed premature arthritis and cloned mice cells have also shown insta-

Reproductive cloning:
Production of an embryo which is genetically identical to the donor to transfer into a uterus. This is currently illegal.

bility. Around the world, lawmakers and regulatory bodies have taken action to prevent human cloning. US researchers experimenting with the same technique by inserting adult human cells into seventeen enucleated human eggs, found that only three developed to the six-cell stage. Certainly, as Norman M. Ford argues, 'One day it may be possible . . . to clone a human embryo from which pluripotent embryonic stem cells could be obtained, grown in a culture, and used to produce stem cells to treat [a] patient's defective bone marrow, cardiac muscle, or degenerated nerve tissue, e.g. Huntington's or Parkinson's diseases' (*The Pre-natal Person: Ethics from Conception to Birth*, Wiley-Blackwell, 2008, p. 61). It may even be possible to grow whole organs for transplantation that would not be rejected by the body's immune system because they would be identical to the patient's own cells.

Therapeutic cloning:
The cloning of an embryo in order to produce stem cells for therapeutic uses, such as research into serious genetic diseases

Saviour siblings

The film *My Sister's Keeper* is based around the ethical dilemmas of so-called 'saviour siblings'. These are children selected through IVF screening because they have a tissue match with an older sibling. In one well-known case from 2000, a couple had a child called Molly with an inherited disease. After PGD, they screened fifteen IVF embryos, establishing that they were free of the disease and a perfect tissue match for Molly. After 'Adam' was born, healthy stem cells from his umbilical cord were transplanted to Molly, his older sister, whose bone marrow was later found to be 100 per cent derived from Adam. The question raised by such cases is whether the new child is to be loved and treated in its own right and not as a means to an end. The HFEA's 2002 guidelines stipulate that saviour siblings will only be permitted for the life-saving treatment of siblings, not of parents. Furthermore, whilst blood from the umbilical cord of the saviour sibling can be used for therapeutic purposes (the cord would normally be discarded after birth in any case), the siblings' organs cannot be used, and neither must its health be endangered (for example by the risks involved in bone marrow transplants).

Genetic engineering and human embryo research in . . .

Christian ethics

Situation Ethics acts on the basis of the agapeic calculus. If justice is love distributed, its sharpest critique of therapeutic – and, even more so, enhancement – genetic engineering would be the inequality it may promote if its results were restricted. If a rich elite widened the gulf between rich and poor through selecting or designing the genetic profile of their 'offspring', this would exacerbate local and global injustice. Parental love which seeks to manufacture and commodify children also neglects the humbling sense in which to love unconditionally is to accept life as a gift. Parents who've gone through genetic screening for Down's syndrome typically detach themselves from an emotional commitment to their foetus until the antenatal tests come out clear. One woman commented, 'If they'd handed her to me and said she was Down's I'd have been upset but I'd have got on with it; but once you've got into the testing trap you have to get to the end' (Wyatt, *Matters of Life and Death*, 2009). So, if this approach were extended in PGD and genetic engineering, parental love, which is often the most selfless humans are capable of, could become far from agapeic. Situationists are pragmatic, however, and would favour stem cell research where it could reduce suffering more widely, though their concern over the risks to future generations would follow the precautionary principle.

The *Natural Law* tradition would view life as a gift and not as raw material for genetic enhancement into a separate species that could divide humanity. Pope Benedict XVI argued that embryo experimentation and genetic enhancement could easily become the eugenics of the future. What it means for humans to flourish is not to enter into an arms race for greater strength, longevity, beauty, disease resistance, intelligence, etc., for oneself or one's children. Human flourishing does not happen in the isolation of individualism or the wealthy self-interest of Western healthcare consumerism. A child is a gift, not a right or a product for design and manufacture. As Pope John Paul II put it in his encyclical *Evangelium Vitae* (*The Gospel of Life*, 1995), 'from the time that the ovum is fertilised, a life is begun which is neither that of the father nor of the mother; it is the life of a new human living being . . . The human creature is to be respected and treated as a person from conception.' Critics of Natural Law would point to the significant numbers of natural miscarriages that occur in early pregnancy and suggest that reproductive technology is not that much less efficient.

Furthermore, they would point to the fact that the embryo has no self-awareness or capacity to feel pain and ask why an ancient Greek Aristotelian ethic should still persist in Catholic moral thinking.

Christian ethics also recognises a number of theological principles that apply to our understanding of genetics. These include:

Creation and giftedness

According to the Bible, humans are made in the image of God (Genesis 1:26–7). God creates unique individuals with their own genetic identity. The sanctity of human life is also evident in texts like Exodus 20:13 – 'Thou shalt not commit murder' – and inferred from others like Psalm 139:13: 'you knit me together in my mother's womb'. The construction of ethical principles on genetics from proof texts is disputed, however, and the legal provision set out in Exodus 21:22–4 for when two men who are fighting accidentally injure a pregnant woman, causing her to miscarry, seems to distinguish between the loss of an unborn child (for which compensation is due) and injury to the woman (which calls for a life for a life, an eye for an eye). Some commentators see this passage as referring to the fight causing a live, premature birth in which case a life for a life would apply. Yet ethical principles are built less upon individual proof texts and more on values and principles of the whole of scripture (what the Reformation termed *tota scriptura*). Whilst genetics shows us that human nature may be more malleable than we'd previously thought, in Christian theology it derives its value and sanctity from God, the giver of all good gifts including life and health: 'The Lord God formed man from the dust of the ground and breathed into him his spirit' (Genesis 2:7).

Theologian Oliver O'Donovan's book *Begotten or Made?* (1984) argues that removing embryos from the social environment of relations to parents and viewing them as genetic material in IVF/PGD technology can lead to them becoming objects of production and experiment. With the unitive act of procreation by parents and reproductive medicine being separated out in laboratory selection, children become less gifts and more commodities. Where they were 'begotten' through the union of their parents and are now 'made' in vitro, gene therapy rapidly morphs into genetic enhancement. There is the prospect of donor sperm and eggs, and a surrogate mother. This could mean three biological parents (two genetic, one physiological), and one or two further adoptive parents. Whilst all sorts of reconstituted families are brought about by circumstances, deliberately engineering children with such complex ancestral origins is questionable.

The key point that O'Donovan, and, for that matter, the dystopian film *Gattaca* and Aldous Huxley's novel *Brave New World* (1932), all make is that, in preferring selection and genetically engineered approaches to conception over receiving children as gifts of nature, in theory we appear to advance choice but, in practice, we limit it. Control and planning make certain outcomes predictable (currently gender, but maybe hair or eye colour, athleticism, intelligence, etc.). The point is that, as the societal preference for 'patient choice' is exercised in conceiving children in an increasingly artificial way – as products rather than receiving them as gifts – the 'tyranny of normality' may exert its pressure on the parent(s).

There is also a danger that we place too much faith in technological progress when the age-old work of character formation and social justice that builds communities and environments of support is more at the centre of what it means to be human. Human finitude or creatureliness is an extension of the idea of giftedness. Inflated claims for genetics can cause us to think of every medical disorder as potentially curable and give us the hope that we 'can get out of life alive'. Yet Judeo-Christian ethics emphasises human limits and inter-dependency. We still have to care when we cannot cure.

Justice

Concern over poverty and social *justice* has been said to account for 2,000 verses in the Bible (see, online, 'The Poverty and Justice Bible'). Rather than place great faith in the human capacity to steward new technological resources, the language of the Fall in Genesis 3 warns of the capacity of human nature to use technological advances to its own selfish ends. Christianity is realistic about human failing or sin. As C. S. Lewis put it in his *The Abolition of Man* (Oxford University Press, 1944, p. 39), the so-called mastery of man over himself can only turn out to mean the mastery of some men over other men . . . 'Man's final conquest has been the abolition of man.' Chief among the issues would be concern for the poor, marginalised and disabled in a society that may see greater divisions between the gen-rich elite and the 'Naturals'. Prudence, charity/love and justice are virtues that would best deal with obvious dangers such as:

1. Genetic or epigenetic research (into how genes express themselves in specific environments) could lead to discrimination in insurance, or employment. Further knowledge of an individual's probability of early heart failure, cancer or a neurodegenerative condition, despite the significant factors of lifestyle and environment, could result in doors being closed to them.
2. If geneticist Lee Silver is right to predict the widespread extension of PGD using multiple fertilised eggs, then will this highly selective process (eliminating embryos with even moderate disabilities or fatal potentialities) send out powerful

Statue of C. S. Lewis entitled *The Searcher*

messages about the value of the disabled in society? Will this default method of conception put pressure on couples and suggest that certain traits 'ought' to be eliminated from the gene pool? Here genetic counsellors have a key role to play in interpreting test results in a manner that reflects the risks without emphasising the worst-case scenario.

Yet, for all such concerns, there is also a deep sense that humans are co-creators in a world latent with possibilities left open by God's unfinished work. Francis Collins, the former Director of the Human Genome Project, is himself a committed Christian, and his appointment by President Obama as Director of the National Institute of Health has seen him support funding for stem cell research.

3. There is an emphasis on *hope and eschatology* (end things). The nature of Christian hope is motivated to work and pray for the coming of the kingdom of heaven on earth. For this same reason, Christian ethicists are wary of visions of earthly utopias or of man 'playing God'. The notion that a genetic revolution in medicine will 'progress' human nature and perfect it, perhaps even raising the dead (at least those who have been cryogenically frozen) is rejected in Christian eschatology. The Tower of Babel in Genesis 11 gives a picture of a people seeking to build a tower up to the heavens. It was not their desire for progress, but a god-like ambition, that is seen as their undoing. The pressure on parents for flawless babies, on healthcare professionals to deliver them, and on health economists to reduce the number of individuals suffering from expensive, chronic disability can just as easily be the stuff of a dystopian novel as of a utopian society (see Robert Song, *Human Genetics, Fabricating the Future*, 2002). Indeed, the theologian Celia Deane-Drummond sees anti-ageing and perfectionist genetics as a form of secularised eschatology 'bent towards goals that cannot be attained merely within finite human existence' (*Future Perfect? God, the Transhuman Future, and the Quest for Immortality*, 2006). For all the astonishing progress of medicine and the prospect of yet more treatments emerging in genetics, the personal experience of what it is to be human involves the hard work of a 'life plan' encountering suffering, and learning to love and relate to others in community and society, and to face our own mortality. Eschatology and Christian hope promise the resources of faith to help in persevering with caring when there is no cure, so we can call the chaplain when the surgeon and the physician can do no more. Christian hope lies not in immortality but in resurrection, not in a super-human enjoyment of a greatly extended lifespan where genetic advancements enable descendants to live longer without the burdens of old age, but through God's gift of resurrection foreseen in Christ's resurrection.

This theology of hope is particularly associated with the German theologian Jürgen Moltmann, who returned to his native Germany after having been a British prisoner of war from 1945 to 1948. In the rebuilding of Germany, he sought to construct theology for 'the survivors of [his] generation' conceived 'in the light of its future goal. Eschatology should not be its end, but its beginning.' He drew on the work of Barth and Bonhoeffer (who had led the confessing church that opposed Hitler's attempts to Nazify the German Protestant Church).

Emphasising Christ's resurrection and return, he believed that, rather than cheating man of happiness in the present, eschatological hope was the foundation of true hope. Christian ethics should be governed by the example of Christ, who will himself renew all things and calls us to a **preferential option for the poor** and to work for the renewal of life in light of God's incarnation in the suffering and injustice of the world. So, technology is never the ultimate salvation or perfection of humankind.

> ### Discussion Question
>
> Do you consider any of the three points above to have things to add to the discussion about genetic engineering in wider society (sometimes referred to as the public square), where debate is largely secular?

Preferential option for the poor: A belief championed by liberation theologians that sees God as being on the side of the poor and oppressed who, by virtue of their marginalization, gain a unique insight into God's purpose.

Utilitarian ethics

Utilitarians consider the consequences of choices and seek to act responsibly. They are aware that the media have a tendency both to hype up unrealistic expectations of what the spectacular advances in biotechnology can deliver, and, conversely, to spread panic about clones and eugenics. In *Rethinking Life and Death* (Oxford University Press, 1995), Peter Singer replaces five old commandments that express a Sanctity of Life position rooted in religious ethics with a new set, four of which are relevant in this debate.

Ten Commandments, Austin State Capitol, Texas

Old Commandments	*New Commandments*
1 Treat all life as of equal worth	1 Recognise that the worth of human life varies
2 Never intentionally take an innocent human life	2 Take responsibility for the consequences of your decisions
3 Be fruitful and multiply	3 Bring children into the world only if they are wanted
4 Treat all human life as always more precious than any non-human life	4 Do not discriminate on the basis of species

As we saw in chapter 3, Singer's Utilitarianism seeks to prioritise the minimisation of pain before the maximisation of pleasure. In a series of books, including *The Life You can Save* (2009), *One World* (2002), *How Are We to Live?* (1995) and *Animal Liberation,* he has sought to raise concerns over the treatment of preventable deaths in the developing world and human mistreatment and exploitation of animals. When animal experiments yield little in the way of medical advance, and at the same time cause unnecessary pain and distress, they should be halted. Although not opposed to animal testing in principle, Singer has said that he would prioritise testing on a brain-dead human before a fully functioning adult chimp. This is less a practical proposal than an attempt to get us to think less glibly about hundreds of thousands of mice, rats and rabbits used in experiments without consent or consideration of their interests. Singer is also critical of the use of higher primates in research when the medical benefits are far from clear. For Singer, we need to move away from a speciesist disregard of animals as objects when they too can suffer and have interests.

Equally, Singer would warn against restrictive access (on the basis of cost) to the results of genetics for medical treatment and diagnosis. If the genetic revolution in medicine widens the gap between rich and poor and extends longevity for the wealthy while neglecting the more urgent treatment of preventable deaths in the developing world, it exacerbates an existing inequality. As a Negative Utilitarian for whom reducing suffering takes priority over increasing the quality of life for the richest, Singer would rather the global healthcare budget took more account of the greatest good of the greatest number. The World Health Organization has expressed concern that poorer countries will miss out on the benefits of genome research.

Despite the above reservations about who stands to benefit from the genetic revolution, Singer is very much in favour of research on embryos, especially if genetic diseases can be eradicated globally. He dismisses the argument for its moral status based on 'potentiality' – the newborn infant that it might become. As he writes (with Helga Kuhse), 'We believe the minimal characteristic needed to give the embryo a claim to consideration is sentience, or the capacity to feel pleasure or pain. Until that point is reached, the embryo does not have any interests and, like other nonsentient organisms (a human egg, for example), cannot be harmed – in any morally relevant sense – by anything we do' (Kuhse and Singer, 'The Issue of the Moral Status' in Singer et al., *Embryo Experimentation*, Cambridge University Press, 1990, p. 73).

He asks us to imagine a couple taking part in an IVF programme in which a fertile egg from the woman and semen from her partner/a donor have been placed in a petri dish and fertilisation has taken place. The news then comes through that the woman has a medical condition which makes pregnancy impossible (Singer, *Unsanctifying Human Life*, Blackwell, 2002). If the couple does not wish to donate their newly created embryo to someone else, would it be morally wrong to dispose of it? In another case, a human egg and then sperm are tipped down the sink of an IVF lab, but a blockage causes fertilisation. Should the egg be rescued from the sink? For Singer, such thought experiments serve to highlight the implausibility of the religious view that unconscious cells constitute a new sacred human life. He argues that there is evidence that intrauterine devices (IUDs) 'often work not strictly as contraceptives . . . but by ensuring that any egg that is fertilised will fail to implant in the womb' (ibid., p. 54). Yet there has been little concern about the use of IUDs. In fact, even in successful IVF labs, 'the probability that a given embryo which has been transferred to the uterus will actually implant there and lead to a continued pregnancy is always less than 20% and generally no more than 10%' (Singer and Karen Dawson, 'IVF Technology and the Argument from Potential' in ibid., p. 178).

Around 17–22 per cent of pregnancies result in miscarriage, and Singer comments that 'If pregnancy is diagnosed before implantation (within 14 days of fertilisation), the estimated chance of a birth resulting is 25 to 30%. After implantation this chance increases to between 40 and 60%. It is not until six weeks of gestation that the chance of birth occurring increases to between 85 and 90%' (ibid.). Singer asks: 'In the absence of religious beliefs about being made in the image of God, or having an immortal soul, should mere membership of the species Homo sapiens be crucial to whether the life of a being may or may not be taken?' (*Spectator Magazine*, 1995). He controversially wrote in *Practical Ethics* (Cambridge University Press, 1993, p. 90) that 'To take the lives of [self-conscious and aware persons with a past and desires for their future] without their consent is to thwart their desires for the future. Killing a snail or a day old infant does not thwart any desires of this kind, because snails and new born infants are incapable of having such desires.' With only 64 per cent of Down's syndrome cases in Europe being diagnosed in pre-natal testing, Singer argues that parents should even have the right to terminate until 30 days after birth (infanticide).

Discussion Question

Do you find Singer's proposal that infanticide be legalised in cases of severe disability to be appalling/wrong/acceptable/the right of the parents? Why?

For Utilitarians, rather than there being fixed principles and intrinsic rights and wrongs, we should judge actions by their consequences and the extent to which they maximise the preferences of any beings affected by them. Aiming for the greatest good of the greatest number involves a careful quantitative and qualitative look at the risks and rewards. As the ethicist John Harris writes:

> We must not act positively to cause harm to those who come after us, but we must not fail to remove dangers which, if left in place, will cause harm to future people. On the one hand we must not make changes to the genetic structure of persons which adversely affect their descendants. On the other hand, we must not fail to remove genetic damage which we could remove and which, if left in place, will cause harm to future people.
> (John Harris, *Enhancing Evolution: The Case for Making Better People*, Princeton University Press, 2010, p. 80)

So embryo experimentation should continue apace and, given how the potential breakthroughs in genetics could reduce human suffering, gene therapy rather than enhancement should be prioritised (though it can be hard to separate the two).

An even more strident line of reasoning is seen in the work of Oxford ethicist Julian Savulescu (a Utilitarian and Director of the Oxford Uehiro Centre for Bioethics). He argues that parents have a duty to optimise their children's health. Indeed, they are 'morally obliged to genetically modify their children', including through the use of genetic and epigenetic technology, to enhance, for example, their children's 'memory, temperament, patience, empathy, sense of humour, optimism' in order to grant them 'the best opportunity of the best life' (see Savulescu, 'Why I Believe Parents Are Morally Obliged to Genetically Modify Their Children', *Times Higher Educational Supplement*, November 2004). Such a view is rejected by Harvard Law Professor Michael Sandel in his book *The Case Against Perfection: Ethics in the Age of Genetic Engineering* (2004). He argues that Savulescu's vision of health as a resource to be maximised 'rejects the distinction between healing and enhancing' and has the effect of creating an arms race in a culture of hyper-parenting where parents who forgo PGD and happen to have a disabled infant are frowned upon. Parental love is both accepting and transformative. Parents do promote the excellence and flourishing of their children, but to hot-house and commodify them as products to be moulded and cajoled from before birth throughout life is to diminish the giftedness of life.

A more circumscribed role for genetic enhancement is put forward by the Utilitarian philosopher Jonathan Glover in *Choosing Children* (Oxford University Press, 2006). Here he picks up John Stuart Mill's Harm Principle – 'the only purpose for which power can be rightfully exercised over any member of a civilised community against his will, is to prevent harm to others. His own good, either physical or moral, is not a sufficient warrant.' Glover sees this principle as limiting autonomy when genetic enhancement chosen by parents may be foreseen as harming others. This would include future generations that are not yet sentient (cannot feel pleasure and pain) but will be one day. If a 'genetic supermarket' of the future includes the prospect of more aggressive, stronger, faster, more energetic and intelligent children with height and eye and hair colour pre-set, as well as propensities to disease and unwanted conditions deselected, why not leave it to the market rather than regulate? Perhaps a gen-rich elite will evolve to become practically a separate species, thereby losing the characteristics common to all human beings, and perhaps equality of respect will go with this. Glover advocates a middle course between 'the strong precautionary principle' which steers clear of any unknown risks and the 'genetic supermarket' of a completely free market choice for parents. This may be like 'rebuilding a boat on

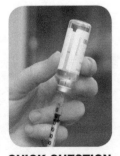

QUICK QUESTION
Designer babies – do they represent the commodification of children?

Michael Sandel

the open sea', but, with advances in medical sciences, we may be able to see our way ahead more clearly as genetic research and technology yield more foresight. To flourish without giving free rein to 'our dark side' in genetics is the course we should steer, with Mill's Harm Principle guiding us.

Kantian Ethics

QUICK QUESTION
Should the super-rich be free to pay for 'gen-rich' offspring if it were possible?

Kantian principles call us to act on those maxims that we can will to become a universal moral law. The research and development of the human genome has been jointly funded by the US government and private companies. Although the human genome itself is in the public domain, spin-off technologies (especially in epigenetics which govern genes being turned on or off) will be patented. Private investment comes with a profit motive that may well drive forward genetic enhancement and gene therapy as lucrative income streams. Here, it is largely the healthcare interests of the world's rich that drive research and development, not the more urgent needs of the poor. For Kant, such self-interest would contradict the principles of universalisability and acting out of 'Good Will'. It would trouble Kant that biotechnology never reaches many desperately needy lives in the global south, and that wealth buys health. On the one hand, the developed world may research gene therapy and embryos to enhance life-extension for rich people, and to develop desirable characteristics for their children. On the other, preventable deaths (e.g. infant mortality, malnutrition, lack of clean water or sanitation, and malaria) remain disproportionately high due to the shortage of doctors, medicines and limited medical facilities in developing countries. So Kant would not have us consider these issues in isolation, but as part of the greater good or *summum bonum* of a Kingdom of Ends. Whilst there is not a clear line to be drawn between remedial and enhancing engineering, Kant would oppose both if there was no prospect of them being universalised. But the prospect of wealth deliberately seeking to increase the gap between the haves and the have-nots (in strength, intelligence, longevity or genetic resistance to the likelihood of contracting a disease) would disobey the three main formulations of the Categorical Imperative.

Other formulations of the Categorical Imperative assert that actions should not treat other people as 'a means to an end' and that they should seek 'to bring about a kingdom of ends'. When multinational agro-businesses seek to introduce GM crops that develop a customer dependence upon herbicides and seeds that are resistant to them by rendering the ground fertile solely to those companies' seeds, then farmers (often in the developing world) are a means to an end. Saviour siblings and clones could be seen as being conceived as a means to an end (e.g. providing transplants for a sibling or a genetic copy of an older relative). It would be irrational to consider it the parents' *duty* to conceive a sibling in every case where their child's genetic disorder could be eased by them doing so.

One further objection could be found in Kant's emphasis on the rational autonomy of individuals. Autonomy is one of four foundational principles in modern bioethics and it chiefly finds its roots in Kant. The case of the Icelandic government's policy of making a genetic database of the nation, with the aim of eventually mapping the DNA of everyone in order to enhance their medical treatment, is instructive. In 2003, Icelanders successfully challenged (on the grounds that it was unconstitutional) their

Informed consent:
When an informed and competent person freely chooses to enter into an action after being made fully aware of the risks and benefits that may result from it

government's policy of linking their medical records to their DNA profile without needing to obtain their consent; it is now voluntary. Whenever **informed consent** is not obtained (for example in employment or insurance profiling), Kantian Ethics would view this as undermining the autonomy of the patient. It is even conceivable that adult clones could make a Kantian case in suing their parents for not obtaining their consent to being conceived.

If Kant had lived to see the progress of reason and enlightenment in the medical science of genetics, he'd be critical of any over-optimism about genetic therapy and enhancement being the solution to human limitations. Kant's moral system is more than realistic about human failings and self-interest. Its exceptionless universal rules seek to secure us against the risk of giving an inch (to therapeutic genetic engineering) and losing a mile (to enhancement genetic engineering). For Kant, progress was in good part to be found in our capacity for building a moral community in which each regarded the other with Good Will as part of a greater Kingdom of Ends.

In contrast to the negative assessment above, a significant minority report in support of certain types of genetic engineering is also evident among some neo-Kantians. Some, like the American Fritz Allhoff, argue that foetuses and the unborn lack a rational nature and 'therefore do not participate in humanity'. This assumes that Kant would be unpersuaded by the argument from potentiality. Equally, were they able to consent to germ-line genetic interventions that enhanced primary goods (such as health, intelligence, etc.), we can assume they would do so. Furthermore, as Kant considered it a duty to develop one's talents, genetic engineering may be considered to be an extension of this. To other Kantians, this appears to be a dubious reading of Kant's position. Whilst he engaged with and embraced many progressive ideas of his day, he would have been cautious about the ends–means justification of embryo experimentation. The major contemporary German political philosopher Jürgen Habermas argues against screening and manipulation for non-medical enhancement. Aware of the shadow eugenics casts over twentieth-century history, he argues that there is an essential freedom to the beginning of life if it is born not made. He believes that humans will not be able to control this freedom (Habermas, *The Future of Human Nature*, 2003). A designer baby or saviour sibling is subject to the designs of the parent and their autonomy is therefore restricted before birth. As Michael Sandel puts it, 'eugenic parenting is objectionable because it expresses and entrenches a certain stance towards the world – a stance of mastery and dominion that fails to appreciate the gifted character of human powers and achievements, and misses the part of freedom that consists in a persisting negotiation with the given' (*Justice: A Reader*, Oxford University Press, 2007). Kant wrote that 'physical experiments involving excruciating pain for animals and conducted merely for the sake of speculative enquiry (when the end might also be achieved without such experiments) are to be abhorred' (John Passmore, *A Hundred Years of Philosophy*, Penguin Books, 1975, p. 202). Humans ought to avoid callousness, as befits the dignity of rational creatures, and as modern Kantians know more about the rational processes of dolphins and higher primates, a stronger case is made for extending duties of care, even rights, to them.

Discussion Questions

1. Would a world in which selecting from 100 fertilised embryos before implanting them commodify children and make their parents quality control managers responsible for what has been called 'the tyranny of normality'?

2. On what basis should the state restrict parental choice in respect of pre-implantation genetic diagnosis? Consider the following cases in which parents:

   a. *wish to select deliberately for a particular gender*
   b. *seek to engineer a child with deafness and see this as introducing them to a community and identity rather than harming them*
   c. *seek out sperm from an Olympic athlete and an egg from a top graduate with a high IQ and have them implanted in a surrogate mother.*

   How might a Utilitarian, Kantian and Natural Law thinker decide on these cases?

3. If, in the future, pre-natal screening can accurately select out embryos with a high propensity to genetic defects, would it ever be justifiable for:

   a. *parents to be discouraged or even prevented from following 'the natural route'?*
   b. *insurance companies to refuse treatment for these conditions on the grounds that they were foreseeable and therefore preventable prior to implantation?*

4. Professor John Harris has made the case that the human race may need to become more resilient, stronger and longer-living if it is to journey through space for prolonged periods to live on other planets, moons or space stations. Given this, genetic engineering and even cloning should not be held back by the 'precautionary principle' (caution due to the fear that the risks may outweigh the rewards). Do you agree or disagree with this assessment? Why?

FURTHER READING

Tony Hope (2004) *Medical Ethics: A Very Short Introduction*. Oxford University Press

Michael J. Reiss and Roger Straughan (2001) *Improving Nature? The Science and Ethics of Genetic Engineering*. Cambridge University Press

Michael Sandel (2004) *The Case against Perfection: Ethics in the Age of Genetic Engineering*. Harvard University Press

Michael Wilcockson (2008) *Medical Ethics*, Access to Religion and Philosophy. Hodder and Stoughton.

OCR Past Paper Questions

JUNE 2010

    (a) Explain how a follower of Kantian ethics might approach issues surrounding the right to a child.   *[25]*

    (b) 'The right to a child is an absolute right.' Discuss.   *[10]*

MAY 2011

    (a) Explain the differences between the Hypothetical and Categorical Imperatives.   *[25]*

    (b) How useful is Kant's theory when considering embryo research?   *[10]*

JANUARY 2012

    (a) Explain the main ethical principles of the religion you have studied with regard to genetic engineering.   *[25]*

    (b) 'Religious ethics prevents progress in genetic engineering.' Discuss.   *[10]*

MAY 2012

    (a) Explain the moral issues surrounding the right to a chilld.   *[25]*

    (b) 'Having a child is a gift not a right.' Discuss.   *[10]*

JANUARY 2013

    (a) Explain how a follower of Natural Law might respond to human embryo research.   *[25]*

    (b) To what extent can human embryo research be justified?   *[10]*

CHAPTER

9

War and Peace

Introduction – the history and conventions of Just War theory

Any civilised state that asks its people to go to war and risk their lives needs to offer some justification for its actions. The First Gulf War (1990–1), for example, was justified in terms of liberating a Kuwait that had been invaded by Saddam Hussein's Iraqi forces. Yet once the 'fog of war' descends, collateral damage, or the killing of civilians and the bombing of communications, manufacturing and administrative centres, may suggest that any pretence of justice in the conduct of a war is limited or soon forgotten. In an atmosphere of political propaganda, states sanction citizens to kill and even put them through training that can be, as one writer calls it, a 'desensitising . . . moral anaesthesia' (Oderberg 2000). Many ethicists would consider the Allied response in World War II to be a paradigm of a Just War. Others view the theory as obsolete, suited to an era of uniformed armies on the battlefield as opposed to an era in which military technology can end life on an industrial scale and in an indiscriminate manner, or where vastly superior weaponry is on hand.

..Father, what's the difference between "a just war" and "just a war"?

"A just war" is one which is being planned and "just a war" is one which has already happened.

leunig

'Just War'

In this chapter, we examine political realism and pacifism, as well as the criteria of **Just War theory**, which emerges very much within the long history of the Natural Law tradition as it engages with the evolution of warfare from the days of the Roman empire to the nuclear age. At the heart of Natural Law on this issue is the Doctrine of Double Effect. Peaceful intentions free from self-interest are at the heart of Just War. This being so, the primary aim is peace and life, though the foreseeable consequence is death on a large scale. To keep this peaceful end in view, principles like proportionality and discrimination have to remain central. After explaining these, we will go on to assess Kantian and Utilitarian approaches to this issue.

> **Just War theory:** Principles for deciding whether a war is morally acceptable, developed by St Augustine and St Thomas Aquinas

Political realism and pacifism

Political realists claim that, normally, states act out of national self-interest, and even at times go to war in defence of this. As the Roman writer Vegetius Renatus (late fourth century AD) put it, 'If you want peace, prepare for war.' Furthermore, states have rights that individuals lack because of the anarchy that would result if they did not use power to enforce law and order and protect their citizens. Realists concede that pragmatic pacifism as a personal or even community commitment may prove very effective (as it did for Martin Luther King and Gandhi). Yet war may be a necessary instrument for the defence of states, which possess rights that individuals do not: it is illegal to carry knives in public, but states can possess nuclear weapons. The ethicist Paul Ramsey (1913–98) argued that the pursuit of peace and justice at the level of states may be seen as the extension of loving one's neighbour. In Jesus' parable, the Good Samaritan acts courageously to help the victim of injustice beaten up and robbed on the road. Yet the establishment of a police force on this notorious Jerusalem to Jericho road would be an extension of this charity, as would a standing army to protect such a police force. Charity and compassion need not be naive: sometimes tough love is called for. As the Catholic philosopher Elizabeth Anscombe (1919–2001) put it, in her article 'War and Murder', 'Pacifism teaches people to make no distinction between the shedding of innocent blood and the shedding of any human blood. And in this way pacifism has corrupted enormous numbers of people who will not act according to its tenets . . . seeing no way of avoiding wickedness, they set no limits to it' (in *Nuclear Weapons: A Catholic Response*, ed. Walter Stein, Sheed and Ward, 1961, p. 48).

> **Absolute pacifism:** War is always morally wrong and ending an innocent life is never morally justifiable

> **Relative pacifism:** Whether a war is morally justifiable has to be decided on the relative merits of the case e.g. use of nuclear weapons would never be justified, but use of Just War theory may be

> **Discussion Question**
>
> Imagine you are an absolute pacifist. How would you justify putting the lives of children, those who are injured or severely disabled, and the very elderly at risk?

There are philosophers, such as Jeff McMahan, who argue against the 'prevailing view . . . that in a state of war, the practice of killing is governed by different moral principles from those that govern acts of killing in other contexts'. He rejects as absurd the notion that 'political leaders can sometimes cause other people's moral rights to disappear simply by commanding their armies to attack them' (McMahan, *Killing in War*, Oxford University Press, 2009, p. vii). But the mainstream view is that nation states or alliances possess distinct rights of self-defence given the scale of the threats against them. So where a pre-emptive strike from one citizen who felt threatened by another or a group would be a threat to law and order and encourage vigilantism outside the due and impartial process of police and courts, a state may be justified in protecting its citizens by warning off an aggressor nation with a pre-emptive strike, as in the case of Israel's attack on an Iraqi nuclear reactor in 1981. Such strikes may, however, provoke rather than quell conflict, and many would view them as unjustified. Just before his death, Gandhi was asked what he would do in the event of an atom bomb attack. He said he'd 'come out into the open and let the pilot see I have not a trace of evil against him. The pilot will not see our faces from this great height, I know. But the longing in our hearts that he will not come to harm would reach him and his eyes would be opened.' Realists see this as fatally naive. Furthermore, if implemented, pacifist policies would surrender the deterrent of a standing army and defence system against an aggressor. The making of the threat need not commit one to carrying it out unless one's bluff is called. That is to say, a separate moral decision would arise in the event of, for example, a nuclear attack, aside from the decision to maintain a nuclear deterrent in the first place.

The US theologian Reinhold Niebuhr is an acknowledged influence on Presidents Jimmy Carter and Barack Obama and supported America's entry into World War II, its development of nuclear weapons and its efforts to suppress soviet communism around the world. Rejecting the optimism of some Protestant liberals regarding the goodness of human nature as naive, he advocated a position that came to be termed 'Christian realism'. In his writings (e.g. *Moral Man and Immoral Society*), humanity's fallenness is seen in its capacity for self-deception, not least in the frequently ambiguous motives and interests of statecraft. State power, particularly that of totalitarian states, needs at times to be met with military muscle not pacifism, albeit in a limited and prudent manner. Given our capacity for both sin and goodness, we must act, but not in a morally self-righteous manner. With ruthless enemies, there was no room for optimistic liberalism. Pacifism's hope in the virtue of love was no guarantor of success. It may be employed at the personal level, or pragmatically in certain contexts, but politicians have to make tough decisions in the murky morality of a sinful world and act courageously given the world of *realpolitik*.

Where *absolute pacifists* argue that the deliberate taking of an innocent life is *always* morally unjustifiable, *relative or conditional pacifists* object to specific wars (e.g. Vietnam) or reject the threat and use of nuclear weapons. Pacifism's governing principle is that some actions in war are unconscionable. As Bishop George Bell of Chichester protested in the House of Lords against the saturation bombing of Dresden, Hamburg and Cologne (by contrast, Allied air forces had followed a policy of precision bombing of German military targets in France), 'to justify methods inhumane in themselves by arguments of expediency smacks of the Nazi philosophy that Might is Right'. There are circumstances in which freedom of assembly, of speech or religion are worth less than freedom of conscience, moral defeat is worse than physical defeat. Pope John XXIII (who summoned Vatican II, 1962–5) even wrote 'It is becoming humanly impossible to regard war, in this atomic age, as a suitable means of re-establishing justice.' Weapons of mass destruction called for a 'completely fresh appraisal of war' in the Roman Catholic Church. Drawing on Jesus' teachings in the Sermon on the Mount, Christian pacifism was particularly strong among the radical reformation (Quakers, Mennonites and Anabaptists) who sought to return to the way of Jesus, who died forgiving those who crucified him. For them, Just War theory can end up sanctioning and legitimising war and suiting the propaganda of nations wanting God on their side.

Pacifist theologian John Howard Yoder (1927–97) wrote *The Politics of Jesus* (1972) as a defence of pacifism and an attack on what he termed Constantinianism. Here he saw the pacifist teachings of Jesus and the New Testament Church as falling silent as Christianity gained a seat at the table of Roman power. With imperial might, Christians gained a liking for the taste of wealth and power and grew strangely silent on their Master's Sermon on the Mount or the significance of his cry of forgiveness to his enemies from the cross. Just War theory gave the pretence of a responsible exercise of force and sought limits to wars within 'Christendom' (in this case, the geo-political empire of medieval Christian states). Christian Crusades, nationalism and the warmongering ambitions of kings and princes were part of the legacy of medieval Catholic and post-Reformation Protestant Christianity. Yoder believed that the politics of Jesus were avowedly pacifist and that there ought to be a presumption against violence.

The pacifist Walter Wink (1935–2012) coined the phrase 'the myth of redemptive violence' to draw attention to the justification of war that runs through 'global culture industries', for example in many war films. It has been claimed that the average US child views some 15,000 killings on TV by the time they're eighteen (ekklesia. co.uk article on Walter Wink). The psychology of the narrative they typically see is of a binary world of good and bad guys. Wink argued that this allowed us to have our repressed anger, lust and violence projected onto the villain while enjoying the guilt-free aggression of a hero. The narrative arc of grave injustices followed by the meting out of righteous vengeance by a screen hero like James Bond or Jason Bourne feeds the myth of redemptive violence that is at the heart of the military industrial complex.

When the US and its allies won a swift victory in the first Gulf War, a by-product of this was the demonstration to the arms trade that the American weaponry was superior to Russian technology used by the Iraqi army. The world's largest exporter of arms is the US and its expenditure on and trade in weapons comprise a significant part of the economy. According to the Stockholm International Peace Research Institute, between 2005 and 2009, the US accounted for 30 per cent of global arms sales. According to the *International Business Times*, total global defence expenditure in 2014 is estimated to be $1.547 trillion. Of this, the US will spend $582.4 billion (44 per cent of the total of the top twenty spending countries). According to the *Washington Post* (7 January 2013), the US government spent about $718 billion on defence and international security assistance in 2011 — more than it spent on Medicare. Certainly, wars in Iraq and Afghanistan add greatly to these costs, but Wink's analysis is that such expenditure requires an underlying narrative to rationalise such spending.

It may seem far-fetched, but pacifists argue that to wish for peace but plan for war has a morally corrosive effect, desensitising our consciences and brutalising our imaginations with the 'myth of redemptive violence' that runs in war movies even in peacetime. Pacifists believe that violence begets violence and, for this reason, many were conscientious objectors in World Wars I and II. When criticised as naive and unimaginative, they ask what would happen if countries like the US switched some of the 24 per cent of Gross Domestic Product it spent on defence in 2012 to top up the 1 per cent it spent on foreign aid in the same year (figures: The Borgen Project, September 2013). Would teachers, doctors and business, agriculture and engineering development programmes make for a safer world than a stronger army?

One obvious problem for pacifists is that, if everyone were to reject the national right to self-defence, then many would involuntarily have their choice made for them (such as children, the severely physically and mentally disabled, and the very elderly). As one

---

Case study: has violence declined?

It has been argued 'that in many tribal societies, despite the absence of machine guns and high explosives, the percentage of the population killed annually in warfare far exceeds that of any modern society including Germany and Russia in the twentieth century' (Lawrence H. Keeley, *War Before Civilisation*, Oxford University Press, 1996, p. 32).

Psychology Professor Steven Pinker

Harvard Psychology Professor Steven Pinker has argued that progressive ideas and the humanitarian and rights revolutions arising from the rationalism of the Enlightenment, together with organised national and international government, have made this a less violent world. In six well-referenced chapters of an 800-page book, Pinker cites evidence from a wide range of disciplines in support of his claim. Archaeological studies of skeletons suggest that 15 per cent of prehistoric humans were killed by another person. The pattern is similar for pre-state societies, but lowers with the advent of states (in the seventeenth century, 5 per cent killed by others in Aztec Mexico; in the first half of the twentieth century, around 3 per cent). Hobbes' view that life is 'nasty, brutish, and short' outside of the government of a state seems justified. Of course one could object that this correlation takes little account of the scale of numbers killed in twentieth-century wars, with around 55 million killed in World War II, but Pinker would respond that it is estimated that 40 million people were massacred by the Mongols in a world with one-seventh of the twentieth-century global population. Furthermore, since 1945, the 'long peace' has seen a world in which the developed nations have rarely fought one another (except in proxy wars).

Many reviewers of Pinker's book *The Better Angels of Our Nature: the Decline of Violence in History and Its Causes* (Allen Lane, 2011) are critical of his optimism about human beings becoming less violent. Modern nuclear weapons can kill many times the number Hiroshima's bombing did, and the disproportionality of weaponry and the use of drones may also encourage 'pre-emptive wars'. The percentages of the total population killed may have decreased but, given the death toll in the twentieth century, this offers little comfort for those who agree with Hegel's statement that 'What experience and history teaches us is that people and governments have never learned anything from history, or acted on principles deduced from it.'

Do you agree or disagree with Pinker's view? Give reasons for your view.

writer puts it, 'it is not moral to permit the human race so to endure the injustice of the passion and death of Christ' (Michael Novak, *Moral Clarity in the Nuclear Age*, T. Nelson, 1983, p. 34). Some might appeal to the future justice of history or God. Some contemporary pacifists argue that international institutions and diplomacy were born out of the horrors of World War II and that the future belongs to UN-authorised peacekeeping forces (acting more like a police force on behalf of the international community than national armies). Steven Pinker argues that there are grounds for optimism.

Named America's best theologian by *Time Magazine* in 2001, Stanley Hauerwas (1940–) is a pacifist who has been deeply critical of the American Church and its hunger for political power. He stands in sharp opposition to the Christian realism of Niebuhr and writes 'it makes all the difference who is asking the questions about the "justice" of war and for what reasons' (Hauerwas with Jean Vanier, *Living Gently in a Violent World*, IVP, 2008). To ignore such questions is to ignore the military history that shaped the Just War tradition in the first place. As he writes, 'Christian non-violence is entailed in the very heart of what it means to worship a crucified God.' Hauerwas confesses that he dislikes the term pacifism because, in most people's understanding, 'It's so damned passive.' For Quakers, Mennonites and conscientious objectors, it was always more than a rejection of violence. It was the positive promotion of peace, even at great cost to oneself. As Martin Luther King put it, 'True peace is more than the absence of war, it is the presence of justice.' As a Christian Virtue ethicist, he reminds the Church that Jesus said 'Blessed are the peacemakers, for they shall be called the sons of God.' If the Church can have the courage and imagination to work and hope – even to die – for peace in a violent world, it will bear witness to God's alternative view of time (eschatology) in which swords will be turned into ploughshares. For Hauerwas, Jesus taught his disciples to love their enemies and pray for those who persecuted them (Matthew 5:44), and he said to Peter as he struck out at the guards and soldiers who came to arrest him, 'Put your sword back in its place for all who draw the sword will die by the sword. Do you think I cannot call on my Father, and he will at once put at my disposal more than twelve legions of angels?' (Matthew 26:52). Paul wrote in Romans 12 that Christians were to bless their persecutors, serve their enemies, and seek to overcome evil with good, but to 'leave room for God's wrath'. For Hauerwas, Jesus' pacifism lives in the hope and patience that those who bear crosses are working with the grain of the universe, and that in God's providence, the arc of history bends towards them. He has a poster on his door from the Mennonite Church that reads: 'A modest proposal for peace: That the Christians of the world resolve not to kill one another.' Christian unity, he believes, has everything to do with Christians learning not to kill one another in the name of sub-loyalties to nations. The state in modernity assumes a god-like capacity to demand sacrifices and absolve of sin. As Orwell put it, the solider 'is serving his country, which has the power to absolve him from evil' (in

England, Your England, Inside the Whale and Other Essays, Secker & Warburg, 1962). It is easy to assume that consequentialist logic should decide whether or not to go to war. Yet Christian pacifism is not about prudence or the politics of fear so much as the faith, hope, and charity/love of following a crucified Lord.

Pacifism in peacetime seems reasonable. In the face of atrocities and brutal enemies, deciding for oneself and therefore also for those who cannot defend themselves may appear less defensible. German theologian Dietrich Bonhoeffer spoke to the Czechoslovakian Youth Peace Conference in 1932 and had his authority to teach at the University of Berlin revoked in 1936 for his pacifism. But, after working for Military Intelligence, his knowledge of the Nazi state and its widespread killing of Jews on the eastern front caused him to join a plot to assassinate Hitler.

Just War theory – a historical perspective

Facing waves of persecution, the early Church had no illusions or ambitions of influencing state power, or of deploying the Roman military. Philip Wogaman claims that 'no Christian is known to have served in the imperial armies until about AD 170' (*Christian Ethics: A Historical Introduction,* 2nd edition, Westminster/John Knox Press, 2010, p. 34), though inscriptions on tombs of Roman soldiers who are Christian predate the time of the 'conversion' of Constantine. He allowed Christians to worship freely, but the 'Christ cult' was one of a number of religious groups to whom he turned for military and political advantage. Under Theodosius I, Christianity became the official religion of the empire and an arm of government. Augustine (354–430) wrote in the context of several conflicts over several decades, for example on the ethics of Christians defending the Roman empire from invading Germanic peoples. Whilst he finds military action justified, he is heavy-hearted and nuanced about its use. He drew on the roots of Just War in Plato, Aristotle and Roman law, as well as Old Testament wars commanded by God. For Augustine, war is more justifiable in the defence of others than of oneself (as is the case with modern humanitarian intervention, as in the former Yugoslavia). War must be a last resort, aimed at peace, declared by a rightful authority, in a just cause, and undertaken with honourable intentions. His groundwork was developed in Thomas Aquinas' (1225–74) *Summa Theologica,* which treats questions as diverse as 'war', 'peace', 'military prudence', 'killing in

Dietrich Bonhoeffer (1906–45) on a church youth weekend away with confirmation candidates in 1932. He was a German pastor, theologian and founder member of the confessing church which opposed Nazism and Hitler, especially his euthanasia policy and genocide of the Jews. Two days after Hitler became Chancellor, Bonhoeffer was cut off air in his radio broadcast while warning Germany against the Verfuhrer (Misleader) forming an idolatrous cult. Bonhoeffer was hung by the Gestapo at Flossenburg Concentration Camp in 1945, just 23 days before the German surrender. This was under the personal order of Himmler for his part in the plot to assassinate Hitler. He remains one of the four great 'B's of twentieth-century theology – Barth, Brunner, Bultmann and Bonhoeffer.

self-defence' and 'battlefield courage'. Aquinas' textbook of medieval theology systematised the consensus of the Church's teaching and carefully defined just cause and right intention. For Aquinas, peace was indirectly the work of justice and may require military force and strategy in the name of charity (e.g. he regards ambushes as legitimate in warfare).

Several other medieval thinkers are worth mentioning, including Francisco de Vitoria (1492–1546), who writes in the Age of Discovery when the Conquistadors ventured out into the Americas. Reports of Spain's conquests brought news of indiscriminate killing, along with the acquisition of land and labour. Such brutality

The defences of native peoples were no match for the weaponry of the Conquistadors. This raised questions over the disproportionality of warfare.

was justified on the age-old grounds that the natives were uncivilised and fit to be enslaved. But with the architectural and cultural discoveries of ancient Mexican and Peruvian empires in the mid sixteenth century, Spanish intellectuals like de Vitoria were questioning such logic. He opposed forcible conversions, commenting: 'War is no argument for the truth of the Christian faith.' In distinguishing Church or civil law from divine or Natural Law, and recognising that Amerindians had rights, de Vitoria's legal and philosophical mind was laying the foundations of international relations and law. Hugo Grotius (1583–1645) was a Dutch Protestant Jurist who systematised a long tradition of Just War theory from classical, biblical, and scholastic sources, in opposition to realists like Machiavelli 'whose focus was on the winning and consolidation of power' (Machiavelli, *The Art of War*, Wilder Publications, 2007, p. 251), and in whose writings political survival overrides ethics. In contrast, and controversially, Grotius argues that states should be considerate towards enemies that are 'useful to many', thus recognising that justice transcends the self-interest of individual states. Grotius wrote that 'there is a common law among nations, which is valid alike for war and in war.' (Grotius, *On the Law of War and* Peace, ed. Stephen Neff, Cambridge University Press, 2012, prolegomena).

US Catholic Bishops' statement of 1983

Paul condemns the view that we may 'do evil that good may result' (Romans 3:8), and the first principle of practical reason in Natural Law is that good should be done and evil avoided. So, as war violates the good of life, there is a 'presumption against war' in Natural Law theory (a phrase taken from the 1983 pastoral letter of US Catholic Bishops on nuclear war). In this vein, a 1983 *US Catholic Bishops' statement* used the words 'Comparative Justice' to recognise that the 'just cause' of any state is *relative* rather than *absolute*, and to urge restraint and aim for peace while using force. This is to protect against the mentality present in the propaganda of crusades and holy wars, in which there was no discrimination between the political leaders, soldiers and civilians of an enemy state. Military force ought only to be used as a last resort when all political and diplomatic means of obtaining peace had been exhausted, and under the restrictions of Just War theory. In the case of nuclear weapons, their use is so indiscriminate and disproportionate (unless in self-defence as a retaliatory strike aimed chiefly at military targets and/or halting mutually assured destruction), that the weapons could rarely if ever form any Secondary Precept consistent with the Primary Precept of life. It may be reasoned by proportionalists that, as a deterrent, the Doctrine of Double Effect may still aim at peace with pre-emptive air strikes at military targets, but such a strategy ought only to be a temporary step, progressing towards disarmament.

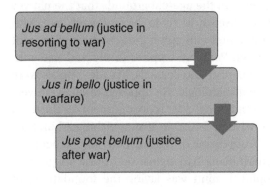

The three phases of Just War: independent or inter-dependent?

***Jus ad bellum*:**
Justice in resorting to war. The principles according to which war might legitimately be waged: Authority, Cause, Intention, Success, Proportionality, Resort. You can use this mnemonic to remember it – ACISPR – **A**ll **C**ats **I**ntend **S**uccess **P**reying *on* **R**ats.

***Jus in bello*:**
Justice during war. The principles which apply during the waging of a war.

***Jus post bellum*:**
Justice after war. The principles which apply after a war has been won.

Jus ad bellum

There are those who argue that once war is declared, those who have just cause on their side are freed from pre-war moral requirements. This would make ***jus ad bellum*** and ***jus in bello*** logically inter-dependent. Once the cause was established as just, violence within certain constraints would be morally justifiable. In contrast, any violence by soldiers fighting for an unjust cause, even if their targets were solely military, would be wrong.

The problem with such a view is that 'enemy' soldiers fighting for a state whose cause is unjust may well be conscripts or coerced into the war through fear and propaganda. Michael Walzer has argued that 'It is perfectly possible for a Just War to be fought unjustly and for an unjust war to be fought in strict accordance with the rules' (Walzer 2013, p. 21). On the same question, Hugo Grotius wrote that 'a war may be just in its origin, and yet the intentions of its authors may become unjust in the course of its prosecution', adding: 'such motives, though blameable, when even connected with a Just War, do not make the war itself unjust' (Hugo Grotius, *The Rights of War and Peace*, 1625). The issue hinges on whether so-called 'unjust combatants' of an enemy state have any legitimacy in killing as long as they follow the rules for just conduct in war (for example, discriminating between combatants and non-combatants and using force proportionately).

Just War theory aims to limit the range of morally defensible reasons for *going to war*, to control and target just conduct *in war*, and to accelerate the process whereby just government and peace can be restored *post war*. Contemporary Just War theory reflects the evolving nature of modern warfare, humanitarian interventions and wars aimed at regime change. The Wars in Iraq and Afghanistan have been criticised as unjust due to the failure to find weapons of mass destruction (Iraq) or to build a stable and enduring peace (Iraq and Afghanistan). The case for the defence would argue that these wars have expelled an illegitimate dictator or corrupt regimes, and that time will vindicate this policy (it took a decade or more, but Germany and Japan were transformed from 1945). They acknowledge the tragic widespread loss of life (including many thousands of Iraqi army conscripts and civilians) and the abuse of prisoners by US military, but assert that isolated human rights violations should not diminish the widespread human rights and free elections that followed on from regime change. With the purging of the old regime from power, the training up of a national police force, reform of education and healthcare, and infrastructural improvement, a new and sustainable order can emerge. Assessing the ethics of such a justification inevitably leads back to the long tradition of Just War theory which we shall now examine.

Just authority

Private armies or the illegal overthrow of a government in a *coup d'état* (lit.: strike of (against) state) is to be distinguished from a war declared by constitutional governments who publicly declare war before their citizens and on an enemy state. Aquinas mentions 'the authority of the sovereign', but today such authority would take the form of elected and constitutional states with international backing or UN Security Council Resolutions. This has become a far more problematic element of Just War theory, given the difficulty in obtaining consensus in the UN or unanimous backing from the Security Council.

An example of a just authority formally declaring war may be seen on 3 September 1939 when Neville Chamberlain (the then British prime minister) reported that the British deadline for the withdrawal of German troops from Poland had expired. He sent the British Ambassador to Berlin to inform the German government, with the instructions that, unless it announced withdrawal of its troops from Poland by 11:00 hours, a state of war would exist between Britain and Germany.

Chamberlain meeting Hitler for talks that failed in 1938. His naive hopes of a diplomatic solution were to bring his leadership to an end. On 3 September 1939, he was to declare officially that Britain was at war with Germany after the deadline for the withdrawal of German troops from Poland had expired.

Just cause

In his *Summa Theologica*, Aquinas describes 'a just war as one that avenges wrongs
. . . or to restore what has been seized injuriously'. One contemporary Just War theorist, Jeff McMahan, has defined just cause in the limited sense of 'the prevention or
correction of wrongs that are serious enough to make the perpetrators liable to be
killed or maimed' (McMahan, *The Ethics of Killing*, Oxford University Press, 2003,
p. 65). In doing so, he excludes from just cause the US war on terror in Iraq and
Afghanistan, 'For people cannot be liable to killing and maiming simply for failing
to organise their internal affairs in a democratic manner' (ibid., p. 71). The US attack
on Japan after Pearl Harbor or the Russian response after the German attack on the
Soviet Union in 1941 may be seen to have had just cause, even if the retribution
exacted is less defensible.

Right intention

This criterion would rule out expansionist wars that steal territories belonging
to sovereign states for motives of wealth or to assert power, gain glory, or pursue
revenge attacks. For Augustine, motives or intentions in going to war ought to be
morally just and aim at a peaceful order. He wrote in *The Confessions* that all people
had to give an account to their all-seeing maker, who 'will expose the motives of
men's hearts' (1 Corinthians 4:5) making this element of Natural Law theory more
explicitly religious. Interestingly, Tony Blair has said of the Iraq war, 'I'm ready to
meet my Maker and answer for those who have died as a result of my decisions' (*The
New Statesman*, February 2010). Despite this, secular Just War theory does recognise
that just intentions are less likely to jeopardise post-war peace or sow the seeds of
further conflicts (according to the economist John Maynard Keynes, the post-World
War I reparations Germany was made to pay following the Treaty of Versailles were
excessive and counterproductive – in particular, he saw France's motives as being
those of economically setting the clock back on Germany and regaining its pre-1870
economic superiority).

Critics of the West may point to far swifter intervention in oil-rich states than
in developing countries where there are no strategic interests at stake. They argue
that the capacity for self-deception makes it hard to judge motives and intentions
which, though morally justified to oneself, may conceal a more self-serving rationale
behind military action. The subjectivity, self-deception and mixed motives of human
endeavour mean that, in practice, this is a difficult criterion to apply, especially in the
politics of spin and the propaganda of war.

Reasonable chance of success

Jesus says in Luke 14:31, 32, 'suppose a king is about to go to war against another
king. Will he not first sit down and consider whether he is able with ten thousand men to oppose the one coming against him with twenty thousand? If he is
not able, he will send a delegation while the other is still a long way off and will

ask for terms of peace.' War must not be pursued when the odds of victory are hopeless. Given the unpredictability of war, such a criterion should again urge restraint and further negotiations for peace, especially among resolute but weak states who, in the face of overwhelming military might, commit their people to an unwinnable war. Predicting the exit strategy and timing with accuracy is difficult (the phrase 'home by Christmas' was to haunt military leaders in the aftermath of the 1914–18 war).

Proportionality

Force should be proportionate to the evil to be overturned. In weighing the good (e.g. securing peace, liberating a state) and bad consequences (fatalities and casualties) of a war, the suffering inflicted must not outweigh the good brought about. Wars caused by an aggressive state grabbing territory and inflicting many casualties may result in a military response, but the suffering caused should be proportionate and include the costs to the enemy troops and state as well as innocent civilians and the environment. Assessment should look beyond the national interest of states and justify the use of military force only in proportion to the overall good to be achieved.

Last resort

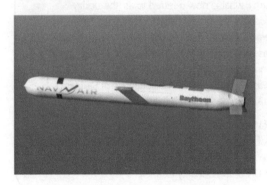

A Tomahawk Cruise missile. It was claimed that these were so precise in hitting targets that military strategists could speak of 'surgical strikes'. Yet collateral impact on civilian targets was common with their use.

All possible peaceful routes to negotiating a settlement should be explored – diplomatic efforts, international pressure through economic sanctions (e.g. against Iran for its nuclear programme) and UN negotiations. Given the loss of life together with the chaotic and unpredictable nature of war, states should resort to it only *in extremis* and after an exhaustive search for an alternative means of achieving peace.

Exercise

Using the arguments below, assess whether or not the Second Gulf War was a Just War

Just authority	Whilst UN Resolutions were passed, the 'allied' attack did not have UN authorisation. It is the international body that arbitrates between its member states. On the other hand, the elected heads of government (principally Bush and Blair) did authorise the war.
Just cause	Was Iraq really linked with Al Qaida or posing a threat to Western nations with WMD? The Kurds in northern Iraq and many political prisoners and the majority of the people were to be liberated from unjust rule.
Right intention	Though sceptics may argue that the US had strategic aims beyond liberating Iraq, such as oil supply and regional stability for economic advantage, most commentators view Tony Blair's entry into the war as motivated by a right intention. Certainly no up-front promises for lucrative post-war contracts were secured and there were very real risks to UK forces (and, as hindsight has proved, costly ones).
Likelihood of success	Hindsight shows that, after dismantling the Baathist party which was the basis of government, and without an effective post-war plan, winning the peace and nation-building was to prove far more complex and difficult than toppling Saddam Hussein's regime.
Propor-tionality	On going to war (**jus ad bellum**), what is now referred to as 'the dodgy dossier' — an erroneous and possibly selectively edited Intelligence Report — suggested that Saddam Hussein had WMD that were ready to use, so a pre-emptive strike could be seen as proportional. In terms of justice in war (**jus in bello**), the mismatch of weaponry was highly disproportionate. The US aerial 'Shock and Awe' campaign savagely destroyed whole battalions of Saddam's army. Furthermore, 'surgical strikes' turned out to bring 'collateral damage'.
Last resort	Given that Hans Blik, the Chief Weapons Inspector at the UN, was asking for more time to examine claims of WMDs, and that sanctions, combined with mounting international isolation, held out hope, the US/UK-led alliance went to war without the backing of the UN or the Security Council.

Jus in bello – the just conduct of war

Minimal force

In achieving one's aims, the military force used must be as limited as possible. For example, in one Church council of 1139, cross-bows and siege machines were banned in wars between Christians (they had been used among petty medieval nobles). Technology can industrialise the scale of war, or minimise fatalities in the accurate use of high-tech weaponry in 'surgical strikes'.

Proportionality

Military force in war should be proportionate to the targets aimed at. A sledgehammer should not be used to crack a nut. This criterion would raise severe doubts over the saturation bombing of Dresden by the Allies in 1945. It was neither a major industrial centre nor a focus for military production. The incendiary bombs used created a firestorm and killed tens of thousands indiscriminately.

An example of proportionality in modern warfare may be seen in the 'flexible response' adopted by the Kennedy administration and by NATO in 1967. Designed to avert an all-out nuclear war of mutually assured destruction, this put in place an escalating response. Robert McNamara, the US Secretary of State under J. F. Kennedy, explicitly stated the response that Soviet nuclear aggression would be met with. A retaliatory strike would inflict 'unacceptable damage' (50 per cent of an enemy's industry and 25 per cent of the population). The logic of such deterrence was that of an explicit, precise and credible response. The term 'conditional intention' distinguished between holding nuclear weapons as a deterrent prior to war and their use in war after the escalation of conflict. It may be argued that, in the era of cold war nuclear brinkmanship, the deterrent of a 'proportionate' response averted an all-out nuclear holocaust.

Discrimination

A distinction between legitimate targets for military violence and civilian non-combatants must be made. Insurgent terrorist groups and urban warfare are a far cry from the open battlefields and uniformed armies of Napoleon and Wellington's era.

Two thousand times more powerful than bombs used before them, the two atomic bombs that landed on the Japanese cities of Hiroshima and Nagasaki are estimated to have killed 140,000 and 74,000 people respectively. The Campaign for Nuclear Disarmament saw this new era of warfare as unconscionable. President Harry S. Truman later commented on his decision to use the bombs: 'I did not like the weapon but I had no qualms, if in the long run millions of lives could be saved.'

Yet where terrorists act indiscriminately, democratic states at war must make every attempt to distinguish military from civilian targets and respect human rights. As one writer puts it, 'Execution by B-52 is not the appropriate penalty for bad politics' (Henry Shue, 'War' in the *Oxford Handbook of Practical Ethics*, ed. Hugh LaFollette, Oxford University Press, 2005, p. 742) – it is capital punishment for the innocent without trial. Yet when facing human shields for military installations and conscript

---

Case study: the formation of international legal and political institutions

In 1901, Henry Dunant was awarded the Nobel Peace Prize for his book *Memoirs of Solferino*. He experienced the suffering of war and his book inspired the creation of the International Committee of the Red Cross. His ideas were later to influence the League of Nations and the Geneva Conventions. These established international standards on the humanitarian treatment of the wounded, of civilians and of prisoners of war. The fourth of these treaties was ratified in 1949 by 194 countries, though with some reservations. More recent developments include the UN Security Council and the International Criminal Court (ICC) based in The Hague, Netherlands (est. 2002 and ratified by 121 states). Here, those guilty of genocide in war (like the former President of Serbia, Slobodan Milošević) can be prosecuted for war crimes as war criminals. Such developments may act as a deterrent as present day or future leaders recognise that the international community will hold them to account.

'Let Us Beat Swords into Ploughshares' (Isaiah 2:4) –a sculpture by Evgeniy Vuchetich at the UN

The formation of the United Nations in 1946 in the aftermath of World War II established a new world order. Firstly, war was no longer a unilateral action of states, and peace became more of an international and collaborative responsibility. Secondly, a charter of human rights brought a greater measure of accountability in how states treated their citizens. Finally, distinctions were made (especially at the Nuremberg Trials) between the justice or injustice of going to war, and the limits of what would be legally termed 'war crimes' in the conduct of war.

On this basis, Charles R. Beitz identifies six goals that have, in recent years, justified intervention:

- To stop or prevent genocide, ethnic cleansing or enslavement of peoples (e.g. Kosovo)
- To alleviate acute distress e.g. starvation
- To restore democratic government after a military coup
- To support an insurgent movement in an attempt to remove an authoritarian regime
- To support a democratic government fighting a rebellion
- To help an oppressed group achieve political self-determination (e.g. Kurds in Iraq)

(Charles R. Beitz, *The Justifiability of Humanitarian Intervention: Ethics in Practice*, ed. Hugh LaFollette, Blackwell, 2007, p. 729)

soldiers in rogue states it is hard to discriminate. Aquinas argued that soldiers had a duty to treat prisoners of war justly and to show mercy towards the conquered nation, especially when peace was no longer threatened. Making such distinctions during war can help when beginning to rebuild trust after the war.

In the aftermath of two world wars, the international community together began to develop legal and political institutions and conventions to limit the escalation of wars between and within its member states, and more widely in the international community as a whole. You can read up on some of the history of this below.

International law prohibits one sovereign state from attacking another even in a preventative or pre-emptive strike. It establishes rules for the just treatment of prisoners of war and prohibits the use of means which are in themselves evil (*mala in se*). such as the use of biological weapons, genocide, ethnic cleansing, rape or the forcing of soldiers to fight against their own side.

Jus post bellum – justice after war

Jus post bellum is perhaps the newest phase of Just War thinking, and Thomas Orend regards Kant as its author (Thomas Orend, *War and International Justice: A Kantian Perspective*, 2000). Notably, Kant's essay *Toward Perpetual Peace* states that wars must not be pursued in ways that destroy post-war trust and peace-making. If war's purpose is to defeat a military threat, not to destroy an enemy nation, then the use of nuclear or biological weaponry, indiscriminate bombing or of landmines crosses this line. His characteristic focus on the duty of Good Will and the universal reach of the Categorical Imperative, even to the ethics of the battlefield, frames conduct in war. As we've seen in Iraq and Afghanistan, winning the peace or nation-building can be more complex and protracted than winning the war, and atrocities or injustices committed during it jeopardise this. Political, diplomatic, legal, medical, engineering and economic advisers can be as important as military commanders. The excellent online 'Stanford Encyclopedia of Philosophy' sets out several emerging criteria for an 'ethical exit strategy' in an area where there is as yet little international law (e.g. occupation law and human rights treaties). Key criteria here include:

Proportionality

Peace settlements should not exact revenge or insist on unconditional surrender. Instead, they should be measured and aim at preventing grounds for resentment of the post-World War I kind that Hitler was able to exploit in some senses for revenge.

Rights vindication

Restoring human rights to life, liberty and territorial sovereignty are crucial if post-war justice is to be restorative. Peace treaties must aim to bring about a greater good and establish legal redress for rights violations.

Discrimination

Justice must target the perpetrators of the violence or injustice that led to, and those who held command during, the war. Leaders, soldiers and civilians need to be distinguished so as to prevent indiscriminate post-war measures unfairly punishing innocent civilians for the war crimes and policies of their leaders.

Punishment

Where there is evidence of war crimes committed by leaders of a regime and soldiers who fought in the war (on all sides), justice demands that these be investigated and prosecuted (either within an interim or established national judicial system or in the ICC).

Compensation

Post-war reconstruction is costly and it may well sow the seeds of future conflicts to leave a defeated country impoverished. A humanitarian exit strategy would involve a range of measures such as infrastructural repairs to roads, factories, energy resources, etc. But it may also seek to address education, the economy and healthcare provision in order to give stable, constitutionally elected government every chance of taking root.

Rehabilitation

Post-conflict reconstruction offers the prospect of the widespread reform of government institutions. There are likely to be many weapons in circulation, so establishing a reformed military and a re-trained police force, and disarming those outside them,

A US soldier leads the training of the post-war Iraqi Police Force

will be important tasks. Bringing about a greater good in the eyes of a devastated post-war nation is controversial. Establishing the just rule of law, upholding human rights, forming a constitutionally elected government, and replacing pre-war propaganda with an education system that empowers students with a sense of their rights are all highly politicised reforms unlikely to find a universally welcome reception. It is surprising for us to hear some Iraqis consider themselves to have been better off under Saddam Hussein's regime than in the new Iraq. Will time persuade them that regime change was for the good?

Exercise

Consider the following examples of warfare. What elements of Just War theory (before, during or after) may they be thought to violate?

1. The saturation bombing of German cities like Dresden in February 1945 — 3,900 tonnes of bombs resulted in a firestorm that destroyed 15 square miles and caused 135,000 deaths in two days (Anthony Taylor, *London's Burning: Pulp Fiction, the Politics of Terrorism and the Destruction of the Capital in British Popular Culture 1840–2005*, Continuum Press, 2005).

2. 3.3 million prisoners of war held in World War II by Germany (57.5 per cent of the total captured) died during their captivity. Between the launching of Operation Barbarossa in the summer of 1941 and the following spring, 2.8 million of the 3.2 million Soviet prisoners taken died while in German hands (Norman Davies, *Europe at War 1939–1945*, Pan, 2006). In 1941, German troops unable to conquer Moscow deliberately took the overcoats and felt boots of Russian prisoners of war, leaving them to freeze to death (Historynet. com).

3. The use of the atomic bomb on Japanese cities Nagasaki and Hiroshima by President Truman on 6 and 9 August 1945.

4. Imprisoning Al Qaida suspects without trial and torturing operatives to obtain information on Osama bin Laden's whereabouts, using waterboarding techniques justified in terms of preventative force.

5. Today around 300,000 child soldiers (under-18s) fight in armed conflict. They are sometimes given drugs to help them cope with their emotions and make it easier for them to kill (source: UN).

6. Today's nuclear weapons have the potential to kill 2 million instantly and 1 million more through injuries if dropped directly on a densely populated area. The UK's nuclear deterrent is an integral part of its defence strategy.

7. A single aircraft leaving a trail of 100 kg of anthrax along a line upwind of Washington, DC, could result in 1 to 3 million deaths (Julian Perry Robinson et al., *The Problem of Chemical and Biological Warfare*, Vol. II, Almqvist & Wiksell, 1973, p. 135) — hence the statement that biological weapons are the poor man's atomic bomb.

8. Civil wars in which political instability or corruption undermines governmental authority bringing about a military coup or revolt. (800,000 killed in 100 days in the Rwandan genocide of 1994; 2.5 million in the fighting, and through disease and malnutrition resulting from it, in Congo).

9. In statistics for 2006, more than 1,000 people a month were killed by landmines. Around 100 million land mines remain in the ground in Vietnam where, in some years, there were 15–20,000 victims annually. In Angola, one in every 470 people is a land mine amputee. Most of the jobs in these countries require a level of physical fitness that rules out amputees and a good deal of arable land is blocked off (Helen Ware (ed.), *The No-Nonsense Guide to Conflict and Peace*, New International Publications, 2006, p. 119).

Kant on war

No state at war with another shall permit such acts of hostility as would make mutual confidence impossible during a future time of peace.
(Kant's pamphlet *Toward Perpetual Peace*, ed. Pauline Kleingeld, Yale University Press, 2006, p. 96)

Somewhat secluded in the little port city of Königsberg, Kant's unbending ethic may be viewed by some as naive when applied to war. He made a political misjudgement in considering the storming of the Bastille to be a 'historical sign' ushering in a 'greater moral tendency of mankind' only to see it descend into the Terror of the guillotine and the imprisonment and execution of the aristocracy and Louis XV, which horrified him (Christopher Coker, *Can War Be Eliminated?* Polity, 2014, p. 179). Fortunately, he did not base his ethics on predicting outcomes. His principled, dutiful ethic extended to warfare in its pursuit of peace and political settlement. As Coker puts it, Kant's point is to 'Do nothing in war that makes peace impossible . . . If peace is the only reason for going to war, then we must wage it in a way that does nothing to make it unattainable – by treating our enemies, for example, as a means to a greater end.' But where rights and duties had some bearing on the conventions of war in an age in which professional armies engaged in close combat, today's weapons of mass destruction, its chemical and biological weaponry, its rockets, air strikes and collateral damage make any adherence to such a code of chivalry highly problematic. Kant's ethic would exclude national self-interest as a just cause for war and emphasise the Good Will or right intention with which warfare ought to be conducted. He would have strongly approved of the Geneva Convention in regard to rights of prisoners of war. The key principle for Kant was 'responsibility' – towards prisoners of war, civilians, and towards future peace – as Coker puts it, 'to stop a limited war becoming unlimited'. The Categorical Imperative calls for us to act rationally and to transcend our self-interest. Kant's essay on 'perpetual peace' is optimistic that humanity's rational intelligence can make peace practical and permanent, whilst also recognising the altogether more tragic prospect of another kind of perpetual peace – that of 'the great cemetery of the human race' resulting from 'a war of extermination'. Kant argued that wars ought only to be sanctioned and instigated by the will of citizens in republican nations with a civil constitution. If the consent of those who had to risk their lives had to be obtained, rather than that of kings and aristocrats who could order others to their deaths in pursuit of their wealth or vainglory, this would lead to more restraint. So too would universal hospitality, including freedom of travel or the establishment of trading links for foreign citizens. Kant's 'league of nations' was ahead of its time, but he saw that political and economic links and alliances would provide a self-interested protection against warmongering. States could negotiate settlements and would be less likely to meddle in the affairs of a neighbouring state or grab resources or land if they were subject to a transnational body of interests.

Philosopher Roger Scruton sees how, on a superficial level, Kant may be read as rejecting the justice of the pre-emptive war against Saddam Hussein's regime

Philosopher Roger Scruton

as non-defensive and therefore unjust. However, as a modern Kantian, Scruton argues that weapons and threats have changed since Kant's day and regime change may be justifiable. Kant's belief in the rational and universal principles ultimately committed him to republican government elected by citizens who authored and abided by its laws. He finds it hard to see how a Kingdom of Ends in which each person is treated as an end in themselves and not a means to an end, could be realised without a representative and accountable government and state institutions. It then follows that a state like Saddam Hussein's Iraq, which rode roughshod over its citizens' rights, imprisoning and executing those who opposed the government without trial, which carried out genocide on Kurds and was a threat to regional and even international peace and order, violates the moral law and has no claim to legitimate authority. Its overthrow would therefore be a good in itself. Scruton therefore argues that a Kantian could make a legitimate argument for a war to topple a rogue state and establish peace and just rule. The problem here is that, without the backing of the UN (akin to Kant's idea of a federation of free states), the accusation of self-interest rather than universal interest may be seen to undermine the legitimacy of war.

Kant on war – assessing the strengths and weaknesses

Strengths	Weaknesses
Kant reminds us that the demands of our rational natures are universal. They transcend the self-interests of states and combatants. Any justification for war must aim at peace and avoid propagandising the enemy nation as evil, or disregarding the post-war peace.	Kant's uncompromising and absolute ethic is unsuited to deal with the instrumental strategy in warfare. Military commanders and soldiers who employ hypothetical reasoning survive and have a far greater chance of success. To navigate the real-time life-and-death decision-making of warfare requires rapid responses. Kant lived in a peaceful port in Prussia and proved inept in his predictions of how the French Revolution would work out. War is a lot more like the strategising of board games than it is the rational process of a court of law.

Utilitarianism/John Stuart Mill on war

Mill believed in the autonomy of self-governing states and argued against interference by foreign powers. He argued for establishing 'some rule or criterion whereby the justifiableness of intervening in affairs of other countries, and ... of refraining from intervention, may be brought to a definite and rational test' (John Stuart Mill, 'A Few Words on Non-Intervention' in *On Liberty*, ed. with intro. by Gertrude Himmelfarb, Penguin, 1963).

In the liquidity of wartime decision-making, calculations of likely outcomes are crucial, to minimise net losses, both military and civilian. Leaders may judge that pre-emptive strikes are justified in limiting losses, or that it is worth sacrificing soldiers to gain control of strategic ground. Taken to extremes, war can be viewed entirely through instrumental sights, clinically ignoring civilian deaths (or justifying torture, saturation bombing, land mines or nuclear weapons) as long as victory is secured. Legitimising the killing of the innocent in terms of a greater good may prove more conscionable for the steely nerves of the Utilitarian. Consequentialist decision-making in war is dependent on good intelligence and accurate and reliable deployment of forces and weaponry. It was along these lines that the western European governments in the cold war linked US and European nuclear defences (in the NATO alliance) in order to deter the USSR from entering into a global nuclear war by attacking any individual western European country. The success of this deterrence (and the Cuban missile crisis was a close call) is held up as evidence that such consequentialist logic can rein in aggressive states where Kantian or Natural Law ethical reasoning would have little or no impact. But it may be objected that, if the worst-case scenario in the cold war had been between (for example) a widespread nuclear war and soviet occupation, few would consider the former the better outcome (see Jeff McMahan, 'War and Peace' in *A Companion to Ethics*, 1997).

Utilitarianism on war – assessing the strengths and weaknesses of the theory in practice

Strengths	Weaknesses
Utilitarianism is the ethic of the modern age. It is most effective when aggregating risk and reward or means and ends in a calculation. This may not seem like ethics, but squeamishness or naive kind-heartedness can cost many lives in war. A cool, dispassionate rationalisation aimed at minimising pain to sentient individuals and optimising the freedoms of maximal numbers is surely worth aiming for. Statistical odds shape military planning, so if accurate data can be gathered and assessed intelligently, Utilitarian logic is well placed to minimise casualties. Military planners under	Choices vindicated on the basis of consequences offer a precarious basis for action when outcomes are unpredictable. Despite the fact that the US spends billions on intelligence gathering, its officials erroneously believed that, by 2002, Saddam Hussein had weapons of mass destruction.
	In calculating the likely outcomes of decisions, historically, Utilitarian logic has often been shown to overestimate goods and underestimate risks and negative results. In war, such optimism might miscalculate the length of war ('home by Christmas' was a slogan that came to haunt recruiters in World War I), civilian deaths, increase in national debt, traumatised post-war citizens, refugees President Truman

Strengths	**Weaknesses**
may not have calculated on 200,000 lives being lost in the atomic bombing of the Japanese cities of Nagasaki and Hiroshima in 1945, but compared to a conventional war dragged out by a militaristic Japanese regime, they could have assessed that it would be likely to have reduced the total lives lost.	and child mortality rates. War is unpredictable, and moral assessment based on consequences rather than principles can prove misguided.
Preference Utilitarianism seeks to maximise the choices of the greatest number, each person's interests to count equally (e.g. pacifists and those who wish for an army to defend them). Its proponents would question the self-interest of nations in going to war and raise the value of the life of foreign citizens; Afghan or Iraqi fatalities would count equally to British or American lives.	Mill's distinction between higher and lower pains and pleasures along with his emphasis on the freedom of the individual would virtually rule out the use of torture, killing the few to spare the many, and the use of saturation bombing, mines and bio-chemical warfare.
	The Utilitarian emphasis on considering the interests of sentient beings (those who can feel pleasure and pain) surely needs to take a longer-term view on the issue of war. This would involve considering future people, animals, and the environment. Do Utilitarians ignore 'future people' in the interests of existing, sentient people?

Case study: The Thin Red Line

The men of C Company have been brought to Guadalcanal in the Pacific during World War II (August 1942 – February 1943) as reinforcements in a campaign to take the island from the Japanese. After marching to the interior, they come to Hill 210, a key Japanese position. The Japanese have placed a bunker housing several machine guns at the top of the hill, giving them control of 1,000 yards of the valley below. Any force attempting to climb the hill can be easily cut down by machine-gun fire and mortar rounds. A brief shelling of the hill begins the next day at dawn. Shortly after, C Company attempts to take the hill and is repelled by gunfire from the bunker.

During the battle, Colonel Tall orders the company commander, Captain Staros, to take the bunker by frontal assault, whatever the cost. Staros refuses, unwilling to treat his men as cannon fodder. When the two reach a stalemate, Tall decides to join Staros on the front line to see the situation for himself. By the time he arrives, the Japanese resistance seems to have lessened, and Tall's opinion of Staros seems to have been sealed.

Col.: This is a war. It's a goddamn battle! Now, I want that frontal attack. I repeat my order. Over.

Capt.: Colonel, I refuse to take my men up there in a frontal attack. It's suicide, sir. I've lived with these men for two years, and I will not order them all to their deaths. Over.

Col.: This is a very important decision, Staros. I don't know if you realise the importance of this operation, Staros. Once our position is secured, we can move the bombers in. That means air power for miles in every direction. Guadalcanal may be the turning point in the war.

It'll cost lives. Is that what's troubling you?

Capt.: No, sir.

Col.: I explained to you the importance of this objective. How many men do you think it's worth? How many lives?

Capt.: I can't say, sir.

Col.: Are you prepared to sacrifice the lives of any of your men in this campaign? How many? One? Two? Twenty? Lives will be lost in your Company, Captain. And if you don't have the stomach for it, now is the time to let me know.

The Thin Red Line

To what extent would Kantian, Natural Law and Utilitarian ethicists approach Staros' dilemma differently?

The future of Just War theory

The concept of 'Just War' may be dismissed by some as a relic of the Crusades and standing armies on the open battlefield. But there has been a renewal of interest in Just War theory among journalists and academics and international law specialists assessing the ethics of intervention in the Balkans, Iraq, Afghanistan and Libya (or the non-intervention in other conflicts). In 2005, the UN adopted the 2001 report of the International Commission on Intervention and State Sovereignty entitled 'The Responsibility to Protect'. This explicitly argues, along Just War lines, that where individual states fail to protect their populations from genocide, war crimes, ethnic cleansing and crimes against humanity, then the international community has a responsibility 'to act in a timely and decisive way to prevent and halt' such atrocities.

Discussion Questions

Consider one paradox and one problem in Just War theory from philosopher Jeff McMahan. How would you deal with them?

A paradox

When combatants of a state that enters into a war unjustly wage it justly (on the level of individuals or in an army), they carry out *jus in bello* in a permissible way. Despite this, collectively, the actions of these individuals remain impermissible given the unjust cause of the state to which they belong. As he asks, 'how can a series of individually permissible acts be collectively impermissible?'

A problem

In a 2012 *New York Times* opinion piece, McMahan claims that:

> The Theory cannot offer any moral reason why a person ought not to fight in an unjust war, no matter how criminal. If a young German in 1939 had consulted the Theory for guidance about whether to join the Wehrmacht, it would have told him that it was permissible to participate in Nazi aggression provided that he obeyed the principles of *jus in bello* (for example, by refraining from intentionally attacking civilians).

Can you suggest any reasons why (if only just authorities can declare war (*jus ad bellum*)) a young German ought to refuse to join up, according to Just War theory?'

In an era of globalisation, David S. Oderberg reckons that the question being asked is 'couldn't a world authority [regulate] relations between states [making] war as unjustifiable as private vendettas and vigilante justice . . . relegating war to the history books' (Oderberg 2000, p. 224). For Oderberg, the economic interdependence of nations after the cold war era has seen the UN play a greater role in regulating international conflict. It has undertaken 59 peacekeeping operations, costing the lives of some 1,900 peacekeepers and around $30 billion. Certainly international law, diplomacy, economic sanctions, global markets and UN peacekeeping forces can exert pressure on rogue states or can prosecute ex-dictators and war lords. Kant's ideal of perpetual peace may be beyond human nature to achieve, but with millions of deaths in the two world wars of the twentieth century and recent conflicts with hundreds of thousands of deaths in Rwanda, the Democratic Republic of Congo, Iraq, Afghanistan and Syria, it is worth striving for.

FURTHER READING

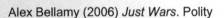

Alex Bellamy (2006) *Just Wars*. Polity

Nigel Biggar (2013) *In Defence of War*. Oxford University Press

Nigel Dower (2009) *The Ethics of War and Peace*. Polity

Nicholas Fotion (2007) *EPZ War and Ethics: A New Just War Theory (Think Now)*. Continuum

David S. Oderberg (2000) *Applied Ethics: A Non-Consequentialist Approach*. Wiley-Blackwell

Gregory M. Reichberg, Henrik Syse and Endre Begby (eds.) (2006) *The Ethics of War: Classic and Contemporary Readings*. Wiley-Blackwell 2006

Michael Walzer (2013) *Just And Unjust Wars: A Moral Argument With Historical Illustrations*. Basic Books

OCR Past Paper Questions

JANUARY 2010
(a) Explain how Utilitarians approach the issue of war. [25]
(b) 'Pacifism causes more harm than good.' Discuss. [10]

JUNE 2010
(a) Explain the ethical principles of the religion you have studied in relation to war. [25]
(b) 'War should not be allowed even as a last resort.' Discuss. [10]

JUNE 2011
(a) Explain the theories of ethical and religious pacifism. [25]
(b) Assess the claim that killing in war is more justifiable than other types of killing. [10]

JUNE 2012
(a) Explain how the followers of the religion you have studied justify going to war. [25]
(b) 'Religious believers should be pacifists.' Discuss. [10]

JANUARY 2013
(a) Explain the purpose and principles of Just War theory. [25]
(b) 'Just War theory cannot be applied to modern warfare.' Discuss. [10]

PART II

A2
RELIGIOUS
ETHICS

ETHICAL TOPICS
AND THEORIES

10 Meta-ethics

How Meta-ethics differs from normative ethics

Meta-ethics focuses on the meaning and use of the language of ethics. We assume we ordinarily know what words like 'good', 'bad', 'right' and 'wrong' mean – but are these meanings universal or relative to time and place? Can their meanings be expressed rationally in argument, or can they only be known intuitively? Are their meanings grounded in our attitudes, values, judgements, God (or some other metaphysical basis), reason, emotion, or something else? Meta-ethics wrestles with questions such as whether there are any moral facts or whether moral claims can be true or false. Meta-ethics takes a descriptive look at different approaches to moral reasoning identifying the battle lines without taking sides or making value judgements. If we get a sense of the meaning of moral language, we can hopefully have clearer definitions that avoid confusion, misunderstanding, or talking at cross-purposes in disputes.

In contrast, normative ethics is where ethics is in the mode of value judgements and carries the weight of obligation and duty. Norms are standards or rules to which our behaviour ought to conform. Normative ethics examines how and why we ought to live and act. Normative judgements relate both to a person's/groups intentions and character, and to their behaviour and actions. Such judgements can be particular, like You ought not to cheat in your biology test, or general, such as Torture is never justifiable. They can relate to values like 'Honesty is a good policy', or to obligations like 'You ought to honour your parents'.

Meta-ethics is like the grammar of ethics and can appear both daunting and dry as dust. Yet if we get a sense of the meaning of moral language, we can avoid confusion or misunderstanding in disputes. In order not to get bogged down as we cover the ground, we will begin with some key definitions.

Cognitivism	Moral judgements are not just feelings – they are making truth claims and so can be true or false (though it may be difficult to prove that the judgements of religion or relativism are true or false).
Non-cognitivism	The view that moral judgements are not true or false as they do not make truth claims. Instead they express emotions, preferences, commands or attitudes.
Egoism	The belief that individuals have a moral duty to optimise good consequences for themselves.
Emotivism	The view that any moral claim (e.g. 'Abortion is murder!') is essentially an *emotional* plea on the part of the one who expresses it for others to share such disapproval or adopt this feeling.
Ethical hedonism	The view that pleasure is intrinsically good and pain bad, so you ought to aim at maximising pleasure (note that this led the ancient Greek Epicurus to lead a life of moderation free of the highs and lows of excess).
Intuitionism	The view that 'good' and 'evil' are objective but indefinable. Basic moral truths are either self-evident or perceived similarly to how our senses experience the physical world.
Ethical Naturalism	This approach defines 'good' in terms of some natural property of the world, e.g. pleasure, human flourishing. A subjective naturalist might argue that moral statements are true in terms of the attitudes society approves of. An objectivist naturalist might argue that what is good is what will promote human flourishing in harmony with the resources of the planet.
Moral objectivism	The opposite of subjective ethics, this view holds that moral statements are true independently of what people think or feel.
Nihilism	In terms of ethics, Nihilists believe that objectivity is impossible. No moral truth claims exist, or if they do they're unknowable.
Prescriptivism	Moral statements as commands or imperatives, as opposed to descriptions. Moral terms are used to guide action and prescribe what people are to do in similar situations. An attempt to move on from emotivism and treat ethical reasoning as rational rather than a form of emotional manipulation, it sticks to 'ought' statements that one lives with consistently.
Moral realism	The view that claims are true in respect of how they correspond to the real world. Moral realists hold that moral statements can in principle be verified or falsified – there is an objective reality to them. This may, for example, derive from God's created moral order or commands, but not all realists are theists.

Cognitivism and non-cognitivism

Cognitivism: Moral judgements are not just feelings – they are making truth claims and so can be true or false (though it may be difficult to prove that the judgements of religion or relativism are true or false)

The main distinction in this chapter is between *cognitivists* (who believe that moral claims are a form of knowledge and can therefore be seen to be true or false by observation) and *non-cognitivists* (who deny this). For cognitivists, moral statements like 'Genocide is wrong' are facts, not merely opinions.

> ### Discussion Question
>
> Can we be said to know any given moral claim (e.g. 'To deny child factory workers an education and exploit their cheap labour is immoral!') in the way we might be said to know those of the natural sciences (e.g. 'Water boils at 100 degrees centigrade')?

David Hume distinguishes facts and values, reasons and opinions.

Non-cognitivism: The view that moral judgements are not true or false as they do not make truth claims. Instead they express emotions, preferences, commands or attitudes.

The eighteenth-century philosopher David Hume made a sharp distinction between facts and values, creating a gap that has been called Hume's Guillotine. Take the following two examples of leaps between 'is' and 'ought' statements:

1. God is our creator, therefore we ought to obey him.
2. Evolution is the competition for survival favouring the fittest, therefore we ought to promote the healthy, intelligent and strong in society, and seek to eliminate the weak.

In his *Treatise Concerning Human Understanding* (1748), Hume writes:

> In every system of morality, which I have hitherto met with, I have always remarked, that the author . . . makes observations concerning human affairs; when all of a sudden I am surprised to find, that instead of the usual . . . propositions, is, and is not, I meet with no proposition that is not connected with an ought, or an ought not. This change is imperceptible; but is however, of the last consequence. For as this ought, or ought not, expresses some new relation or affirmation, 'tis necessary that it should be observed and explained; and at the same time that a reason should be given; for what seems altogether inconceivable, how this new relation can be a deduction from others, which are entirely different from it.

(Quoted in Oderberg 2000)

Here Hume notes a drift from *factual* statements, for example, 'a human foetus is unborn and dependent upon its mother for life' or 'murder is the deliberate taking of innocent human life' – to *value* statements like 'Therefore you ought not to have an abortion – it is murder!' To leap from factual definitions to a value-based conclusion is attempting to get an 'ought' from an 'is'. Hume believed that 'good' or 'bad' arose purely from human reactions of praise or blame. No moral facts existed independently of human sentiment or feeling. As he put it,

> Take any action allow'd to be vicious: Wilful murder, for instance. Examine it in all its lights, and see if you can find that matter of fact . . . which you call vice . . . You will never find it, till you turn your reflexion into your own breast, and find a sentiment of

disapprobation, which arises in you, toward this action. Here is a matter of fact; but 'tis the object of feeling, not reason.

(Quoted in Oderberg 2000)

For Hume, human morality 'is sentiment' – it is in our wiring as humans to react emotionally and to judge on this basis; we cannot outrun our nature. He recognises, as a fact, that human beings will praise and blame and that this is the way their morality works. You may see the killing of a bird by a cat and the murder of a person by another, but it is not sight that distinguishes between killing and murder. Hume was sceptical about the discovery of moral truths. He wrote that 'since vice and virtue are not discoverable merely by reason . . . it must be by means of . . . sentiment . . . that we are able to mark the difference' (Hume, *A Treatise of Human Nature*, 1960, p. 147). Although he rejects the idea of deriving 'ought' statements from facts, Hume recognises that human perceptions add things to the world. Just as the colour yellow is a secondary quality that results from our sense impressions of a banana rather than belonging to the object itself, so morality results from our sentiments. For example, the compassion we feel towards a grieving friend originates in our feelings rather than from outside of us. So Hume argues that vice and virtue are discoverable not by reason but by our sentiments or feelings – as he puts it, 'Morality. . . is more properly felt than judg'd of.' Hume sticks to the fact that nature orientates us to pursue pleasure and avoid pain. He's content to observe human nature rather than moralise about what we ought to do. Our emotions and desires motivate our actions, and reason has only an instrumental role to play in guiding them. As he asserts, 'both vice and virtue are equally artificial . . . 'Tis impossible therefore, that the character of natural and unnatural can ever, in any sense, mark the boundaries of vice and virtue.' Moral judgement about vice and virtue does not move from 'is' to 'ought', but from cause (the usefulness of an action) to effect (our emotional approval).

David Hume (1711–76) in his native Edinburgh. Hume was voted the second-greatest philosopher of all time by BBC Radio 4 *In Our Time* listeners. He is the key figure of the Scottish Enlightenment and a defining thinker in empiricism who sought to show how the mind is entirely furnished with its ideas from experience and sense impressions. Sceptical about miracles and religious testimony of them, he wanted to consign metaphysics to the flames and put his trust in the evidence that sense experience offered. In *An Enquiry Concerning the Principles of Morals*, Hume argues that the foundations of morality lie in human sentiment rather than reason. What motivates action in us is passion not reason. Hume roots morality not in a divine source, but in our feelings of sympathy and self-interest.

Statue of David Hume in Edinburgh

Cognitivist approaches

Cognitive means 'the mental process of knowing' as opposed to non-cognitive (e.g. **emotivism** which holds that moral judgements cannot be known rationally as they are emotional). Cognitivists take moral language (such as 'duty', 'wrong', 'good') to refer to real, existent properties independent of themselves, out there in the real world or in the human reason. **Cognitivism** is a broad classification that can include Naturalism, intuitivism, and religious and secular ethical theories. Here we're concerned with the first two and we begin with **ethical Naturalism**.

Ethical Naturalism

F. H. Bradley (1846-1924) did much to promote one example of ethical Naturalism in the late nineteenth and early twentieth century. In his influential text *Ethical Studies* (1876), he offers a destructive critique of Utilitarianism's answer to the question 'Why be moral?' For Bradley, human self-realisation rather than the calculation of consequences is the source of our motivation to be moral. In part, he offers a psychological theory of moral maturation. By means of practical reasoning and deliberation, we move from childish appetites and egoism to the moral deliberation of seeing that our self-realisation is better achieved through making the world into a better place. Moral motivation is rooted in our will to self-realisation. Personal satisfaction is bound up with the creation of an interdependent society in which we each contribute in our particular station and duty. We will ourselves to become the idealised self we hope to be. When we fall short of this, we feel disappointment at the moral gap between this ideal self and our actual self. In this process of growth, we develop a social self that takes into account the interests of others as they are bound up with our own self-realisation. This is a descriptive theory of ethics, and Bradley believes that our natural urge towards the realisation of our ideal selves (helped along by practices embedded in human institutions like the family/society, and language) is the end goal of ethics. It is not the pleasures of virtue alone that motivate us, but a sense of self-realisation that they help to achieve. So goodness is defined in terms of a property in the natural world – in Bradley's case, this is the satisfaction our practical reasoning finds in developing a mature self that lives up to its ideals and seeks for the same progress in the world around it.

Naturalists believe that moral terms such as 'good' and 'right' can be defined in terms of human nature or properties in the natural world that can be known by our mind or senses. They may be religious (grounded in the way God has made the world and human beings, as in Natural Law theory). Equally, they may be secular, based upon what makes for a flourishing life or good consequences. The claim of Jeremy Bentham that *nature* has placed us under two sovereign masters, pleasure and pain, is a form of Naturalism. What Naturalists share in common is their rejection of the view that we cannot prove moral judgements true or false – that they're just exclamations (as in emotivism). Instead, moral judgements are realist and can be proven true or false from within the natural world. As you can see, Naturalists make up a broad movement who disagree over which natural features of life are good. Cultural relativists, at one end, would define goodness in terms of society's values. At the other end of the spectrum, objectivist naturalists would locate the good in universal aspects of human identity, like reason or maximising choices and freedom and minimising pain. What they have in common, however, is a commitment to defining morality in terms of natural features of the world.

Emotivism:
The view that any moral claim (e.g. 'Abortion is murder!') is essentially an *emotional* plea on the part of the one who expresses it for others to share such disapproval or adopt this feeling

Ethical Naturalism:
This approach defines 'good' in terms of some natural property of the world, e.g. pleasure, human flourishing. A subjective naturalist might argue that moral statements are true in terms of the attitudes society approves of. An objectivist naturalist might argue that moral statements are true in terms of the attitudes society approves of. An objectivist naturalist might argue that what is good is what will promote human flourishing in harmony with the resources of the planet.

Strengths of Naturalism

1. Moral virtues like justice and truthfulness are too serious to be reduced to a matter of taste and opinion. Naturalism's **moral objectivism**, i.e. its' belief that moral claims can be true or false allows them to be discussed rationally. There are moral truths, and though they may be hard to get at in terms of proof, Naturalism's belief that basing our ethics on features that can be reasoned over and evidenced offers a solid foundation for contesting controversial issues and resolving disputes.

2. Rejecting **Naturalism** and believing that moral claims are nothing but opinions risks nihilism (literally nothingness – no objective values or truths). This gives us little rational defence against tyranny and abuse where 'might makes right'. Affirming Naturalism can motivate protests against injustice or form a basis for natural rights.

> **Moral objectivism:**
> The opposite of subjective ethics, this view holds that moral statements are true independently of what people think or feel

Weaknesses of Naturalism

1. Naturalism typically reduces 'good' and 'evil', 'right' and 'wrong', to natural categories or psychological states such as pleasure and pain, or social approval and disapproval. *Principia Ethica* (1903) by G. E. Moore (1873–1958) advances the 'Open Question Argument' against Naturalism. Suppose a Naturalist says 'What is good (natural) is what maximizes pleasure and minimises pain.' It would remain an open question as to whether what is pleasurable is good. It would be equally senseless (and circular) to ask 'Is pleasure pleasurable?'

2. If Hume is right, then 'ought' statements cannot be derived from 'is' statements. This fact–value gap cannot be bridged by drawing ethical conclusions from non-ethical premises.

3. Naturalism's sense that moral knowledge can be observed in nature or human nature finds it difficult to convince the sceptic that there are moral laws or facts based in nature. Maybe we just have to live with the limits of what humans can know and be certain about.

> **Nihilism:**
> In terms of ethics, Nihilists believe that objectivity is impossible. No moral truth claims exist, or if they do they're unknowable.

Intuitivism

Intuitivists believe that you cannot reduce goodness to a natural property – moral knowledge is just innately or intuitively known with the force of an 'ought' or duty to act. We have a special form of consciousness called intuition that accesses knowledge and gains emotional conviction. This leads to moral judgements and actions. Like prime numbers, goodness is real, but it is known directly to our intuition as opposed to being observable like an object in time or space. H. A. Prichard (1871–1947) saw moral thoughts as twofold: reason gathered the facts of the situation whereas intuition decided *what* to do, providing the motive for action. He thought it mistaken to try to justify moral obligation by analysing it in terms of something else, such as pleasure or social approval – it was intuited directly, rather like how our five senses operate.

Moore's *Principia Ethica* agrees with Plato, against the empiricists, that goodness is objective and independent of humans. He agrees with Hume's fact–value gap, accepting that one cannot move from a descriptive statement like 'Torture causes physical and mental pain' to a moral statement like 'Torture is wrong!' Let's suppose we define a value like goodness or justice in terms of a natural property X (where X = pleasure maximisation, impartial desires or maximising people's choices). In what is known as the *Open Question Argument*, Moore asks whether or not it makes sense to ask the question 'Sure this action maximises pleasure/people's choices, but is it right?' Naturalism's neat reduction of goodness to a natural property fails to work because these are two separate kinds of properties – value and fact. Defining one in terms of the other does nothing to bridge the gap between facts and values. It just leads to circular logic, like saying 'The good is what is pleasurable because What is pleasurable is good.' Despite this, Moore still believes in objective moral knowledge. How it is arrived at is clearly a problem for him. As he writes, 'If I am asked "What is good?", my answer is that good is good and that is the end of the matter. Or if I am asked "How is good to be defined?", my answer is that it cannot be defined and that is all I have to say about it' (Moore 1903, p. 20).

Moore defended a common-sense view of 'good' as something known intuitively to us, and directly rather than defined in terms of another property or description. Moore likens 'goodness' to 'yellow'. Yellow may be defined in terms of reflecting light in a particular manner, but to someone blind from birth given such a definition, 'yellowness' would be pretty meaningless. In this sense goodness is a simple, indefinable quality. Intuitivists claim that moral knowledge is just self-evidently true, like the belief that all memories of the past are not fictional or that our sense experience of the world is not some *Matrix*-like conspiracy. That is to say, it is a basic belief that is not dependent upon some prior proof or justification. Intuitivists like Moore are not claiming that all moral dilemmas resolve themselves as self-evident intuitions guide us. Instead, there are some basic self-evident intuitions like the good of friendship or contemplating beauty that give us moral knowledge (cognition), judgement and motivation to act.

Strengths of intuitionism

Intuitionism: The view that 'good' and 'evil' are objective but indefinable. Basic moral truths are either self-evident or perceived similarly to how our senses experience the physical world.

1. It is morally realist, believing moral values to exist independently of us, so it offers a sense of moral duty or a motive to act. This motivation to act in line with our moral intuitions fits with everyday common-sense morality. Academic ethicists may scratch their heads to offer a watertight argument for why Nazism is wrong, but giving reasons why genocide or concentration camps are wrong seems to sidestep our obvious intuitive sense that objective values have been violated.
2. If successful, like our appreciation of beauty, we can trust our consciousness of moral truths as real, and, without the need for divine commands, we can have a sense of there being duties and objective rights and wrongs.

Weaknesses of intuitivism

1. Intuitivists vary greatly regarding what they take to be self-evident moral truths. Ethical disputes being so controversial, it seems unlikely that anything is quite so self-evident in ethics as the intuitivists claim. Unlike simple concepts like the primary colour yellow, which our eyes see directly, 'goodness' is complex and not always self-evident.

2. Freud and behaviourists like B. F. Skinner would see many of our so-called 'intuitions' as products of parenting, schooling or other forms of cultural and social conditioning. Propagandist states that vilify their enemies or scapegoat minorities set out to indoctrinate their 'moral' claims as self-evidently true in the minds of their citizens. This makes it difficult for intuitivists to separate genuine from fake intuitions.

3. Consider J. L. Mackie's argument from strangeness or 'queerness'. As he puts it, 'If there were objective values, then they would be entities or qualities or relations of a very strange sort, utterly different from anything else in the universe' (Mackie, *Ethics: Inventing Right and Wrong*, Penguin, 1977, p. 38). Moral truths as non-natural properties are just 'queer' in the sense of odd. They are claimed to exist, but in a non-physical, indefinable way. Perhaps a simpler explanation would be to go with the emotivists' suggestion that the origin of morality is in human emotions and that it is a by-product of the way we engage with the world as passional animals in it.

4. According to Hume, it is not beliefs that motivate us, but desires. Beliefs relate to facts (whether natural facts like the tides of the earth being affected by the moon, or non-natural facts such as those intuitivists claim we can have of morality). But the motivation to act comes from desire. The problem is that desires are subjective, so even if I grant that the intuitionist can intuit the moral knowledge that the pain of others should be avoided, this need not motivate me to act in line with it.

Non-cognitivist approaches

Emotivism	A. J. Ayer (1910–89/C. L. Stevenson (1908–79)
Prescriptivism	R. M. Hare (1919–2002)

Cognition refers to acquiring knowledge and understanding through sense experience and logic. Non-cognitivists hold that moral truth claims cannot be known – that is, demonstrated to be true or false as naturalists and intuitivists claim. Take the statements

1. 'Your room attracts mice because it has not been cleaned for weeks!' and
2. 'You ought to clean your room more often!'

The non-cognitivist sees the difference as being that

(1) is a truth claim that can be verified or falsified, whereas
(2) is a moral claim that cannot be verified or falsified.

Now say a parent and a child were to argue over (2), the simple subjectivist would say they were each correct as long as they were speaking sincerely. All moral claims are relative, so each is true for them. Here, emotivism asserts that there are no moral facts

Prescriptivism: Moral statements as commands or imperatives, as opposed to descriptions. Moral terms are used to guide action and prescribe what people are to do to in similar situations. An attempt to move on from emotivism and treat ethical reasoning as rational rather than a form of emotional manipulation, it sticks to 'ought' statements that one lives with consistently.

in the universe, only attitudes, feelings and desires. It also claims that moral statements are non-cognitive – rather than being knowable to reason, they are emotional expressions often aimed at commanding or urging others to feel the same.

Discussion Question

Can we trust our brains to give us an accurate picture of reality, as evolved, naked apes? Darwin wrote, 'the horrid doubt always arises whether the convictions of man's mind, which has been developed from the mind of lower animals, are of any value or at all trustworthy. Would anyone trust the convictions of a monkey's mind, if there are any convictions in such a mind?'

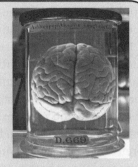

A chimp brain

Emotivism

Emotivism is sometimes caricatured as the 'Hurrah-Boo theory' of ethics. It holds that what may appear on the surface to be a reasoned moral argument is really an emotional appeal to share the positive or negative feelings of its advocate – 'They are calculated to provoke', in the words of the young A. J. Ayer who popularised Hume's scepticism about moral knowledge in his 1936 book *Language, Truth, and Logic*. Ayer believed Moore to be correct about the Naturalistic Fallacy, but thought his belief that we intuited moral knowledge to be nonsense. If I say to a cannibal 'It's appalling that you eat people!', what I'm really doing is asserting my disapproval and wanting them to begin to share my feelings. The logical implication of emotivism is that there need be no real disagreement between two contradictory propositions (e.g. 'Euthanasia is morally wrong'/'Euthanasia ought to be legalised in the UK'). As a logical positivist, Ayer made the bold assertion that such statements were logically neither true nor false by definition and not empirically verified, but rather meaningless. As he wrote, 'The presence of an ethical symbol adds nothing to its content. Thus if I say to someone "You acted wrongly in stealing the money", I am not stating anything more than if I had simply stated, "You stole the money"' (Ayer, Gollancz, 1936, p. 67).

There are, of course, facts involved in moral debate. In genetic engineering, there's a difference between research on stem cells from umbilical cords and on cells taken from aborted foetuses. When we dismiss moral statements as meaningless and pure emotion, this takes little account of how disagreements can relate to facts.

In *Ethics and Language*, C. L. Stevenson argued that disagreements amount to more than expressions of emotion in cases where our attitudes are based upon beliefs held within a social context. As Adam Smith wrote in *The Wealth of Nations*, 'It is not from the benevolence of the butcher, the brewer, or the baker that we expect our dinner, but from their regard to their own interest' (W. Strahan and T. Cadell, 1776, bk 1, ch. 2). Another distinction Stevenson makes is between the meaning and use of a word in a sentence. Words like 'good' or 'wrong' can be used descriptively ('a good

QUICK QUESTION
Emotions voicing praise or blame can be contagious – do these shape behaviour?

pair of pliers' or 'the wrong screwdriver for the screw'), or dynamically ('a good character' or 'the wrong done to a victim'). Used dynamically in a social context in which an emotive meaning is conveyed, words seek to influence others. Hence Stevenson is open-minded about changing other people's minds using rational arguments and attitudes of praise or blame in a social context. Yet the problem is that most of our value judgements are emotive, gut reactions, and consequently immune to reasoning. Stevenson's *moderate emotivism* argues that, to the extent that we can adopt the position of ideal and impartial observers and critically analyse the rationality of our beliefs, we can avoid arguments being propaganda wars that manipulate emotions. There are both cognitive and non-cognitive elements to beliefs in moral debate, and we can reason to the extent that we can unravel the one from the other. To the extent that our feelings can be informed and impartial, we can reason that this kind is preferable to those that are purely emotive. Yet Stevenson agreed with Hume that we are moved to action by desire, and that 'good' has an inescapably emotive sense in persuading and magnetising that would never be wholly rational.

Strengths of emotivism

1. It avoids committing the Naturalistic Fallacy (the claim that right and wrong can be defined in terms of natural facts like pleasure and pain or social approval).
2. It reconceives how we think about ethics after accepting the fact–value distinction. As it is desires, not reasons, that move us to act, it offers a clear account of moral motivation that's free from non-natural properties that moral realists think are somehow built into the fabric of the universe despite being imperceptible to our senses.
3. In grounding ethics in emotion, it accounts for why moral disputes (say over abortion) are often interminable and filled with more heat than light. Emotivism cautions those who would negotiate between disputing parties that reason will have a more modest role given the emotional nature of the human animal in moralising. As a minimalist account of morality that does not go beyond the evidence, this is a strong candidate for the simplest and best explanation of what's going on in moral debate.

Weaknesses of emotivism

1. Reason may be a slave of the passions, but that is not to exclude its role prematurely. It can ask of us that we be consistent, imaginative and informed. It can require that we apply logic to our sentences and arguments. It can ask of us that we live in accord with our claims and judgements on others (where we find ourselves in similar circumstances). Emotivism is too quick to give up on moral reasoning.
2. The US philosopher Brand Blanshard (1892–1987) offered a counterexample to challenge the emotivist. Consider a rabbit caught in a hunter's trap and dying painfully quite out of sight of humans. If right and wrong are merely human emotional reactions, then, in the absence of humans, this is neither wrong nor distressing, like the world before humans arrived on the planet. If humans do

observe the rabbit's suffering and feel bad, the wrongness lasts for as long as their feelings do. If some hikers come upon it and the children eventually get bored of the rabbit and forget about it while the parents feel much happier after lunch, its on-going pain and distress no longer count, according to the emotivist. Blanshard points out the absurdity to the everyday man or woman in the street, of grounding right and wrong in something as fickle as our feelings.

3. If 'good' is defined in terms of emotions, then there is no need to universalise this good and this is more likely to lead to ethical egoism. I might feel better about personal profit than about alleviating global poverty. I might feel like I would hate to be tortured myself, but happy about minimising my risk from terrorism by torturing those suspected of it. Morality as a matter of taste is wide open to persuasion by propaganda, reason having been given up on. But do our moral claims about right and wrong really boil down to trying to get you to share my feelings (e.g. about nuclear weapons or capital punishment)? I may hate Marmite, but this is hardly analogous to hating torture or genocide.

4. If emotions are based upon beliefs or knowledge claims, then they can be reasoned over. For example, if a racist comes to see that their belief is mistaken, this may well change their conduct. But if morality is non-cognitive, then it is hard to see how moral progress can be possible. Were the abolition of the slave trade, voting rights for women, the Equal Pay Act and the establishment of legal rights for disabled people all due only to a change of emotions?

5. If the fact–value distinction can be shown to be mistaken, then emotivism is seen to be built on weak foundations.

Prescriptivism

Prescriptivism is another example of a revised non-cognitivist ethic developed by R. M. Hare. Hare accepted Hume's fact–value distinction and Moore's rejection of the idea that we could define goodness in terms of some property of the natural world. Yet Hare was no ivory tower academic. He had been a prisoner of war held by the Japanese from 1942 to 1945 whilst building the infamous Burma–Thailand Railway. It is hard to assess the role this experience had in his later rejection of the philosophy of logical positivism and emotivism that Ayer had popularised (one which reduced all knowledge to scientific or logical statements and declared moral claims to be meaningless), which had been very influential from the 1930s to the 1950s at Oxford. Yet Hare wanted to show that moral thinking could be a rational activity as opposed to a set of arbitrary emotions or cultural customs. He wanted to go further than simply saying 'I disapprove of the Nazis, please do likewise.' This just seemed woefully inadequate. He wanted to emphasise the importance of both *freedom* and *reason* (the title of his 1963 book). For him, the key was to focus on the character of moral statements as command-like expressions – imperatives. Such 'prescriptions' were 'free' in the sense that we willed or decided upon them as opposed to being emotions we had experienced involuntarily. They were also rational in the sense of being *informed, imaginative and consistent, rather than true or false* (as cognitivism claimed). In making them, we had a duty to take an impartial point of view. As a non-cognitivist, Hare did not seek to bridge the logical gap in sentences between facts and values. Instead he argued that moral judgements do not so much describe how the world is as prescribe how it should be – moral prescriptions were universal guides to choice and action.

Indeed, Hare's 'universal prescriptivism' distinguished moral judgements from other non-moral commands (such as 'Close the windows!') by their universalisability. Ideal observers would have the impartial, near-omniscient and benevolent nature of archangels. Prescriptivism's emphasis on exercising our free and rational natures by adopting the standpoint of the ideal observer drew on Kant's Categorical Imperative and the New Testament's golden rule to 'love your neighbour as you love yourself' (Hare was Christian). Yet Hare argued that 'ought' was a word that looked both in the direction of universal prescriptions and in the direction that suited its users' interests in highly specific maxims as free and rational individuals acted in their particular time and place. Hare himself wrote on political, military and biomedical ethics.

Survivors of a concentration camp demonstrate to General Eisenhower torture methods used on prisoners, 1945

For Hare, 'ought' statements like 'Torture ought to be condemned and illegal' meant 'Be logically consistent in similar cases' (e.g. reject torture by a criminal gang, a legitimate democratically elected state and a tyrannical regime) and 'Live as we would want others to live.' As he puts it, 'If we have to will our maxims as universal laws, we have to will that they should be observed in all situations resembling one another' (R. M. Hare, *Sorting out Ethics*, Oxford University Press, 1997, p. 133). If I would not want to be tortured, it would be inconsistent and therefore irrational to will or desire that another person be tortured. We also need to be informed about how unreliable information gained under torture often is, as well as imaginative in understanding the impact of even short-term torture on the mind and emotions of an individual and their family for life. Hare's emphasis on the need to be consistent is illustrated in the true case of the Nazi fanatic who was committed to the final solution of wiping out all Jews only to discover that he was himself descended from a Jewish grandmother. He confessed this to the Nazi authorities, which resulted in his death. As a non-cognitivist, Hare could not claim that this action was morally incorrect or false. He could, however, show that, if universalised, such terrifying fanaticism strikes us as deeply irrational and destructive. In Hare's Preference Utilitarianism, universalising maxims require us to be consistent, informed and imaginative.

Strengths of prescriptivism

As the points listed below indicate, prescriptivism offers a form of non-cognitivism that eludes most of the criticisms made of emotivism.

> **Moral realism:**
> The view that claims are true in respect of how they correspond to the real world. Moral realists hold that moral statements can in principle be verified or falsified – there is an objective reality to them. This may, for example, derive from God's created moral order or commands, but not all realists are theists.

1. Emotivism tends to see us caught up in emotions that we may later rationalise (for example, I may have a gut reaction in favour of capital punishment and then seek to justify this). For emotivists, what's really going on in moral judgements is the expression of emotions. In prescriptivism, we are more *free and rational* in respect of how informed, imaginative and consistent we are. In this sense, whilst we cannot access **moral realism** in terms of the natural world, we can speak of moral judgements or prescriptions that are irrational or those that have greater or lesser degrees of rationality. Even after rejecting the idea that we access objective moral knowledge, there is still immense value in reflecting upon our choice of moral actions as individuals and societies, and in holding people responsible for the rationality of the principles and actions they prescribe.

2. Moral debates need not be viewed as emotional manipulation or persuasion like marketing, lobbying or propagandising. You can offer advice to someone perplexed by a dilemma in a rational manner, asking if their position is informed, imaginative and consistent, or whether the principle they seek to act by is universalisable. Here you are not manipulating them to align with your feelings about an issue, but informing their independent, free and rational judgement. Thus the private moral anxiety felt in facing a dilemma makes sense as the desire to be consistent or to be rational regarding universalising the maxim or principle by which we act.

3. Prescriptivism is practical and motivates action by giving a greater role to reason than emotivism does. If everyone universally acted consistent with their commands to others and those commands were imaginative and informed, this would take us a lot further towards a better world than mere emotivism.

Weaknesses of prescriptivism

1. In her 1958 lecture 'Moral Beliefs', Philippa Foot argues that prescriptivism justifies fanaticism. Hare mentions the objection of 'a fanatical black hater who is prepared to [follow the universal prescription] to keep all black people in subjection even if he himself were a black person'. Prescriptivism's condemnation of such racism in terms of being irrational in the sense of uninformed, unimaginative or inconsistent seems weak. Prescriptivists would respond by saying that they offer powerful reasons to reject racism and teach others to do so. Prescriptivism cannot prove racism to be false, but, rather, to be irrational because it cannot be reasonably and universally prescribed. Nevertheless, to be fanatical in your prescriptions is to be fanatical (e.g. in the case of a racist who considers him/herself inferior by accepting the racism of others).

Exercise

1. Yossarian – 'From now on I'm thinking only of me.'
   Major Danby replied indulgently with a superior smile, 'But Yossarian, suppose everyone felt that way?'
   'Then I'd certainly be a fool to feel any other way, wouldn't I?'
   (Joseph Heller, *Catch 22*)
   Is there any flaw in Yossarian's logic here?

2. How would you respond to the following statements?

   1. *Swimming underwater is unnatural, anything unnatural is wrong, therefore swimming underwater is wrong.*
   2. *As there are no proofs in ethics, we may as well admit that any moral claim is just as subjective as any other.*
   3. *If it makes you happy, it can't be that bad (Sheryl Crow).*
   4. *Boxing and fox hunting just make me feel sick – of course they're immoral – anyone who needs an argument for why these are wrong is heartless.*
   5. *Prostitution is wrong simply means 'I disapprove of prostitution.'*
   6. *We don't need moral facts. There are enough foundations for society if people just act consistently with their desire for freedom in respecting that of others.*
   7. *All moral claims are relative to their time and place. Slavery and human sacrifice were right by the standards of some cultures in the past. Who are we to judge them by our standards?*
   8. *Cultures are different from each other, so it follows that no one culture is any better than another.*
   9. *You can't put moral intuitions into words – you just innately or instinctively know right from wrong.*

3. 'Now an action done from duty must wholly exclude the influence of inclination' (Kant). Does this set Kant on a collision course with Virtue Ethics, which emphasises that training in virtues or certain dispositions of character more likely to lead to human flourishing is a morally good thing?

4. 'By morality the individual is taught to become a function of the herd, and to ascribe to himself value only as a function' (Friedrich Nietzsche).

   Is morality a veiled way for the herd or mass of people to enforce conformity by emphasising duties and obligations?

5. What, if anything, do the following uses of the term 'good' have in common?

   The Lord of the Rings is a good film
   Mother Teresa was a good person
   Eagles are good predators
   Luis Suarez is a good footballer
   God is good
   My lunch was good today
   That's a good smartphone you have there

2. The man-in-the-street would be scandalised to hear professional ethicists say that rape, theft and murder were not objectively wrong. Does this mean that what's wrong about the rabbit example mentioned above is that what makes the suffering of the rabbit bad is the prescription that this is bad by the observer? Here prescriptivists might argue that if everyone prescribed animal traps as illegal, the problem could be solved. But prescriptivism can seem arbitrary when a gamekeeper who culls rabbits prescribes traps as good and a walker who keeps pet rabbits prescribes them as bad.

Conclusion

Since the 1960s, many philosophers have seen the gap between facts and values as able to be bridged by our practical reasoning in interpersonal and social contexts. The philosopher Philippa Foot, who studied at Oxford and worked as a government economist during World War II, reflected on her experience of returning to Oxford in 1945: 'in the face of the news of the concentration camps, I thought, "It just can't be the way Stevenson, Ayer, and Hare say it is, that morality is just an expression of attitude"' (Alex Voorhoeve, *Conversations on Ethics*, Oxford University Press, reprint 2011, p. 91). She and other philosophers have challenged the fact–value distinction of Hume and Moore. One attempt to bridge the gap is set out by John Searle in the following argument (in *The Construction of Social Reality*, Penguin, 1996, p. 77):

1. Jones utters the words 'I hereby promise to pay you, Smith, 5 dollars.'
2. Jones promised to pay Smith 5 dollars.
3. Jones placed himself under (undertook) an obligation to pay Smith 5 dollars.
4. Jones is under an obligation to pay Smith 5 dollars.
5. Jones ought to pay Smith 5 dollars.

Searle argues that the gap between facts and values is bridged by '*institutional facts*' as opposed to 'brute facts'. That is to say, social practice makes the descriptive statements tie in with the evaluative ones here – the 'is' or factual statement in the community to which Jones and his debtor belong carries the force of a moral 'ought' or obligation. Many philosophers now argue that the fact–value gap was exaggerated in Hume and Moore. Facts and values are entangled in much of human behaviour, e.g. art, architecture, mathematics and science, so why should they not be in the practical rationality of moral thought? Pragmatists would argue that 'knowledge of facts presupposes knowledge of values'. For example, building a telescope or a microscope or designing an experiment presupposes that you value the knowledge that this instrument may possibly yield. As Hilary Putnam puts it, 'The logical positivist fact/value dichotomy was defended on the basis of a narrow scientistic picture of what a "fact" might be, just as the Humean ancestor of that distinction was defended on the basis of a narrow empiricist psychology of "ideas" and "impressions"' (Putnam, *Ethics Without Ontology*, Harvard University Press, new edition, 2004). In response to the economist Milton Friedman's claim that, over differences of value, 'men can ultimately only fight', what meta-ethical discussion deliberates over is the role of reason, emotion, and knowledge in our moral judgements. Insofar as we are rational beings, moral deliberation can yield reasons to motivate us to act rationally. Perhaps this could be along the lines of Derek Parfit's formula in *On What Matters* (Oxford University Press, 2013, vol. I, p. xxii) – 'Everyone ought to follow the principles whose universal acceptance everyone could rationally will and no-one could reasonably reject.'

Discussion Questions

1. Do you find Searle's attempt to bridge the gap between facts and values to be persuasive? Give reasons for your view.
2. Think back to Philippa Foot's example of a fanatic who universally wishes ill upon a certain group and consistently follows through on this even when (to their shock) their ideology calls for self-hatred. How might a prescriptivist like Hare have responded to this criticism of their theory?
3. Assign student A to be a cognitivist, and student B to be a non-cognitivist. Debate the strengths and weaknesses of your conception of what's going on in morality.
4. Assume, for argument's sake, that morality is purely based upon human feelings and is non-cognitive. Does this give us enough to work with in building a stable society and a practical way of living in which humans can live peaceably and flourish together?
5. Which of the above theories might consider human rights to be no more than a legal fiction? Which would reject this belief?

FURTHER READING

Andrew Fisher (2011) *Meta-ethics, An Introduction*. Acumen Publishing

David S. Oderberg (2000) *Moral Theory: A Non-Consequentialist Approach*. Wiley-Blackwell

Hugh LaFollette and Ingmar Persson (2013) *The Blackwell Guide to Ethical Theory*. Wiley-Blackwell

Harry J. Gensler (2000) *Ethics: A Contemporary Introduction*. Routledge

Alex Miller (2003) *Contemporary Metaethics: An Introduction*. Polity

OCR Past Paper Questions

JANUARY 2010
To what extent is ethical language meaningful?   *[35]*

JUNE 2011
'Ethical statements are no more than expressions of emotion.' Discuss.   *[35]*

JANUARY 2012
'All ethical language is prescriptive.' Discuss.   *[35]*

JUNE 2012
To what extent do moral statements have objective meaning?   *[35]*

JUNE 2013
Critically assess the view that the word 'good' has no real meaning.   *[35]*

11 Free Will and Determinism

Introduction: how free are you?

Would it trouble you to be told that your actions are determined and that there are no alternatives to your 'choices'? Consider the complex chains of causes that precede your decisions; your family upbringing, education and wider environment shape you, while the chances are that what you buy or wear owes much to the advertising that shaped your desires into needs. The political and economic context you find yourself in, when and where you live, together with your genes, determine many of your life decisions. Still confident that you are free?

You might argue that, despite such constraints, the experience of wrestling over your choices and decisions is undeniable: that you have significant freedom over which university, relationship or job to choose. You might say that, unless it is possible to distinguish between deliberate and unintentioned actions, then praise or blame is pointless.

Yet perhaps the mainstream view in contemporary philosophy is that the everyday

Is life a predetermined path with no real forks in the road?

sense of freedom as having real *alternative possibilities* or a future with forking paths is an illusion. Much of this debate hinges upon our definition of freedom. Two opposing definitions are:

Liberty of spontaneity. This defines freedom as the feeling that we are free. We're not conscious of being forced to act by anyone outside of ourselves, but voluntarily choose our own actions, beliefs or thoughts.

Liberty of indifference. The ordinary sense of free will is taken to mean the ability to have done otherwise than we did. The term 'indifference' is used because we could take it or leave it, or go either way on the choice at hand. This is in line with our common intuition of being torn over choices. It also explains our frequently strong feelings of praise or blame for the 'choices' of others. Both the hard determinist and the libertarian are agreed upon this fuller definition of freedom. The libertarian firmly believes that such freedom does exist. The hard determinist affirms that any claim of a person making a 'free' choice ought to satisfy this definition, whilst denying that such freedom exists.

Exercise

Rate the following scenarios in descending order of the person's/animal's responsibility for the harm done. If you attribute no blame, put NB, but justify your reasoning.

Scenarios (1 = most responsible, 7 = least responsible)

[_] A cat stalks a bird in your garden, catching and killing it.

[_] Unaware of the one-way system in a town you visit, you drive you car the wrong way down a street, causing traffic chaos and incurring a fine and three points on your licence.

[_] Thumper Hard is a thief who, in most cases, true to type, steals. But on one occasion when he breaks into a house and sees an old woman who reminds him of his mother, he remembers the promise he made to her on her death bed that he would lead an honest life and does not go through with his theft.

[_] A woman who has been kidnapped falls in love with her kidnapper and thereafter 'willingly' takes part in several robberies before being caught by the police.

[_] A kleptomaniac with a compulsive desire to shoplift (though they can afford to pay) faces prosecution, having stolen from a shop.

[_] A nuclear physicist advises what appears to be a legitimate energy company but it turns out to be a rogue state developing a nuclear weapon.

[_] A student 'chooses' a break-time drink and chocolate bar from a school vending machine, 'choosing' a leading brand, which uses product endorsement by sports stars and huge advertising campaigns to shape customer choice.

[_] You make a promise to drive your grandmother to a hospital appointment but stop en route to help at the scene of an accident, which prevents you from making it to your granny's.

[_] You see a player collapse at a school football match and know how to do CPR, but fear you might be sued if anything goes wrong, so you do not intervene.

[_] Modern humans have an excessive appetite for junk food because, for tens of thousands of years, sugar and fat were scarce and vital parts of their ancestors' diet. Even though refined sugar and saturated fats are now easy to come by, this evolutionary drive in our psychology remains.

Are we responsible for our actions? Case study: the 1924 Leopold and Loeb murder trial

In 1924, Nathan Leopold and Richard Loeb, sons of prosperous Chicago families, murdered an acquaintance of theirs, fourteen-year-old Bobby Franks. Franks was walking home from school when the two asked him to discuss a tennis racquet in their hired car. Killing him with a chisel, they poured acid on his body to make identification difficult, before dumping it and burning his clothes. Described as 'the trial of the century', leading defence lawyer Clarence Darrow changed their plea to guilty, thereby succeeding in switching the trial by jury (at a time when the public were intent on the death penalty) to a hearing before a judge.

Eighteen-year-old Richard Loeb was raised by a controlling and strict governess and had previously planned and executed petty crimes. Then in 1924, the 'weird and almost impossible' relationship between him and Nathan Leopold spurred the two on to commit murder. Leopold was influenced by his reading of Nietzsche's *Beyond Good and Evil*. He viewed himself and Loeb as elites above the requirements of conventional morality. Loeb had trouble distinguishing the real world from that of the detective novels he read voraciously. But they were soon caught. While struggling to conceal the body, Leopold had dropped a pair of horn-rimmed tortoise-shell glasses with a hinge that was traced to a Chicago optometrist who had supplied only three such prescriptions, one of them to Leopold. Further evidence concerning a typed ransom note and the collapse of their alibis led to the conclusion that they were guilty.

Defence Attorney Clarence Darrow successfully defends Leopold and Loeb against execution

Darrow argues the *Leopold–Loeb* case before Judge Caverly

The trial is most remembered for Clarence Darrow's 'guilty' plea. He blended science and emotion, spoke of their genetic inheritance, drew in expert psychologists, and eloquently addressed Judge Caverly with the words 'where responsibility is divided by twelve, it is easy to say "away with him"; but, your Honour, if these boys are to hang, you must do it — . . . it must be by your cool, premeditated act, without a chance to shift responsibility'.

Whilst he impressed upon the judge his responsibilities, diminishing his clients' responsibility was at the heart of Darrow's defence. Overruling the prosecution, Judge Caverly admitted expert psychiatric evidence of the accused's obsessions with Nietzschean philosophy, and crime and detective novels, as well as with one another. Their emotional immaturity, sexual longings, alcohol abuse and glandular abnormalities were cited as mitigating factors. The most famous lines of Darrow's 12-hour plea are:

> Nature is strong and she is pitiless. She works in mysterious ways, and we are her victims. We have not much to do with it ourselves. Nature takes this job in hand, and we only play our parts . . . What had this boy to do with it? He was not his own father; he was not his own mother . . . All of this was handed to him. He did not surround himself with governesses and wealth. He did not make himself. And yet he is to be compelled to pay.

In pleading that Leopold be spared, Darrow said, 'Tell me that you can visit the wrath of fate and chance and life and eternity upon a nineteen-year-old boy!'

1. Do you consider Darrow's defence on the grounds of diminished responsibility legitimate? What role (e.g. protection, deterrence, reform, retribution, reconditioning) does punishment play if we regard human actions as determined? Does diminishing responsibility undermine justice?
2. What difference is there between an ordinary thief (who deliberates and wrestles with his sense of the outcome and the imprudence of stealing) and a kleptomaniac who compulsively steals, other than that the latter is determined and the former is not?
3. Does the consequence argument (that if determinism is true, then all actions are consequences of past events and the laws of nature and hence not up to us) establish that free will is incompatible with determinism?

In the debate over free will and determinism, the dispute focuses on *what it means to be free*. Hard determinists and libertarians both agree that freedom requires *alternative possibilities* and that choices need to be (at least in part) *rationally willed* by the agent. Compatibilists see free will as compatible with determination as long as we're unaware of being forced into our decisions and *feel them to have been freely made*. The following diagram illustrates how the debate hinges on the compatibility of free will and determinism.

Table 4   Compatibilists vs incompatibilists

Compatibilists hold that freedom need not have alternative possibilities or originate from within in the agent.	*Incompatibilists* argue that voluntariness (making freely willed decisions), alternative possibilities and Self-Formed Actions are necessary to freedom.	
Soft determinism	Hard determinism	Libertarianism
All choices are caused – the idea of uncaused choices that are self-originating in the individual is rejected – this would be out of character or irrational. Insofar as our actions are internally rather than externally caused (i.e. we will them without feeling forced to do so), they are 'free' and we can be held responsible as the immediate cause of them. E.g. a drug addict may appear 'determined' to steal to feed their habit, but nonetheless be held accountable for their crimes as the immediate cause of their crime was internal to themselves (they willed it).	This has been defined as 'the belief that a determined set of conditions can only produce one possible outcome given fixed laws of nature'. It also applies to human action in terms of natural laws, hereditary and environmental causes that inevitably bring about their effects. Of course we do not observe every cause and effect, so this is an inference from our observations which suggests, in principle, that all effects have preceding causes. Punishment is not about just deserts but limiting future consequences by deterring crime or reconditioning criminal behaviour.	People are capable of acting rationally and are in certain cases free to do otherwise than they do. They ought to be held accountable because they can make conscious and rational choices. The loss of individual responsibility seems to follow from hard determinism. Yet writers like Sartre argue that we often act in 'bad faith' — as passive objects acted upon by external forces — because we fear the radical freedom we have. There is safety in divesting ourselves of such responsibility and handing it over to authority figures.
Compatibilists past and present include: Hobbes, Locke, Hume, Mill and Dennett.	Hard determinists include Honderich, Pavlov and Skinner.	Libertarians include Bergson and Sartre, and, in a moderated way, Kant and Kane.

Hard determinism's two key concepts

1. Universal causality
2. Causal necessity

Hard determinism asserts that in any event, given the momentum of earlier causes, there can be only one possible outcome. There are only *apparent* forks in the road, and genuine alternative choices are an illusion. On a personal level, Determinists still have moments of indecision and the feeling of making choices. This is because, despite cause and effect being like a domino chain (albeit with multiple causes), we cannot outrun our nature and live as determinists.

Imagine a chain of events in time as a series of dominoes. Event 1 (E1) is, for example, an addictive personality who takes their first drink. This leads to E2 (alcoholism) and this, in turn, to E3 (liver disease).

> **Hard determinism:**
> The view that human beings do not have any free will because they are controlled by some external force. Humans cannot be held responsible for their actions.

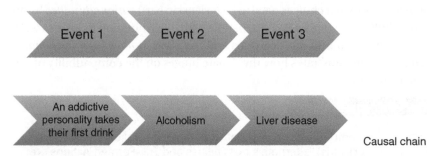

Causal chain

Universal causality is the idea that *every* event results from prior causes. This includes your every desire, choice, action, feeling, because your every brain state results from prior causes.

Causal necessity is the claim that the chain of cause and effect is such that effects must necessarily follow on from prior causes. This may be obvious in more predictable outcomes such as dominoes tumbling. But for the hard determinist, human brains are made of atoms and every bit as much objects in the physical world. *If all the causal inputs could ever be known and computed, then our neurobiological systems would in theory be predictable.*

The idea that our actions are largely determined may appear bleak and depressing. Yet for physicalists, who hold that everything in the universe is matter and energy, our brains are shaped by the totality of prior causes that precede them. It is at this point that a divide appears between *compatibilists* and *incompatibilists*. *Compatibilists* see determinism sitting comfortably with our *feeling* of freely willing our choices, on the one hand, and being determined to make them, on the other. This may seem contradictory, but s*oft determinists* hold that *we can never outrun our nature*. Even as determinists, they freely admit to having indecisive moments at the supermarket or over which job or university to apply for. Yet, with David Hume, the eighteenth-century philosopher, they recognise that we are *passional more than rational*, or, as he put it, 'reason is and ought only to be the slave of the passions, and can never pretend to any other office than to serve and obey them' (*A Treatise of Human Nature*

1789). The multiple causal inputs into our present moment mean that we will never be fully aware of the degree to which we have choices. The alcoholic's choice to have a drink may not appear to him/her to be any less free than that of the social drinker.

In contrast, for *libertarians,* there is a fork in the road, with two or more genuine paths to travel down. These are not necessarily fixed prior to the point of decision (though in the case of an alcoholic's or kleptomaniac's choices, they may well be). You could decide on a course, a university, a job or a partner, or have taken a different turn. We define our individual character by our choices. Event 1 (getting good A Level results) is followed by Event 2 (going to a university fair where you learn about courses on offer) to a fork in the road – (choosing your future university). For libertarians, there really is a choice to be made – you could go either way based on your own free and rational decision-making process. For determinists, subtly, your parent(s) or guardian(s), school, the careers fair, where you live, costs and access to information would have shaped your preferences. Compatibilists would be in-between – we may have marginal choices and elbow room in overcoming behavioural patterns through analysing their subconscious causes and consciously overcoming them (e.g. a phobia of heights, spiders or exams).

Hard determinism – a key thinker: Ted Honderich

Ted Honderich is concerned about the implications for our lives if determinism is true (which, in his view, it is, sadly). Honderich reduces our choices to psycho-neural events determined by earlier causes. As he writes, 'It follows . . . about states of the brain as effects . . . that on every occasion when we decide or choose, we can only decide or choose as we do.' And, unlike the cheerful compatibilist who sees choice as the feeling that we are not forced against our will by external causes, Honderich is 'dismayed' by the austerity of the hard determinist view. Our 'life hopes', that is our sense that we are agents with some voluntary and self-originated choices about our futures must take a battering if we are to appreciate the implications of hard determinism. He is adamant that we have to give up on the hope that there is some kind of dualist self at home in our minds and able to originate top-down control of our brain states, a 'ghost in the machine' turning the steering wheel and taking forks in the road of life's journey.

As he writes, 'States of the brain are, in the first place, effects, the effects of other physical states ... all actions are movements caused by states of the brain.'

Yet for all of Honderich's dismay over determinism, he sees two types of life hopes, one of which is doomed, but the other lives on after determinism has been accepted. We must abandon the hope of an open future of forking paths or the origination of actions within the minds or deliberation of agents. Yet this does not destroy all 'life hopes'; we can still shape our attitudes, embracing enabling circumstances rather than frustrating ones, or being free of obvious constraints or able to act independently of others. This is not the contented compatibilism of Hume in which, as long as an action is voluntarily willed and without obvious external constraint or coercion, it may be cheerfully said to be free and at the same time determined. Honderich has

Philosopher Ted Honderich. It is worth looking up Honderich's website on Determinism and Freedom at ucl.ac.uk as it offers essays from a wide range of thinkers.

felt depressed at reaching the conclusion that our intentions, desires, and delibera-tions are consequences of brain states and causal chains that we did not ourselves originate, any more than our 'choices' and 'decisions' themselves.

Honderich argues that the familiar debate between compatibilists and incompati-bilists is missing the point. It is not a question of compatibilism or incompatibilism being true or false, for that is incoherent and meaningless. Rather, it is a question of how our attitude towards freedom is worked out practically.

In *A Theory of Determinism* (Clarendon Press, 1990, vol. II) and *How Free are You?* (2002), Honderich addresses various challenges to, and problems faced by, determin-ism, e.g.:

1. The argument that quantum theory in physics offers us 'uncaused causes' – a level of indeterminacy or randomness in the world which may also exist in the brain. Honderich rejects randomness as making room for free will as he sees brain states occurring at the subatomic level and not transferring up to the level of brain states that affect decisions and choices.
2. The incompatibilist's objection that we cannot both be determined and be held responsible for our behaviour. Indeterminists argue that, once freedom (that allows for voluntary and self-originated actions) is removed, we cannot praise or blame people or hold them morally responsible for their actions. In contrast, Honderich believes that we are quite capable of what he terms 'intransigent' (unmovable and fixed in our human nature) attitudes of moral approval or disap-proval, even though an agent could not have done otherwise than they did. Such toughness runs deep in our veins and it is hard to outrun our natural instincts. On the other hand, compatibilists like Hume seem to brush over the real sense of loss and dismay arising from what Honderich terms the 'life hope' of origination, with the idea that our voluntary and self-forming actions leave a certain degree of openness to our futures. So Honderich rejects both compatibilism and incom-patibilism. The view that we have free will, either in the form of alternative pos-sibilities or as simply the feeling of making voluntary choices, is mistaken. But we can still shape our attitudes to be affirming of the future rather than despairing, and this can affect our sense of self and our approach to life.

What's the point of punishment if actions are determined?

Honderich rejects the idea that we have either–or choices in life. In his 2005 book *Punishment: The Supposed Justifications Revisited,* he argues that punishment can have a limited role in allowing society to keep offenders from living bad lives (that diminish such goods as longevity, health, knowledge, etc.). The commonly felt emo-tions of praise and blame help to satisfy victims or their families in retributive justice, but this is often far from constructive. Equally dubious motives for punishment arise in the Utilitarian logic that argues for the benefits of deterring crime by setting stiff punishments that become part of the risk vs reward logic of would-be offenders.

Honderich sees the impact of deterrence as being hard to measure. In its place, he sees the reality as being that rich and powerful elites shape the retributive systems of punishment in US and UK society in ways that benefit their self-interest. We ought to aim at 'the principle of humanity', in which we take rational steps to keep people from living bad lives, and in which their health, power relationships, knowledge and self-respect are promoted in laws that accord with this principle. Justice should be forward-looking rather than backward-looking.

> Thought experiment: *Imagine you are one of only two people left on planet Earth. You are a terminally ill judge who has imprisoned the other survivor (who murdered a third, now deceased survivor). You have it in your power to execute this prisoner. What do you do?*

> Only a highly retributivist view of justice would go ahead arguing that 'regardless of the consequences, it's the principle of a life for a life'. Other purposes of justice would be future-focused and these could be supported by compatibilists and even some hard determinists : protection (as a form of quarantine); reconditioning (perhaps through cognitive behavioural therapy to retrain the desires of a prisoner or condition them to respect authority and be repelled by violence); or deterrence (to make examples of criminals with harsh penalties in order to shape the conditions that determine the behaviour of some criminals).

In addition to the points mentioned above, Determinists find support for their position from the following.

Evolutionary psychology and neuroscience

> I would lay down my life for two brothers, or eight cousins.
> (British biologist J. B. S. Haldane in the 1950s)

Daniel Dennett, Steven Pinker and Richard Dawkins stress that we had limited knowledge of human nature prior to 1859 and the publication of Darwin's *On the Origin of Species*. As we are different in degree, rather than kind, from our mammalian ancestors, our genes have evolved over millions of years (chiefly, for humans, during the Pleistocene Era). Our inclinations and desires make us 'freely' want to pursue certain courses of action that aid the survival and reproduction of our genes. Appetites for food, drink, sex, knowledge and the nurturing of the young are there in our brain chemistry as they are in that of all higher primates. We have genetically based dispositions to approve or disapprove of certain behaviours as seen in phobias, our eye for beauty, our tendency to fall in love, or the desire for honour and revenge. In his book *On Human Nature*, sociobiologist E. O. Wilson writes that 'there is an innate predisposition to manufacture the cultural apparatus of aggression' (*On Human Nature*, Harvard University Press, 1978). Yet this is not uniformly expressed, as our brains are evolved to be highly adaptive to the environment they find themselves in. This would explain how, despite the similarity of our fight-or-flight responses, the rates of violent crimes vary a great deal between countries. The genotype does not determine the phenotype; even in the womb, twins can experience different environments. Another survival trait with evolutionary logic is kinship altruism, which can be seen in the devotion shown to offspring

(children possess 50 per cent of a parent's genes and 25 per cent of grandparents').
Reciprocal altruism (the logic of you scratch/watch my back, I'll scratch/watch
yours) also develops out of the reproductive advantage of knowing who to trust
and how to detect 'cheats'.

Some thinkers see free will as a by-product of evolution in developing the cerebral cortex/frontal lobe of our ancestors. This enabled complex language, the
passing on of learning to future generations, a greater empathy and emotional
intelligence, and perhaps even the capacity to expand this circle of altruism to
include a strong sense of obligation to those who have no capacity to pay it back,
difficult as this is. As Richard Dawkins writes, 'Let us try to teach generosity and
altruism because we are born selfish' (Dawkins, *The Selfish Gene*, Oxford University
Press, 1976, p. 200). In *The Selfish Gene*'s chapter on Memes, he even concludes
by saying

> our conscious foresight . . . could save us from the worst selfish excesses of the blind
> replicators . . . We have the power to defy the selfish genes of our birth and, if necessary,
> the selfish memes of our indoctrination. We can even discuss ways of deliberately
> cultivating and nurturing pure altruism – something which has no place in nature . . . We
> are built as gene machines and cultured as meme machines, but we have the power to
> turn against our own creators. We, alone on earth, can rebel against the tyranny of the
> selfish replicators.

Genetics and epigenetics

The study of epigenetics (how our genes switch on and off or express themselves in relation to variables like our lifestyle, diet, environment, stress levels,
etc.) has focused greater attention on the interaction between genes and their
environment. One such example is seen in the incest taboo in which a negative
imprinting stage occurs during early childhood that normally prevents sexual
attraction to family members in adulthood. Another might be that genetic pre-
dispositions to heart disease could be switched on or off depending upon diet
and exercise. The more we know about this, then arguably the less genetically
determined we are.

Behaviouralism

Behavioural psychology finds its roots in experimental studies of animal conditioning. In the early 1900s Nobel Prize-winning physiologist Ivan Pavlov (1849-1936)
turned to experimental psychology, studying how dogs came to associate the sound
of a bell with the food they were given when it rang. They came to form such strong
associations with the unconditioned reflex of salivating on receiving food that the
mere ringing of a bell would bring it on. Behaviouralist experiments and method
were later applied to human psychology and found that we too could be conditioned
to associate emotional responses with events, for example fear with dental appoint-
ments, or pleasure with shopping.

Scientific psychology holds to a belief in causal determinism. Science can be seen as an inductive argument based upon the assumption that modelling cause-and-effect patterns can yield a high degree of predictability. People may be the 'efficient cause' of their behaviour, but the final cause lies in past events and external influences that nurtured or conditioned their responses. Our environment has conditioned us to respond in specific ways through behavioural reinforcements. In 1920 Watson and Rayner even conditioned a young boy called Albert (by using a loud noise paired with a white rat) to respond anxiously towards it, even generalising this to a fur coat. Behaviouralist B. F. Skinner (1904–90) performed experiments on pigeons, training them to peck at a green light and avoid a red one through the dispensing of seed when the 'operant' was successful. Skinner's emphasis on positive reinforcement continues to influence educational theory today, praise rather than blame being at the heart of good practice for, as he said, 'we don't want to be punished for doing what we want'. In a similar way, our purchasing choices as consumers can be conditioned through positive associations with certain brands, celebrity endorsement or the loyalty associated with a successful team.

Behaviouralists view the punishment of humans as more complex than, but analogous to, the puppy training of dogs, and as shaped entirely by their environment. Temper tantrums in young children can be overcome by consistently ignoring such behaviour for a period of non-reinforcement. Here the negative conditioning is achieved by such behaviour delivering no positive goals (such as attention-gaining or sweets at the supermarket counter). As their nurture and conditioning is still in formation, young offenders in particular have more potential to be reconditioned – perhaps de-sensitised to empathy or conditioned to develop a stronger aversion to gang culture. Sadly, however, prison environments can dehumanise inmates and strengthen their loyalties within the criminal world, causing greater levels of re-offence.

It would be wrong to see psychology as wholly deterministic. Contemporary approaches in psychology emphasise the individual and draw on a range of person-centred, behaviouralist and cognitivist approaches. Cognitivist psychologists believe that human thought impacts upon behaviour and therefore cannot be the same as unconsciously conditioned behaviour. Consequently, they give greater value to a person's rational will and intentions in making progress and breakthroughs in counselling or treatment. If subconscious phobias over heights, dogs, exams or relationships are identified, patients who are willing to work at confronting their fears can overcome them. They need to engage actively with treatments such as exposure therapy (e.g. gradually taming their fear of heights in increasing challenges), or by reinforcing positive responses. Where the thoroughgoing determinist would argue that, if one were able to control the exact same stimuli from the outset of a life, the same or highly similar outcomes would result, cognitivists would be happier to admit less uniformity of behaviour.

Exercise

Research:
- The Milgram experiment
- Zimbardo's Prison Experiment
- *Walden Two* by B. F. Skinner – a novel about a utopia set up by a hard determinist psychologist.

Do such studies demonstrate that the individual is so moulded by the social environment and conditions in which they are placed that any choices they suppose to be free are likely to be caused or determined for them? If so, in what sense are the individual guards responsible when they become vicious and tyrannical, or prisoners when they riot?

Thomas Nagel on consciousness and moral luck

Philosopher Thomas Nagel (1937–) thinks that the attempt to take an objective stance external to ourselves is bound to fail 'since some knower must remain behind the lens if anything is to be known' (Gary Watson (ed.), *Freewill*, Oxford University Press, 2007, p. 246). Unlike a cat stalking a bird, entirely in the present and unselfconscious, we can observe ourselves in a detached mode. We sense a capacity to 'subject our immediate impulses to objective scrutiny' (ibid., p. 252). A 'Blind Spot' appears when we're not in a detached, objective mode, but rather, in the world of interpersonal emotions and holding ourselves or others responsible for their actions, and praising or blaming. Nagel's 2012 book *Mind and Cosmos* rejects attempts to reduce consciousness to physical processes or brain states. Biological organisms are made up of genetic information and yet humans have a sense of there being more than purely physical properties in nature. Mind, or the subjective sense of what it is like to deliberate, should make us sceptical of reductive hard determinism. To recognise desires and emotions arising in our nature and stand back from them points us to the mystery of mind or consciousness, which is at the heart of the problem of free will and determinism.

On the other hand, Nagel recognises that we often have little control over choices, outcomes and circumstances in terms of what he calls 'moral luck'. This term refers to circumstances that can have a huge bearing on our choices and decisions but over which we have no control. Our personality or the chain of events we find ourselves in can lead to promotion or to prison. Living through a civil war or having to fight to stay alive during genocide, as opposed to living and working in peaceful and prosperous times, may alter the course of our decisions and character. Being a victim of crime or abuse can leave permanent psychological scars that shape our character. Moral luck shows us that much of our decision-making is often beyond our control. Nagel cautions against too zealous an emphasis on considering humans praiseworthy or blameworthy for all of their actions or circumstances. Often moral luck plays its part as much as the merits or demerits of a person's character and choices.

Weaknesses of hard determinism

1. Susan Blakemore (1951) states that 'it makes no sense (in scientific terms) to distinguish sharply between acts that result from conscious attention and those that result from our reflexes or damage to the brain'. (*The Mind Machine*, 1999, BBC Books). If this is how hard determinists view human behaviour, we can wonder whether determinism lacks the language to do justice to the evidence of having to deliberate and to wrestle with dilemmas and decisions that our moral intuitions and personal experience provide us with. If deliberate and involuntary actions are virtually indistinguishable, will courts soon stop using the language of mitigating circumstances (e.g. a woman who kills her husband after his repeated and long-running acts of violence and cruelty towards her and her children) or aggravating factors (such as racially motivated hate crimes or premeditated murder) if all crimes are equally determined? Can a murderer have their sentence reduced if the crime was committed in hot blood/under the influence of drugs/due to insanity, if every action is causally necessitated by prior actions?

2. According to Kant, 'freedom is . . . a condition of the moral law which we know'. In other words, our feeling of moral obligation or duty to the moral law would make no rational sense if we were determined. 'Ought' implies 'can' – moral obligation suggests enough free will to be held responsible for our actions. So moral agents (people) have a degree of rational self-determination.

3. Causal necessity (the idea that cause *x* must always and necessarily bring about effect *y*) is not empirically observable as David Hume argued. We would have to have exhaustive knowledge or be omniscient to know this. So the most that hard determinists can argue is that *if* exhaustive knowledge of universal causation were available prior to this moment, the future would *hypothetically* be predictable. Therefore hard determinism is a *metaphysical* claim rather than an *empirical* one. Furthermore, causation is not necessarily a string of pearls, one following the other. Causes could be multiple, indeterminate and more probable than predictable.

4. Hard determinism sits well with those who like to see individuals as easy to mould or society as easy to engineer. Governments, marketing agencies and a wide range of propagandists are empowered by this belief. Noam Chomsky argues that hard determinism's dismissal of individual free will is too often a power-play that seeks to win the ideological battle against grassroots resistance to social engineering before it is even begun. If I believe I'm determined, I'm more likely to blithely accept the will of society and government as fact.

5. It is difficult to see what evidence would count against determinism. Is the theory so insulated from criticism that it offers no grounds for its falsifiability?

6. The absence of evidence is not evidence of absence. Neurologists would freely acknowledge that our present scientific understanding of the brain is far from exhaustive in a way that would secure 'determinism' as a 'scientific' model. It is hard to conceive of a brain scan that would offer evidence in support of free will, yet it might be that mind states emerge from, but are qualitatively different from, brain states. Hard determinism reduces reality to lower levels of explanation

(minimising mind and thoughts to the level of neurons), but doesn't go further than this to consider sub atomic levels of indeterminacy that might affect the macro levels of the brain's biochemistry.

7. Can we make sense of 'moral backsliding' (if morally wrong actions are involuntary and not self-originated, how can we meaningfully distinguish them from blinking?), or of the difference between intentioned and non-deliberate actions?

8. If hard determinism is correct, how secure are the foundations of our knowledge claims since we are determined to make them and our rationality is a product of past events not of independent thought? If every event (including our reason) is an effect of prior causes, why need it be rational?

9. Determinism may be more true of the thought of animals than of the human mind. The emergence of language, self-consciousness, second-order desires about desires (e.g. when smokers summon the willpower to give up smoking) set humanity apart from the rest of the natural world.

Soft determinism or compatibilism

The philosophers Thomas Hobbes (1588–1679), John Locke (1632–1704) and David Hume were all compatibilists. Thomas Hobbes defines compatibilism in these terms:

> He is free to do a thing, who may do it if he have the will to do it, and may forbear if he have the will to forbear. And yet if there be a necessity that he shall have the will to do it, the action is necessarily to follow; and if there be a necessity that he shall have the will to forbear, the forbearing will also be necessary.
>
> (Hobbes, *Leviathan*, Cambridge University Press, 2nd rev. edition, 1996, p. 42)

John Locke (1632-1704)

John Locke and the case of a contented compatibilist locked in a room

John Locke can be hard to place in relation to quite what position he took on the free will and determinism debate. Not only did he revise his chapter on this in *Essay Concerning Human Understanding* over several editions, but at times he appears to contradict himself in both affirming and denying free will. Most academics take him to be a compatibilist who thinks that humans are able, to a degree, to suspend their desires, to deliberate, and to will the next action. This he says, is 'the hinge upon which turns the liberty of intellectual beings' (*Essay Concerning Human Understanding*, bk 2, ch. 21).

Though he does not deny causal determinism, Locke thinks that we have sufficient liberty to be held responsible for willing our actions. As he writes, 'a Man may suspend the act of his choice from being determined for or against the thing proposed, till he has examined, whether it be really of a nature in it self and consequences to make him happy, or no.' (ibid.). This is not libertarian freedom. Our psychological make-up means that we pursue happiness and therefore that we suspend and deliberate over actions that aim at that goal. We do, however, voluntarily (freely desire to) suspend our desires, deliberate, and experience a sort of freedom in doing so. So Locke is not a hard determinist arguing that complete causal determinism is evident in all human actions. He does justice to our personal experience of both suspending desires and deliberating on the one hand, and, on the other, he shows that this is wired into our natures. We can, through our suspension of desires and deliberation, alter the desires and freely 'will' 'certain goals that precede certain actions. These 'movements' occur not because of freedom of the will, but through 'unease', 'the mind having in most cases, as is evident in Experience, a power to suspend the execution and satisfaction of any of its desires'. (ibid.). We gravitate towards our happiness, by deliberating about desires unlikely to lead to this. So some form of reasoning triggered by 'unease' about the consequences of our present desires affects our actions in willing other desires.

Here our freedom lies somewhere between that of God and of the beasts. Locke believes that God's judgement on humans is just, as they are responsible for their beliefs and have the capacity to ask whether the course of action that is presently desired will lead to happiness. So human nature can suspend certain desires and deliberate, and different people can exercise this rational capacity more than others. But this is to be seen in the general context of Locke's idea of the mind as a *tabula rasa* – a blank slate that experience writes upon. So human nature is part of a causal chain that includes prior experiences, beliefs, reasons, and suspension of desires. Human actions are movements that we can desire to stop. The heart pumps blood around our bodies without us deliberately willing it. Yet there are actions or movements that our thought and desires can be said to will. We can deliberate and judge some actions preferable to others. What we are not free to determine is our nature itself. Rather like the Utilitarians who followed him, Locke writes that 'what has an aptness to produce pleasure in us we call good, and what is apt to produce pain in us we call evil' (ibid.). Our unease may range widely from hunger, to the desire for achievement, to pangs of conscience. Locke isn't explicitly clear as to the source of such uneasiness, though it is likely that the creator is one source, equipping us with feelings akin to a conscience, though these also arise from our upbringing, habits, and education. Yet Locke is able to account for the difference between voluntary and involuntary actions, and to show how our deliberations following unease intervene between desire and will in causing movements or actions.

Locke's position is well illustrated in the example of a man who is 'carried whilst fast asleep into a room where is a person he longs to see and speak with, and be there locked fast in, beyond his power to get out; he awakes and is glad to find himself in so desirable company, which he stays willingly in' (Hackett Publishing Co., 1996, p. 153). In this case, the man has no alternative possibilities and yet can be said to feel wholly free in willing his choices. There are constraints, but the mind intervenes between desiring and willing the action. The man has suspended his desire to leave the room, judging that he is happily fulfilled in staying there. As for him, the sources of our desires and judgments are often unknown to us, but we will them voluntarily and deliberate rationally over them.

Locke is happy to accept that we have a certain kind of liberty of deliberation and judgement in considering the objects of our desires as we 'examine them on all sides, and weigh them with others'. Yet, as he writes, this kind of liberty is '(as I think it *improperly*) call'd Free will' (*Essay*, bk 2, ch. 21, p. 47). Locke remains an empiricist, indeed his Essay attempts to refute rationalist claims of the mind having innate ideas, and to show how it is, instead, a blank slate written on by experience. So our mind and desires are wholly shaped by our sense experience and reflections on this. Hume's psychology will take empiricism farther to see reason as the slave of the passions and argue that when it comes to motivating the will to act, we are passional rather than rational. For Locke, reflection on our desires is still able to affect our will, though this itself is a product of our human nature, itself a product of past events which include sense experience, emotions, and deliberation.

The compatibilism of David Hume (1711-1776) – the absence of external constraint

Being the thoroughgoing empiricist that he was, David Hume stuck to what we could observe. Rejecting the idea of causal necessity, he argued instead that science was inductive and that no matter how many times we observed cause and effect (like lead sinking in water or fire burning), we could not claim to have seen or observed a 'necessary connection' between them. To prove determinism to be objectively true was beyond our empirical observation, as we would have to be omniscient about all prior causes. Yet Hume claimed to solve the age-old conflict between liberty and necessity, seeing this long-running and contentious dispute as one over words, determinists and libertarians describing the same thing from different vantage points.

Hume sees liberty as being the feeling of the absence of any external constraint. So we have 'liberty of spontaneity' in which we can voluntarily will an action, aligning ourselves with what prior causes dictate in any case. What we can't have is 'liberty of indifference' in which we have genuine alternative possibilities and originate new causes and effects separate from the chain of events leading up to this point in time. As Hume put it, 'By liberty then, we can only mean a power of acting or not acting, according to the determinations of the will; that is to say if we choose to remain at rest we may; if we choose to move, we may.' (*An Enquiry Concerning Human Understanding*, ed. L. A. Selby-Bigge, Oxford University Press, 1902 p. 95) This position is termed **soft determinism** or *compatibilism* because it claims to reconcile freedom with determinism: I am free as long as I feel I am and do not have a sense of being forced to act against my internal will by external causes.

Hume's argument against **libertarianism** is that there are *two possible causal explanations* for our choices and actions. They could be determined by prior causes (such as habits of character like addictions or compulsive behaviour, one's environment, genes, education, etc.). If this were the case, then our present choices would be *determined by prior causes* and hence not free. What appear to me to be choices are part of a causal chain stretching back well beyond my present conscious choice.

On the other hand, if there were 'independent origination' to our choices – that is to say they emerged *uncaused and random* at the moment of decision or shortly before, they would indeed be disconnected from what went before. For Hume this makes no sense – it's chance, not choice. To act out of character would be like

Soft determinism:
The view that human beings have limited free will but are to some extent controlled by external forces. Humans are partially responsible for their actions.

Libertarianism:
The view that humans have free will, unrestrained by any external force

switching from being an accountant to a lion tamer to a teacher to an astronaut from day to day without any rationale. Causes preceded reasons for Hume and the mind came to be populated with ideas from sense experience that built up over time, so our decision-making was part of a causal chain that stretches back behind us and which we do not ourselves determine. Our experience tells us that much of human action and nature is predictable – if someone returned from a foreign land with tales of people who were unerringly good and flawless in their behaviour, without exception, Hume says that we would doubt this as human nature has common traits. What we have is the freedom to will our actions and the sense that we are free of obvious external constraint in doing so. This definition of free will is termed 'voluntarism', though it does not fully address the question of internal constraints. A kleptomaniac who wants to shoplift a particular pair of trainers, or an alcoholic who 'chooses' from a range of drinks at the bar, passes the compatibilist's test of free will, yet this gives us little basis on which to distinguish their freedom from what could be said to be more rational choices.

Compatibilists differ over their account of moral responsibility. Some argue that praise and blame are wired into our emotional responses to the behaviour of others; rather than justly judging it, we are having a causal effect on future behaviour, deterring harmful actions and promoting beneficial ones. Others are more optimistic that, in minor senses, we possess a degree of choice and can form good habits or place ourselves in good environments that bring out the best in us. This could amount to little more than beast-like morality conditioning the behaviour. But compatibilists would warn against too Platonic a view of human nature and emphasise that we're different in degree, not kind, from the evolutionary psychology of our ancestors.

Incompatibilists (both determinists and libertarians) agree that freedom requires there to be genuine *alternative possibilities* (APs) when we make our decisions. But compatibilist Harry Frankfurt disputes this.

Discussion Questions

1. If you happened to choose the only remaining ice cream in stock from the range advertised on the poster board of choices on the ice-cream van, would your choice have been determined or free?

2. Kant called Hume's compatibilist view that freedom was just the feeling of voluntarily willing our thoughts and actions despite there being no alternative possibility a 'wretched subterfuge . . . a petty word-jugglery' (*The Critique of Practical Reason*, p. 86). Do you think that you can only properly be said to be free if you have alternative possibilities?

Philosopher Harry Frankfurt (1929–) seeks to establish a compatibilist version of free will in opposition to the objection that there can be no moral responsibility for actions without *alternative possibilities*. For the libertarian, you can be held responsible only if you could have done otherwise than you did, because responsibility implies the freedom to have acted differently. Frankfurt denies this and seeks to show how you could still be held responsible for your actions without alternative

Philosopher Harry Frankfurt

possibilities being open to you. Using several thought experiments, 'Frankfurt cases' set out to show how we can be said to 'choose' a course of action despite it being the only one available to us.

In one example, a Democrat-voting neuroscientist has implanted microchip switches inside thousands of voters' brains. On election day, should the voter entering the voting booth show 'prior signals' of wanting to vote Republican, a switch will be activated to force them to change their mind. But, in many cases, there is no need for the switch to activate, as the voter is a sure-fire Democrat voter. In such a scenario it is quite possible that the agent freely chooses the single possibility left open to them. And, as long as the agent's choice aligns with that of the switch controller's, their choice is both free and without alternative possibilities. But it may be objected that the agent or their family would start to notice (i.e. 'You voted Democrat? Why ever did you do that?'). What Frankfurt seeks to show is that in those cases where there is no need to deploy the control mechanisms because the agent is 'freely' choosing the desired action, *they can be held morally responsible for that action without there needing to have been alternative possibilities.* If this strategy succeeds, he claims that it demonstrates that libertarian versions of free will are false. To be said to have made free decisions does not require us to have alternative possibilities.

The problem is that in the real world rather than in the hypothetical one of thought experiments, 'prior signals' are often not present before choices are made. There remains the possibility that an agent could (right up to the moment of decision) act differently from how their 'prior signals' indicate they will. This has been termed 'the information objection', where the controller acts in advance of the information about which way a decision will go to block off alternative possibilities.

> **Discussion Question**
>
> How persuaded are you by Frankfurt's suggestion that to be said to be free, you need not have alternative possibilities?

Libertarianism

In contrast to our popular sense that we're capable of free and rationally motivated decisions, the consensus opinion among philosophers is in favour of compatibilism and the rejection of freedom in the sense of having two important qualities:

1. genuine alternative possibilities; and
2. originating in our rational will independent of prior causes.

The subjective stance of persons and the objective stance of machines

The French philosopher Henri Bergson (1859–1941) opposed what he saw as determinism's pacifying effect on people. Tragically, he was to die of pneumonia while compelled to queue to register as a Jew in Nazi-occupied France. So he would have witnessed both French collaborators and the Resistance. He argued that, as temporal beings, humans measure time not just by clocks but also by our feelings. We can *feel* time passing slowly when waiting for the bus, but quickly in an exam or when we're having fun. Furthermore, human behaviour is far less predictable than that of objects. Bergson held that human willpower could allow us to deliberate and depart from the past. He also objected to determinism's claim that human actions were, at least hypothetically, entirely predictable. To make such a prediction would require an omniscient knowledge of all causal inputs into an individual's mind, including their conscious and unconscious selves.

We shall now consider four major lines of defence set out by a variety of libertarians.

Dualists

Dualists would see the mind as separate from the body and made of different 'stuff'. So, while the physical world of matter is determined, the mind is free. They hold that 'mind states' can control or influence 'brain states'. When neurons fire in the brain, behind these may exist the mysterious non-physical substance of 'mind' that causes them to do so. Yet this dualism of mind and body begs the question of precisely how non-physical minds operate neurotransmitters without energy (contradicting the law of the conservation of energy)? Plato and Descartes are dualists, but the distinction between mind and matter is also defended by contemporary dualists like Alvin Plantinga and Saul Kripke. Kripke uses the analogy of how water and H_2O relate. Just as we can experiment with hydrogen and oxygen and not make water, so, too, all the neurological expertise we can gather does not add up to the subjective experiences of our minds.

Kant – 'ought' implies 'can'

Immanuel Kant considered freedom to be one of the postulates (underlying assumptions) of practical morality, or 'a condition of the moral law which we know'. That is to say that although we cannot prove that we're free (because freedom exists not in the phenomenal world of our senses, but in the noumenal world), free will is a working assumption behind the moral law. Kant puts it like this: 'The will, in the phenomenal sphere, is subject to the law of nature, and in so far, not free, and on the other hand, as belonging to the thing in itself, it is not subject to the law, and so is free.' For Kant, still operating in the framework of Cartesian dualism, the mind (as opposed to the body) could originate decisions; reason itself could motivate choices. Kant also believed in transcendentals such as God, freedom and the after-life. He posited these as the basis for morality (set them down as foundations that could not themselves be proven to be true). So for Kant, our rational will enables us to rise above the phenomenal world of animal instinct. This noumenal realm allows freedom to break into the causal chain of past and future and enables us to will our decisions rationally. To this extent, human reason can determine and direct future goals. Roger Scruton explains Kant's belief in a particular kind of free will: 'The free agent we see to be distinguished, not by his lack of constraint, but by the peculiar nature of the constraint which governs him. He is constrained by reason, in its reception to the moral law' (Scruton, *A Short History of Modern Philosophy: From Descartes to Wittgenstein*, Routledge, 2001, p. 157).

Humans can reason. Their wills can be autonomous or independent, capable of being rationally rather than passionally motivated to act dutifully. We can set aside self-interest and favouritism and act according to the requirements of the Categorical Imperative. Kant held that, in exercising our autonomous reason, we are free and responsible. The dignity of humans over animals lay in being free to reason and not being governed by instincts and feelings.

Sartre and Camus – existentialism and radical freedom

'Existence precedes Essence' was the unlikely rallying cry of Jean-Paul Sartre, the French existentialist philosopher. He rejected Platonic or religious beliefs that we have an essential objective nature, believing instead that we are 'abandoned' in a cold and indifferent universe where any meaning to life is that which we ourselves create in rebellion against the despair of our mortal existence. Our freedom lies in the fact that our existence is not pre-defined by our essential nature (as Plato believed). Instead, we shape our world's meaning and act consistently with our (subjectively chosen) values. We could do this by being consistently honest in order to value truth, or by respecting the freedom of others just as we wish to exercise our own. As we make up our own values, these are subjective, but can nonetheless be authentic or inauthentic. Sartre argued that we often act in 'bad faith', sometimes as a response to the anguish and existential angst of our fear of death and – in the absence of God or any objective order – because we bear the weight of the responsibility of making decisions that define us. To act in bad faith is to resign ourselves to be passive objects acted upon by circumstances or the past, or to seek security in authority figures who numb our despair by offering the reassurance of a false objectivity to the world. We can 'choose ourselves' as victims, passive pebbles swept by the tides of life. But, as Albert Camus (an existentialist journalist, playwright and novelist) argued, once we've made the choice to live (and rejected suicide), we cannot evade our responsibilities for the choices we make.

Sartre gives the example of a waiter who so embodies the role he plays that he takes himself too seriously and so can be said to be acting in bad faith, allowing himself to be objectified by his job. Writing in occupied France where Nazi Fascism had overrun a free press and democratic society, Sartre championed freedom. He gives the example of a student who asks him whether he should look after his elderly mother or join the Free French. Sartre sends the young man away to make his own decision rather than devolve responsibility onto his teacher (in any case, we may well be aware that our choice of whom to go to for counsel will push us towards a particular decision). The student is left with a dilemma – condemned to be free and to deliberate and decide. Yet if determinism is true, if the next event in the causal chain is inevitable, why should he feel torn?

Since the work of the psychologist Sigmund Freud, we have seen that our actions are often controlled by our unconscious mind and conditioned by our past experiences, especially those of our early childhood. Yet Sartre argued that our past need not dictate our present and future. We can choose to reinvent ourselves despite our fear of the responsibilities of freedom. As he said in a 1969 interview, 'the idea I have never ceased to develop is that in the end . . . a man can always make something out of what is made of him' (Warnock, *Existentialism*, Oxford University Press, 1998, p. 130).

In many ways, Sartre encounters what he calls the 'facticity' of life with a call to the individual to overcome their fears about taking responsibility for the radical freedom they possess to break with the habits and conformist pressures of their environment or past. He asks us to imagine a group of walkers confronted by a fallen boulder that blocks their path on a mountainside. One might choose to be 'defeated' and return the way he came. Another sees himself as 'a courageous hero', who risks his life by scaling the boulder and carries on. Another may choose to be an 'artist' and paint or photograph the scene. Despite the facticity of the circumstances, there remain choices to make which define us. Sartre would have admired the capacity of artists like Madonna to reinvent themselves several times over in a career. Existentialism sees us as 'beings unto death' who are 'condemned to be free'. The novels of the existentialist writer Albert Camus (e.g. *The Stranger, The Plague, The Myth of Sisyphus*) focus on how individuals decide who they are in facing crises – heroes and antiheroes find their identity in their choices.

The argument from interpersonal emotions

Peter Strawson's argument from interpersonal emotions sees the determinism debate as somewhat irrelevant to the question of how human beings and societies regard responsibility. In *Freedom and Resentment* (Routledge, 2008), he sees human nature as responding to people's deliberate actions with *reactive attitudes* of thanks, forgiveness, hurt, resentment, etc. We take a more objective stance towards tables that bruise us as we knock against them, or when mechanisms or natural disasters cause loss of life. In the same way, we view non-deliberate actions (like someone tripping us up and knocking a drink out of our hand, or failing to call an ambulance when they themselves were injured in the accident and unconscious) from an objective stance rather than a reactive one.

Peter Strawson (1919–2006) makes the point that interpersonal emotions and attitudes of praise and blame are hard-wired into human nature. Even if prior causes determine present events, we still couldn't hope to outrun our nature.

But, in contrast to our dealings with animals or machines, our feelings of resentment or admiration towards people are due to a subjective or reactive attitude. Normal responsible and rational adults successfully interact every day by using interpersonal emotions. We may exempt from responsibility very young children (when they throw their meal off the high chair and laugh), or the criminally insane judged not fit to stand trial. But for normal adults, such interpersonal feelings of empathy are fundamental to the way we live socially, guiding us through thousands of interactions each week. Psychopaths who lack empathy may treat other human beings as objects to be used. They may be clever in their manipulation of others, but this does not make their reasoning more reliable – indeed, it is rather less so. The determinist gets it wrong on two counts. Firstly, they ask us to treat humans as objectively as machines, an approach which is not only impossible, given human nature, but would result in normal human relationships and interactions being rendered ridiculous (a world of Mr Spocks or narrowly left-brain thinking). Secondly, it would be contradictory to say that abnormal cases are normal (that our feeling that a human being is responsible for their behaviour in one circumstance was no different from their being not held responsible in another). Our experience in relationships or as members of families, communities, societies and nations is that life cannot be lived purely from a theoretical, objective stance. As Strawson puts it, 'it would be useless for us to ask whether it would not be rational for us to do what it is not in our nature to [be able to] do'. Reactive attitudes and our subjective sense of responsibility, and the emotional intelligence to operate relationally with other human beings, are here to stay. Given this, determinism seems remote and theoretical rather than practical or livable. As David Wiggins puts it, 'What Strawson maintains is that ... our ordinary ways of talking about responsibility, agency ... human character ... are best left unreplaced and unreduced. They require no justification at all beyond their manifest viability, and their proven capacity to animate the practices of everyday life'. (Watson (ed.), *Freewill*, p. 118).

Discussion Question

Do you think Strawson is right to see the debate over determinism as remote from real life, where our human nature will always praise and blame even if in theory, all actions are determined by prior causes?

The theological debate about determinism

Predestination:
A doctrine particularly linked with St Augustine and John Calvin, which argues that, before their birth, some people are selected for salvation by God, while others are selected for damnation

It is interesting to note that the same broad positions (hard determinism, compatibilism, and libertarianism) adopted in the modern secular debate over free will and determinism were established in previous centuries of theological debate. Perhaps the fact that this debate has continued for well over 1,500 years in Christian theology should suggest to us that those who claim (like Hume) that it is easily resolvable as a question of language are a little over-optimistic and premature.

In the fifth century, Pelagius (dates uncertain – c.354–418 CE) was a British monk and ascetic whose emphasis on the freedom and responsibility of mankind was libertarian. Concerned over the falling moral standards of Christians in cities like Rome, he held Augustine's teaching on divine grace and **predestination** partially responsible for this. If salvation is nothing to do with our moral exertions and entirely assured for the elect ahead of time, then for Pelagius, here lay the cause of moral complacency and backsliding. For Pelagius, despite Adam's fall, human nature still possessed free will. He rejected Augustine's view of original sin (an inclination to rebel against God and to do evil) and mankind's depravity without divine grace. God's grace was seen in the gift of the law, and humans could will to act in obedience to this (indeed, Jesus had taught 'be perfect therefore, even as your Heavenly Father is perfect' Matthew 5:48). God justly elects and damns after actual lives of virtue or sin, not before them. Living an ascetic life of virtue himself, Pelagius saw Christ's example and teaching, together with the law, as providing motivation and instruction for mankind to overcome sin and gain salvation.

Against this, Augustine (354-430 CE) argued for original sin (the teaching that we inherit Adam's fallen nature and have no hope of salvation without divine grace). God foreknew and permitted Adam's fall but did not predestine it; by his eternal decree, he predestined all mankind to be among either the elect (chosen for eternity in heaven) or the reprobate (subject to damnation). Augustine sees his teaching emerging from certain biblical texts like Romans 9:11-20:

> though they were not yet born and had done nothing either good or bad – in order that God's purpose of election might continue, not because of works but because of him who calls ... What shall we say then? Is there injustice on God's part? By no means! ... it depends not on human will or exertion, but on God, who has mercy ... he has mercy on whomever he wills, and he hardens whomever he wills ... who are you, O man, to answer back to God?

A second chapter of this debate in church history arises in the late sixteenth and early seventeenth century between John Calvin (1509-64) and Jacobus Arminius (1560-1609). The Dutch theologian Jacobus Arminius argued that, because of his exhaustive foreknowledge of human choices and actions from birth to death, God acts as a just judge. Arminius believed that Christ died for all, not just the elect as Calvin held in his doctrine of limited atonement. As divine grace is universally available to all, and as God judges on the basis of the freely willed decisions of each person, the goodness and justice of a loving God is upheld. Arminianism spread worldwide chiefly through Methodism, whose co-founder, John Wesley, wrote 'if man were not free, he could not be accountable for his thoughts, words, or actions. If he were not free, he would not be capable either of reward or punishment; he would not be capable of being either morally good or bad.' (John Wesley, 'On Predestination', Sermon 58 in Works, 6:227).

For John Calvin (1509-64), divine sovereignty entailed an omnipotence and omniscience which decreed all of creation. As he writes, 'It is certain that not one drop of rain falls without God's sure command.' Calvin's sovereign and inscrutable God predestines the elect to eternal salvation and the 'reprobate' to eternal damnation. Calvin's definition of predestination is:

> the eternal decree of God, by which he determined with himself whatever he wished
> to happen with regard to every man. Not all are created on equal terms, but some are
> preordained to eternal life, others to eternal damnation; and, accordingly, as each has been
> created for one or other of these ends, we say that he has been predestined to life or to
> death.

> (*The Institutes*, III.21.5).

Calvin denied that God elected on the basis of his foreknowledge of an individual's faith. As total depravity (the corruption of our reason, will and virtue by sin) condemns all mankind, it logically follows that salvation is solely an act of God's grace in unconditional election (which is irresistible for those chosen) and not on account of their own merit or even some synergy (joint work) between God and human beings. Equally, the reprobate (sinful) are justly damned for no other reason than the divine decision or will and Adam's fall (1 Cor. 15:22). As Calvin wrote, 'God's foreknowledge cannot be the reason for our election, because when God surveys the whole of mankind, he will find them all ... under the same curse', adding that God is not 'liable to render an account', nor are we 'competent judges to pronounce judgment on this concerning our understanding'. Calvin acknowledges that this is a 'fearful' doctrine, but one for which a sovereign and free creator is not 'liable to render an account'.

Arminius recognised in Calvin, as have many since, the problem that predestination appears to make God the author of evil. Calvin may reply that double predestination justly punishes humankind's voluntary bias or inclination to do evil and to rebel against the divine law. Yet such freedom seems that of puppets unaware of their strings and yet responsible for their movements. The later Spanish Jesuit theologian Luis de Molina (1535–1600) addressed such concerns in a form of compatibilism known as 'Molinism' that has been popularised by the contemporary philosopher William Lane Craig. Molina's *Concordia* (1588) argues that God knows all possible worlds – that is to say, every possible thought, deed, word and event in any hypothetical future contingent. Thus, uniquely, he can align his own will for the future of humankind with free choices within the actual world in which we live. God could have known before time that if Jesus' disciple Judas were placed as his disciple, he would betray him, thereby fulfilling his overall plan of crucifixion and resurrection for his son, and yet Judas would have freely willed that choice. Equally, God could place 'person A' in one set of circumstances in which he/she would be a kind shop manager, or in another set where he/she would be an evil dictator, either of which could: (a) bring about the future God wished, and (b) ensure that the 'person A' freely willed his/her decisions. The idea is termed 'middle knowledge' as it refers to three moments in God's knowledge:

1. Natural knowledge – in which God knows all possible worlds he could make.

2. Middle knowledge – God's foreknowledge of all future free actions and how his creatures would act if he were to place them in any possible set of circumstances.

3. Free Knowledge-God's knowledge of the actual world he chooses to create.

This not only vindicates divine justice, but is also the only adequate safeguard for free will according to Molina. Of course it might be objected that for those who 'choose' to do evil, thereby condemning themselves, this is a kind of divine 'sting' operation, which smacks of entrapment. Yet this denies the omnibenevolence of God, whose grace wills that 'none should perish'. Furthermore, Alvin Plantinga (another reviver of middle knowledge) gives the fictional example of 'Curly Smith', who suffers from 'trans-world depravity'. Whichever hypothetical world God places Curly in – as a ticket collector, or with the power of a tyrant – he would show himself to be irredeemably corrupt and harsh in his use of power. Middle knowledge comes before foreknowledge. In it, God knows how all of his free creatures would act in every possible world and circumstances he might (hypothetically) place them in. The attraction of this position lies in its potential to reconcile divine sovereignty and human free will. In this way, God can act providentially, as he does in the biblical case in which the deception of Joseph's brothers in selling him into slavery results in his rise to a powerful position in Egypt, which allows him to save his people from famine. As he says, 'You meant it for evil against me, but God meant it for good in order to bring about this present result' (Genesis 50:50). It is argued that this also evades the worst challenges to the justice of divine predestination, such as the charge of fatalism.

Discussion Question

Explain how middle knowledge could account for how Jesus' disciple Judas Iscariot could both be predetermined to betray him, and at the same time be considered to have freely willed, and be morally responsible for, his act.

Libertarian or compatibilist thought may be seen in Pelagius, Aquinas and Arminius, who rejected hard determinism and argued that, despite their fallenness, human beings could choose (to a greater or lesser extent) 'not of necessity but freely' (Aquinas, *Summa Theologica*). The Dutch theologian Jacobus Arminius (1560–1609) argued that, because of his exhaustive foreknowledge of human choices and actions from birth to death, God can be said to act justly in election and reprobation. As divine grace is universally available to all, and as God judges on the basis of the freely willed decision of each person, the goodness and justice of a loving God is upheld. Arminianism spread worldwide chiefly through Methodism, whose co-founder John Wesley wrote 'if man were not free, he could not be accountable for his thoughts, words, or actions. If he were not free, he would not be capable either of reward or punishment; he would not be incapable of being either morally good or bad.'

The scale of twentieth-century suffering brought the problem of evil to the forefront of theology and the Free Will Defence has been crucial in defending the goodness of God. One may even see the theological movements of Process theology and Open Theism as a response to this problem. They strongly feature human freedom, together with a God who is 'down in the trenches' and travels with us in time, unable to foreknow or predestine from outside of time.

The 'Open Theist' Clark Pinnock takes the view that God restricts his control of the world in order to make room for human free will. God is everlasting rather than eternal, and within time rather than beyond it as Augustine believed. God reacts to events creatively not coercively. The creative suffering and vulnerability of God moves away from the immutability (unchangeability) in God associated with the Greek idea that change from perfection would result in imperfection. God is not remote but responsive, not closed-off, but open to his creatures relationally in time. In a post-Holocaust era where all theology listens more closely to the cries from the cross and the concentration camp, Open Theism and, more radically, Process theology, engages criticisms that Calvin's God is just too transcendent in thought and deed.

Questions concerning human responsibility in light of predestination, or concerning the possibility of a compatibilism between divine foreknowledge and human free will, prefigure those of the contemporary secular debate over determinism and free will. Perhaps the fact that this debate has continued for well over 1,500 years in Christian theology should suggest to us that those who claim (like Hume) that it is easily resolvable as a question of language are a little over-optimistic and premature.

Taking things further (beyond the specification and just for general interest, not the exam)...

Unlike most other debates, that of free will and determinism uses our brains to examine our brains. There are cases of the expert testimony of neuroscientists in criminal courts resulting in lowered sentences on the grounds of diminished responsibility due to abnormalities shown in brain scans. Philosophers disagree about the effects widespread belief in hard determinism would have. P. F. Strawson (1919-2006) thinks that our everyday ways of talking about responsibility prove to work well and are best left alone without reducing them to talk of brain states over which we have no control. Saul Smilansky argues that hard determinism would be dangerous if it became a widely held belief and, therefore, that the illusion of free will is largely positive. It keeps people of goodwill working for the general good and this in turn becomes a kind of reality as attitudes shape human behaviour. Inter-personal attitudes of approval or blame can shape the habits of social morality for the good. If word got out that determinism were true, many could become apathetic, depressed, or even fatalistic, devaluing others viewed purely as biological processes.

One frequently quoted example from neuroscience that some take to be evidence for determinism is an experiment devised by Benjamin Libet (1916-2007). This detected activity or 'prior signals' of a decision to act before people were conscious of it. Libet noticed that sometimes 'prior signals' were detected but no action was taken

In conclusion – three choices

The preceding debate has essentially left us with three choices, each of which has its benefits and costs.

Options	Benefits	Costs
To deny free will altogether.	May be seen to fit better with evolutionary and behaviouralist psychology and recent science on the neurobiology of the brain. Might offer a less emotive way of dealing with criminals, who are less monsters, more malfunctioning machines needing reprogramming.	Does not fit with our natural feelings of dilemmas, torn choices and actively shaping our future. Undermines human moral responsibility. It is hard, even impossible, to ignore our feelings of praise, blame, or justice requiring punishment, remorse, or making amends for wrongs and to replace this with ideas of reconditioning faulty machines. A metaphysical, non-scientific claim – without exhaustive knowledge of causation (universal and necessary), hard determinists can neither prove their view nor state what it would take to falsify it. Could make us more passive and resigned rather than responsible agents who believe that personal, social and political change is possible. If determinism is true, then it is pointless to argue for or against it. Yet determinists do rationally argue for their view, so they contradict their own position.
To affirm free will as compatible with determinism.	Solves an age-old language problem due to the mistaken definition of freedom as needing alternative possibilities. Instead, as long as our actions are free of obvious external constraint and we will them 'freely', they can be said to be free. This definition accepts that all actions are either part of causal chains that preceded our choices or random, hence non-rational. As we cannot predict all future events and do not know all past causes, there's still room for us to allow our strong human instinct for feeling free to look at the future as probable rather than predictable.	I need an explanation of how it can be that, if I have no choice about having an addictive personality, that if I have an addictive personality and this predetermines that, if exposed to gambling and alcohol, I will become a compulsive gambler or alcoholic, I may still be said to have freely chosen this course. I'm also open to the criticism that I've just redefined free will to exclude the common-sense view of it needing to have alternative possibilities.
To affirm free will as incompatible with determinism.	This empowers those who believe that personal, social and political change is possible. Those who emphasise the need for 'willpower' or rational decision-making in our actions argue that it stops us being putty in other people's or institutions' hands.	An explanation is needed for how an action can be neither determined by prior causes nor random. To be free, actions must have alternative possibilities and be self-formed by the agent. Here, Frankfurt's examples (in which actions can be freely willed by the agent and yet determined by prior causes) need explaining.

Discussion Questions

1. If, as Augustine thinks, God is eternal and outside of time, does this solve the incompatibility problem of his creatures having genuine free will whilst also being pre-destined?
2. If you became convinced that hard determinism was correct, how would it affect your emotions and behaviour?
3. Could any justice system afford to take determinism seriously, even if it were correct?
4. Is it sufficient that actions be voluntary to be free or do they also need to be self-determined?
5. Do you think it is possible to reconcile the existence of God, who is all-knowing and all-powerful, with human free will? What problems are there with Calvin's view?

Are we responsible/Can we change? It took Barack Obama several years to quit smoking. Is it possible to allow reason and willpower to reshape desires and train us in new habits too?
Are we responsible even for our emotions/attitudes?
Are our choices the consequence of prior causes which we have no control over?
Do we just have freedom of desire, not freedom of the will? Can reason help recondition our negative behaviours?
If the general public became convinced of hard determinism, not just scientists and philosophers, would this cause serious problems?

and therefore spoke of 'free won't' rather than free will. Some more recent studies have tried to predict human action seconds before it occurs. If an action is shown to start in the unconscious mind before a person is aware of it or consciously wills it to happen, does this undermine free will? Neuroscientist and philosopher Raymond Tallis (1946) thinks not. He thinks that 'Neuromamia', as he terms attempts to reduce human behaviour to brain chemistry, overreaches the science. Our actions interconnect intentions, decisions and plans. He gives the example of one study in which people learned to juggle and, over a period of six weeks, white matter in the part of their cerebral cortex associated with visuo-motor skills showed clear changes. Can we intentionally act on our own brains to change their wiring? Isn't this what habits and training do? Of course this doesn't make us completely free. But Tallis points out that the hard determinist is unreasonably arguing that 'In order to be truly morally responsible for one's actions, one would have to be the cause of one's self ... to have brought myself into being' (*Aping Mankind*, Acumen, 2011, p. 257). Such a definition rules out free will. Yet Tallis argues that our intentions do make a difference, as when we harness the laws of gravity to build and use a slide or a swing to enjoy play. Human ingenuity and action build cities, technology, culture and law. They use laws of nature rather than simply being determined by them. Looking in on our consciousness as brains with scanning equipment is one viewpoint that may offer evidence that we are more determined by our unconscious brains than we had supposed. Looking out from the subjective viewpoint of ourselves, choices and responsibilities seem strikingly real. Perhaps this is what Samuel Johnson meant in his statement, 'All theory is against the freedom of the will; all experience for it.'

Evidence in favour of free will could arise from the idea of indeterminacy in quantum physics. If, at the subatomic level, matter is more probabilistic than determined, there may be a sense in which cause and effect aren't as certain and predictable as Newton's mechanistic view of the universe has led us to suppose. Actions and decisions may be underdetermined. Robert Kane takes this view. He aims to meet Hume's challenge that our 'choices' EITHER:

1. originate from outside of us, being determined by a chain of cause and effect that comes before us, shapes our character, personality, genes , and decisions.; OR
2. arise quite randomly within us and are therefore irrational and can't be said to have been freely willed or intentionally chosen.

Kane does this by arguing that, in moments in which we are 'torn' over which way to go in a choice or dilemma, we have consciously and rationally seen that there are good reasons to go either way (hence the torn feeling of willing both choices). This, he supposes, generates a state of indeterminacy in our minds and, like a coin toss, we land on one side of the choice or the other. In this case, the decision is both self-formed (it originates within us), and also freely willed (we found good reasons to support it). It's random, sure, but not irrational, and it does allow for self-forming actions and some kind of free will to exist. This means, in the words of philosopher Mary Midgeley, that 'Minds can affect brains as well as brains affecting minds.' (*Are you an Illusion?*, Acumen, 2014, p. 105).

FURTHER READING

Joseph Keim Campbell (2011) *Free Will*. Polity

Daniel Dennett (1984) *Elbow Room*. MIT Press

Ted Honderich (2002) *How Free Are You? The Determinism Problem*. Oxford University Press

Robert Kane (1998) *The Significance of Freewill*. Oxford University Press

Roger E. Olsen (2011) *Against Calvinism*. Zondervan

Thomas Pink (2004) *Free Will: A Very Short Introduction*. Oxford University Press

OCR Past Paper Questions

JUNE 2010
Critically assess the claim that religious people are free to make moral decisions.   *[35]*

JUNE 2011
Critically assess the view that we are not responsible for our evil actions.   *[35]*

JANUARY 2012
Critically assess the claim that free will and determinism are compatible.   *[35]*

JUNE 2013
'Without freedom it is impossible to make moral choices.' Discuss.   *[35]*

CHAPTER **12**

The Nature and Role of Conscience

LEARNING OUTCOMES

In this chapter, you will learn:

- the different views of the conscience as God-given, innate or the voice of reason, or instilled by society, parents, authority figures
- whether conscience is a reliable guide to ethical decision-making
- the views of Augustine, Aquinas, Butler, Newman, Freud, Fromm, Piaget
- to discuss these views critically and their strengths and weaknesses

Introduction

"I've been getting annoying pangs of conscience when faced with ethical dilemmas. Got anything for that?"

In democratic states, unions can strike, trainee doctors can refuse to take part in an abortion, and conscientious objectors can refuse military conscription. Freedom of conscience is enshrined in article 18 of the UN Declaration of Human Rights. Yet for all this talk of conscience, as the ethicist Paul Lehmann once observed, the modern history of the idea of conscience has led thinkers to either 'do the conscience over' or 'do the conscience in' (*Ethics in a Christian Context*, Westminster/John Knox Press, 2006). Some of the thinkers we will consider see it as a form of infantile neuroticism, the internalising of the moral codes of society. At the heart of the debate is the question of whether the conscience is innate to human nature or instilled in us from external authority figures such as parents, teachers or social structures (government, law, the media, etc.). The debate over the reliability of conscience in decision-making is bound up with questions over its nature.

> ### Exercise
>
> 1. Research *The Awakening Conscience* by Holman Hunt at The Khan Academy. How does Hunt show us temptation and conscience in his symbolism?
> 2. What is meant by the terms 'prisoners of conscience' and 'conscientious objector'?
> 3. So-called 'whistle-blowers' in Industry and the military inform the public about malpractice or illegal activity. They are said to be acting 'in good conscience' in going against the interests of their employer. One such example is that of the research chemist Jeffrey Wigand, who witnessed against his employers in the tobacco industry. He claimed that they knowingly 'spiked' cigarettes to make them more addictive. He was played by Russell Crowe in the film *The Insider*. What do you think about whistle-blowers?
> 4. Consider the case of prosecutors at the Nuremberg trials after World War II. Some Nazi officers and commanders defended their atrocities and crimes against humanity by arguing that they were following orders. Some even argued that their consciences were so warped by their obedience to authority that they acted out of a false sense of duty. Does this undermine the value of conscience altogether?

QUICK QUESTION
Eric Liddell, Olympic 400m Gold Medalist, Paris, 1924. Liddell was a Scottish Presbyterian who would not run in his Olympic heat on the Sabbath day because of his obedience of the fourth commandment. The story of his achievements and beliefs is told in the film *Chariots of Fire*.

What makes people follow their conscience at great personal cost to themselves?

Conscience in the New Testament

Whilst the term 'conscience' derives from the Greek *'suneidesis'* (knowledge with/to know something about oneself) and is not found in the Old Testament, it underlies the Genesis story of Adam and Eve's disobedience and runs through biblical historical, prophetic and wisdom literature. In 2 Samuel 12, for example, the prophet Nathan confronts David with his adultery with Bathsheba and murder of her husband Uriah to cover his tracks. The classic confession of Psalm 51 is David's sorrowful response.

C. A. Pierce's classic 1955 study *Conscience in the New Testament* shows that Paul uses the word 'conscience' twenty times. Aside from his use, it only occurs in Hebrews and 1 Peter. He speaks of conscious awareness of righteousness (Romans 13:5), of conscience as a witness (Romans 2:15, 9:1; 2 Corinthians 1:12) which can accuse or defend, and of having a good and a pure conscience.

In Romans 2:14–15, he says that if 'the Gentiles [non-Jews], who do not have the law [of Moses], do by nature those things [the commandments] that are of the law . . . They show the work of the law . . . written in their hearts, their consciences bearing witness to them'. So he does believe in a universal faculty in human beings for making moral judgements. Nonetheless, the conscience can be misinformed (for example, when those of a 'weak' conscience wrongly believe that meat bought from public markets which is from sacrifices to idols is not unclean as these are not real gods). He also thinks that it can be trained by self-examination (1 Corinthians 11:28; Galatians 6:4) and by seeking the will of God (Romans 12:2). Its judgements should be tempered with love and peacefulness towards others (1 Corinthians 14:19). Pierce makes the point that 'Conscience is taken today as justifying, in advance . . . in the New Testament . . . it refers only to the past and particular, and to the acts of a man's self alone'. It is 'the painful reaction of man's nature, as morally responsible, against infringements of its created limits' (Pierce 1955).

WE WERE KIND OF HOPING TO LET OUR *CONSCIENCE* BE OUR GUIDE.

The conscience is part of a larger framework in Christian ethics, or what the philosopher Charles Taylor calls a 'moral ontology' (a sense of how the world *is*). That's to say that, in Christian thought, the study of man (*anthropology*) derives from the study of God (*theology*). For this reason, theologian John Webster argues that conscience 'ranks well after "prayer" or "following Jesus" in a Christian's moral framework (Webster, 'God and conscience', 2006). The theologian Karl Barth even wrote, in his *Ethics*, 'To have a conscience is no more or less than to have the Holy Spirit' (Wipf & Stock Publishers, 2013, p. 482). Indeed, Barth speaks of 'the secret energy of the Spirit' by which the conscience judges not by its own authority but through prayer and worship, aligned with the judgement of God. Conscience is not about individual freedom or being true to yourself for Barth, but about allowing one's love of God to shape the love of one's neighbour. As Paul puts it in 1 Corinthians 2:16, we are to allow the mind of Christ to be formed in us so that we grow in the art of moral discernment.

The New Testament mentions the word we translate as 'conscience' thirty-two times (*Strong's Concordance*, 1985) but also uses the word 'heart' (*kardia*) for the seat of the emotions and moral awareness many more times in both Old and New Testaments. In a similar vein, St Paul talks of consciences becoming weak, seared or defiled with habitual disobedience of divine commands. As he writes, 'I do not understand my own actions. For I do not do what I want, but I do the very thing I hate . . . I can will what is right, but I cannot do it. For I do not do the good I want, but the evil I do not want, is what I do' (Romans 7:15, 18). For Paul, a healthy conscience is not so much about internal moral auditing, as uncovering those secret sins that honest self-knowledge and the Holy Spirit show up. Different consciences need not all agree, given the distinct circumstances in which individuals find themselves. Nonetheless, 'my conscience permits me to commit adultery' would be an example of self-justification, not conscience at work.

Synderesis: According to Aquinas, this is our inner knowledge of and natural disposition towards doing good and avoiding evil – 'that good should be done and evil avoided' – a natural dis-position of humans to understand the first principles of morality instinctively.

Aquinas (1225–74)

For Aquinas, conscience is 'the mind of man making moral judgements', or 'the application of knowledge to some action', the inner faculty of moral reasoning that stems from our comprehension of the eternal moral law that God has established in his created order. Aquinas distinguishes *synderesis* from *conscientia*.

Synderesis refers, according to Aquinas, to our inner knowledge of and natural disposition towards doing good and avoiding evil – 'that good should be done and evil avoided' – a natural disposition of humans to understand the first principles of morality instinctively. This is the inner prompting of the eternal moral law in us that good should be done and evil avoided. It takes the form of moral knowledge (e.g. of the Primary Precepts) and is an innate faculty of reason that directs us to do good and avoid evil. In *De veritate*, Aquinas writes that conscience is at work before and after our deeds. We 'proceed from principles to conclusions' *before* moral choices and 'consider whether they are right' *after* the event.

Conscientia refers to 'the mind of man making moral judgements'. It is a practical form of judgement, like Aristotle's term *phronēsis*. As he writes, 'Conscience is reason making right decisions and not a voice giving us commands' (*Summa Theologica*, I–II, Q.19, A.5&6). This can be mistaken or dulled through our failure to listen to it. For example, our moral judgement is impaired when *apparent* goods (like wealth through dishonest gain), rather than *real* goods, are aimed at. So in *Summa Theologica*, he argues that prudence (the intellectual virtue of making correct judgements about right and wrong) requires moral training in virtue and practical wisdom.

Conscientia: Aquinas thinks that humans use their reason to make moral decisions. We have to train ourselves to recognise our conscience.

Aquinas argues that acting against conscience is always wrong and, at the same time, that acting according to it cannot be sinful. As he writes in *Summa Theologica*, 'Every judgement of conscience, be it right or wrong, be it about things evil in themselves or morally indifferent, is obligatory, in such wise that he who acts against his conscience always sins.' Yet this raises the difficult question of what happens when our conscience is mistaken over the facts of a case or prejudiced by self-interest. There are cases in which people do evil acts in obedience to their consciences, or they do the right thing and yet feel the pang of a guilty conscience. When British volunteers answered Lord Kitchener's call to arms in World War I, most did so with a sense of obeying their consciences. In contrast, Huckleberry Finn (in Mark Twain's novel) is troubled with a bad conscience when he fails to give up Jim, the runaway slave. His conscience tells him that he's breaking the law, but his feeling of sympathy for his travelling companion overrules it.

Here, Aquinas would argue that the individual has a responsibility to inform the conscience and seek to know right from wrong. The individual's faulty conscience could be dulled by habitual failure to listen; it could be misinformed or misled. He sees that the conscience can be mistaken. This can be knowingly (vincible errors) and unknowingly (invincible errors). Moral judgements can be faulty and we have a capacity for self-deception. The individual's feelings, such as righteous indignation at wrongs done, may mistakenly be used in moral justification of revenge, for example. We may also lack all of the facts of a given dilemma. For this reason, Catholic moral theology came to distinguish between *material sin* (where conscience is in error) and *formal sin* (where the voice of conscience is known and disobeyed). We are at fault when we could have taken more trouble to be informed

I LET MY CONSCIENCE BE MY GUIDE, AND IT TURNED OUT TO BE A SOCIOPATH.

before making our moral judgement (as in the case of someone who doesn't ask too many questions about why goods they are purchasing are so cheap in case they might discover them to be stolen, produced by exploited workers, or avoiding tax).

Our ignorance can be either voluntary (vincible) or involuntary (invincible). Where it is involuntary, we are not responsible. Take Aquinas' example of two cases:

- someone believes their conscience to be telling them to commit adultery;
- a man mistakenly thinks it good to sleep with what he takes to be his wife in his own bed when it is in fact her identical twin sister.

In the second case, the erroneous judgement is involuntary and therefore excusable, whereas in the first case, the person ought to have known that this was morally wrong as it goes against Primary Precepts and the moral law. They are therefore morally responsible for their actions.

Yet an erring or immature conscience grows through practical wisdom gained by experience, reasoning and listening to the Church's teaching and scripture. We have a high regard for the individual conscience in the modern secular world, yet, for theologian Michael Banner, authenticity and 'being true to yourself' are the precise opposite of what Aquinas means by the conscience. We have a duty to inform it, to train it through habit and experience in the virtue of prudence, to be wary of being misled, and to listen to the voice of the eternal moral law within us.

Bishop Joseph Butler (1692–1752)

> Your obligation to obey this law is its being the law of your nature. That your conscience approves of and attests to such a course of action is itself alone an obligation. Conscience does not only offer itself to show us the way we should walk in, but it likewise carries its own authority with it, that it is our natural guide, the guide assigned us by the Author of our nature; it therefore belongs to our condition of being.
>
> (Bishop Joseph Butler, *Fifteen Sermons* [1726], quoted in David E. White, *The Works of Bishop Butler*, University of Rochester Press, 2006, p. 62)

Bishop Joseph Butler

The Anglican Bishop Joseph Butler was well aware of the problems of relativism raised by Thomas Hobbes. Hobbes saw individuals outside of the protection of the state as condemned to a chaotic life that was nasty, brutish and short. By entering into a social contract co-operatively, they protected themselves from this 'state of nature'. Laws and the authority that citizens invested in the state were a practical necessity to bring this about, a form of enlightened self-interest.

For Butler, there was more than just self-interested co-operation going on in our moral reasoning. He spoke of 'the sentiment of understanding' and 'a perception of the heart'. The emotional traction and authority of conscience in our natures was evidence of its author. Yet in his defence of conscience as an innate human faculty, Butler does not draw on external authority such as the Church's teaching, scripture or Natural Law. Instead he turns inwards to look at our *inner experience* of moral approval of virtue and disapproval of vice. Conscience carries its own authority written into sentiments of approval and detesting, authored into human beings and their nature. As D.C. Alison puts it ('Debating Christian Theism', 1995, p. 209), 'on the grounds of empirical evidence, there is a governance of the world which encourages virtue, discourages vice, and implies logical probability of ultimate congruity between moral duty and self-interest'. Modern readers may think this a mistaken strategy because private moral judgements can seem so diverse and relative. Take cannibals (Butler would have at least read of them in *Robinson Crusoe*) – surely the fact of moral disagreement undermines any claim to universal conscience. Not so for Butler – cannibals may perhaps 'lie awake with a sort of moral indigestion' or maybe they haven't yet exercised their consciences (Michael Banner, *Christian Ethics: a Brief History*, Wiley-Blackwell, 2009, p. 76). When (or if) they come to their moral senses, they will see the abhorrence of their deeds as the rest of the world does.

In order to undermine the claim that all our decisions are a form of rational self-interest, Butler begins by establishing less controversial aspects of human moral identity that can be easily observed, such as self-love or benevolence towards others. He has a high view of the capacity of the human conscience to adjudicate between self-interest and altruism. For example, we often experience the kindness of strangers who give, seeking nothing in return. As he says, 'this moral approving [of virtue] or disapproving [of vice] faculty is certain from our experiencing it in ourselves and recognising it in each other' (Butler 1736 in White 2006, p. 41). This faculty of conscience or 'practical discerning power within us' may be disputed when it comes to particular cases, but 'in general, there is in reality a universally acknowledged standard of it'.

David Hume essentially accepts Butler's idea of there being universal feelings of approval and disapproval among human beings. He simply thinks that these do not require God and can be naturalised – for him, 'Morality is determined by sentiment.' As Michael Banner puts it, 'It is not that Butler's argument [that there is widespread evidence of emotional approval of virtue, disapproval of vice] fails, but rather that even if it succeeds, it is insufficient to provide a genuine justification of moral obligation.'

> **Exercise**
>
> Having read the section on Butler, explain the extract on page 237 from his 1726 sermon.

John Henry Newman

John Henry Newman (1801-90) has been called 'Doctor conscientiae' (teacher of conscience). For Newman, the conscience had been 'desacralised' in modern times. Where once it had a deep sense of duty to the moral law, it had become the 'right of self-will' and autonomy. As he writes, 'it no longer implies the responsibility of the creature towards its Creator, but complete independence, total autonomy, overall subjectivity and arbitrariness.' (*Certain Difficulties*, vol. II., London, 1896, p. 250). He saw it as a 'Lawgiver and Judge'. It is 'imperative and constraining, like no other dictate in the whole of our experience', having 'an intimate bearing on our affections and emotions' (*Grammar of Assent*, London, [1870] 1891, pp. 107f). For this reason, in *The Grammar of Assent*, Newman argues from conscience to the existence of God. Its existence offers evidence of a transcendent rather than an immanent, this-worldly source. He says of conscience that 'though it may suffer refraction in passing into the intellectual medium of each, it is not therefore so affected as to lose its character of being the Divine Law, but still has, as such, the prerogative of commanding obedience' (*Certain Difficulties*, vol. II, p. 247). We can look at it as emotions attached to vice and virtue, or as an 'echo of God's voice' (*Sermon*, Notre Dame, IN: University of Notre Dame Press, 2000, p. 327). So Newman sees duty as more than long-term self-interest or a useful aid to the happiness of the greatest number. It is a 'messenger from Him', prophetic in its information, and kingly in its command, the original 'Vicar (representative) of Christ' (*Certain Difficulties*, vol. II, p. 248). The severity of conscience's judgements on our thoughts, words, and deeds is merciless and speaks of punishment not forgiveness. As we begin to obey it, we become conscious of our incapacity to fulfil the demands of the moral law and so it points us to our need for forgiveness and peace with God. For Newman, it was the imprint of a personal God. In the sacrificial death of Christ the Son, we are reconciled to the Father and originator of the moral law.

In his *Letter to the Duke of Norfolk*, Newman addresses the claim that, after the doctrine of papal infallibility, the consciences of Roman Catholics would belong to the Pope not the Crown. In it he writes that 'if I am obliged to bring religion into after-dinner toasts ... I shall drink ... to Conscience first, and to the Pope afterwards.' (*Certain Difficulties*, vol. II, p. 261). For Newman, the Church is the infallible guardian of revealed truth (where conscience has no authority) but the conscience is an advocate of the moral law in humanity's innermost being and one has a duty to follow it. Here, 'the Pope is not infallible in that subject-matter in which conscience is of supreme authority'; there is 'no dead-lock'. So if 'the Pope speak[s] against Conscience ... [he] would be cutting the ground from under his feet. His very commission is to proclaim the moral law, and to protect and strengthen that "Light which enlighteneth every man that cometh into the world"' (*Certain Difficulties*, vol. II, pp. 252f.). This said, the conscience is informed by faith and the Church in matters of doctrine. It is obedience to the voice of conscience that orientates – as in the prodigal son coming to his senses in a foreign country – and leads us to find our way back home. As he writes, 'its very existence carries our minds to a Being exterior to ourselves; for else, whence did it come?' The order of Newman's logic is interesting – the force of moral obligation leads us to God/ revelation, not the reverse.

Pope Benedict XVI (1927–) acknowledged the influence of Newman's teaching on conscience in the aftermath of Nazism when one leader had said 'I have no conscience. My conscience is Adolf Hitler.' For Newman, the conscience may be individual, but it was not egocentric or subjective; it carried a deep sense of duty to the moral law. Benedict saw the conscience as 'an interior rampart against any form of totalitarianism'. Newman himself was moved at great personal cost by his conscience at the age of forty-four, when he left friends and family, his career and the Anglican Church, to be received into the Roman Catholic Church.

Freud

The psychoanalyst Sigmund Freud (1856-1939) wrote that:

Sigmund Freud, 1856-1939

The philosopher Kant once declared that nothing proved to him the greatness of God more convincingly than the starry heavens and the moral conscience within us. The stars are unquestionably superb, but where conscience is concerned God has been guilty of an uneven and careless piece of work, for a great many men have only a very limited share of it or scarcely enough to be worth mentioning . . . the critical voice of the superego is silent, the ego is re-instated, and enjoys once more the rights of man.

(Freud, *New Introductory Lectures on Psycho-analysis*, Leonard & Virginia Woolf, 1933, p. 88)

For Freud, the conscience was not an internal rational faculty, but an emotional imprint formed by early childhood development. Deep-seated feelings of guilt about 'taboo' acts or thoughts can be impossible to uproot in adulthood without the aid of psycho-analysis. The child internalises authority figures that imprint upon its emotional make-up through conditioning (by reward and punishment of behaviour). In Freud's understanding of the self, a tension existed between

The Super-Ego	The Super-Ego represses desires, is fearful of authority, and constantly warns of punishment.
The Ego	This is the focal point that balances out pleasure and reality. It adjudicates between the conflicting voices of the Super-Ego and Id over instinctual drives (such as for food, water, sex, self-preservation and loving relationships).

The Id	The Id wants to give full release to unchecked lust, anger, greed, etc. Unchecked, it would be self-indulgent and self-destructive, entirely desire driven without recourse to reason.

In this scheme of things, the conscience is the Super-Ego, doing the work of censoring, reprimanding and warning of the need to keep ourselves in check as our parents once did for us. In Freud's version of the self, the moral role of conscience is replaced by the Ego, an internal psychoanalyst who, in the mature psyche, maintains an uneasy truce between the aggressive warring interests of the Super-Ego and the Id. We alone must take responsibility for this balancing act to become fully integrated selves. For Freud it is infantile of us to seek a father figure in God or his implanted conscience to lift the burden of decision-making from us.

Freud believed that, while the Super-Ego remains necessary, repressed instincts can result in psychological illnesses. He believed that too much attention to the Super-Ego's unbending and judgemental voice would lead to unhealthy repression and neurosis (a mild to severe mental illness with symptoms such as irrational anxiety, stress, depression and a guilt complex). Through his psychoanalysis and exploration of the unconscious, he sought to get patients to express their repressed desires. As Keith Ward (1998) writes, 'Freud sometimes wrote as though all supposed reasons for acting were no more than rationalisations of primitive drives to sex, aggression, or power, and as though all "moral" conduct was a disguised form of self-interest.'

Perhaps Freud's mentally ill patients (for many of whom religion was part and parcel of their neurosis and phobia) led him to see only their imprisonment in a neurotic and joyless obsession with moral restrictions and rules. Freud's disciple Jung, who later broke with his thought, came to see a more positive role for religious experience.

Erich Fromm

The authoritarian conscience

Authoritarian conscience: Eric Fromm's term for the internalised voice of an external authority, something close to Freud's concept of the Super-Ego. This internal voice may be backed up by fear of punishment, or spurred on by admiration of an authority figure.

Eric Fromm (1900-80) was part of a group of sociologists and psychologists in the 1930s who wrote on authority and the family. Their thesis was that authoritarian personalities masked their own weaknesses by means of a domineering will over their families. An authoritarian parent created an authoritarian child who, as Fromm put it, is characterised by a 'strict super-ego, guilt feelings, a docile love of parental authority, desire for and pleasure at dominating weaker people' (Fromm, *Crisis in Psychoanalysis*, 1973). He distinguished the **authoritarian conscience** from the *humanistic* one. In his view, human beings were largely determined by social or psychological influences due to their background or upbringing. These moulded their feelings of guilt and controlled their behaviour. Authoritarianism was, for Fromm, a form of sickness. External social mores (codes of behaviour shaped by parents, the

Eric Fromm (1900-80)

Church, the state, public opinion) are internalised (become a part of oneself) through the fear of punishment and the hope of reward. These created a deference towards authority that carries a feeling of security and power whilst avoiding the anxiety of guilt and punishment. Yet over time, as the codes of behaviour established by external authorities become internalised and followed instinctually rather than because of external rewards or punishments, the authoritarian conscience develops. As Fromm puts it, the key point is that 'the prescriptions of authoritarian conscience are not determined by one's own value judgement but exclusively by the fact that its commands and taboos are pronounced by authorities'. Whilst parents mostly teach good values to their children, Fromm was to witness the evils of Nazism and the ability of citizens to internalise the state's lethal ideology. Many SS and Nazi officers believed they were doing their 'duty' or acting 'according to their conscience' despite the obvious repulsion of killing. Where 'disobedience becomes the "cardinal sin"' and 'obedience . . . [the] "cardinal virtue"', great abuses and suffering can follow from the authoritarian conscience as the oppressive parent, teacher, or state worm their way into the individual's mind. Fromm writes that 'The very fact of having a guilty conscience is the symptom of one's virtue because the guilty conscience is a symptom of one's "fear and trembling" before the authority.' So it is that, according to Fromm, we do not trust our own judgement and follow the crowd or the authority instead, reducing ourselves to willing slaves and crippling our productiveness and creativity. Fromm's Marxist roots are evident in statements like 'we have made ourselves into instruments for purposes outside ourselves . . . we experience and treat ourselves as commodities and . . . our own powers have become alienated from ourselves'. Conscience, far from being about the individual taking responsibility, is simply our duty to internalised authority figures.

The humanistic conscience

Whilst Fromm was pretty determinist about human behaviour, influenced as he was by Marx's view that the individual was shaped by social structures such as the state, the Church, owners of capital, schools, laws and the media, he saw the **humanistic conscience** as able to break free. As he wrote, 'Humanistic conscience is not the internalised voice of an authority who we are eager to please and afraid of displeasing; it is our own voice . . . independent of external sanctions or rewards' (Fromm, *Man for Himself*, 1947). The humanistic conscience is the readiness to 'listen to the voice of one's own humanity and is independent of orders given by anyone else'. 'Con-scientia' refers to self-knowledge; to listen to oneself over the noise of authoritarian voices and to develop authentic values that lead to flourishing and avoid failure by learning from past experience.

In many ways, Fromm turns conscience on its head, seeing the individual crippled by the internalisation of authorities that demand that his/her own interests be

Humanistic conscience: Fromm's term for a person's own voice, present in every human being, and independent of external sanctions and rewards. This voice is a person's true self, found by listening to and heeding one's deepest needs, desires and goals.

sacrificed. Social taboos are to be put aside – for example, sexual behaviour is to be regarded as a matter of personal preference, akin to our taste for food. The humanistic conscience is not external – whether in heaven, the state or one's parents. It is one's own ideals and purposes in life that make for human flourishing.

> **Discussion Question**
> How does Fromm see conscience as potentially dangerous or liberating?

Piaget and Kohlberg

Jean Piaget (1896–1980) began his career as a biologist looking at the evolution of organisms. He went on to study cognitive development from childhood to adolescence. He was fascinated by the debate between empiricists like Locke who held that all knowledge came from experience, and thinkers like Kant who agreed that we are born with a blank slate of a mind (a *tabula rasa*), yet who held that experiences were actively processed in our minds. Piaget was drawn to Kant and came to believe that, as children observe how the world acts, they are not passive. They actively construct or invent reality as their experience of the external world interacts with their ideas. In Geneva he studied the approach of children to moral dilemmas like what to do when the 'rules of the game' of marbles were broken.

Jean Piaget

What he found was that children fitted new experiences into their existing framework of understanding the world (assimilation). If these encounters did not fit their existing model, they adapted their model and accommodated the new knowledge or experience into a new one (accommodation). Through experimental study, he came to map out several stages of cognitive development.

Piaget's three stages of cognitive development

Premoral judgement	Heteronomous morality	Autonomous morality
Up to 4 or 5 years old	4–5 to 9–10 years old	After 9–10 years
No clear understanding of rules	Morality in the form of external restraint – rules come from authority figures like parents or teachers. They are fixed, and failure to obey requires retributive punishment. The intentions may be the same in Situations A and B, but if the fallout or consequences of A are greater than those of B (e.g. fifteen cups broken rather than one), then the punishment will be greater.	Rules are created by consent and can be altered with agreement. Intentions and not just outcomes matter, and morality is characterised by co-operation and reciprocity as children interact with peer group, not just parents and teachers. The punishment must fit the crime and intentions and consequences are seen to complicate dilemmas.

From *The Moral Judgement of the Child* (Free Press, 1932)

Studies in the development of the moral reasoning of children and into the age at which they become morally responsible for their behaviour still draw on Piaget's developmental model of moral judgement and reasoning. In moral education within schools, and where criminal charges are brought against children, the findings of cognitive psychologists remain very influential. Moral thought is not innate (we're not born with it), but [is] part of the normal development of human reasoning as we interact socially.

Piaget has been criticised for the complexity of the various dilemmas he set small children. In one such test he overcomplicates the question by asking which boy is more naughty when John breaks fifteen cups and Harry one cup and both do it accidentally. This may have pointed them away from motives and intentions and towards consequences.

Piaget's experimental work was taken up and developed by Lawrence Kohlberg (1927–87), who began a long-term study of 10- to 26-year-old US males interviewed every three years and asked questions like 'Why shouldn't you steal from a store?' or 'Would it be morally right for a man called Heinz to steal medical drugs that he thought might cure his dying wife of cancer?' Kohlberg elaborated Piaget's theory into a six-stage developmental process culminating in universal principles of justice such as the respect for the dignity of human beings as individual persons and respect for the universality of human rights. Like Piaget, he too faced criticism over the abstraction or subjectivity of the dilemmas he set and how connected they were to the types of moral decision-making the children encountered in their daily life.

The psychologist Elliot Turiel (1983) observed that children as young as four could distinguish between moral rules and social conventions when set dilemmas they were familiar with. Carol Gilligan (1982) noted that Kohlberg's original studies were on males. Her research suggested that males characteristically put principles before people (bringing justice and judgement centre-stage) whereas females generally put people before principles (centred on compassion and care) and that Kohlberg's universals may be very male-orientated values. Other critics have seen Piaget's and Kohlberg's approach as Western-centric and individualistic. They point out that the social context of family, kinship, culture and tradition (including religion) has a far greater impact in moral decision-making than moral principles. Later research by Kohlberg and other psychologists took such criticisms on board and widened the research base more internationally and cross-culturally in extended studies to show how cognitive development shaped moral thought. Kohlberg highlighted the importance of social interaction with others and the co-operation and negotiation it develops in the fair resolution of conflict. As children become more self-aware through social interaction and co-operation, they can see better the value of reciprocal rather than selfish behaviour. So children at play, having more power in shaping teams, peer support schemes or elections to school councils, and democratic processes, have become more of a feature of education.

The universal nature of the stages Piaget proposed may be seen to add support to the idea of conscience. However, this is not an innate, God-given faculty, but rather one that evolves in the social interactions of human cognitive development.

Heteronomy:
Being subject to or under the authority of the 'law of the other' coming from outside of the rational will (autonomy) of a person. This might be from authority figures such as parents, teachers, the Church, societal codes, or it may be from appetites or desires that are not rationally willed.

Taking things further (beyond the specification) ... the conscience in evolutionary psychology

For most secular thinkers, morality is a product of evolution. This goes back to Darwin's *The Descent of Man* (1868), in which natural selection is seen as partly responsible for the development of mankind's moral capacities. In this view, proto-morality (a kind of raw first stage) is present in ape colonies and among many species, for example in the co-operative hunting and play of dolphins. Kinship altruism is commonplace, animals often defending their offspring at great risk to themselves, or working co-operatively to rear their young in large colonies (as featured in the documentary film *The March of the Penguins*). Behaviour that has a positive or negative impact on the colony or group, such as aggression, cheating, protection or reciprocity, all contributes to establishing order and hierarchy. To observe animal behaviour in social groups is to see 'game theory' in action. In the competitive struggle for existence, co-operative strategies generally succeed over conflict. Consider the following two examples from James Rachels:

A rhesus monkey

1. A group of rhesus monkeys were trained to obtain food by pulling a chain when a light showed. They were then enabled to learn that their pulling one such chain also resulted in a severe and painful shock (produced by an electric shock) for another monkey whom they could see through a one-way mirror, while pulling a different chain did not. Before they had grasped that one pain for the other monkey occurred only when they pulled the first chain, a clear majority of them deliberately refrained from operating the device, although this meant that they went without food, in some cases for several days.

> **Discussion Question**
>
> Do you think the monkeys exhibit sympathy – can they be said to be morally virtuous?

2. Rachels thinks that genes can be responsible for traits of character, and perhaps even that altruistic behaviour with survival benefits may have genetic markers passed down by responsible or altruistic parents to their offspring. In 2012, researchers at the Rockefeller University in New York claimed to have identified a single gene linked to the parenting skills of mice. By injecting a molecule that silenced their estrogen receptor in a specific area of the brain, they found that the mice stopped licking their pups or defending them.

So, for evolutionary psychologists, the concept of the conscience has its roots in the quest for survival and reproduction at the heart of evolution. Put simply, it is not always the Alpha Male that wins – nice guys sometimes finish first in the race for a mate because they prove to be a better bet in terms of loyalty and devoted parenting. The kin-altruism present in the social instincts of higher primates can, in humans, extend beyond immediate relatives or offspring and into an 'expanding circle' (Singer's phrase) encompassing even global ethical concerns or future generations. In this view, 'conscience' is developed from our ape ancestors and not a moral faculty placed innately and uniquely in the human animal by God. Peter Singer points out that Darwin showed animals to be 'capable of love, memory, curiosity, reason, and sympathy for each other' (Peter Singer, *A Darwinian Left: Politics, Evolution, and Cooperation*, Weidenfeld & Nicolson, 1999, p. 60). Yet he also concludes that a Darwinian left should 'reject any inference from what is natural to what is right' (eugenics and a 'might is right, natural selection' outlook would express the views of the Darwinian right). So while many of our interpersonal emotions of praise and blame may emerge from our evolutionary past, at a critical rather than intuitive level, Singer sees us better served by Utilitarian reasoning than by a faith in some innate or God-given conscience.

Despite its critics, and whether it springs from a natural or a supernatural source, the language of conscience remains part of our public moral vocabulary; it is there in the whistle-blowers, the prisoners of conscience, conscience clauses, prominent leaks from military sources, and political resignations because of conscience. Though it may be dismissed as a by-product of evolution, without it, individuals may lack the courage to confront the powerful, for, as Edmund Burke wrote, 'All tyranny needs to gain a foothold is for people of good conscience to remain silent.'

Exercise

1. 'I can't in good conscience allow the U.S. government to destroy privacy, internet freedom and basic liberties for people around the world with this massive surveillance machine they're secretly building.' Edward Snowden

   Look into Edward Snowden's case – do you think that he was justified in leaking the secret information he did while employed by the U.S. government on the authority of his conscience?

2. Read the following extracts from two papal statements.

   (a) What significant points are made about conscience in each statement?
   (b) How would the critics mentioned above begin to challenge this idea of conscience?

   In the depths of his conscience, man detects a law which he does not impose upon himself, but which holds him to obedience. Always summoning him to love good and avoid evil, the voice of conscience when necessary speaks to his heart: do this, shun that. For man has in his heart a law written by God; to obey it is the very dignity of man; according to it he will be judged. Conscience is the most secret core and sanctuary of a man. There he is alone with God, Whose voice echoes in his depths.

   Vatican II, *Gaudium et Spes* (Joy and Hope), section 16

   Certain currents of modern thought have gone so far as to exalt freedom to such an extent that it becomes an absolute, which would then be the source of values . . . The individual conscience is accorded the status of a supreme tribunal of moral judgement which hands down categorical and infallible decisions about good and evil. To the affirmation that one has a duty to follow one's conscience is unduly added the affirmation that one's moral judgement is true merely by the fact that it has its origin in the conscience. But in this way the inescapable claims of truth disappear, yielding their place to a criterion of sincerity, authenticity and 'being at peace with yourself.' ... Conscience is no longer considered ... an act of a person's intelligence, the function of which is to apply the universal knowledge of the good in a specific situation ... Such an outlook is quite congenial to an individualistic ethic, wherein each individual is faced with his own truth, different from the truth of others.

Pope John Paul II, *Veritatis Splendor* (*The Splendour of Truth*; 1993), section 32

3. Having read this chapter, which of the following definitions of conscience do you find most agreeable and why?

   (a) *'[T]hat inmost citadel of the personality where the self is to reign in unmolested sovereignty, king of its own castle, uncorrupted by the compromises and pressures of the crowd.'* Henry Chadwick

   (b) *'Conscience ... refers to a person's sensitive awareness of one's public ego-image with the purpose of seeking to align one's behaviour and self-assessment with that publicly perceived ego-image. Conscience is a sort of internalisation of what others say, do, and think about one, since these play the role of witness and judge.'* B. J. Malina

   (c) *'I have my own laws and lawcourts to pass judgement on me and I appeal to them rather than elsewhere.'* Michel de Montaigne

   (d) *'[T]here is no witness so fearful, nor accuser so terrible as the conscience that dwells in the soul of every man.'* Polybius

   (e) *'It has long been our contention that "dread of society" is the essence of what is called conscience.'* Sigmund Freud

   (f) *'Conscience is the power to feel our thoughts and think our feelings in moral questions.'* T. S. Eliot

   (g) *'Conscience is where the "is" of the universal moral law is turned into the force of one's duty to act or refrain from what ought/ought not to be done.'* Immanuel Kant

   (h) *'Conscience is the only witness, since what takes place in the heart of the person is hidden from the eyes of everyone outside. Conscience makes its witness known only to the person himself. And, in turn, only the person himself knows what his own response is to the voice of conscience.'* Pope John Paul II

   (i) *'Conscience comes from a depth which lies beyond a man's own will and his own reason and makes itself heard as the call of human existence to unify himself.'* Dietrich Bonhoeffer

FURTHER READING

Carol Gilligan (1982) *In a Different Voice.* Harvard University Press

Basil Mitchell (1985) *Morality Religious and Secular: The Dilemma of the Traditional Conscience.* Clarendon Press,

Paul Strohm (2011) *Conscience: A Very Short Introduction.* Oxford University Press

Elliot Turiel (1983) *The Development of Social Knowledge.* Cambridge University Press

Keith Ward (1998) *In Defence of the Soul.* One World Publications, 'Conscience'

OCR Past Paper Questions

JANUARY 2010
Assess the view that conscience need not always be obeyed.   *[35]*

JANUARY 2011
Critically assess the claim that conscience is the voice of reason.   *[35]*

JANUARY 2012
'For moral issues surrounding sex the demands of conscience override other ethical
considerations.' Discuss.   *[35]*

MAY 2012
How convincing are Butler's claims that people have an innate sense of
right and wrong?   *[35]*

JANUARY 2013
Critically assess the claim that conscience is a reliable guide to ethical
decision-making.   *[35]*

13 Virtue Ethics

QUICK QUESTION

Can bad characters be good? In the film *Despicable Me*, Supervillain Gru adopts three orphans to help with a theft but, despite himself, he grows to care for them over time. Virtue ethicists say that we are what we habitually do. The moral life is not about individual actions but character-forming habits over time that shape the story of our lives – only at death can a life be judged, in hindsight.

LEARNING OUTCOMES

In reading this chapter, you will learn:

- about the principles of Virtue Ethics from Aristotle
- about the 'agent-centred' nature of Virtue Ethics
- about the concepts of *eudaimonia* and the Golden Mean
- about the importance of practising the virtues and the example of virtuous people
- modern approaches to Virtue Ethics
- to discuss these concepts critically and their strengths and weaknesses

Discussion Question

Is pre-existing behaviour or character a predictor of future behaviour? Can a good person do harm despite the best of intentions because they are naive or fail to calculate the consequences of or universalise their actions? Does a bad person look at moral choices and dilemmas differently?

What is virtue?

The English word 'virtue' comes from the Latin *'virtus'*, though the concept comes from the Greek word **arêté**, which actually comes from the name of the Greek god Ares. Ares was the son of Jupiter and Juno and was the god of war and destruction, so *'arêté'* probably originally meant the idea of bravery in war, which was a soldier's defining characteristic. *'Arêté'* came to mean an 'excellence' at something, so that a worker with *arêté* had the characteristic of being excellent at his work.

Virtue, then, has to do with a person's character. Someone's virtue is what they do best, something they excel at. So a musician (who can give a 'virtuoso' performance) excels at playing an instrument, a chef excels at cooking, and so on. Such a person undergoes training and often a kind of apprenticeship under those who have mastered the skills and practices they seek to develop. They practise for a long

Arêté:

Virtue, or any good characteristic or excellence. *Arêté* involves committed and purposeful training and practice, usually under the tutelage of a master-practitioner.

time to become excellent at what they do, so that, eventually, by making choices and developing good habits, these excellences become part of the person's character.

History of Virtue Ethics

> [T]he beginning is the most important part of any work, especially in the case of a young and tender thing; for that is the time at which the character is being formed and the desired impression is more readily taken . . . And shall we just carelessly allow children to hear any casual tales which may be devised by casual persons, and to receive into their minds ideas for the most part the very opposite of those which we should wish them to have when they are grown up?
> (Plato, *The Republic*, bk 2)

Almost all discussion of Virtue Ethics focuses on Western philosophical traditions, including Socrates, Plato and Aristotle. It is important to note, however, that Virtue theories exist from all around the world, from Confucianism, Buddhism and Taoism in Asia to the Akan people in West Africa and Native American tribes in North America.

As the American philosopher Nina Rosenstand points out in her book *The Moral of the Story* (p. 386), 'the overwhelming number of ancient stories that we have, as well as examples of tribal cultures around the world, seem to have favoured the Virtue approach'. Two examples can be seen in:

1. The ancient Chinese philosophy of Confucianism in which the cultivation of character and skilled judgements were aimed at a 'harmonious' life. Virtues included Ren (benevolence and charity), Li (good manners), Yi (honesty and uprightness), Zhi (knowledge) and Xin (faithfulness and integrity).

Exercise
The claim has been made that it takes 10,000 hours of purposeful practice to make a genius. Certainly there is a correlation between those who make it to be professional musicians and the number of hours they practised. Look up 'The Dan Plan' online for an entertaining example of a would-be golfer testing this hypothesis.

2. The Akan society of West Africa, in which story-telling was the method of teaching children how to practise a good character (*suban pa*). Among the key virtues for this community were kindness, faithfulness, compassion and hospitality. Without these virtues, society would not be harmonious. The community would only thrive when the virtues were put into practice by the people.

Context

In Western philosophy, Virtue Ethics began in the ancient Greek world. Greek epic poets and playwrights like Homer and Sophocles painted their heroes and antiheroes in terms of their virtues and vices. Thinkers like Socrates, Plato and Aristotle were key to the development of Virtue Ethics. According to Greg Pence (in Singer, *Companion to Ethics*, pp. 249–58), the ancient Greeks made three sorts of contribution:

- first, they focused on character traits (virtues) as opposed to moral laws or individual actions. As we will see below, Plato's *Republic* discusses the virtues that develop out of different political systems (e.g. democracy, oligarchy, tyranny and meritocracy) and he sees politics as social ethics.

- second, they put virtues into a kind of 'rank order', the most important of which they called the **cardinal virtues** – temperance, wisdom, courage, prudence and justice.

- third, they analysed various kinds of human character. We will see below how Aristotle listed five types of person, ranging from the moral monster to the great-souled man.

Cardinal virtues: These are the most important virtues. Plato and Aristotle, followed by many ancient philosophers, regarded temperance, wisdom, justice, prudence and courage as the most desirable character traits.

All these thinkers placed a special emphasis on education, because virtuous character traits are developed throughout a person's life. It is the responsibility of adults (especially teachers and parents) to teach the virtues to the young. If people fail to develop virtuous characters as they grow up, they will instead develop bad character traits, or vices.

As a result of the demise of Aristotle's ideas and the rise of neo-Platonic philosophy, particularly as it developed within Christianity, there came to be little discussion of Virtue Ethics until the thirteenth-century Christian scholars, especially St Thomas Aquinas, re-discovered Aristotle's philosophy and adapted it for Christian thought and teaching. Aquinas accepted many of Aristotle's ideas on the virtues and added the **theological virtues** of faith, hope and charity/love to the cardinal virtues.

With the waning of the Middle Ages and the rise of the Renaissance, the Scientific Revolution and the Enlightenment, the influence of Aristotle's Virtue Ethics again declined. In the eighteenth century, Immanuel Kant's rationalism led people to accept a rule-based system of ethical decision-making. By the nineteenth century, moral theories like Utilitarianism focused on individual actions and their consequences, and these supplanted the character trait emphasis of Virtue theory. Within the past few decades there has been a revival of interest in Virtue Ethics, owing to important writings by Elizabeth Anscombe, Alasdair MacIntyre, Rosalind Hursthouse and others, who believe that Virtue Ethics may bring a way of combating some of the problems of both the rule-based and consequence-based approaches of Kant and Utilitarianism. The rest of this chapter will look in more detail at some major Virtue ethicists in Western philosophy – Aristotle, Aquinas, Anscombe and MacIntyre.

Aristotle was, for twenty years, a pupil, then a teacher, at Plato's Academy in Athens. He later set up a rival school, the Lyceum, and also taught the young teenager who was to become Alexander the Great. He was one of the first philosophers to think about the virtues. His book *The Nicomachean Ethics* is a major contribution to ethical theory on the virtues, and a great deal of subsequent ethical discussion on the virtues has been debate and reflection on Aristotle's fundamental analysis.

The real key to understanding Aristotle's ethics is to grasp his teleological (goal-orientated) view of human identity. According to Aristotle, everything in nature has its own unique function, purpose, or the goal that it attempts to achieve. For example, the unique function or characteristic of the eye is to see, that of the skeleton is to support the body. Humans, Aristotle says, also have their own unique function, which is to transcend the biological impulses shared with the rest of the animal kingdom. Humans are to act in accordance with reason. Though they share many functions with the rest of nature (for example, a need for nutrition and growth are shared with both plants and animals, while consciousness and feeling are shared only with animals), only humans can use their powers of reason to work out which is the best course of action in any situation. Aristotle calls this capacity to reason 'the rational principle'.

Aristotle (384–322 BCE)

Aristotle begins *The Nicomachean Ethics* with the following words: 'Every art, and every enquiry, and similarly every action and pursuit, is thought to aim at some good, and for this reason the good has rightly been declared to be that at which all things aim' (*The Nicomachean Ethics*, ed. David Ross, Oxford University Press, 2009, p. 1). What Aristotle is saying here is that people choose to do certain things because they will bring about particular 'ends' or 'goods'. For example, you are studying A Levels in order to go to university or get a job. You want to get a job in order to make money. You make money because you want to buy a car or a house, and so on. According to Aristotle, this process of pursuing things for particular ends or goals cannot go on to infinity, because you would never be able to justify the individual steps in the chain. There must, therefore, be some 'ultimate' good or end for humans, which we desire for its own sake. As Aristotle says, 'We call that which is in itself worthy of pursuit more final than that which is worthy of pursuit for the sake of something else . . . we call final without qualification that which is always desirable in itself and never for the sake of something else' (ibid., p. 2). This ultimate good, then, is something that is 'good *in itself*' or intrinsically good. It is not good because of what it achieves, but simply good because it is good.

Aristotle calls the ultimate good that all humans aim to achieve *eudaimonia*. This is often translated as 'happiness', but is more accurately understood as 'living well'. It means much more than just living a very moral life. Living a *eudaimon* life certainly involves being moral, but it also involves the kind of thing that a parent wishes for his child – that they should develop into a 'good person'. Another way of putting this is to say that a person is living the eudaimonic life if he is 'flourishing' – that his life is 'going well'. For Aristotle, in fourth-century Greece, this meant living a pleasurable life, in

Da Vinci's 'Vitruvian Man', depicting a human being's 'ideal' proportions

QUICK QUESTION

Is there an essential human nature that informs what a flourishing life would look like for human beings, or is the good life a more subjective creation of values by different individuals, communities, cultures and societies?

the company of friends and one's children. Importantly, for Aristotle, it involved the constant pursuit and attainment of excellence through a very wide range of human activities. All these activities should come under the umbrella of reason, which Aristotle thought was the one capacity that truly differentiated human beings from other animals. Aristotle puts it this way:

> We state the function of man to be a certain kind of life, and this to be an activity or actions of the soul implying a rational principle. The function of a good man is to be a good and noble performance of these, and if any action is well performed it is performed in accordance with the appropriate excellence.
>
> (*Nicomachean Ethics*, bk 1, ch. 7)

Immediately after this summary of the eudaimonic life as an activity of the soul which exhibits human excellence, Aristotle adds another important point. He says that such a life can only be thought of as a good life if it can be maintained for as long as a person lives. Only the 'complete life' can be considered to be a life that has achieved its proper end or goal.

In Aristotle's thought, the way for humans to achieve this eudaimonic or happy life is to possess the virtues. Just as the life worth living involves more than just high moral quality, so the virtues cover a wide range of human characteristics. Aristotle divides the virtues into three main types or classes: bodily, of character and of intelligence. The attainment of each of these is necessary to living the good life.

The bodily virtues

These are health, strength and 'good looks'. Aristotle gives some clues as to what someone with a virtuous appearance might look like: 'Small people may be neat and well proportioned, but cannot be beautiful. The virtuously proud man has a deep voice and a level utterance, for the man who takes few things seriously is not likely to be hurried. While a shrill voice and a rapid walk are the results of hurry and excitement.'

The virtues of character (moral virtues)

Moral virtues: Aristotle's definition is: a disposition to behave in the right manner and as a mean between extremes of deficiency and excess, which are vices

This type of virtue has to do with putting reason into practice. The excellence of intelligence (the intellectual virtues) shows rationally which course of action is best, while the excellence of character puts this into practice. For example, if I want to preserve a healthy body and am concerned about what I eat, my reason tells me that I should eat sensibly, according to a healthy diet. My greedy instincts, however, might get in the way when I have a meal at a restaurant or when I am in the sweet shop. This is where the moral virtue of 'temperance' is necessary. Temperance is the middle point between the two extremes of self-indulgence and complete rejection of all sensory enjoyment (a state sometimes referred to as 'insensibility'). Equipped with this virtue, I can combat my indulgent instinct to eat chocolate and pursue a healthier diet.

The next important point made by Aristotle is that excellence or virtue of character is learned by constant training and repetition or habit (the Latin word *ethice* = habit). To some extent, human beings are like blank slates when they are born. As a person practises temperance, he gradually becomes a temperate person. Someone who habitually exercises courage becomes a courageous person. The 'blank slate' gradually becomes filled with virtues over time, simply by the practice of the virtues. Aristotle believed that we build our own character in much the same way as a lyre player practises to become a good lyre player: 'it is from playing the lyre that both good and bad lyre players are produced; men will be good or bad builders as a result of building well or badly'.

While a person might initially struggle to demonstrate a particular virtue because they have to combat their natural instincts, by repeating virtuous actions that person should become someone who wants to behave in accordance with virtue rather than unthinkingly following their natural impulses. Excellence of character (moral virtue) is therefore a settled disposition to want to act and to act in a way appropriate to the situation. The truly virtuous person, then, does not live in a state of constant self-denial because their true selves have become virtuous through constant practice.

Classical Greek vase depicting lyre player

As part of his understanding of the excellent character, Aristotle develops the idea of the mean. By the 'mean', Aristotle has in mind the middle point between opposite extremes. The temple of Apollo at Delphi in ancient Greece bore the inscription 'Meden Agan' meaning 'Nothing in excess'. The mean is the virtue of character, the opposite extremes are vices. The **doctrine of the mean** is not a way of determining the best course of action (e.g. always act with a mean of cowardice and rashness), but rather a guide to the nature of the excellent character. Furthermore, in some situations it is best to act with an extreme of a particular type, e.g. anger in response to extreme injustice. The proper interpretation of the idea of the mean, then, is 'the disposition to feel and display the right degree of emotion on each occasion … a mean between being too much disposed and too little disposed to feel and display each emotion' (*Nicomachean Ethics*, pp. 45f.). Again, 'in the mean one will feel and display each emotion at the right times and not too often or infrequently, with reference to the right matters, towards the right people, for the right reason and in the right way' (ibid., pp. 45f.).

Aristotle's list of means is given in the table below. Many of these do not seem to be what we would normally call moral qualities (e.g. the vice of self-effacement). They

> **Doctrine of the mean:**
> When talking about the moral virtues, Aristotle says that the virtuous man establishes a 'mean' or middle point between deficiency and excess, e.g. courage is the mean between cowardice (deficiency) and foolhardiness (excess)

are what contribute to *eudaimonia*, which is understood as the sort of life a parent wishes for their child, not the life of a moral saint.

Aristotle's virtues and vices

Vice of deficiency	Virtuous mean	Vice of excess
Cowardice	Courage	Foolhardiness
Insensibility	Temperance	Intemperance
Meanness	Liberality	Wastefulness
Pettiness	Magnificence	Vulgarity
Mean-mindedness	Magnanimity	Vanity
Lack of ambition	Proper ambition	Over-ambition
Indifference	Patience	Irascibility
Surliness	Friendliness	Obsequiousness
Modesty	Sincerity	Boastfulness
Boorishness	Wittiness	Buffoonery
Shamelessness	Modesty	Shyness
Callousness	Proper indignation	Spitefulness

Aristotle gives two analogies to help us to understand the doctrine of the mean. First, we say of great works of art that it is impossible to add or to take away anything from them. This implies, for Aristotle, that excess and defect destroy the beauty of the work, while the mean preserves it. The second analogy concerns health. The body's health and strength are impaired by either too much or too little food or by too much or too little exercise. The right amounts of food and exercise create and preserve health and strength. Similarly, says Aristotle, virtues and vices relate to affections and actions in which there is an excess, an intermediate (the mean) and a deficit. So we may feel fear or anger and pleasures or pains in general, in different degrees, but to feel them too much or too little is bad.

The virtues of intelligence (intellectual virtues)

Intellectual virtues:
Aristotle listed five intellectual virtues: practical intelligence, scientific knowledge, intuition, wisdom and art or technical skill

After his discussion of the **moral virtues**, Aristotle turns to what he calls the **intellectual virtues**, or virtues of intelligence. He defines five kinds of intellectual virtues:

Art (*techne*)	Although this is a capacity for 'making' or 'doing', it is intellectual because it involves a true process of reasoning.
Scientific knowledge (*episteme*)	This is concerned with what is unchanging: it is a capacity to demonstrate the connections between things.

Rational intuition (*nous*)	This is the faculty from which we get knowledge of first principles. This is where scientific knowledge begins.
Practical intelligence (*phronēsis*)	This concerns things that could be otherwise (i.e. contingent things): it is by practical intelligence that we are able to reason out the right means to secure the ends we aim at.
Wisdom (*sophia*)	This is a combination of *nous* (rational intuition) and *episteme* (scientific knowledge), as both of these relate to the highest and most valuable objects.

Of these five kinds of intellectual virtue, practical intelligence and wisdom play the most important part in Aristotle's ethics. The moral virtues are what make us aim at being a virtuous person. Practical intelligence is what makes us take the right steps

Socrates lived a virtuous life and died for his principles in 399 BCE. When Aristotle was accused of the same crime of impiety by an Athenian court in 323 BCE, he left the city, saying that he would not let the city sin twice against philosophy. Socrates' sense of purpose, virtue, and integrity epitomises the good life (*eudaimonia*) for Plato and Aristotle.

to achieve the right end. Aristotle sees a close relationship between the moral virtues and practical intelligence – in fact, he suggests that they are inseparable. In practice, it is impossible to have one without the other. Practical intelligence without moral virtue would be mere cunning or astuteness (*deinotes*). Conversely, moral virtue without practical intelligence is at best 'natural virtue', a natural disposition that children and animals may share, but which needs training and reason to develop into virtue.

For Aristotle, then, **eudaimonia** or 'living well' is a complex reality made up of many excellences, each of which is to be valued in its own right and as part of the greater whole. It will include reasonable wealth, good looks and good birth, as well as the virtues of character and intelligence.

Yet, while it is a complex thing, Aristotle suggests that there are three main candidates for the type or structure of life that comprises the eudaimonic life: the life of contemplation, the political life and the life of sensual pleasure. Aristotle thinks that the life of contemplation is the best life, with politics coming second. The point that Aristotle is making is that you have to choose one dominant approach to life, but this does not exclude other excellences and pleasures any more than a brain surgeon never has to eat again after qualifying or no longer needs friendship. Furthermore, in choosing politics and contemplation, he is simply reflecting to some extent the social values of his time and of the upper classes of society with which he was associated all through his life.

It must be remembered, however, that, for Aristotle, the life of contemplation is most like the life of God, who is the most eudaimonic being. Aristotle understood God as pure intuitive reason; he is reason itself, not someone who possesses that reason. Since man has a limited capacity for intuitive reason, he has a divine spark within him.

Aristotle's Virtue theory sees virtue as socially formed. Citizens of Greek city-states like Athens nurtured their virtues in community and society, sharpening their judgement about the golden mean through practice. Kant may be guilty of seeing the autonomous rational agent as a rational individual. Aristotle sees ethics as practical, social and participative, as they exercise the bodily, intellectual and moral virtues. People must choose their direction through life, whether that be contemplative or in politics, and pursue it with excellence. As they do this, they will be living the eudaimonic life, although final judgement on that person's life must await their death.

Aquinas

St Thomas Aquinas offered a systematic account of the virtues. His discussion of the virtues holds many insights and has been almost as influential as that of Aristotle, particularly in the field of Christian ethics.

Aquinas' account of virtue appears in various writings, but the most important of these appears in his final theological work, the *Summa Theologica*, a multi-volume handbook for Christian priests and other scholars. The first part of the second volume (*Prima Secundae Partis*) contains Aquinas' presentation of his thoughts on virtue. He defines a virtue as a stable disposition that inclines a person to act in one way rather than another. He also talks of a virtue as a habit which perfects human capabilities. Human beings have various 'capabilities': these are the intellect, powers of the will, and two irrational appetites – the 'concupiscible appetite' (which accounts for our physical desires), and the 'irascible appetite' (which accounts for our emotions like anger and fear). Some of these powers are good for us, while others are not. For instance, sometimes we can desire healthy food, and, at other times, we might desire food that we know is unhealthy. Aquinas argues that we need good habits to help us to act in good ways so that we can achieve our 'ends' or goals in life. According to Aquinas, these good habits are the virtues.

To take a simple example, if our aim or goal is to become a good athlete, then we must eat healthily, train hard and develop suitable habits to ensure that we can achieve our goal.

Aquinas goes on to say that the ultimate goal of human beings is to attain perfect happiness. By this he means achieving the vision of God that faithful Christians experience in heaven.

Aquinas talks of three main categories of virtue: intellectual, moral and theological. He follows Aristotle in his views about the intellectual and moral virtues. Intellectual virtues perfect the intellectual powers of the human being. These can be either theoretical or practical. Theoretical intellectual virtues have to do with acquiring general principles. For example, studying Science and Mathematics leads us to grasp true general principles. We learn these principles from a scientist or mathematician, experts in their field. The practical intellectual virtues could be called 'skills'. Examples of these might be the skills of carpentry or medicine, which have to be practised in order to learn them. These virtues dispose the person who has them to produce works that are well done, e.g. a well-built house or a healed patient.

For Aquinas, the moral virtues perfect the appetitive powers of the soul. To cite three examples, he discusses the virtues of temperance (which concerns the pleasures that come from the table and the bedroom), courage (which concerns the emotions of fear and confidence) and justice (which concerns the interactions of people with each other).

To the intellectual and moral virtues which Aquinas shared with Aristotle, Aquinas added the 'theological' virtues of faith, hope and charity/love. These three **theological virtues** differ from the intellectual and moral ones because they have God as their object, not humans. Aquinas is clear that the theological virtues come from God; in his term, they are 'infused' virtues, put into people's minds and wills by God. God does this in order for humans to achieve salvation. The infused theological virtues are directed toward the perfect happiness that consists in the vision of God in heaven – a happiness which can be achieved only with God's help.

Aquinas wrote a great deal about the virtues, and put forward a principle for deciding which the most important ones were: for any two virtues, the more excellent virtue has the more excellent object. The table below summarises these.

Theological virtues: After the New Testament was written, the four ancient virtues became known as the cardinal virtues, while faith, hope and charity/love were referred to as the theological virtues. They were developed particularly by St Thomas Aquinas and became part of Natural Law theory.

Virtues	Most important	Reason
Intellectual	Wisdom	Its object (God) is the most excellent object of knowledge
Moral	Justice	Its object (the ways people interact with each other) is the most excellent
Theological	Charity/love	This unites humans with God most closely

For Aquinas, the theological virtues are the most important, as they are given by God, and, of these, charity/love, 'the mother and form of all the virtues', is the most important virtue of all.

Some key thinkers in the modern revival of Virtue theory

Elizabeth Anscombe

Elizabeth Anscombe

Elizabeth Anscombe (1919-2001) was taught by Ludwig Wittgenstein and later became Professor of Philosophy at Cambridge University. She was initially responsible for re-igniting the discussion about Virtue theory. In 1958, she published an article, 'Modern Moral Philosophy' at a time when religious-based approaches to public and contemporary ethics were no longer considered credible. She argued that both Kantian Ethics and Utilitarianism failed as moral systems for non-theists because they ultimately depended upon some external (divine) lawgiver. Utilitarianism justified evil deeds by calculating on the basis of consequences it could not know ahead of time (she coined the term 'consequentialism'). Kantian Ethics offered what was, for Anscombe, the incoherent alternative of being 'self-regulating'. Anscombe's article kick-started a debate about Aristotle's virtues and how they could form a basis for a non-theistic system of moral decision-making. A convert, and thereafter a lifelong Catholic herself, she is seen by many scholars as arguing that our language of moral obligations finds deeper roots in religious traditions. She may not have succeeded in rehabilitating insights from religious ethics and tradition to the mainstream. Nevertheless, what she began (influenced by Wittgenstein) was a new attention to ethics as practice, and, by focusing on Aristotle, she called for a richer psychological account of character formation and human flourishing than legislative systems of ethics like the Utilitarian and Kantian approaches had put forward.

Alasdair MacIntyre

Alasdair MacIntyre

Alasdair MacIntyre (1929–) is a British-born philosopher who has developed and adapted what Aristotle has to say in relation to present-day moral theories. His most important books are *After Virtue* (1981) and *Whose Justice, Which Rationality?* (1988).

MacIntyre begins *After Virtue* with a story of a catastrophe. The public blame scientists for a series of disasters. Riots occur, scientists are killed, laboratories destroyed and books and scientific instruments burned. Shortly after these events, a 'know-nothing' political movement gains power and abolishes science teaching in schools and universities. The few remaining scientists are imprisoned and executed.

Some time later, there is a reaction against this movement and a more enlightened generation tries to revive science. They possess only fragments of the 'old' scientific tradition – odd formulas, half-chapters of books, broken instruments, some calculus. There is only partial knowledge of Einstein's Theory of Relativity and Darwin's theory of evolution. Many suspect that any real scientific knowledge is irretrievably lost.

MacIntyre argues that something similar has happened in the world of morality, and, astonishingly, most people have not noticed. Modern ethical debates seem endless and are characterised by widespread disagreement and a lack of consensus.

According to MacIntyre, this is because we make moral decisions without having the necessary structures for moral thinking. There is no overarching tradition to give meaning and purpose to our moral lives. So, we are Utilitarians when it comes to allocating valuable medical resources, Kantians in wanting to establish universal moral rules through reason, and Christian when we elevate charity as a virtue in our society. The industrialised, urbanised and individualistic Western society we live in has broken down the communities in which virtues can thrive and flourish. This breakdown has left many people disillusioned and lacking a purpose (*telos*), or even a concept of what 'the good life' actually means.

MacIntyre claims that this catastrophe actually happened over a long period of time. He spends time in *After Virtue* discussing the intellectual context of moral thinking. He says this is important because, without remembering where ethics comes from, we will not be able to understand the 'narrative context' or flow of ethical debate and the reasons why moral theories change. He does not like 'quandary ethics', whereby different theories are tested by looking at highly unusual and improbable dilemmas. If we are to be able to make ethical decisions, we have to know that the system is clear and workable. For this to be the case, we have to know its context.

Winston Churchill is lionised for his courageous leadership of Britain during WW2. His courage may be seen as a golden mean between the vice of deficiency (in Chamberlain's appeasement of Hitler) and the vice of excess (as in the disastrous 1915 Gallipoli campaign in which Churchill as the first Lord of the Admiralty was a prime mover – it saw 140,000 Allied casualties in nine months of fighting).

Up until the seventeenth century, Aristotle's ideas held sway. Ethics was about learning to be a 'good person' by doing good things and by being taught how to be virtuous. Of course, there were different understandings of what the virtues were, and all were relative to the different cultures in which people grew up – for example:

- the virtues of ancient Greece, as set out in Homer's *The Iliad* and *The Odyssey*. The moral role models of the day were adventurers and warriors, so physical strength, courage, cunning and friendship were seen as virtues.
- the virtues of Athens and other city-states. Virtues here were courage, friendship, justice, temperance and wisdom.
- the virtues of medieval Europe, which included courage, justice, temperance, wisdom as well as the Christian virtues of faith, hope and charity/love.

Whichever set of virtues was accepted, there was always a belief that they were intimately linked to communities. The virtues were developed in the practical co-operation of groups of people living and working together. Further, there was a *telos* or goal in life – a 'good life' to which one ought to strive. The purpose of life was the attainment of the good life.

MacIntyre claims that there are two different but related contexts in which human beings live their lives and which require the exercise of the virtues:

- the 'practices'
- the search for the good life.

The practices

Human beings are part of many different activities throughout their lives. MacIntyre calls these activities 'practices'. These practices might include working as a teacher, playing rugby, being a mother and studying photography at evening classes. All these practices have a particular history. The history or tradition of teaching stretches back through centuries and, growing out of this past, it has an open-ended future. In some ways, the teacher of today is helping to shape that future. All practices share certain characteristics:

1. They are 'coherent and complex'.
2. They are a form of co-operation between people that has been established in the past.
3. Each practice needs 'goods' that are unique to that practice. For example, there are certain skills in rugby that are unique to that game – good handling, goal kicking, spin passing, etc. MacIntyre calls this type of unique skill an 'internal' good. He contrasts these with 'external' goods, like a rugby player being able to make money from his abilities. Such 'external' goods are not unique to one activity. When an individual achieves an 'internal' good, he benefits the entire community (i.e. we all watch and admire his skills). Internal goods enrich everyone involved in a particular activity, while external goods will often only benefit the individual concerned.
4. These goods are produced when people strive for excellence in the tradition of which they are a part.
5. As people pursue excellence in their particular practice, the practice itself is developed and changed in ways that have continuity with the past, but also take the practice on to new heights of achievement. For example, new training techniques in rugby have enabled the practice of rugby to be extended and developed.
6. True happiness comes as a by-product of striving for and achieving excellence in a particular activity. The person tries to achieve excellence, and happiness 'creeps up' on them. Happiness is therefore inseparable from the activity pursued. So, for example, the particular happiness that comes from winning a game of chess could not be gained from winning at Snakes and Ladders or by scoring a goal in hockey, or by any other activity.
7. To participate meaningfully in any practice requires an individual to demonstrate certain virtues that are essential to the practice in question. For example, the practice of academic learning requires a commitment to many other things. Someone

who cheats in all his examinations to achieve his degree is not properly participating in the tradition of education. Equally, someone who thinks that they can learn nothing from their teachers will probably fail to realise the *internal goods* of education. This is also true in sport – Maradona's 'hand of God' goal against England helped Argentina to gain the *external good* of victory, but was seen by many people (though not in Argentina) as a denial of what the practice of soccer is all about. Internal goods are co-operative and develop skills which benefit others, whereas external goods tend to be competitive goods where my success means your failure; my increased, your decreased share of the pie.

MacIntyre summarises his account of a practice as follows:

Any coherent and complex form of socially established co-operative human activity through which goods internal to that form of activity are realised in the course of trying to achieve the standards of excellence which are appropriate to, and partially definitive of that form of activity. With the result that human powers to achieve excellence, and human conceptions of the ends and goods involved, are systematically extended.

(*After Virtue*, 3rd edition, University of Notre Dame Press, 2007, p. 187)

The search for the good life

According to MacIntyre, all the individual practices pursued by people are set in a larger, over-arching context. It is this that enables a person to decide on a specific occasion between the particular demands of all the practices they are involved in. For example, a person may need to decide whether to mark a set of Year 8 books, or to go and pick the children up and cook them dinner, or to go to rugby practice, or to take some pictures with their new camera. In order to prioritise these choices, the person must have an over-arching idea of what sort of life they want to lead. So, for example, they may decide that cooking dinner for their children is more important than any of the other choices because they want their children to be healthy and happy, and this outweighs the good of their own pleasure or that of marking exercise books.

MacIntyre describes this over-arching dimension of an individual's life as the 'search for the good life'. The good life is the life that allows individuals to 'flourish' as human beings. Just as a watch flourishes when it tells the time, so a human being flourishes when he/she does what is appropriate for him/her. The search will lead different people and different communities in different directions, but there is at least one common characteristic of the flourishing life: that those living it are engaged in the search for what it means to be a human in their own particular context.

MacIntyre says that there are three characteristics of a flourishing human being:

1. The ability to evaluate, modify or reject our own practical judgements – to ask, in effect, whether what we think are good reasons to act really are sufficiently good.
2. The ability to imagine realistically alternative possible futures so as to be able to make rational choices between them.
3. The ability to stand back from our desires, so as to be able to inquire rationally what the pursuit of our good here and now requires, and how our desires must be directed and, if necessary, re-educated if we are to achieve it.

It is clear that MacIntyre is very similar at this point to Aristotle. Both claim that the abilities to reason and evaluate are what set human beings apart from other creatures. MacIntyre, however, having the benefit of modern biological knowledge, does not draw such a strict distinction between humans and other species as did Aristotle. Nevertheless, it remains true for MacIntyre that humans are one of the only species to have 'moved beyond their initial animal state of having reasons for acting in this way rather than, towards the specifically human state of being able to evaluate those reasons' (*Dependent, Rational Animals*, Bloomsbury Academic, 1999, p. 47).

In order to flourish as a human being, it is necessary for an individual to possess the 'intellectual and moral virtues'. MacIntyre does not provide a comprehensive list of these. Instead, he says that they are whatever quality enables a person to become a 'practical reasoner', or, in other words, to move beyond a childish approach to life to that of an adult who flourishes as an adult. These qualities are, for MacIntyre, the intellectual virtues. Temperateness and honesty would be good examples of the kind of quality MacIntyre has in mind. Both of these require the mental capacity to evaluate different options, and imagination (i.e. the ability to imagine realistic, future possibilities so as to decide between them). These correspond generally with Aristotle's 'virtues of intelligence'.

For MacIntyre, the person who possesses the full range of intellectual and moral virtues is equipped not only to flourish himself, but also to enable others to flourish. Humans are, according to MacIntyre's 1999 book, *Dependent, Rational Animals*. Humans depend on other human beings at different stages of their lives for almost everything that enables them to flourish. For example, a child depends on his parents as well as those who act *in loco parentis* on his journey to develop into a flourishing adult. MacIntyre discusses virtues that humans need to help other human beings become 'practical reasoners'.

Among the values discussed by MacIntyre is the Native American Lakota people's idea of 'Wancantognaka'. This can be loosely translated as 'generosity' and 'generosity combined'. MacIntyre explains what Wancantognaka involves: 'It involves a generosity that I owe to all those others who owe it to me. Because I owe it, to fail to exhibit it is also to fail in respect of justice; because what I owe is uncalculating giving, to fail to exhibit it is also to fail in respect of generosity' (1999, p. 120). For MacIntyre, something

Wheelchair basketball at the London 2012 Paralympics, which transformed attitudes towards disability

like Wancantognaka ought to govern the way in which we relate to all human beings we come into contact with. They, in turn, owe us the same treatment.

In quite a radical departure from Aristotle's account of the virtues, MacIntyre also stresses the 'virtues of acknowledged dependence'. Since all human beings are dependent on one another to a greater or lesser extent, it is a vice not to acknowledge that. Indeed, a failure to realise our dependence on others in friendship, community and healthcare will severely impair our capacity to flourish as human beings. For example, able-bodied people may be tempted to deny that they are dependent in any way on disabled people, but, according to MacIntyre, the vulnerability of severely disabled people exposes to us just how temporary the Enlightenment myth of the autonomous rational individual is. At birth, death and many times in between, we are dependent upon the help of others. Further, the possibility of caring for a disabled person 'gives us the possibility of learning something essential, what it is for someone else to be wholly entrusted to our care, so that we are answerable for their well being' (ibid.).

How the people of Le Chambon in occupied France illustrate MacIntyre's Virtue theory

MacIntyre's claim that communities train people to be virtuous is illustrated in the life of a small Protestant village in southern France. During the Nazi occupation, it sheltered around 5,000 Jews, putting its own survival at risk. False identity papers were produced, some Jews were smuggled out to Switzerland, and others hidden during 'round-ups' aimed at gathering up Jews to send off to concentration camps. Yet this tightly knit community of Protestant Christians with a strong ethic of hospitality to strangers 'as if to Christ' considered it 'the done thing' and right and proper to shelter Jews when discovery of this fact could well have led to reprisals. The margins of their parish paper contained biblical phases like 'One must obey God rather than man', and 'He who does not love his brother whom he has seen, how can he love God whom he has not seen?' Their stories, hymns and life together fostered a strong sense of unity and hospitality, and having themselves been victims of persecution as a minority Protestant community under a Roman Catholic French government, they knew what it was to be victim to such injustices. Stories of how pastors in their history had, under interrogation and imprisonment, refused to give up the names of members of their illegal congregation steeled them for their present task of sheltering the Jews.

Discussion Questions

1. How might a community provide a strong sense of identity and a moral compass for its members?
2. In the highly mobile world of modern cities in which people may not belong to a community and feel rootless and lacking in identity, are there moral resources that we lack which ancient societies possessed?
3. (a) Moral community   (b) Moral agent   (c) Moral action – how might (a) shape (b) and (c)?

Martha Nussbaum

Martha Nussbaum (1947–) is a Virtue ethicist who has written on Moral Philosophy (especially on justice and inequality) and law. In *The Fragility of Goodness*, she deals with what some call 'moral luck', the sense that the flourishing life is often constrained by human vulnerability to circumstances, ill health, injustices or inequality of opportunity. Her reading of Aristotle and Plato sees vulnerability as a key to the eudaimonic life – it is this which brings us into community and social co-operation. Here, Nussbaum argues that system-based approaches to ethical reasoning can at times boil down to putting the dilemma in at one end, cranking it through the procedure of universalisable rules or calculations of consequences, and delivering a decision. In doing so, they can overlook how systems and institutions of power can be stacked in favour of the rich and powerful. They certainly neglect 'the three frontiers', namely justice for the disabled, transnational (or global) justice which includes the welfare of developing nations, and the interests of animals. She argues that human dignity and a fuller account of justice and a virtuous society would value 'a wide range of motives, including the love of justice itself, and prominently including a moralized compassion for those who have less than they need to lead decent and dignified lives' (*Frontiers of Justice*, Harvard University Press, 2006).

In 2003, Nussbaum founded the Human Development and Capability Association with Nobel Prize-winning economist Amartya Sen. This took a 'capabilities' approach to international development, rooted in an Aristotelian perspective. She argued that substantial freedoms, such as the resources to live to old age, or to participate in economic and political activities, often determine a people's capability or incapability to develop. Such a view contrasts with a Utilitarian focus on economic growth and income levels, recognising as it does that freedom and flourishing require a wider perspective on human and societal flourishing. It also goes some way to addressing the claim that Virtue Ethics is relativistic given such an emphasis on the need to develop a minimum threshold of capabilities for all citizens that would allow for an adequate level of dignity in terms of freedom, justice and flourishing. Examples of the denial of capabilities could include female genital mutilation, the objectification of women in pornography, or imprisonment without trial.

Rosalind Hursthouse

Rosalind Hursthouse (1943–) illustrates how, despite being accused of failing to move from theory to practical application, Virtue Ethics can deliver practical recommendations for action. In a famous 1991 essay on 'Virtue Ethics and Abortion' (*Philosophy and Public Affairs*, 20), Hursthouse reshapes the terms of the debate which have been centred around the familiar questions of the status of the foetus as a person, or whether a woman has a right to control her own body. Rather than prescribing a view on abortion, she focuses on the quality of relationship that the partners in the conception have. Were the circumstances in which the pregnancy began consensual, were both partners fully self-aware, and not under the influence of alcohol and drugs? The virtuous person thinks about what is virtuous or vicious in particular circumstances – what is practical, prudent, compassionate, calculating or cruel. Acting within your rights does not guarantee virtue or prevent vicious action. Abortion can be kind and wise, or callous and selfish, dependent upon circumstances. The question is: what enables the flourishing of one's life in a holistic sense in these circumstances? On the one hand, avoiding having children on the grounds of inconvenience represents a deficient understanding of how parenthood enables human beings to grow in character and virtue. Yet exceptions exist in cases involving the trauma of rape, or in which the mental or physical health of the mother or existing children is at risk. There does, however, need to be a weighty reason to abort the pregnancy, and even when abortion is justified, it may still be appropriate to feel guilt if the behaviour that led to it resulted from a character flaw.

Hursthouse speaks of *virtues as multi-track dispositions* that shape choices, values, emotional reactions, even desires. An honest person, for example, desires honesty, teaches her children to be truthful, is saddened by and confronts dishonesty, and seeks out honest companions. But virtue also requires *phronēsis* (practical judgement that avoids excess and deficiency in virtue and learns to make this better with good role models and time and experience). She also values the importance of acting for the right motives as being in the spirit of Virtue theory. She makes the point that *eudaimonia* is broader than happiness. It values flourishing, co-operative virtues and practices. A life aimed at wealth, fame or power could not be said to be a flourishing one in terms of Virtue Ethics. Virtue is its own reward and encompasses the life spent in pursuit of virtue and the flourishing of the wider society.

Michael Slote

Michael Slote (1941–) focuses on virtues such as caring or empathy towards others. Psychopaths are the most vicious of people despite being able to make very rational, tactical decisions. Indeed, a psychopath could apply a Hedonic Calculus very readily in business while lacking any empathy for his fellow human beings, and herein lies a problem. In Slote's view, the ethics of care and empathy provides a corrective to the tendency in Kantian and Utilitarian ethics to overemphasize rational control in human life, or the tendency to reduce the moral life to procedures or rules. Care is arguably based in empathy and provides the 'cement of the 'moral universe, (Morals from Motives', 2010, p. 13). Slote is influenced by feminist writers who see patriarchal society as more focused on virtues such as justice and autonomy. Virtues such as nurturing, self-sacrifice, and patience, which are more commonly valued and exhibited in the lives of women than of men, have been marginalised as society neglects the contributions they make. Slote's form of Virtue theory also focuses more on the motives of moral agents in the circumstances in which they make their judgements (i.e., it is *agent-focused*). These can change depending on circumstances and take account of consequences, but the focus is on the intentions or motives, as opposed to Aristotle's *agent-focused* approach, which assumes a more absolute view of virtues like justice, temperance, generosity, as engrained in the character rather than emerging from the motives of the agent.

Slote distinguishes between the following two types of Virtue theory and argues in favour of what he calls a 'warm' Virtue Ethics. As he writes, 'an act is morally acceptable if and only if it comes from good or virtuous motivation involving benevolence or caring (about the well-being of others) or at least doesn't come from bad or inferior motivation involving malice or indifference to humanity' (*Morals from Motives*, Oxford University Press, 2001, p. 38).

A cold virtue focused account

It is enough to do what a virtuous person would do.

Humans need rational grounds for moral action, including a consideration of consequences.

You act as any virtuous person would in your shoes and this may not be from feeling or sentiment.

Virtue theory is grounded in the good consequences such motives may bring about, or on rules or principles.

It avoids the accusation of being self-centred, and subject to our feelings, for motivation.

It balances the flourishing of the lives of others with that of one's own life.

A warm agent-based account of the virtues

You act from motives or dispositions of character because you are virtuous in motive or by disposition of character.

Virtue is its own reward, e.g. kindness is fulfilling to the kind person.

Warm Virtue Ethics – e.g. care, empathy, compassion – may be both the motive and reward for moral acts.

Virtue theory is grounded in universal benevolence and caring, which is intrinsically good. Love and friendship are life's great goods but should not stop with our family, community or nation – 'it is objectionable to treat the fate of other nations as a matter of practical attitudinal indifference' (p. 94).

Does not regard as virtuous actions done for the right reasons or consequences, but from the wrong motives – e.g. administering the law justly but with vengeful delight at prosecuting an offender for whom one has a personal dislike.

Virtue theory in modern theological ethics

Stanley Hauerwas and Sam Wells raised eyebrows when they organised their *Blackwell Companion to Christian Ethics* (2004) around Christian worship. Prayer and scripture reading, celebrating the death and resurrection of Jesus in the Eucharist, offering gifts and Baptism were worked into issues such as race, parenting, politics, abortion, cloning, marriage and war. At the time, it seemed a novel approach to focus on the formation of character and virtue through the practices of the Church community. The standard model of approaching ethics today is through quandaries, or dilemmas and extreme case studies (like the life-and-death choices). By contrast, they were trying to show how it is not so much that the Church has a set of ethical principles, but rather that it embodies a social ethic in the life of its community. Coming from a virtue tradition, they put the focus on moral *agents* rather than moral *actions*, on what kind of people we ought to be (collectively) rather than what we should do. In modern consumer culture, our desires are moulded into brand acquisition and we are told to love the label, to discover our identity and self-worth in the brand or consumer choice. Christian worship is seen as subverting such a view and reforming our imagination and desires to will the justice and peace that God wills in the world. To the extent that we take on the characteristics of what we worship, individuals who are told to value power, celebrity status, wealth and sexual attractiveness by advertisers are challenged in Christian worship to love justice and mercy and to be humble in following Jesus.

Summary – key distinctives of Virtue Ethics

In his book *Ethics* (Polity, 2008), Noel Stewart identifies several key differences between Virtue Ethics and rival ethical theories. . .

Agent vs action

In modern ethics, a distinction is frequently made between, on the one hand, act-based ethics (such as Utilitarianism and Kantianism) in which the morality of actions or decisions is the focus, and, on the other hand, agent-based ethics in which the character and skills of the person or 'moral agent' are the focus, as 'good fruit grows from good trees'. Act-based ethics tend to neglect the benefit of virtues for the agent's character and flourishing. A fulfilling life involves cultivating the virtues like loyalty, friendliness, wisdom, integrity and compassion, which are attractive qualities. Here Kant's distrust of emotional rewards for virtue and his austere sense of duty are in contrast to virtue as its own reward, as habits and dispositions of character which are fulfilling and enjoyable to develop. Likewise, Utilitarianism does not see virtue as intrinsically good, only good insofar as it leads to good consequences.

Being vs doing

The question 'Who should I be?' comes before that of 'What should I do?' Parents are natural Virtue ethicists when they ask not 'What is my child doing right/wrong here and now?', but 'What kind of person is my child becoming?' Modern ethics often wrongly marginalise motives, habits, attitudes and emotions.

Virtues vs rules

We cannot navigate the complexity and lifelong training in virtue that a flourishing life requires by setting out lists of rules. Circumstances change and social contexts are different. Good role models (whether fictional heroes like Harry Potter, or real people like Dame Ellen MacArthur who, in 2005, broke the world record for the fastest solo circumnavigation of the globe) and mentors can offer examples of admirable lives.

Community vs individualism

Alasdair MacIntyre ends *After Virtue* with a stark choice between Nietzsche and Aristotle. Nietzsche's superman leaves behind the masses and pursues external goods like money, power and status with a will that is competitive not cooperative. In contrast, Aristotle sees that the flourishing of the individual is integral with that of their community and city; you cannot grow the virtues of loyalty or friendliness on your own. Socrates described himself as a citizen of the world. Our proper end as social animals is not individualism.

The moral life as a whole life story versus moments of ethical crisis and dilemmas along the way

Ethics is not just about calculating on a case-by-case basis – habits and moral character develop over time, so reflecting deliberately on our habits and lifestyle can shape our destiny.

Exercise

1. Aristotle would have disagreed with many modern ethicists, for example Utilitarians who sharply divide facts and values. Take each of the statements below and place them in the relevant box. . .

(a) Water boils at 100 degrees C. (b) Murder is wrong. (c) As a pupil, in my school, I ought to wear the uniform. (d) Caring for my siblings is the right thing to do in my family – families ought to look out for one another. (e) Illegal tax evasion is unjustifiable in the UK. (f) Academics who plagiarise are stealing intellectual property and ought to face serious consequences. (g) I have the same rare blood type as my mum who will die without a blood transfusion. At no risk to myself, I ought therefore to help my dying mother to live by giving some of my blood to save her life.

Fact	Hard to tell	Value

2. Consider the list below of MacIntyre's goods internal to practices. Usually, he judges these to be generally preferable to those external to them in terms of developing virtue. Would you say that you/your school is more driven by goods internal to or external to practices in sport or academic life? How would you justify the balance between both?

Goods external to practices – trophies/exam grades and university places.
Goods internal to practices – co-operative teamwork or self-discipline and perseverance.

3. How does Aristotle avoid the Hedonistic Paradox (that when you aim directly at happiness, it eludes you)?

4. Moral knowledge, unlike mathematical knowledge, cannot be acquired merely by attending lectures and is not characteristically to be found in people too young to have much experience of life. Now if right action were determined by rules that any clever adolescent could apply correctly, how could this be so?. . . moral knowledge involves the training of the emotions in a way that the acquisition of scientific knowledge does not (Rosalind Hursthouse, *On Virtue Ethics*, Oxford University Press, 1999, p. 128).

How might practical wisdom (*phronēsis*) replace the 'decision procedure' of a Utilitarian (seek the greatest good of the greatest number, the maximisation of choices) or a Kantian (act only on those principles that you can at the same time will to become a universal moral law) when helping a moral agent know the right way to act in a particular situation?

5. 'Anyone can get angry – that is easy – or give or spend money; but to do this to the right person, to the right extent, at the right time, with the right motive, and in the right way, that is not for everyone, nor is it easy' (Aristotle, *The Nicomachean Ethics*, ed. David Ross, Oxford University Press, 2009, p. 36).

When was the last time that you felt your anger or someone else's was not only justified but exercised in the manner stated above?

Strengths of Virtue Ethics

1. *Agents, not actions.* Most ancient cultures have, in their epics and stories, adopted the holistic, lifelong narrative of a character rather than looking at individual actions. Agents, not actions, have been at the centre of moral thinking, which develops over time in character formation and through the circumstances and challenges of life. The moral life is not about occasional crises, in-between which one is an amoral, non-calculating person. It is about daily habits, micro-choices that add up to shaping a character.
2. *Emphasis on character.* The banking crisis or shocking cases of violence, abuse and scandal raise the question of character and moral leadership in the press. Here, Virtue Ethics seems ideally suited to addressing the debate about moral formation and the nurturing of young people and leaders for the future good of society.
3. *Relationships are of key importance.* Act-based ethical systems can fail to see how the roots of selfless actions develop from the interpersonal obligations of special relationships such as those of a family or community. Here emotions matter. In a 'balloon debate', Kantians and Utilitarians would throw their parents out well before Virtue ethicists. Yet purely logical and dispassionate impersonal calculations or principles may obscure the central role that compassion, love and loyalty play in nurturing ethical behaviour. Virtue Ethics is able to articulate the reasons why relationships matter and – with Plato – that politics is social ethics. The moral life is too complex for Bentham's Felicific Calculus or slogans like 'the pursuit of pleasure, the avoidance of pain, the greatest good of the greatest number'.
4. *Character has to be trained.* If, as Hume argues, human behaviour is more passional than rational, then we need training. In his view, agents are often

more crucial than calculations because doing the right thing can be costly and may require willpower, so the training of habit and character is crucial. Emotions are not to be downplayed but trained and harnessed in pursuit of a flourishing life.

5. *Training helps to solve dilemmas.* The moral life is more than ethical accountancy in which we total up the pros and cons of outcomes or duties and out comes the decision. Virtue Ethics is sometimes accused of being no good in a crisis or of not having ready-to-hand answers to 'What should I do in X case?' moral dilemmas. In answer, Virtue ethicists might quote the military training adage 'The more you sweat in training, the less you bleed in battle.' Training in virtuous habits like courage or generosity, or truth-telling, and in judging the golden mean, will show you how to act in any given situation by shaping your character and the questions that occur to you. Take the following example.

In May 1569, the Anabaptist Dirk Willems escaped imprisonment for his faith and was running for his life. Prison rations had left him thin enough to cross a frozen pond. The pursuing prison guard fell through into the icy water and Willems instinc-

Dirk Willems turning to rescue his prison guard in an act that will cost him his life

tively turned back to save him, knowing he would be recaptured. He was later burned at the stake. For many Anabaptists and Amish, Dirk illustrates well how a lifetime of training in reverence for life leads to instinctive behaviour at crisis points.

Weaknesses of Virtue Ethics

Like any moral theory, there are many criticisms of Virtue Ethics. Here are five important ones.

1. *Degrees of virtue.* For Aristotle, there are many virtues. How do they stand in relation to each other? For any one virtue, a person can be more virtuous than another person. (This is not passing judgement on any person, but on the nature and relative values of the virtues themselves.) Look at the following examples and ask yourself: 'Who is the most honest?'

(a) Rich person 1: very greedy by nature, but always just manages to resist his impulse to kleptomania.

(b) Poor person 1: sees hugely uneven distribution of wealth as a serious injustice. Is often tempted to steal to redress the balance a little, but never actually does so.

(c) Rich person 2: works hard, very effective in her job, materially well-off, sees no need to steal, has never been tempted to steal, never does steal.

(d) Poor person 2: aware that many people are much better off materially. Is content, however, with her life. Has never even considered stealing as an option.

Are all four equally honest? Could they be ranked in order of virtue? The levels of temptation are very different. According to Aristotle, the truly virtuous person always thinks, feels and does the right thing. This would make (c) and (d) the most virtuous by nature. But, surely, (a) and (b) show greater personal strength and courage in overcoming their temptation?

2. *Goal* orientation. After Darwin, *Aristotle's goal-orientated view of nature became obsolete*. Species are not consciously goal-orientated, but, instead, the DNA of gene mutations that confer a reproductive advantage have a better chance of surviving. The metaphysical foundation of Aristotelian ethics seems outdated. Still, just because nature lacks a *telos* or consciously chosen sense of what a flourishing life looks like, this does not rule out humans reflecting on this and deciding upon virtues and vices that lead to or away from the eudaimonic life.

3. *Virtue Ethics is radically relativistic*. Virtue Ethics is a *normative* approach to ethical decision-making. The implication of this is that what constitutes virtue for one culture or person may be different from what constitutes virtue for another. Without a universally true and binding set of ethical principles, morality becomes merely personal opinion. Different cultures emphasise virtues in different ways. The Homeric virtue of physical strength, for instance, is no longer seen (by most people) as a key virtue. Could it be that all virtues are derived from particular cultures and sustained and adapted by them? Alternatively, it could be that there actually is a set of core virtues, but no-one can give a definitive description of them.

4. *Real-life crises*. Virtue Ethics provides less action-guidance in dilemmas than most other ethical theories. Many critics of Virtue Ethics argue that it is inadequate because it will not help a fourteen-year-old girl who has to decide whether or not to have an abortion, or an employee working in a corrupt business. It is all very well saying that *phronēsis* or practical wisdom will sort this out, but it often does not. Attention to universalisability or consequences can provide ready-made assessments of the right course of action in a crisis.

5. *Conflict between virtues*. What happens *when virtues* (e.g. patience and justice, or loyalty and truth-telling) come into *conflict*? Virtue ethicist Rosalind Hursthouse replies to such an objection by asking 'Does kindness require not telling hurtful truth?' She gives the example of telling a student of philosophy that they are not good enough to go on to graduate work in the subject. This could be the kind thing to do in the longer term if it were true.

Case study – Friar Bartolomé de las Casas (1484–1566)

Utilitarians could hardly ask for a better case study in what is wrong with Virtue theory in practice than the disastrous consequences of the actions of the well-intentioned Friar de las Casas. Intending to alleviate human suffering, he added to it a hundredfold. Friar de las Casas was a principled man. His 'Short History of the Destruction of the Indian Peoples' offered an eyewitness account of the atrocities committed as the first European settlers colonised the West Indies. By 1515, he gave up his own slaves and argued for justice on their behalf before King Charles V, the Holy Roman Emperor. Attacking forcible colonisation, he argued instead for the rights of the indigenous Indians. He proposed that they be granted self-governing townships that would pay taxes to the King of Spain. To compensate for the loss of labour that such reforms would result in, and to lessen the suffering of Indian slaves, he suggested that African slaves be allowed to be imported instead. Despite his later belief that all slavery was equally immoral, he had unwittingly contributed to the beginnings of the transatlantic slave trade, which was to see more than 12 million people forcibly removed from Africa. He was to spend fifty years of his life fighting for the rights of native

Illustration from Bartolomé de las Casas, 'A Short History of the Destruction of the Indian Peoples', 1552. The cruelty of and atrocities committed by the European settlers against the native peoples of the Americas horrified Friar Bartolomé de las Casas.

Indians to be free of violent atrocities and slavery. He is remembered as a forerunner of human rights. But his legacy is also of a virtuous man unintentionally accelerating the mass human suffering of the slave trade from the sixteenth to the nineteenth century.

Discussion Question

Does this illustrate the Utilitarian's point that a very careful calculation of consequences is more important than virtuous character? Do motives matter less than outcomes, as Utilitarians would say in criticism of Virtue theory?

6. *Ethical values are not verifiable.* A. J. Ayer (and other Logical Positivists) argued that ethical statements were impossible to assess, or test for validity, because they were not consistent with the Verification Principle. Moral concepts were pseudo-concepts. If we say 'Matthew was wrong to steal that money', all we are saying is 'Matthew stole that money.' The value judgement is simply a reflection of the value systems of the speaker. Whether the theft was wrong or not cannot be verified. It is purely an emotional response, not a factual one. For Ayer, there can be no absolute validity for moral assertions, and none of them can have any objective content. For this reason, it is impossible to list any criteria (like a list of

virtues) for assessing morality. If Ayer is right, this would account for the changing views on (say) fox-hunting or homosexuality in the last thirty years or so. One response Virtue ethicists might offer is that 'positive psychology' can explore what makes normal life more fulfilling. Psychology may be able to investigate empirically what patterns of life make us live better and establish more flourishing behaviour from infancy to our latter years.

7. *Romanticisation.* Alasdair MacIntyre's *After Virtue* offers small-scale fishing and farming communities as examples of face-to-face relationships in which the virtues thrive. Here, accountability, long-term relationships and concern for reputation, as well as role models, offer a school of virtue. Yet some critics see this as a *rose-tinted view* of such societies and argue that Virtue Ethics is less relevant to a globalised, urbanised world with more transient, rootless lives, in which Utilitarian logic seems better suited to addressing modern moral dilemmas between people who do not share as many values and beliefs in common. We should also remember not to get too nostalgic over Aristotle, who knew that the wealth of Athens relied a good deal on military conquest and slavery. He wrote: 'the slave is a living tool'.

FURTHER READING

Heather Battaly (2014) *Virtue*. Polity

Rosalind Hursthouse (1999) *On Virtue Ethics*. Oxford University Press

Christopher Stephen Lutz (2012) *Reading Alasdair MacIntyre's After Virtue*. Continuum Books

Daniel C. Russell (2013) *The Cambridge Companion to Virtue Ethics*. Cambridge University Press

OCR Past Paper Questions

JUNE 2010
'The weaknesses of Virtue Ethics outweigh its strengths.' Discuss.   *[35]*

JUNE 2011
To what extent is Virtue Ethics helpful when making decisions about extramarital sex?   *[35]*

JANUARY 2012
To what extent do modern versions of Virtue Ethics address the weaknesses
of Aristotle's teaching on virtue?   *[35]*

JANUARY 2013
'Following the example of virtuous people is the most useful aspect of Virtue Ethics.'
Discuss.   *[35]*

APPLIED ETHICS

14 Environmental and Business Ethics

LEARNING OUTCOMES

In this chapter, you will learn:

- about the issue of how humans should relate to the environment, its resources and species
- about secular approaches – the Gaia Hypothesis
- about issues in business ethics: the relationship between business and consumers; the relationship between employers and employees
- about the relationship between business and the environment; business and globalisation
- about the application and the different approaches of the ethical theories (Natural Law, Kantian Ethics, Utilitarianism, Christian ethics, Virtue Ethics) to environmental and business ethics
- to discuss these issues critically and their strengths and weaknesses

SECTION ONE: ISSUES IN ENVIRONMENTAL ETHICS

Introduction – human responsibility for damage to the environment

As in the Cree Indian saying 'Only after the last tree has been cut down. Only after the last river has been poisoned. Only after the last fish has been caught. Only then will you find that money cannot be eaten.' Today we have a growing sense that natural resources are not limitless and may run out all too soon, leading to conflicts over oil, water and land.

Given this, 'environmental sustainability' has become a buzzword in business and politics. The negative impact of post-industrial human activity is extensive: habitat destruction and urban spread, species extinction, acid rain, global warming, the overharvesting of fish, the degradation of land through use of pesticides and fertilisers, nuclear waste, water and air pollution and the unsustainable burning of fossil fuels. This raises pressing questions such as: how are human beings to flourish in a sustainable way when consumers are energy-hungry and want ever-higher standards of living? How can we respect and live in balance with nature's ecological systems to make the planet habitable and beautiful for future generations? Will business leaders and lawmakers respond with innovation and political will to the scientific evidence of climate change caused by human activity?

Exercise

Read the following six facts and projections. In boxes in the left margin, order these from 1 (most serious concern) to 6 (least serious concern).

[_] Sea levels have risen between 10 and 20 centimetres over the last 100 years and are predicted to rise between 9 and 88 centimetres by 2100. If this occurs, up to 70 million Bangladeshis and the same number of Chinese will lose their land and a large-scale environmental refugee crisis will see millions move into densely populated areas.

[_] Since 1850, 2.2 billion acres of lands have been converted to human use and today tropical deforestation (e.g. in the Amazonian rainforest) occurs at a rate of 25 million acres per annum. According to NASA, tropical forests hold 460–575,000,000,000 metric tons of carbon worldwide. http://earth observatory.nasa.gov/Library/Deforestation.

[_] Oceans, which are thought to have absorbed about half of the carbon dioxide humans have produced over the past 200 years currently absorb around 1 ton of carbon dioxide per person per year. In time, they will become more acidic and less hospitable to the finely balanced ocean life they sustain. At the same time, fish stocks are being overharvested from them in an unsustainable way.

[_] It is estimated that 10,000 species are lost annually as a consequence of human activity and that 'By 2050 . . . a million species will become extinct as a direct result of climate change' (Curry 2011, p.34). The real damage to biodiversity comes when so-called 'keystone' species become extinct and, with them, a delicate ecosystem that supports thousands of other species collapses, threatening large-scale problems. In one example on the US west coast, a population of sea otters came near to extinction due to disturbance from boats which caused sea urchin numbers to rise rapidly, kelp forests to decline, and, with them, a sharp fall in stocks of fish, squid and other organisms.

[_] By 1991, the hole in the ozone layer (which protects us from the sun's harmful ultraviolet rays which can cause skin cancers and upset our immune system) had grown to the size of a continent (21,000,000 sq.km). The hole opened up over Antarctica but especially threatened the world's southernmost cities. Its cause was traced to chlorofluorocarbons (CFCs) found in aerosol propellants, refrigerators and air conditioners. Addressing this has been a notable success with governments acting to sign the Montreal Protocol in 1985 and to phase out CFCs by 1999 (ten years later in the case of developing countries).

[_] Greenhouse gases (methane, nitrous oxide and carbon dioxide) mean that whilst solar radiation penetrates the atmosphere, the energy and heat radiated back into space are absorbed in the earth's atmosphere, leading to increases in temperature. According to the Third Assessment Report from the Intergovernmental Panel on Climate Change (IPCC), of the 140 years that meteorological records have been kept, 90 per cent of the hottest years have occurred since the 1990s. The IPCC estimate 'that between 1990 and 2100, the average global temperatures will rise by at least 1.4 degrees Fahrenheit and perhaps by as much as 5.8 degrees . . . even a 1 degree rise in average temperatures would be greater than any change that has occurred in a single century for the past 10,000 years' (Peter Singer, *One World*, Yale University Press, 2002, p. 20).

Earth as an ecosystem

People over eighty-five were born in the early 1930s, at a time when a third of the current global population of over 7 billion people were alive. Today we are well aware of the earth's limited natural resources and fragile ecosystem. The evidence amassed by such bodies as the IPCC (www.ipcc.ch) and photos of the earth seen from space have brought home the limited resources of our planet. Yet the mind-set of empires and colonists who in past history journeyed out into what seemed like limitless frontiers and resources persists. And transferring from fossil fuels to renewable energy and reducing our carbon footprint becomes a little less urgent to voters in times of financial crisis. Yet the danger of short-term profits and bonuses has been one of the lessons economists have learnt from the global financial crisis of 2008. Many climatologists suggest that, if it is not already too late to change, irreversible and potentially catastrophic environmental damage is on the horizon.

'Earthrise', one of *Life Magazine*'s '100 Photographs that Changed the World' has been described as 'the most influential environmental photo ever taken'. Rather

Earthrise photo by astronaut on
Apollo 8

than seeing ever-new frontiers to expand into, it is clear that we are cutting away the ground beneath our feet. *Apollo 13* astronaut Jim Lovell captured a newfound sense of the earth's fragile biosphere in his observation that: 'From the moon you can put your thumb up and hide the earth behind it. How insignificant we really are, but then how fortunate we are to enjoy living here amongst the beauty of the earth.'

The Gaia Hypothesis

The British scientist James Lovelock had previously worked for NASA designing instruments for lunar probes and came up with the successful idea of using infrared telescopes to detect carbon dioxide on Mars, an indicator that life exists there. This got him thinking about earth as a living biosphere with self-regulating control mechanisms. For example, algae in the oceans generate dimethyl sulphide, which creates clouds that have a cooling effect. Similarly, icecaps reflect the sun's rays back into space and trap methane and carbon dioxide. Lovelock sees such 'feedback loops' as stabilising the equilibrium of the atmosphere. The name *Gaia* (from the Greek earth goddess, though Lovelock says it is a metaphor 'no more serious than a sailor who refers to his ship as "she"') was suggested to him by his neighbour William Golding (the Nobel Prize-winning novelist who wrote *The Lord of the Flies*). He refers to Gaia as 'the dynamical physiological system that has kept our planet fit for life for more than three billion years'. Looking at earth as a living biosphere calls into question the compartmentalising of ecology into rival campaigns and concerns. Instead, a co-ordinated effort at every level – personal, charitable, local, governmental and international – is needed to halt what Lovelock calls, in the title of his 2006 book, *The Revenge of Gaia*. If we fail to act, the human population will collapse from 7 to 1.5 billion as the temperature of the earth rises by several degrees. This sense of a reckoning is dramatised in a new genre of 'Cli-Fi' novels, films and documentaries about ecological catastrophes and doomsday scenarios (e.g. *The Day After Tomorrow, Waterworld, The Age of Stupid, An Inconvenient Truth, The 11th Hour*). They convey our sense of an impending ecological catastrophe or simply the depletion of **biodiversity**, icecaps, stable weather patterns and a ready supply of energy for power-hungry industrial nations.

Lovelock refers to *Homo Sapiens* as 'a plague of people', an infestation reaching 'a tipping point' after which global temperatures will sharply soar. Earth is a self-regulating biosphere which is undergoing climate changes not seen for 55 million years. Yet 'The world is fighting back', asserts Lovelock; 'Only a handful of the teeming billions now alive will survive.' Controversially, he advocates a shift to using nuclear power – the only large-scale carbon-free energy available. It may already be too late, but Lovelock urges the use of innovations in science and technology to reduce energy consumption, as well as action to avert global population growth. Without it, we face 'a global decline into a chaotic world ruled by brutal warlords on a devastated Earth'.

Whilst he has many critics (e.g. Greens who object to his pessimism and advocacy

Gaia Hypothesis: James Lovelock's theory that the earth is a self-regulating biosphere with feedback loops to maintain balances and life systems. The revenge of Gaia against the industrial-scale pollution of humans is to to turn to red-hot mode (the theme of Lovelock's 1996 book).

Biodiversity: The diversity of living organisms in a habitat or the world, e.g. the range of plants and animals in a national park. Some estimates suggest there are 12.5 million species globally, with particularly intense biodiversity in areas such as the Amazon rainforest.

of nuclear power), Lovelock has done much to challenge outdated **anthropocentric** thinking about our planet's ecosystem. He talks not of sustainable development but of sustainable retreat, urging humanity to develop new technologies for carbon capturing and generating ocean algae to raise CO_2 levels. We need policies that will stave off the worst effects of global warming, to prepare to relocate hundreds of thousands of people and animals from low-lying areas, and to alter radically our lifestyles as conspicuous consumers. He warns against alarmist environmentalists who offer guilt trips and few practical solutions.

Anthropocentric: Human-centred. In such a viewpoint, non-human nature is instrumentally valuable insofar as it supports human survival, needs and interests. Humankind are intrinsically valuable and their interests prioritised.

Deep Ecology

This movement extended beyond a reverence for human and animal life to integrate these with the land, water and ecosystems in a holistic perspective. It grew out of the work of thinkers like Rachel Carson (1907–64) – whose 1962 book *Silent Spring* examined the dangers of pesticides in the food chain and saw a new interconnectedness to the ecosystem – and the Norwegian philosopher Arne Naess (1925–2009), who coined the term '*Deep ecology*' in 1973. The diversity and flourishing of nature, quite apart from human interests, is of intrinsic worth in what has been termed '**biocentric** egalitarianism'. This view encourages us to take a less species-centric look at ecology. This would involve peacefully and democratically reducing population growth and lightening our carbon footprint. Sustainability ought to be judged in terms of meeting not future human population needs but the needs of biodiversity and the health of earth's ecosystems. This shift away from putting ourselves at the centre could be the key to seeing the importance of protection in law against areas of rainforest being cleared to graze beef cattle, or to finding the political will to regulate global carbon emissions. Rather than placing human interests on one side of the scales and those of the non-human natural world on the other, 'Ecosophy', as Naess called it, took a holistic or unitary view of ecological balance and harmony. Developing an environmental conscience

Biocentric: The view that consideration of the interests of all life on earth, rather than human interests in particular, should inform our environmental decisions. A political and ethical worldview which argues for the inherent value of all living things.

An aerial photo of the Brazilian rainforest, sometimes described as the lungs of the earth

required this shift from people to land, or from an anthropocentric to a geocentric ecology.

Critics warn against being unrealistic, arguing that humans are simply too short-sighted and self-interested for democratic politics to take this agenda seriously. Global capitalism is based upon economic growth and this seems to clash with a sustainable approach to the environment. In this world, everything is priced and commodified, including rainforests. Change requires realism about human behaviour. Free market solutions in terms of renewable technology and carbon sequestration or trading offer more realistic routes to progress. Perhaps legal rights could be extended to world heritage sites of natural beauty or ecological importance like rainforests, if financial incentives were also in place. In your exam, you need to distinguish clearly between:

Differences between Deep and Shallow ecology

Deep ecology	Shallow ecology
Both the earth itself and living flora and fauna on it are believed to have an intrinsic value independent of being a resource for humans.	Nature is instrumentally valuable insofar as it is the ground beneath our feet and the air we breathe. So reducing pollution and becoming more energy-and water-efficient should make long-term economic growth more sustainable.
The ecosophy of Arne Naess calls for human beings to make radical changes in their species-centric view of the planet's resources. They need to reduce radically their conspicuous consumption, pollution and population. They must live with a light carbon footprint and resist the unsustainable demands for year-on-year economic growth.	Biodiversity is important for humans to preserve to avoid keystone species being wiped out, causing knock-on effects or species made extinct which could provide medicines for the future or whose loss would diminish the beauty of the planet (e.g. Bengal tigers or rare parrots).
With a global population of 7 billion and growing levels of industrial pollution and energy consumption, humankind needs to scale back radically their depletion of nature's scarce resources.	Although the interests of humans and the natural world are seen to be interdependent, in times of economic hardship, job and wealth creation trump longer-term environmental concerns.

Discussion Questions

The eco-experience machine thought experiment

1. The philosopher Robert Nozick (1938–2002) came up with the 'experience machine' thought experiment to demonstrate that pleasure was not a good in itself, but derived from other goods. He asked us to imagine a virtual simulator that could be programmed to deliver any pleasurable experience to our thoughts and senses. The question was: would being elected president, winning the Olympic 100m final, playing first violin at a world-famous concert, or being a football star be worthy, valuable and real if it were a convincing if inauthentic virtual experience in a pleasure simulator?

In his book *Ethics*, Noel Stewart sets out a similar thought experiment in the chapter on 'Environmental Ethics'. He asks us to imagine ourselves doing something similar to Nozick's experiment in the pleasure machine for an aesthetic experience in artificial but very realistic forests, or visiting the Galapagos Islands restored to the time before settlers had hunted the dodo to extinction and eaten many of the giant turtles. If nature is not valuable in itself and we can enjoy all its experiences of peace, space, biodiversity, colour, bird and insect sound, temperature and smell without it having to be there, would that be an adequate substitute? If not, what does this say about the intrinsic value of nature in itself, quite apart from the resources and pleasure humans derive from sharing its habitat? This Aesthetic or Beauty defence suggests that wild animals in their habitat have a certain awe for us that caged ones or those reared in captivity as in zoos do not. If you agree, can you suggest why this is so? How does this thought experiment shed light on the debate between shallow and deep ecology?

> **Geocentric:** In this kind of view, the earth's resources, organic and inorganic, are treated as a whole, and life systems (human / flora and fauna) are not privileged in a separate hierarchy. This is in opposition to an anthropocentric or biocentric view.

2. Should we adopt an ***anthropocentric*** (preserving nature so as not to cut the ground beneath our feet), ***biocentric*** (valuing living organisms in their own right) or ***geocentric*** approach (including mountains, rivers, rocks as inherently valuable)?

When was the last time you made a purchase as a consumer that involved a choice about the environment (think recycled, distance transported, packaging, waste)?

Avatar, directed by James Cameron

Avatar (2009) – science fiction with an environmental conscience

James Cameron's science-fiction film consciously sought to make cinemagoers reflect on how they interacted with nature and their fellow man. Set around 2209 among the Na'vi, the indigenous people of Pandora, it features a utopian natural world of jungles with spectacular beauty and wonders, whose people live in symbiosis with a living and conscious nature. The film is suffused with spiritual imagery reflecting an intrinsic respect for nature and deep ecology. The Eywa refers to the ancestral guiding force – a pantheistic female deity that encompasses all living things. It acts to keep the ecosystem in equilibrium and has healing powers. The Na'vi represent our aspirational selves, whereas humans appear in the film as plunderers of nature, 'trashing our world and maybe condemning ourselves to a grim future', as Cameron put it.

Coming after the invasion of Iraq in 2003, and the country's ongoing occupation by coalition troops, *Avatar*'s language caused controversy when it consciously mirrored that used in the war. The Sky people (humans) attack in waves of military helicopters and bulldozers. They want to exploit the rich biodiversity and mine unobtanium to survive their energy crisis. Colonel Quaritch says to his marines, 'Our only security lies in pre-emptive attack. We will fight terror with terror.' There are references to a 'shock and awe campaign' and 'daisycutters'. Cameron acknowledges that, in such references, the film implicitly criticised the Second Gulf War, the Sky People attacking conventional forces with superior missile firepower.

Avatar was banned in China where its plot about indigenous peoples rising up against eviction from their homes for industrial-scale 'developments' of local resources was considered too controversial. There, the ongoing building of the world's largest hydroelectric power station, the Three Gorges Dam, has been estimated to have displaced between 300,000 and 1.3 million people. Critics say it has flooded archaeological and cultural sites, increased the risks of landslides, and, together with other massive infrastructure projects, ridden roughshod over the welfare and interests of indigenous peoples. Its defenders assert that the total electricity-generating capacity of the dam is 22,500 MW, which will limit greenhouse gas emissions.

In the following section, we examine two rival accounts of whether or not Christian belief bears much of the responsibility for the environmental crisis. According to philosopher Alasdair MacIntyre, humans are story-telling animals and this is evident in the two rival accounts of where the blame for the ecological crisis lies. There is some truth in both of them.

Exercise

In a one-page evaluative essay outline, weigh up the arguments for each story and decide which you consider to be the most plausible.

Story A – Christian theology is responsible for the ecological crisis

There is a longstanding tradition of scholars who trace the blame for viewing nature as an expendable, material resource to the Bible and Judeo-Christian theology. Max Weber, the nineteenth-century sociologist, argued that the pantheism of earlier myths sacralised nature. In making nature the work of God and separate from him, Jewish and Christian texts disenchanted nature, and, in giving mankind 'dominion' over the earth, they made it ripe for scientific investigation and commercial plundering. His book *The Protestant Work Ethic and the Spirit of Capitalism* (1905) even rooted the Protestant work ethic in a deep psychological need to find evidence that one was predestined for an eternity among the elect rather than the damned. Where the Catholic Church had offered assurance of salvation through the sacraments, ordinary Protestants felt themselves in a more

Max Weber (1864–1920)

precarious position. Here, confident faith in being chosen took the place of a priest's assurance of God's grace. According to Weber's analysis, if one fulfilled one's worldly calling, working hard and living modestly and reinvesting profits, material success fed on such confidence and a belief that God's blessing and favour was to be seen in one's business endeavours. Reformer Martin Luther taught that a secular 'calling' was the vocation of most Christians. Modern capitalism inherited this work ethic and secularised it, driving up economic productivity in the process. Weber cites the example of US President Benjamin Franklin whose father was Calvinist (though he himself was a deist). In many of his sayings, such as '*Time* is money', 'Money can beget money', he captures the restless spirit of workaholics whose psychology is rooted in Protestantism.

In his 1966 lecture entitled 'The Historical Roots of our Ecological Crisis' (American Association of Science, 1967), Lynn White Jr asserted that 'Christianity bears a huge burden of guilt' for the destruction of the environment. He argued that 'Especially in its Western form, Christianity is the most anthropocentric religion the world has seen.' It 'not only established a dualism of man and nature, but also insisted that it is God's will that man exploit nature for his proper end'. This all led to

> the Christian dogma of man's transcendence of, and rightful mastery over, nature . . . Our science and technology have grown out of Christian attitudes towards man's relation to nature which are almost universally held not only by Christians and neo-Christians but also by those who fondly regard themselves as post-Christians. Despite Copernicus, all the cosmos rotates around our little globe. Despite Darwin, we are not, in our hearts, part of the natural process. We are superior to nature, contemptuous of it, willing to use it for our slightest whim.

For White, ecology depends upon our view of the man–nature relationship and 'we shall continue to have a worsening ecological crisis until we reject the Christian axiom that nature has no reason for existence save to serve man' (quoted in Ken Gnanakan, *God's World: Biblical Insights for an Environmental Theology*, SPCK, 1999, p. 19) This said, he does not advocate abandoning Christian ethics, but instead believes that only religion has the power to motivate changes in behaviour. He sees St Francis of Assisi as an important example in this respect.

This account of the roots of the ecological crisis interprets the word 'dominion' in Genesis to mean 'domination' or human superiority over nature. In Genesis 1:28, the Bible licenses mankind to 'Be fruitful and increase in number; fill the earth and subdue it. Rule over the fish in the sea and the birds in the sky and over every living creature that moves on the ground.' The consequence of this, according to White, is overpopulation and a desacralisation of nature whereby *human interests trump those of animal kind or the environment*. Adam and Eve relate to their creator, Adam gets to name the other animals (Genesis 2), and, after the Fall, God clothes them in animal skins. On this account, it would appear that nature has no inherent value but is there to provide for human needs.

Furthermore, it is argued that Christians' hopes of a life in another world undermine their commitment to this one. The focus of believers (especially influential in the US) is on Christ's second coming and the New Heavens and New Earth of Revelation 21. This combines with a Platonic dualism, absorbed by Augustine, that devalued the physical world as something changeable and imperfect and looked beyond to the eternal world, changeless and perfect. Such a worldview is fertile soil for scepticism as to 'the inflated claims of eco-activists'; why worry about rust when the ship is sinking and you are expecting a helicopter rescue? In this analysis, Judeo-Christian thinking is a fundamental part of the anthropocentric mindset that expends the resources of the natural world in an unsustainable way.

Story B – Jewish and Christian scriptures affirm the intrinsic worth of creation aside from and beyond man. Theocentric, not anthropocentric, in worldview, they offer resources to motivate changing perspectives and ecologically responsible practice.

Earth's crammed with heaven,
And every common bush afire with God;
But only he who sees, takes off his shoes
(Elizabeth Barrett Browning)

[T]he glory of the LORD fills the whole earth
(Numbers 14:21)

This alternative account to Story A seeks to defend religious texts from the charge of providing the ideological basis for the destruction of the environment and to lay the blame at the feet of an altogether more mechanistic, modernist view of the world that emerges out of a less sacred, more secular worldview and industrial age. As Alister McGrath puts it, 'the fundamental impulse of modernity was to dominate – to understand in order to master, as a conquering army might learn the language and customs of those who stood in their way, in order to ensure their more effective subjugation' (McGrath, *The Re-enchantment of Nature*, Hodder & Stoughton, 2003, p. 101). In contrast, the Bible's theocentric perspective rules against anthropocentrism. Its vision of nature provides for mankind but retains a scale, grandeur and mystery that testify to the wider being of a creator who made the world *ex nihilo* (out of nothing). The Psalms offer ample examples of such a worldview.

When I consider your heavens,
The Work of your fingers,
The moon and the stars,
Which you have set in place,
What is man that you are mindful of him,
The Son of Man that you care for him?
Yet you have made him a little lower than the angels
And crowned him with glory and honour.

(Psalm 8:3–5)

The heavens declare the glory of God; and the firmament shows his handiwork. Day to day utters speech, and night to night shows knowledge.

(Psalm 19:1–2)

The earth is the LORD's, and everything in it, the world, and all who live in it.

(Psalm 24:1)

Dust you are and to dust you will return.

(Genesis 3:19)

Biblical law also regulates time for nature to rest. On the Sabbath, no work is permitted 'so that your ox and your donkey may rest'. (Exodus 23:12). It also requires longer fallow periods of rest for the land, termed 'sabbatical' or 'Jubilee' years. To quote Jonathan Sacks on this, 'As Maimonides points out, land which is over-exploited is eventually eroded and loses its fertility. The Israelites were therefore commanded to conserve the soil by giving it periodic fallow years and not pursue short-term gain at the cost of long-term desolation.' As well as this environmental reason, Sacks cites a second theological one – 'The land', says God, 'is Mine; you are but strangers and residents with me' Leviticus 25:23 (Sacks, *The Dignity of Difference*, Continuum, 2006, ch. 9, 'Conservation: Environmental Sustainability').

Alister McGrath (1953–)

Sustainability is not a new idea then – Deuteronomy also contains a law which forbids taking a young bird together with its mother (6:14). This warns against our modern habit of overharvesting nature. In Genesis 1, even before he has made man, God sees that what he has made is good – it delights him. He feeds and sustains nature (Psalm 104; Matthew 6:26), he hears its groaning (Romans 8:22) and will liberate it (Romans 8:20–1).

In *The Re-Enchantment of Nature*, McGrath argues that nature has been viewed mechanistically and we need to be re-enchanted by its witness to the glory of God's creative power. The Psalms capture our human longing for transcendence, the sense of awe and wonder that nature's aesthetic inspired in Romantic poets like Coleridge and Wordsworth, who saw the damaging effects of the industrial revolution on people and landscapes. Whereas the Enlightenment view emphasised words like power, control and survival ('nature red in tooth and claw') as seen by a detached observer, the Romantic view focused on mankind's encounter with nature, standing in awe of its wonder and beauty. An example can be seen in Wordsworth's poem 'The Tables Turned':

> Let Nature be your Teacher . . .
> Sweet is the lore which Nature brings;
> Our meddling intellect
> Mis-shapes the beauteous forms of things:–
> We murder to dissect.
>
> Enough of Science and of Art;
> Close up those barren leaves;
> Come forth, and bring with you a heart
> That watches and receives.

Sustainability: Taking the long-term view in managing present economic, social equity and environmental interests without endangering those of future generations. The three 'r's (reduce, reuse, recycle) are at the heart of this kind of movement, pithily captured in the question 'What use is a saw mill without a forest?'

The Enlightenment project placed God at best as a clockmaker, a deity far removed from the day-to-day running of creation. This deism is in stark contrast to the Christian doctrine of nature as God's creation in which God the Son becomes incarnate in Jesus to restore creation's original integrity. Theologians like Tom Wright and Alister McGrath see Romans 8's statements that 'creation itself will be liberated from its bondage to decay and brought into the freedom and glory of the children of God' and that 'the whole creation has been groaning as in the pains of childbirth right up to the present time' to hint at the renewal of the present earth, a hope that brings for them a new motivation for ecological action. This may ultimately be a divine work, but it is one that Christians are called to join in with.

According to this account, the thesis that Christianity is chiefly responsible for the ecological crises is therefore misguided. Christianity teaches that humans are **stewards** of nature and called to rule over it with the same loving wisdom as God. Instead, it is the Enlightenment project, especially in its post-industrial late capitalist phase, that is held responsible for an anthropocentric approach to reality that is limitless in its desire to control and exploit the material resources of nature for its own ends. Human self-centredness is the essence of sin; it fractures human beings' relationship with God, with each other and with nature. The central metaphor of the universe as a clockwork mechanism emphasises those aspects of reality that can be quantified and mechanised. The subject–object relationship, so essential to the scientific project, became a worldview. McGrath makes the point that the problem is not so much in this (scientific) approach, but in the danger that this abstract, reduced model of the world started becoming the only legitimate view of reality. This made man the measure of all things, disenchanting nature by removing the idea that the natural world had any intrinsic value or power of its own, or that it represented the work of a creator. Christianity and other religions placed limits on what man could do to nature because man was never the ultimate authority.

> **Stewardship:**
> A reading of Genesis 1:26 in which humankind being given 'dominion' to rule over nature is interpreted as people being God's vice-regents or stewards. Responsible and caring rule, rather than selfish exploitation, ought to be characteristic.

At both an academic and a popular level, Christian thinkers and activists are engaged in environmental and animal welfare campaigns. Charitable campaign groups like A Rocha, Operation Noah and Christian Aid lobby government, inform about energy usage, and audit Church environmental policies. Theologian Andrew Linzey (Director of the Oxford Centre for Animal Ethics) has written or edited over twenty books on animal rights, ethics and theology and appeared on Channel 4's *Food for Thought*. An advocate of Christian Vegetarianism, he argues that, although Christians have seen animals in an instrumental way as commodities, their thinking should be shaped by the Cross of Christ whereby God identifies with the innocent suffering of the weak, and they should see them as fellow creatures with intrinsic worth. David Clough's work on the theology of animals also alerts Christians to the global estimate of 56 billion non-human animals slaughtered each year (100,000 per minute), which has quadrupled in the last fifty years. Farming methods and aggressive breeding to improve the meat productivity of animals in artificial conditions has often worsened their lives. The Worldwatch Institute estimates that 74 per cent of the world's poultry and 68 per cent of its eggs come from factory farming, which renders the lives of animals more of a burden than a benefit to them. Alongside such statistics, research on higher primates and dolphins has established that animals are

A commercial chicken production house in Florida

intelligent (adult chimps have outperformed children of 2½ in logical reasoning tests) and have emotional lives within social groups. Christian charities are active in campaigning over climate change, with governments, churches and individuals being called on to reduce their carbon footprints and re-evaluate their view of animals and the environment.

SECTION TWO: ISSUES IN BUSINESS ETHICS

In this section, we will examine the series of relationships set out in the specification.

business	*&*	*consumers*
employers	*&*	*employees*
business	*&*	*environment*

Whilst we will deal initially with environmental and business ethics separately from the moral theories, you will be required to apply theory to them, and the two will be integrated in the second half of this chapter.

Business and consumers

In the economics of supply and demand, ethical consumers who are informed, discerning, and have choice can exert influence through their purchasing or boycotting power. The Co-op's 2012 report estimates the **Ethical Consumer** Market (people deliberately making choices based on moral beliefs or values) to have risen from £13.5 billion in 1999 to £47.2 billion in 2012. Significantly, it appears to be recession-proof, growing by £10 billion over the five years of the economic crisis. Duncan Clark's *The Rough Guide to Ethical Shopping* (Rough Guides, 2004) sees consumers as voting with their money. For example, it offers websites which grade energy providers on their green credentials. The estimated UK retail sales of **Fair-trade** products rose 19 per cent in 2012 to £1.57 billion. Responsible tourism with carbon-neutral flights, sustainable fishing, organic and local farm produce, energy-efficient appliances, charity shops, hybrid cars and use of wind and solar power are all part of the Ethical Consumer Market. Sustainable Consumerism also assesses how basic needs can be met and quality of life improved without costing the earth in terms of waste, pollutants, and use of natural resources. The needs of future generations should not be put at risk. In its 2011 survey, the Co-op found that 50 per cent of consumers would avoid a product based on the ethical reputation of a firm (Co-op Ethical Consumer Markets Report, 2012). So consumers are not powerless and the free market listens carefully when they boycott goods causing 'brand damage' that hurts profits (e.g. over child labour in Uzbekistan or sanctions in Burma). Customers are stakeholders. Companies that are interested in longer-term survival and growth need to treat their customers well and provide quality and value in their goods and services. Indeed, Seth Godin, a leading business writer, goes as far as saying, in *Unleashing the Ideavirus* (Do You Zoom, 2000):

> Marketing by interrupting people is not cost-effective anymore. You cannot afford to seek out people and send them unwanted marketing messages, in large groups, and hope that some will send you money. Instead, the future belongs to marketers who establish a foundation and process where interested people can market to each other. Ignite consumer networks and then get out of the way and let them talk.

Another aspect of consumer power is seen in shareholder advocacy at annual general meetings of corporations, from institutional investors like pension funds, socially responsible mutual funds, unions or faith-based investors' resolutions. These put pressure on boards to adopt 'corporate social responsibility' and act as 'Corporate citizens' engaging in philanthropic and green agendas. Since the launch

Ethical consumerism: The deliberate choice to purchase certain goods or services rather than others based upon moral beliefs and values

Fair-trade: A movement which seeks fair treatment for developing-world workers and producers in the supply chain. It seeks fair prices, living wages, safe conditions and rights for workers, together with greater transparency and justice in trade.

Renewable energy, like that harnessed by wind turbines, offers an example of sustainable energy

of Friends Provident's ethical fund in 1985, the ethical investment sector in the UK has grown to over 100 products and is valued at over £11 billion in 2013. These may exclude investments in tobacco, arms, alcohol or oppressive regimes, or promote community projects or loans to marginalised groups and small businesses, as well as encouraging environmentally friendly and sustainable businesses, including the alternative energy sector.

The above paragraph may lead us to believe that consumer sovereignty is alive and well. The reality is that not all markets are fully competitive and, in many cases, consumers are misinformed, vulnerable, excluded, determined or ignorant when making their choices. Critics of big tobacco companies cite their targeting of developing-world countries where consumers are less informed about the link between cigarettes and cancer (in 2007, 37 per cent of all cigarettes were sold in China). Furthermore, such is the marketing power of big brands like Apple, Coca Cola and Microsoft that **globalisation** can actually constrict choice as smaller competitors are put out of business and consumer tastes are moulded. Pricing can be deceptive, as in the sale of certain budget airline tickets, and can be fixed by a 'cartel' of companies or exclude the poor from vital resources (e.g. when some multinational drug companies were criticised for pricing HIV/AIDS/anti-malaria drugs out of reach of the sick and poor of developing countries). Drinks and fast-food companies selling high-sugar products targeted at children raise questions of the duty to inform, as well as the ethics of marketing to vulnerable customers. More aggressive advertising aimed at creating insecurity and dissatisfaction or manufacturing 'needs' out of 'wants' has created a consumer culture which is less transparent, informed, free and unpressured than we might believe.

> **Globalisation:** The interconnectedness of global finance, markets, institutions, business, technology, culture, politics, law and environment

Employers and employees

From the rise of trade unions and workers' rights in an era of exploitation in Victorian mills and mines, UK employment law has come a long way. Employers are obligated to uphold rights, such as the right to a healthy and safe working environment, to belong to a union, to have holidays and time off, a minimum wage, maternity and paternity leave. Employers should not discriminate on the basis of race, religion, gender or sexual orientation, though limited exemptions exist for faith groups (presently it is not compulsory to appoint female bishops, such issues being seen as a matter of religious liberty with faith groups being able to appoint leaders from practising members). Employers typically own business assets like buildings, stock, equipment, etc., but their employees are a different type of resource. Employees may part-own and operate the business and are often among the most costly aspects of its operations, requiring management and training, leadership, career development and pastoral care.

There are 'moral hazards' for both parties in contracts. Employees may have to move to a new location with all the upheaval this creates, and their need to earn a living makes them dependent to a degree on their employer. Employers may, for example, discover that an employee puts at risk the reputation of the company through their professional or personal conduct, or lose intellectual property if confidential information or planning is leaked. Kantians would see the employer as having a duty not to treat their employees as a means to an end, instead valuing them as **stakeholders** in the business. To only satisfy *shareholder* interests is to take a very short-term view (given that many shares are bought and sold for profit over short periods). Although some businesses create a short-term outlook with bonuses, employees are often more likely than shareholders to take a longer-term perspective and to value other goods alongside profit (such as excellence or quality in the goods or services the business provides). Virtue ethicists would emphasise the role of chief executives or senior managers in setting an agenda of Corporate Responsibility and mutual respect in the DNA of their business culture. 'Tone at the top' is a term that describes the board of directors and senior executives setting the tone or values culture for the company to prevent fraud or unethical practices such as bullying, tax evasion or other abuses of power. The belief is that this sets an agenda which permeates throughout the whole culture of the company. Virtue theorists could see this emphasis on character and training in virtue in terms of practices aimed at excellence that develop virtues internal to them, such as truth-telling, respect and justice.

Stakeholders: Parties such as customers, local communities, government, suppliers, employees, civil society and shareholders who are affected by business practice and therefore have an interest or stake in it, making business more democratic and accountable

> **Exercise**
> 1. Have you ever avoided a company or purchase on ethical grounds? If so, why?
> 2. Investigate the issue of accountability in terms of company responsibilities to workers in the garment industry in Bangladesh. Fires and the collapse of buildings, together with workers not being paid a living wage, have raised questions about the ethics of supply chains.

Businesses and the environment

Tracking sustainable consumption – look up:

1. 'zerofootprint' to do an online calculation to measure and manage your carbon footprint;
2. National Geographic's Greendex system, which is an annual sustainable consumption index of actual consumer behaviour and material lifestyles across eighteen countries.

Triple bottom line: In addition to the bottom line of *profit*, in 1994, John Elkington's SustainAbility consultancy suggested that successful businesses also have a *people* account (for social responsibility to stakeholders) and a *planet* account (for environmental responsibility)

Businesses seek to maximise profit by externalising the wider social costs of their goods and services, so they do not have to be met by the producer or the consumer at the point of sale. At worst, this can be seen as a form of theft: those who benefit from stealing from those who will have to bear the costs. In *The Value of Nothing* (Portobello, 2011), Raj Patel gives the example of McDonald's. He cites one estimate that the cost of voluntarily offsetting the 2.66 billion pounds of CO_2 created in the making of 550 million Big Macs sold in the United States every year would be between $7.3 and $35.6 million.

A further external cost borne by the environment is seen in the forests cut down to graze beef cattle. The Centre for Science and the Environment in India estimates this

Externalities:
The consequences (negative or positive) of commercial and industrial activity for other parties (e.g. where true costs of production are dodged by the producer)

raises the price of each Big Mac to $200 (cited in Patel 2011). This does not even take into account the $562 million saved by the US beef industry, which fattens its produce on government-subsidised corn (according to a Tufts University study). Nor does it take into account the social subsidy estimated at around $273 million p.a. in the form of Medicare, food stamps, and government payments to turn the poverty-line wages of employees into living wages. One further cost to add to the **externalities** bill comes in the form of obesity and heart disease resulting from 'excessive meat consumption', which is estimated at $30–60 billion per year in the US.

It is also important to consider the externalising of environmental costs to businesses at the macro level. World Bank estimates put the cost to China's environment at 8 per cent of its GDP (M. Bekoff, *The Emotional Lines of Animals*, 2004). As each business looks to lower its costs in production, packaging, marketing, labour and interest payments, etc., moving goods around the earth's surface by land, sea and air adds to greenhouse gases. Carbon offsetting (whereby, through using alternative energy sources or planting trees, the environmental costs are factored into the price) is rarely taken up (though U2's and Coldplay's tours aim to be carbon-neutral, with varying success). At the Rio Earth Summit in 1992, governments discussed measures to reduce carbon emissions. In *The No-Nonsense Guide to Globalisation*, Wayne Ellwood proposes that the World Trade Organization should incorporate an agreement that 'requires all governments to stabilise greenhouse gas emissions at 1990 levels' and provides 'for customs inspection, seizure and disposal of goods that were produced in ways that violate that agreement' (*New Internationalist*, 2005, p. 122). He wishes to see regulation set limits to free trade policies that add to global warming or biodiversity loss. Yet the consensus seems to be that dealing with environmental crises should be the responsibility of other specialist bodies rather than being regulated in international trade agreements.

The Kyoto Protocol is 'an international agreement linked to the United Nations Framework Convention on Climate Change, which commits its Parties by setting internationally binding emission reduction targets' (UN). It was adopted in 2005 and revised in 2012. As countries such as China, the US and Russia have been reluctant to commit to binding reductions on carbon emissions, governmental action on climate change at an international level still has a long way to go. The year 2014 saw the introduction of the United Nations' Clean Development Mechanism which 'allows emission-reduction projects in developing countries to earn certified emission reduction (CER) credits, each equivalent to one tonne of CO_2. These CERs can be traded to allow industrialised countries to a meet a part of their emission reduction targets under the Kyoto Protocol.' Individuals, corporations and events can also trade in CERs. Another UN initiative is its Global Compact, which is a bottom-up rather than a top-down approach. Working directly with companies, it offers them a platform to support and enact ten core values in areas of human rights, labour, the environment and anti-corruption.

Natural Law and business/environmental ethics

Worship of God is one of the primary goods for Aquinas, and, in his teleological view, each creature's end expressed its purpose in the order of creation. Hereby, Aquinas'

Natural Law may arguably be seen to take a deep ecological view which gives an intrinsic value to nature, because, despite being based on reason rather than revelation, it is theocentric not anthropocentric. Natural resources, animals and the environment aren't just commodities to be valued for their instrumental worth to humans. As Aquinas puts it, 'the whole universe is more perfect in goodness than man; for though each individual thing is good, all things together are called very good. Therefore the whole universe is to the image of God, and not only man.' (ST, Q.93, Art.2, Obj.3). Unlike Kant, who saw human reason as the basis of law, Aquinas sees eternal law (the law by which God rules creation) and Natural Law as the foundation on which the legitimacy of the laws of governments are built. This again moves away from an anthropocentric environmentalism. Practical rationality calls us to use scarce resources prudently, and alerts us to human obligations to non-human animals, plants, and perhaps even ecosystems. The Primary Precept of practical reasoning is that good be done and evil avoided. This would emphasise sustainable business practices and conservation, recycling and use of renewable energies wherever possible.

Kantian Ethics and business/environmental ethics

Kantians would naturally take a rights-based approach to employment law and think universally, rather than in terms of personal or national self-interest, with regard to the environment. Kant's first and third formulations of the Categorical Imperative seek to act on principles that can be universalised or establish a kingdom of ends. This global viewpoint would welcome the UN initiatives mentioned above. The phrase 'Tone at the top' originates in accounting and refers to the ethical climate of a business as established by its directors and senior management. If the tone set at the top is one of transparency, the rejection of fraud and the promotion of responsibilities towards the environment or stakeholders, it will filter down through the business. Kant's own father acted with good will in heated disputes between saddle- and harness-makers' guilds, and the tests of this adherence to duty are the three formulations of his Kant's imperative. Kant also rejected hypothetical imperatives and formulations of Kant's imperative. Kant also rejected hypothetical imperatives and believed that reason could lead us to synthetic a priori judgements (ones that applied to the world of sense experience but could be known by reason alone). So, prior to experience, we can grasp the principle that we ought to use finite resources prudently and not squander them. As fossil fuels, rainforests and ecosystems are finite, this establishes duties of care that we owe to them. Kant's emphasis on the autonomous rational self doing its duty can prove difficult to put into practice if the corporate culture solely seeks profit and cuts costs by shirking the above responsibilities. So it is vital that business leaders avoid contradictions of between reason and the will. Take the example of a business executive whose decisions increase pollution and deforestation while he lives in the countryside to enjoy clean air and a beautiful landscape and is conscientious in his local recycling. Businesses and consumers ought not to will one thing for themselves, such as a fair wage or to enjoy a high standard of living from profits/income made from the exploitation of workers in the developing world paid less than a living wage

– and something else for others: they are ends in themselves and should not be used as means to our ends.

Kant has been criticised for his view that while humans have intrinsic worth and cannot be treated as a means to an end, the worth of the natural world of animals and the environment, as an end in itself, is more vulnerable. Kant's concern over callous or cruel treatment of animals is not primarily about their interests, but due to injury we do to our humanity. He also places the focus of moral reasoning on the individual autonomous self when business and environmental ethics are better served with collective and co-operative behaviour. Rational dignity and the capacity to be moral agents lifts humankind above nature, but it also gives it a special responsibility within it for Kant. For others, his emphasis on intrinsic worth and dignity and its connection with duties can extend to a non-anthropocentric ethic that is transferrable to animals in terms of their interests or 'will to live', or to the environment in term of deep ecology or ecosystems. Kant's awe at the starry heavens above and the moral law within is taken up by other scholars such as Emily Brady (*The Sublime in Modern Philosophy: Aesthetics, Ethics, and Nature*, Cambridge University Press, 2013). She attempts to save Kant from the charge of anthropocentrism by reading him as seeing the vastness, beauty, and power of the natural world as awakening a sense of one's rational nature and moral vocation. Destroying habitats and species, natural resources and over-hunting/fishing all dehumanise this rational dignity of human beings in a failure to see the interplay of reason and awe at the sublime in nature.

Utilitarianism and business/environmental ethics

Utilitarian ethics are consequentialist and take a prudent cost–benefit approach to weighing ethical decisions. Given the scientific evidence for the impact of human industry and energy usage on the environment and the risks of flooding, rising global temperatures, desertification, species extinction, etc., taking stock of likely consequences is a crucial part of the ethical discussion. Practical and empirical, Utilitarian logic provides a useful basis on which to measure and regulate businesses on their ethics, the UN's certified emissions reduction credits being an example of such logic. A focus on the greatest good of the greatest number also encourages global responsibility. In an age in which multinationals often wield more power than nation states, Bentham's dictum of 'Every man to count for one and no one to count for more than one' serves to empower employees, consumers and activists to challenge business policies where they are exploitative or damaging to the environment. Utilitarianism is democratic in outlook and would argue for businesses to extend their scope of responsibility beyond shareholders to all stakeholders, taking into account the welfare of employees (including those in their supply chain who work in the developing world).

Bentham wrote that 'The question is not, Can they *reason*? nor, Can they *talk*? but, Can they suffer?', and Peter Singer's writing in books like *Animal Liberation* and *One World* expresses a desire for ethics to be less anthropocentric. Concern for animal welfare challenges the cruelty of the meat industry's factory-farming methods. He attacks 'speciesism' for being as ungrounded as racism in giving little or no value to the lives, interests and welfare of non-human animals. Rule Utilitarians may even go further and speak of animal rights. They would also advocate reforms in legislation, regulation, and company policies that take account of the impact of rules on ethics and the environment. Change requires movements, not just individuals making decisions on an ad hoc basis. Mill's writing would balance the liberties of individuals or companies against the harm principle. Law ought to intervene or regulate when significant harm is done to others, and environmental law and policy on carbon emissions reflects this. Critics claim the ends–means reasoning of Utilitarianism gives it a very shallow ecology, preserving the ground on which we stand for instrumental rather than intrinsic reasons. Yet part of Mill's recovery from his breakdown came through reading the Lakeland poets Wordsworth and Coleridge, so his qualitative emphasis on higher pleasures included an aesthetic appreciation of nature. Greedy consumerism and overconsumption would resemble the pleasures of the pig and Mill would warn against undervaluing natural resources or the ecosystem in a purely qualitative cost-benefit analysis.

Virtue theory and business/environmental ethics

In drawing our attention to the question not simply of what goods, services, and profits we are producing, but of who we are becoming as a society (*polis* in Aristotelian terms) or a global community, Virtue theory reminds us that we flourish together and in co-operation with, not dominance over, the finite resources of the natural world. In *After Virtue*, MacIntyre asserts that 'the tradition of the virtues is at variance with central features of the modern economic order' (1984, p. 254). He sees the rich consumer and the bureaucratic manager (matching ends and means) as sadly characteristic of our age. MacIntyre highlights how co-operative practices are necessary to the cultivation of virtue. He explains this in terms of external goods which 'are such that the more someone has of them, the less there is for other people ... External goods are therefore characteristically objects of competition in which there must be losers as well as winners' (ibid., pp. 190–1). In contrast, internal goods are about pursuing the excellence intrinsic to an activity. The true musician, artist or craftsperson is not motivated solely by the creation of a commodity for sale, but by a sense of calling and satisfaction that comes in the pursuit of excellence in their creative work, in the pursuit of a practice that is for the good of a wider community of practitioners. When businesses focus entirely on external goods, they can become dehumanising to work in. They can also value what is measurable and think short-term, undervaluing the environment.

A key thinker on business ethics and Virtue theory was Robert Solomon (1942-2007). On the one hand, he was critical of Aristotle who, as an aristocrat, was disparaging about the commerce of commoners and foreigners: he approved of *oeconomicus* or household trading, but was critical of trade for profit, or *chrematisike*, seeing those engaged as moneylenders or in commerce as 'parasites'. On the other hand, Solomon was more positive about the application of Aristotle to the culture of corporations. Aristotle's ethics challenges the idea of an inescapable conflict between individual self-interest and the wider public good. Instead, it places eudaimonia, or human flourishing, in the polis – the neighbourhood, business, city, country or globe. As Solomon puts it, 'Corporations are real communities, neither ideal nor idealised, and therefore the perfect place to start understanding the nature of the virtues' (Solomon, *Ethics and Excellence: Cooperation and Integrity in Business*, Oxford University Press, 1992, p. 116). The best business leaders invest heavily in their people and do not think as pure technocrats manufacturing profit. They value their employees, fostering a culture of excellence (*arête*). Big corporations can learn from Aristotle's belief that teleology or a sense of purpose lies at the heart of our best work – excellence goes beyond efficiency. They can innovate new energy-efficient and green technologies. Solomon advises his graduate students: 'to live a decent life choose the right company' (ancient Greeks used to say: 'to live the good life one must live in a great city'). He cites examples of business mission statements like 'Better living through chemistry', 'Quality at a good price', 'Productivity through people', 'Progress is our most important product' (Solomon, 'Aristotle, Ethics and Business Organizations', *Organization Studies* 25 (2004), pp. 1021-403). Successful businesses like The Co-operative and John Lewis Partnership, invest in staff development and foster a collective sense of excellence and social/environmental responsibility. In doing so, they attract staff and customer loyalty.

The resurgence of trust in many works on business ethics (e.g. Robert Solomon, *Building Trust*, 2001; Francis Fukuyama, *Trust: The Social Virtues and the Creation of Prosperity*, 1996; and John Whitney, *The Economics of Trust*, 1994) also suggests that Virtue theory remains relevant. Relationships exist at every level of corporations, and between employers and employees, and businesses and suppliers or customers. Transparency as to corporate decisions and policies on all stakeholders and the environment is a part of this trust. Trust can break down, as it did in the banking crisis when financial products turned out to be worthless and banks were hiding the true extent of their debt. As John Roberts notes in *The Modern Firm: Organizational Design for Performance and Growth*, 'Culture is the "softer" stuff, but it is no less important for that. It involves the fundamental shared values of the people in the firm, as well as their shared beliefs about why the firm exists, about what they are collectively and individually doing, and to what end' (Oxford University Press, 2004, p. 79). Corporate cultures shape their employees' values and, in the case of ENRON, the Texas-based energy, commodities and services company who filed for bankruptcy in 2001, this culture silenced questions about values and focused solely on profits and bonuses larger than annual salaries (even to the point of false accountancy in inflating its figures to attract investors). Sherron Watkins, the former vice-president and whistle-blower, alerted the CEO to the fraud and deception, but he was at the heart of it, later being prosecuted for insider trading, securities fraud and making false statements to auditors. She advises university graduates to work for companies priding themselves in the excellence *(arêtê)* of their products and services, not solely on their profits. So values, and virtues of truth-telling and transparency, of accountability and questioning, need to be there before crises arise.

Discussion Questions

Socrates and Aristotle believed in the unity of the virtues. Courage, justice, temperance, etc., were one. The pursuit of profit cannot be an end in itself, but part of a wider flourishing of character and society. To act virtuously is to have the wisdom and character to act in the right way at the right time to the right person for the right reason. When all of the virtues work together, values, priorities and principles become clear. Yet, like most people, business leaders exhibit some virtues, but lack others, and it's here that virtues can be vices when employed to the wrong ends (such as profit at all costs).

Take the example of Apple Computers. It has been challenged over the pay and conditions of workers in its supply chain. Critics say that the companies it outsources production to in China pay less than a living wage, use under-age labour and require excessive working hours. There are reports of oppressive management, environmental pollution, and even suicides reported at some plants. The founder of Apple Computers, Steve Jobs, said, 'I would trade all of my technology for an afternoon with Socrates.' If his wish had been granted, he may have got more than he bargained for. Plato called Socrates the gadfly, for just as a gadfly stings a horse into action, so Socrates stung the rich and powerful elites of Athens with his relentless questioning. Socrates may have applauded Steve Jobs for his pursuit of excellence in himself and in Apple and praised his company's contribution to people's efficiency and to paperless offices.

Yet Socrates may well have asked:

how the goals or purposes of Apple contribute to the wider flourishing of the world (Socrates called himself a citizen of the world);

how, if the workers in Apple's supply chain aren't flourishing in their lives, the company itself could be said to be flourishing;

why Apple had such huge cash reserves when there was so much preventable suffering in the world;

whether, unless you possessed all of the virtues, you could truly be said to possess any of them.

Set up a dialogue between Socrates and Steve Jobs using these questions: how would each respond to the other?

Steve Jobs, (1955–2011) Entrepreneur and co-founder of Apple Inc. and Pixar Animation Studios

Strengths of Virtue Ethics in business

Whistle-blower:
A person with insider knowledge who reveals illegality or wrongdoing in an organisation or government. Often done in the public interest and at personal cost (e.g. loss of employment).

The 'good life' consists of more than profit, and Virtue theory has a healthier holistic approach to human flourishing. It also recognises that human flourishing requires individuals or corporations to be part of a wider community in order to develop, encouraging a relational and stakeholder approach. Business is seen as an integral part of the *polis* or wider society.

Aristotle linked the virtuous life with happiness. This wasn't pleasure, but the realisation of our true potential. Virtue ethicists would advise young graduates setting out on a business career to do their research into the firms they apply to and to find mentors they respect (ones who show good judgement or *phronēsis* and who exhibit lives they wish to emulate). Workers' rights and consumer protection are significant. So too is a concern that life is more than 'another day, another dollar, then retire and die'. When Steve Jobs persuaded the boss of Pepsi-Cola to join his business, he said to John Sculley, 'Do you want to sell sugared water for the rest of your life? Or do you want to come with me and change the world?' Business has social responsibilities and isn't disconnected from other local, national, or global stakeholders. Relationships and trust matter a great deal after the 2008 crash and Virtue Ethics has a great deal to offer in this discussion. Wall Street's motto has, since 1801, been 'My Word is my Bond' 'dictum meum pactum' and perhaps such wisdom is returning in the greater emphasis on Corporate Social Responsibility (CSR), or corporate citizenship/conscience. Whilst this may simply be a bid to increase long-term profits and avoid brand damage, CSR aims to go beyond compliance with the law to take initiatives that consider the interests of stakeholders and the environment.

The emphasis on the golden mean of virtues lying between the vices of deficiency and excess in Virtue theory should encourage Western consumers to moderate their energy usage, or shopping, etc., and think instead about the global poor.

In MacIntyre's terms, purely external goods are sought after by bureaucratic managers, and the value of people/the planet are screened out in their narrow concentration on profit. Perhaps Virtue Ethics can suggest why it might be in the longer term interests of business to value co-operation and internal goods, excellence, their employees, clients, and community more.

Weaknesses of Virtue Ethics in business

Virtue ethicists can undervalue the ingenuity of the free market. If there's a niche for ethical investment, some entrepreneur will fill this void. From Aristotle's aristocratic disdain for those who had to make a living in trading to modern Virtue theory, there can be a snobbish dismissal of market forces when their innovation and efficiency often deliver where well-meaning critics stand idly by.

Virtues are relative to time and place. Cultures and in the Far East emphasise collective stability rather than individual rights, together with loyalty, even conformity. So **whistle-blowing** runs against the grain, whilst it is seen as virtuous and protected in law in several Western countries. How useful is Virtue theory in practice if it is so culturally relative? In a global market, do managers respect local cultural values that clash with their own, e.g. where bribery or child labour are standard?

Discussion Questions

Films review

Wall Street and *Wall Street: Money Never Sleeps* are Oliver Stone films that touch on the Zeitgeist of the 1980s and our own day. The original film defined the excesses and speculation of brokers just before the stock market crash of 1987; the sequel focuses on the 2008 crash. The film raises deep questions about the sustainability of a model of global capitalism which transcends nation states. The ethics of sustainability, of PR departments **greenwashing** corporate images, of the price we put on the interests of the environment and future generations are all raised by this film. Interestingly, the young businessman Jacob Moore (in the second film) is promoting research into green energy, which is seen very much as the next stock market bubble by his cynical mentors. There are some memorable quotes in both films:

Greenwashing:
When companies seek good public relations by making trivial and low-cost eco-friendly changes to products, services and processes that are merely for show

Wall Street, 1987

'The point is, ladies and gentleman, that greed, for lack of a better word, is good. Greed is right, greed works. Greed clarifies, cuts through, and captures the essence of the evolutionary spirit.

Greed, in all of its forms; greed for life, for money, for love, knowledge has marked the upward surge of mankind. And greed, you mark my words, will not only save Teldar Paper, but that other malfunctioning corporation called the USA.'

(Gordon Gecko's speech to shareholders)

Wall Street: Money Never Sleeps, 2010

'What's your number? How many millions do you want in your bank account before you walk away? $10m, $50m, $100m?'

(Jacob Moore to Bretton James)

'It is clear as a bell to those who pay attention. The mother of all evil is speculation. Leverage debt. The bottom line is, it is borrowing to the hilt. And I hate to tell you this, but it is a bankrupt business model. It will not work. It is septicemic, malignant and it's global.'

(Gordon Gekko's speech to university students)

'One thing I learned in jail is that money is not the prime asset in life. Time is.'

(Gordon Gekko)

Bearing in mind the issues raised by *Wall Street* and *Wall Street: Money Never Sleeps*, debate the following questions:

1. Discuss how the social, economic and environmental aspects of sustainability work together in the Body Shop's business model: www.thebodyshop.com/values/index. aspx. You could look up the websites of Toyota, L'Orēal and Microsoft to examine their environmental and corporate responsibility commitments.

2. Consider how an Act/Rule Utilitarian would evaluate this debate:

Should the Arctic National Wildlife Refuge be opened to oil drilling?

Yes	No
i. The proceeds from drilling could dramatically lower the price of oil, leading to another economic boom.	i. It takes the focus off the real cause of the oil shortage — our excessive consumption.
ii. It would lessen our dependence on foreign oil, especially in the Middle East.	ii. A wildlife refuge could be disturbed by humans, with animal lives possibly being changed in the process.
iii. Drilling could easily be done without disrupting the refuge or damaging the environment.	iii. The drilling may not yield much of anything.
iv. It would dramatically help the economy and the people of Alaska.	iv. It could take years or decades before any significant amount of oil is ready for use.
v. The drilling and land development would create hundreds of thousands of jobs.	v. The reserve can be saved as a last resort decades from now when we've exhausted other supplies.
vi. Alternative energy sources are the future, but for right now they're too expensive and underdeveloped; oil from ANWR could help fuel the world economy in the meantime.	
vii. Every dollar we spend on oil from the Middle East, Russia and Venezuela only strengthens the communists and terrorists trying to harm the United States.	

(Source: Balanced Politics, ishttp://www.balancedpolitics.org/anwr_drilling.htm)

3. Do you think big business environmentalism can ever be more than PR and marketing if profit is the bottom line?

4. Can global economies continue to experience growth for centuries into the future if the natural resources are finite and population growth continues at present rates?

5. 'The natural world has value in itself and reveals God.' Examine and comment on the significance of this view for stewardship of the natural world, with reference to the topic you have investigated.

6. 'The protection of the environment should be only for the good of humankind.' Assess this claim.

7. If we are part of the problem, we are part of the solution. What holds Western consumers like ourselves back from moderating our conspicuous consumption and lifestyles that are energy-hungry?

FURTHER READING

Robin Attfield (2014) *Environmental Ethics*. Polity, 2nd edition

John Benson (2000) *Environmental Ethics: An Introduction with Readings*. Routledge

Michael Boylan (2013) *Environmental Ethics*. Wiley-Blackwell

Andrew Crane and Dirk Matten (2010) *Business Ethics: Managing Corporate Citizenship and Sustainability in the Age of Globalization*. Oxford University Press

Patrick Curry (2011) *Ecological Ethics: An Introduction*. Polity

Michael Sandel (2013) *What Money Can't Buy: The Moral Limits of Markets*. Penguin Books

OCR Past Paper Questions

JANUARY 2010
'Utilitarianism is not the best approach to environmental issues.' Discuss.   *[35]*

JUNE 2010
Assess the usefulness of religious ethics as an ethical approach to business.   *[35]*

JANUARY 2011
'The environment suffers because business has no ethics.' Discuss.   *[35]*

JUNE 2011
Assess the claim that secular approaches to environmental issues are of more help
than religious approaches.   *[35]*

MAY 2012
To what extent are ethical theories helpful when considering ethical business practice?   *[35]*

'There is no moral imperative to care for the environment.' Discuss.   *[35]*

JANUARY 2013
Critically assess the view that businesses have a moral duty to put their consumers first.   *[35]*

JUNE 2013
'Businesses are completely incompatible with Virtue Ethics.' Discuss.   *[35]*

15 Sexual Ethics

Discussion Question

In the preface to *Practical Ethics*, Peter Singer writes:

> Even in the era of AIDS, sex raises no unique moral issues at all. Decisions about sex may involve considerations about honesty, concern for others, prudence, and so on, but ... the moral issues raised by driving a car, both from an environmental and from a safety point of view, are much more serious than those raised by sex. Accordingly, this book contains no discussion of sexual morality. There are more important ethical issues to be considered.

> Do you agree or disagree with Singer? If so, why? If not, why not?

Love, sex, marriage – a public or private affair?

Marriage is seen by some secular thinkers (e.g. Michael Walzer) as a contractual agreement mutually beneficial to each side, not least because, at its best, it secures a fairer exchange of affection and commitments. In contrast to the insecurity of the marketplace of short-term relationships, it offers the promise of greater permanency, legal rights and intimacy. On the down side, he sees family life as perpetuating social inequalities, as wealth, education and power are passed on from one generation to another. In Christian belief, however, marriage and sexuality are not simply private matters between consenting adults. According to David McCarthy (*The Good Life: Genuine Christianity for the Middle Class*, Revell, 2004), they are bound up with the life and community and mission of the Church as an embodied social ethic that seeks for the just and loving rule of God in heaven to appear on earth. Marriage vows are made before God and witnessed by friends, family and the body of the Church. They take place in a service of worship with prayers, Bible readings and, in the Catholic and High Church traditions, a Nuptial Mass. Marriage is characterised firstly by friendship, and its purpose extends beyond personal intimacy to the couple encouraging one another's Christian discipleship and spiritual and character growth. Churches run marriage preparation courses touching on all aspects of life together, from finances, sex, children and family life, careers and handling conflict to housework. But membership of the Christian community aims to train believers in the joys and challenges of life together from baptism to death. At the centre is a sense that the love of God sustains human loves (1 John 4:7–17). With singleness being referred to as a gift (Matthew 19:1–12; 1 Corinthians 7:1–15), and a monastic tradition going back to at least as far as the fourth century CE, marriage is a separate calling, with discipleship and human flourishing (including the reproduction and preservation of life) being central purposes.

Attitudes to sex in the Bible

For most Jews and Christians, the Bible is the primary source of authority when it comes to sexual ethics. The creation story of Genesis has had a foundational effect on all Jewish and Christian discussion of sexual ethics. In Genesis 1:26–8, humans are commanded to 'be fruitful and multiply', and Genesis 2:24 reads 'That is why a man leaves his father and mother and is united to his wife, and they become one flesh.' Sexual union is seen to signify a monogamous and lifelong union with the hope of children resulting from it.

In the great patriarchal narratives of Genesis (the stories of the founding figures of Israel such as Abraham, Isaac, Jacob, and Joseph (Genesis 12–50)), there is a strong emphasis on the idea of the Covenant, the special agreement and relationship between God and humans. God promises to give three things to the people: land, heirs and many descendants. These three promises provide much of the structure of the early history of Judaism. Marriage was thought of as the normal adult state in the Bible, which contains more than 500 references to 'marriage', 'married', 'husband' or 'wife'. Many writers contrast a modern consumer mind-set in entering sexual relationships with this covenantal marriage mind-set. The consumer puts self-interested desires first and tends towards short-term commitment, weighing costs and benefits. In contrast, covenants are entered solemnly with vows of commitment and a deep sense of one's responsibilities and expectations.

Introduction – four key issues in sexual ethics

Pre-marital sex

> **Pre-marital sex:** Sexual relations prior to marriage. Also traditionally termed 'fornication'.

The British Attitudes Survey of 2008 suggested that British people are increasingly tolerant of **pre-marital sex**. Of the 3,000 people surveyed, 70 per cent had no objections to pre-marital sex. This was a significant increase from 48 per cent in 1984. Only 28 per cent agreed that married parents brought up children best. The Family and Parenting Institute commented that 'The quality of the relationship that parents have matters most – not necessarily their marital status' (*BBC News*, January 2008).

On the other hand, several studies show that couples who live together before marriage (7.5 million couples in the US in 2012 and up 1,500 per cent since 1960) are more likely to divorce than those who do not. Writing in the *New York Times*, clinical psychologist Dr Meg Jay puts this down to 'gender asymmetry' (women typically seeing this as a step towards marriage whereas men view it as a way to test a relationship or postpone commitment). Cohabitation may on the surface appear to increase freedom but marriage offers a stronger incentive to invest in a lasting relationship in which one has greater expectations and responsibilities. Several studies suggest that cohabiting couples 'are as likely to return to singleness as to enter marriage', and that those who do marry after a period of cohabiting are more likely to get divorced than those who move from singleness to married life (A. Thatcher, *Living Together and Christian Ethics*, Cambridge University Press, 2002).

Case study: living together before marriage

In April 2011, shortly before Prince William married Kate Middleton, the Archbishop of York, Revd Dr John Sentamu, gave his backing to the couple having lived together before their marriage. He was reported as saying that 'many modern couples want to "test the milk before they buy the cow"'. He argued that the royal couple's public commitment to live their lives together would be more important than their past. Other Anglican clergy, on the traditionalist side of the Church, criticised the Archbishop for failing to reinforce biblical teaching that prohibits sex outside marriage (see *Daily Telegraph*, 29 April 2011, accessed online).

Do you think Dr Sentamu was correct in making this statement? Explain your reasons.

Conservative Protestant and Roman Catholic Christians say that the Bible is clear in its condemnation of pre-marital sex. They point to several quotations to justify this conclusion. Among these are the following:

1 Corinthians 7:2 'Let each man have his own wife and each woman her own husband.' This statement comes towards the end of a long section in which St Paul criticises the Christians in Corinth for their failure to live up to God's laws – in particular, regarding sexual immorality.

In *1 Corinthians 6*, Paul makes the uncompromising statement: 'Make no mistake: no fornicator or idolator, no adulterer or sexual pervert . . . will possess the kingdom of God.' A few verses later, he says: 'The body is not for fornication . . . it is for the Lord' (v. 13). In v. 18, he says 'Every other sin one may commit is outside the body; but the fornicator sins against his own body.' A 'fornicator' is someone who has sex with someone to whom he/she is not married. Paul understands pre-marital sex as a sin on two grounds: it is a sin against the other person, and it is also a sin against oneself. Paul believed that the body, having been created by God, belongs to God, therefore to abuse the body is a sin against God.

> **Exercise**
>
> Look up the following passages in the Bible and explain how they relate to pre-marital sex:
>
> Acts 15:20
> 1 Corinthians 5:1; 6:13, 18; 10:8
> 2 Corinthians 12:21
> Galatians 5:19
> Ephesians 5:3
> Colossians3:5
> 1 Thessalonians 4:3
> Jude 7

Extra-marital sex

Extra-marital sex: Sexual intercourse with someone other than one's marriage partner. Traditionally called 'adultery'.

Extra-marital sex occurs when a married person engages voluntarily in sexual activity with someone other than the person to whom they are married. It is commonly known as 'adultery'.

In the Old Testament, adultery is condemned as a very serious crime. It is specifically prohibited in the Ten Commandments (both versions: Exodus 20:14; Deuteronomy 5:18) and in the Holiness Code in Leviticus (18:20). Women could be guilty of this sin as well as men. Two witnesses had to testify in court for the case to be considered by the judges. If a man suspected his wife of adultery, but did not have sufficient evidence to convict her, and if she was pregnant, he could demand that she submitted to a trial by ordeal, which would decide whether she was guilty or innocent. If she was found to be guilty, this would be revealed physically, in a miscarriage or a premature child (Numbers 5:11–31). The penalty for

Still from Franco Zefirelli's 1977 TV mini-series *Jesus of Nazareth* with Jesus saying to the woman caught in the act of adultery, 'Where are your accusers now? Go and sin no more.'

anyone found guilty of adultery was death by stoning. This method of execution is assumed in the New Testament – see John 8:7, in the story of the young woman accused of adultery where Jesus says 'Let whichever of you is free from sin throw the first stone at her.'

In the New Testament, St Paul condemns adulterers as sinful in 1 Corinthians 6:9–10, as part of a list of immoral people who will not inherit the kingdom of God. The basis of Paul's objection seems to be the same as that for pre-marital sex: that it is a sin against another person and God, and also that it is a defilement of one's own body (see 1 Corinthians 6.18). Many Christians condemn adultery because it breaks the bonds of marriage, which is a sacrament ordained by God. In Matthew 19:9, Jesus says that sexual unfaithfulness in marriage is the only exception for which divorce is allowed.

On the issue of divorce and sexual ethics, the Situation Ethicist Joseph Fletcher wrote that:

> If . . . the emotional and spiritual welfare of the parents and children in a particular family could best be served by divorce, then wrong and cheapjack as divorce often is, love justifies a divorce . . . And this is the criteria for every form of behaviour, inside marriage or out of it, in sexual ethics or in any other field. For nothing else makes a thing right or wrong.
>
> (*Situation Ethics*, SCM Press, 1966, p. 133)

Contraception

The Bible has virtually nothing to say directly about **contraception**, as artificial means of birth control were not available at that time. However, there are two passages which are often referred to in the debate about whether contraception is allowable for religious people today. These are Genesis 1:26–8 – 'be fruitful and multiply' – and the story in Genesis 38 concerning Onan, who 'spilled his seed'.

The context of these passages needs to be taken into consideration. The Bible has a very positive view of the value of children. They are a gift from God (Genesis 4:1; 33:5), barren women are sometimes blessed by God (1 Samuel 1:6–8) and God forms children in the womb (Psalm 139:13–16).

Contraception: The deliberate use of devices or techniques aimed at preventing a woman from becoming pregnant as a result of sexual intercourse. Examples include the pill to prevent ovulation, intrauterine devices to stop implantation in the uterus and barrier methods such as the condom, or male/female sterilisation.

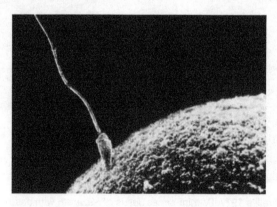

Sperm fertlising the ovum

> **Exercise**
>
> Look up the following passages and explain how they may be relevant to the debate on contraception
>
> Genesis 21:1–3; 25:21–22; 30:1–2; 33:5
> Psalm 127:3–5
> Proverbs 17:6
> Jeremiah 1:5
> Luke 1:7; 1:42
> Galatians 1:15

Given this positive view of children, the interpretation of the two passages above often assumes that anything that prohibits or prevents the generation of children is wrong. Therefore, God's command to 'be fruitful and multiply' means that contraception should not be used, as that would prevent new life coming into existence. Onan's sin was practising contraception by withdrawing from his sister-in-law (*coitus interruptus*).

Homosexuality

Homosexuality: Attraction towards, desire for or sexual activity with a person of one's own sex

Biblical teaching on **homosexuality** seems to be clear and uncompromising: homosexuality is an 'abomination'. Leviticus 20:13 says: 'If a man has intercourse with a man as with a woman, both commit an abomination. They must be put to death; their blood be on their own heads.' Here, it does not matter whether the homosexual intercourse takes place with or without consent or what age the participants are. All are guilty equally, because of the inherent sinful nature of the homosexual act, which defiles the nature of God's creation.

The story of Sodom in Genesis 19 has sparked much debate. Lot was visited by two angels (disguised as men), and the men of the city surrounded Lot's house, demanding that he send the angels outside so that the townspeople could 'know' them – that is, to have sexual intercourse with them. God later destroyed the city because of the depraved behaviour of the people of Sodom (the Sodomites).

In the New Testament, St Paul says in Romans 1:24–32 that impure homosexual relationships are deserving of death. This applies to female–female relationships as well (v. 26). This is the only passage in the Bible that refers to same-gender sexual behaviour by women.

Applying moral theories to these four practical issues

Contraception

Christian perspectives

As we saw earlier, the Bible has nothing directly to say about contraception. This means that any Christian views on it come from Church teaching, and this has often been subject to debate and disagreement, review and interpretation over time.

For Roman Catholic Christians, contraception of any kind is 'intrinsically evil' – that is, wrong in itself, regardless of any consequences. The only methods of birth control allowed for Roman Catholics are 'natural' ones. These include abstinence (not having sex) and the 'rhythm' method (having sex only when the woman is in the non-fertile part of her menstrual cycle, using charts to determine when this is likely to be). Although these natural methods are quite effective, they require discipline from the couple to keep records and to contain their sex lives to particular times of the month.

Roman Catholic official teaching against contraception largely comes from the importance of Natural Law, particularly as formulated by St Thomas Aquinas. He taught that there were two functions of marriage: the 'generative' and the 'unitive'. The 'generative' function is more important. Aquinas argues that God created the universe in a particular way, and to go against that is a sin. This Natural Law argument has been upheld by successive Popes. For example, Pope Pius XI said:

> No reason, however grave, may be put forward by which anything which is intrinsically against nature may become conformable with nature and morally good.

> Since, therefore, the conjugal act is designed primarily by nature for the begetting of children, those who exercise it deliberately frustrate its natural power and purposely sin against nature and commit a deed which is shameful and intrinsically vicious.

> (*Casti Connubii* (*Of Chaste Wedlock*), December 1930))

Many more recent Roman Catholics argue that contraception is morally acceptable, because there is no necessary link between sex and reproduction. For instance, during part of her menstrual cycle, a woman will be infertile, incapable of conceiving, so it is not wrong to practise sex then.

Part of the Roman Catholic objection to the use of contraception is its consequences if widely used. Critics argue, however, that the consequences of *not* using contraception will result in overpopulation and greater levels of poverty, starvation and death. This is a particularly widely used argument in South America and Africa.

Other Roman Catholics use the 'Doctrine of Double Effect'. Aquinas had formulated this principle: 'Nothing hinders one act from having two effects, only one of which is intended, while the other is beside the intention. Now moral acts take their species according to what is intended, and not according to what is beside the intention, since this is accidental' (*Summa Theologica, Secunda Secundae Partis*, Q.64). The argument in favour of contraception is that use of condoms is morally acceptable to prevent the spread of HIV/AIDS even if a secondary consequence of this is the prevention of conception.

The Anglican Church is in favour of contraception. At the Lambeth Conference in 1930, it was decided that, if there was a morally acceptable reason not to have children and to continue to have sex, then other methods could legitimately be used, provided it was done in the light of Christian principles. By the end of the 1950s, the Anglican Church had concluded that the responsibility for whether to have children or not lay with the conscience of couples, not with Church doctrine. Other Protestant and Orthodox churches agree with the view of the Anglican Church.

Kantian perspectives

Immanuel Kant's moral theory centred around the idea of the Categorical Imperative. This said that every human being had an innate ability to reason. This rational faculty meant that humans are able to decide which action is the morally correct one by doing our duty. The way to tell what our duty was in any specific case was to uphold the Categorical Imperative. The Categorical Imperative shows that our duty applies to everyone at all times, without exception. For Kant, the Categorical Imperative is also unconditional, i.e. it does not depend on any consequences of our actions. To find out whether any proposed action is morally correct, we should 'universalise' it: if it is consistent for everyone to comply with it, it is the morally correct thing to do.

Kant was a lifelong bachelor and had a negative view of human sexuality. For him, sex and erotic behaviour were largely manifestations of the animal instincts in humans and objectified the other, taking away their rational dignity. Sexual behaviour was only justified by the imperative of preserving the human race, within marriage. He is not clear whether sex is morally acceptable if a couple cannot have children. He wrote that 'Sexual love makes of the loved person an Object of appetite; as soon as that appetite has been stilled; the person is cast aside as one casts away a lemon which has been sucked dry.' In the commitment of married life, partners begin to see each other as *persons* rather than as mere objects. Erotic love 'taken by itself . . . is a degradation of human nature', but it can be expressed with reciprocity in the monogamous, lifelong union of married life where it 'reestablishes the rational personality' (Kant, *Lectures on Ethics*, ed. J. B. Schneewind and P. Heath, Cambridge University Press, 2001, p. 163).

Kant observed how prostitutes and concubines or mistresses were used as a means to an end, such exploitation most commonly being by men of women. As body and self are inseparable for Kant, when the man gave himself partially to two concubines or mistresses who gave themselves exclusively to him, they were exploited and objectified 'into a thing' rather than being an end in themselves. As he puts it, 'the body is a part of the self. In its togetherness with the self it constitutes the person; a person cannot make of his person a thing.' Kant's attack here is, according to Roger Scruton, on fornication, or sex before marriage. Here Kant sees the other as being used as an 'object of appetite' rather than in the mutual covenant of marriage. Fornication falls short of the duties and responsibilities of the rational person (body and mind).

Kant is very forthright in his condemnation of masturbation, which he argues is contrary to reason (the moral law) and contrary to nature as well. He argued that contraception is contrary to the proper purpose of the sexual organs. Contraception degrades humans to below the level of animals, which do not use contraception. He thought that contraception was worse than suicide, as suicide required courage and, where there is courage, there can be some respect. However, with contraception, there is no courage, merely a 'weak surrender to animal pleasure'.

Some modern Kantians, however, have taken a different view. They start with Kant's maxim that it is always wrong to treat people as a means to an end (i.e. to see people as only having instrumental value). In his day, women were often treated as a means to an end, by not having control over whether to have a family or not, as they were considered the property of their husband. It is argued that Kant would have desired autonomy for women on the issue of contraception, so that it would be acceptable to use contraception to avoid having a family if they did not want to.

Utilitarian perspectives

Mill was well known as a social reformer as well as a Utilitarian. When he was seventeen, he was arrested for distributing a pamphlet supporting contraception. He was influenced in this by the ideas of Thomas Malthus, an eminent economist and thinker, with whom Mill was closely acquainted. Mill was impressed by Malthus' theory of population (i.e. the working class). Mill was convinced that population control was essential in improving the living conditions of the working class. He wanted them, along with everyone else, to be as happy as possible in their situation. He thought that the use of contraceptives would be more effective at controlling the population than legislation. With the UN projecting that the current global population of 7.2 billion is set to reach 9.6 billion by 2050, together with the immense human suffering caused by the spread of the HIV/AIDS virus, the issue of contraception is very much on the agenda. Utilitarian critics of the Catholic Church, such as Peter Singer, argue that it could do much to decrease human suffering and death as well as lower unsustainable population growth if it promoted contraception and family planning across Africa and Latin America.

In his 1859 book *On Liberty* (J. S. Mill, *On Liberty and the Subjection of Women.* Penguin Classics, 2006), Mill wrote that freedom should be a matter of individual choice, and would not need the interference of the state, 'so long as we do not attempt to deprive others of theirs or impede their efforts to obtain it'. He was in favour of people having the freedom to experience sexual pleasure, except where this might result in social harm, for instance in the cases of rape or child molestation. He was also an activist in the promotion of the rights of women and, in this context, he campaigned for their right to use contraception. The contemporary Utilitarian John Harris even goes as far as arguing (1984) that sexual activity is less a moral issue than one of etiquette and manners. Yet, given the risks of sexually transmitted disease, sexual abuse, violence, trafficking, and the objectification and exploitation of women in pornography, this is a questionable claim.

Mill married Harriet Taylor soon after the death of her first husband. He had known her as a friend for two decades

Virtue Ethics perspectives

Virtue Ethics is a person-centred way of looking at ethics, asking questions about how a person may become virtuous throughout their life. As far as contraception is concerned, no one view is taken by all Virtue ethicists. As the Christian Virtue ethicist Stanley Hauerwas writes:

> I am impressed that in spite of the hundreds of articles published defending or opposed to abortion, the way people decide to have or not to have an abortion rarely seems to involve the issues discussed in those articles. People contemplating abortion do not ask if the foetus has a right to life, or when does life begin, or even if abortion is right or wrong. Rather, the decision seems to turn primarily on the quality of the relationship (or lack of relationship) between the couple.

The focus of Virtue Ethics is on the agent (the character of the person) rather than the action. In the case of a failure to use contraception leading to abortion, Hauerwas' point is that many relationships are not strong enough to raise a child – or another child. Particularly in the case of 'casual sex', failure to use contraception is seen as irresponsible and lacking in such virtues as prudence or wisdom. In this case, where a failure to use contraception leads to pregnancy, studies show that those having abortions are well aware of contraception, but may dislike the side-effects or the inconvenience of getting the pills, or do not wish to admit to themselves that they are planning to be sexually active. Some Virtue ethicists like Rosalind Hursthouse controversially condemn such behaviour as callously irresponsible and lacking in such virtues as sincerity, honesty, self-discipline and compassion. Critics of such a view emphasise the complexity of social causes of casual sex including a highly sexualised media, sexual pressure and exploitation by men, and poverty, lack of education and powerlessness.

Michael Slote, for example, emphasises one particular virtue – care – in relationships and argues that a three-way balance is required:

- care for those who are near to us (intimate care)
- care for other people in general (humanitarian care)
- care for our own well-being (self-care).

Considering each of these together enables a more holistic and comprehensive consideration of the issue of contraception.

Discussion Question

Rosalind Hursthouse offers the following analogy for the responsibility of a woman whose failure to use contraception leads to the conception of an embryo. She asks us to imagine a safe house used to shelter Jewish refugees in France, 1944. The signal agreed by the Resistance is closed windows to indicate 'danger, keep away', and an open window to mean 'climb through and shelter inside'. If the owner were carelessly to open the windows one summer afternoon, would they have an obligation to risk their life to shelter the Jew or expel the refugee knowing the risk of capture and death they face?

In what ways is this a fair/unfair analogy for the responsibilities towards the foetus if pregnancy should result from unprotected sex?

Homosexuality

Christian perspectives

There is a heated debate within Christianity about the status of homosexuals. For *Catholic and fundamentalist and conservative Protestant Christians*, homosexuality is understood as an illicit lust forbidden by God. God made humans male and female in Genesis 1:27, and Adam was given Eve as a companion, heterosexual marriage (where the two become one flesh) being the proper place for the sexual expression of this complementarity. For this group, Leviticus 18:22 and 20:13 (which says 'If a man has intercourse with a man as with a woman, both commit an abomination') condemn homosexual acts as being against the will of God. This is not to deny that homosexual orientation or same sex attraction exists, but to believe that, as for heterosexuals outside of heterosexual marriage, sexual intercourse is forbidden, Paul describing homosexual acts in Romans 1:26–7 as being unnatural and indecent.

Many Christian theologians, such as Michael Banner and John Milbank, seek to offer a critique of a secular culture which pushes family and religious life to the margins while placing individual sexual orientation and expression at the centre of human identity. They argue that the whole debate is driven by such assumptions in the secular media and that Christians need to focus on Christ, humbly aware of their fallen natures and how Jesus taught them not to judge. Instead, heterosexuals and homosexuals alike should seek forgiveness for lustful desires that make others objects, and, rather, be holy even as God is holy. In an age in which everything is commercialised and sex sells products and pornography produces a non-relational form of sexuality, the worship of a loving and self-giving God should make the marriage between husband and wife a reflection of Christ's love for the Church, which took him to the cross (Ephesians 5:22). It is here that the theological meaning of sex is properly understood. In the sacrament of marriage, the loving, creative union of husband and wife is not for self-gratification, but a calling to service of the Church and the world. Within the Christian community, affectionate bonds and fellowship are there for those whose orientation, celibate calling or time of life rules out a sexual relationship.

Liberal groups within Christianity, however, argue that the few biblical passages that refer to homosexuality need to be interpreted and contextualised if they are to be properly understood. They point out that there are very few references to same-sex consensual relationships in the entire Bible and that Jesus never mentions homosexuality at all. Some liberal interpreters dispute the interpretation of the New Testament Greek words *'malakoi'* and *'arsenokoitai'* (1 Corinthians 6:9–11; 1 Timothy 1:10). They suggest that such texts do not refer to adult committed and consensual sexual relationships but to unequal relationships, such as with male prostitutes or minors, not uncommon in the ancient world. Those engaging in such practices are listed by Paul as being among those who 'will not inherit the kingdom of God'. Furthermore, liberal thinkers would argue that Christians have altered their views over such questions as polygamy, divorce, conversion by military crusade, slavery, the role of women in leadership, evolution and hell. So, in the view of one liberal church denomination, 'Coming of age about sexuality requires affirming a diversity of responsible sexualities within the church, including the lives of gay men and lesbians.' Such churches, together with groups like the Lesbian and Gay Christian Movement, read Paul's statement in Galatians 3:28 – that 'there is neither Jew nor Greek, slave nor free … There is neither male nor female; for all are one in Christ Jesus' (an example of shifting attitudes towards the acceptance of non-Jews into the Church) – as a mandate to shift attitudes in today's Church and to promote an inclusive community. In 2003, the New Hampshire Episcopal diocese controversially elected the openly gay priest Gene Robinson as bishop. UK churches are not currently obliged to officiate in gay marriages (legalised in 2013 in the UK). In order to protect their freedom of belief, the law allows them to 'opt in' to officiating the ceremony, which can be performed in a secular civil ceremony or a religious setting in more liberal denominations. Some liberal Church leaders even argue that, in a society that has largely accepted homosexuality, the Church's rejection of this as anything from 'intrinsically disordered' and sinful to 'short of the ideal' is a barrier to belief for many liberal-minded unbelievers. The 1963 *Quaker Report on Sex* sees the key to obeying Jesus' command to 'love your neighbour as you love yourself' as being faithful, self-giving love rather than exploitation or abuse – whether the relationship is heterosexual or homosexual is considered morally irrelevant.

Natural Law

Aquinas mistakenly supposed that there was no 'homosexual' behaviour in the animal world, concluding from this that homosexual acts went against the Natural Law. For Aquinas, sexuality ought to be experienced within marriage and should help to bring the couple together in love and companionship. He did not say that sex was only for the procreation of children. This does not rule out homosexuality, as such a couple could have a fulfilling loving and companionable relationship, except they could not procreate.

However, Aquinas goes on to argue that any sexual act must be 'generative', if it is to be moral. That is, legitimate sex must include vaginal intercourse. This clearly rules out male homosexual relationships. He does not provide a reason for this conclusion. Some recent Natural Law theorists have attempted to provide one. Paul Weitham, for instance, says that homosexual acts, like contraception, impede the true purpose of the sex organs, which is to reproduce. This 'perverted faculty argument' may be what Aquinas meant. In the goal-orientated or teleological view of Natural Law, genitalia are aimed at procreation and, for Aquinas, homosexual relationships 'run counter to the natural mode of intercourse between male and female' (*ST*, 1a2ae, Q.94).

The neo-Thomist Natural Law theorist John Finnis argues that homosexuality is always harmful and degrading. Homosexual sex cannot lead to procreation and, therefore, means that the couple's bodies are used instrumentally rather than for the purpose for which they were created. This leads to the disintegration of the person. Any such disintegration is a bad thing and against the laws of nature. Therefore, no sexual activities outside heterosexual relationships are permissible. He also argues that the exclusive and lifelong commitment of marriage is a good thing in itself. Sexual intercourse, understood as heterosexual intercourse, contributes to and confirms this good thing. Therefore, homosexual acts cannot achieve this good and are not a morally acceptable way of life.

The most telling argument against Finnis' view is that he puts procreation at the centre of marriage. If one were to put love or mutual support or companionship at the centre instead, there would be no reason to object to homosexual relationships. In response, the Princeton law professor and Natural Law advocate Robert George agrees that:

> Marriage is a comprehensive union of two sexually complementary persons who seal (consummate or complete) their relationship by the generative act – by the kind of activity that is by its nature fulfilled by the conception of a child. So marriage itself is oriented to and fulfilled by the bearing, rearing, and education of children. The procreative-type act distinctively seals or completes a procreative-type union.

He goes on to suggest, however, that marriage has wider value beyond its primary purpose:

> marriage has its characteristic structure largely because of its orientation to procreation; it involves developing and sharing one's body and whole self in the way best suited for honorable parenthood – among other things, permanently and exclusively. But such development and sharing, including the bodily union of the generative act, are possible and inherently valuable for spouses even when they do not conceive children.
> (George, *The Meaning of Marriage: Family, State, Market and Morals*, Scepter Publications 2010, p. 144, and p. 154)

Utilitarian perspectives

Jeremy Bentham wrote the first known argument for homosexual law reform in England. He argues for the decriminalisation of 'sodomy', which in his day was punished by hanging. His writings on this subject stretch throughout his lifetime, from his early twenties, but were not published until 1931. He argued that homosexual acts should be judged on whether they contributed to happiness and alleviated pain. He wrote, in 1795, that 'I have been tormenting myself for years to find if possible, a sufficient ground for treating [homosexuality] with the severity [both in law and in morals] with which they are treated at this time of day by all European nations: but upon the principle of utility I can find none' ('Essay on Pederasty', quoted in J. R. Fitzpatrick, *John Stuart Mill's Political Philosophy*, Bloomsbury, 2006, p. 35). Bentham dismisses Voltaire's objection that homosexuality is 'prejudicial to the population', arguing that human population growth is under no threat and if it were, then monks and nuns would be equally guilty. So Bentham sees no consequentialist grounds for objecting to homosexuality.

John Stuart Mill wrote about the 'Harm Principle' in his celebrated essay *On Liberty*: 'the only purpose for which power can be rightfully exercised over any member of a civilised community against his will, is to prevent harm to others. His own good, either physical or moral, is not sufficient warrant . . . Over himself, over his own body and mind, the individual is sovereign.' Mill argues that, if homosexual acts between consenting adults cause no harm or distress (except to those people who think that homosexuality is wrong for religious or other reasons), then it should be left to individuals to do as they wish. The law should have no place in private relationships and homosexuals should not be penalized or criminalised. If, however, these acts were to take place in public, this would be a matter for the legal authorities, as public decency would be offended.

Critics of Natural Law may argue that focusing sex acts on reproduction is too 'biologistic' and ignores the wider purposes of bonding, pleasure and expression of love that sexual relations allow. They see this strict view of what is 'natural' to be a social construct. For Utilitarians then, judging an action good or bad depends not on the intrinsic nature of the action, but on its consequences.

Kantian perspectives

Kant argues against the morality of homosexuality. He says that it is immoral because it is a crime of the flesh against nature. In the *Groundwork to the Metaphysics of Morals* (1785; Harper Perennial, 2009), he says: 'Intercourse between *sexus homogenii* [i.e. same-sex partners] . . . is contrary to the ends of humanity; for the end of humanity in respect of sexuality is to preserve the species.'

According to Kant, a homosexual is not a genuine person because, by engaging in homosexual acts, he falls below the criteria of personhood, by deliberately going against what it is to be a human, i.e. to procreate.

The Kant scholar Alan Soble explains that Kant's explicit condemnation of homosexual (or same-sex) relations can be found in his *Lectures on Ethics*. Kant's arguments are grounded in the second formulation of the Categorical Imperative, which says: 'Act in such a way that you treat humanity, whether in your own person or in the person of any other, never as a means to an end, but always at the same time as an end.' Engaging in homosexuality is to treat the other person as a means to an end – your own sexual gratification – and this alone makes it immoral.

Others have argued that Kant's prohibition also goes against the first formulation of the Categorical Imperative: 'Act only according to that maxim whereby you can at the same time will that it should become a universal law without contradiction.' If your maxim were that everyone should be homosexual, then this could not be universalised, as no children would be born and the human race would die out. This would obviously be contradictory. It has been argued, however, that if the maxim were changed to say that those who wish to be homosexual may be so, this would still allow others to be heterosexual and the human race could continue. It could be moral, therefore, to allow homosexuality to those who wished to be homosexual.

Virtue Ethics perspectives

Virtue Ethics takes a distinctive approach to ethical issues which is significantly different from most other ethical theories. This is because it emphasises the character of the individual rather than the rules someone must follow or the consequences of actions performed.

On the issue of homosexuality, Virtue Ethicists are divided between those who are influenced by the Natural Law tradition, such as the British ethicist Rosalind Hursthouse, and the tradition which focuses more on an individual's character, such as the American Michael Slote, who emphasises the element of care in relationships.

Rosalind Hursthouse argues that the character trait or virtue by which to assess sexual ethics is temperance (moderation or self-restraint). Where sexual relationships are 'wildly, wilfully promiscuous' (1999, p. 156), they are a vice not a virtue. Whilst it is a natural goal in human flourishing to reproduce, the objection that homosexuality does not result in reproduction is irrelevant (not least because of IVF for lesbian couples, and surrogate mothers for gay couples, or adoption for both).

Exercise

Read the following passage and decide whether you think the analogy used is legitimate. If so, why? If not, why not?

John Corvino's essay 'In Defense of Homosexuality' (in A. Soble, ed., *The Philosophy of Sex*, Rowman and Littlefield, 5th edition, 2007, p. 171) includes this passage:

> A Roman Catholic priest once put the argument to me as follows: 'Of course homosexuality is bad for society. If everyone were homosexual, there would be no society.' Perhaps it is true that if everyone were homosexual, there would be no society. But if everyone were a celibate priest, society would collapse just as surely, and my friend the priest didn't seem to think that he was doing anything wrong simply by failing to procreate. Jeremy Bentham made the point somewhat more acerbically roughly 200 years ago: 'If then merely out of regard to population it were right that [homosexuals] should be burnt alive, monks ought to be roasted alive by a slow fire.'

Discussion Questions

'Principles without traits [virtues] are impotent and traits [virtues] without principles are blind.' William Frankena
   Do you agree?

How does the discussion of Virtue Ethics and sex illustrate this weakness with Virtue Ethics?

Slote, on the other hand, emphasises the ideas and examples of 'intimate care' as well as 'self-care', which are found in many same-sex relationships. These, it is argued, are characteristics that develop the virtues and help homosexual couples and individuals to become more virtuous. This is consistent with generally accepted virtues of love, commitment, loyalty, friendship, pleasure and so on.

Pre- and extra-marital sex

Christian perspectives

Many Christians rely on their idea of conscience as a moral guide. In Romans 2:12–16, St Paul taught that conscience was universal and given by God. That is why people who have no knowledge of God's law can still obey its demands. Aquinas believed conscience was a deep sense of right and wrong which derived ultimately from God.

Natural Law would also emphasise the danger of dualism in masturbation or casual sex (which causes a disharmony between the conscious self and the body). Such activity aims purely at bodily pleasure and, without further significance or commitment in terms of relationship, leads to a non-relational form of sexuality which dehumanises. The sexual nature of men and women ought to be expressed in the intentional, significant commitment of lifelong marriage. 'With my body I thee wed' is a phrase from the Anglican marriage service which refers to the wedded couple being 'united with one another in heart, body, and mind'. To treat your body as a mere instrument for pleasure is, Natural Law would argue, to lead to the disintegration of a person. By contrast, as Robert George puts it, 'Coitus is a unitary action in which the male and female literally become one organism . . . as a potential father and mother' (*In Defence of Natural Law*, Oxford University Press, 2001, p. 98).

In book II of his *Confessions*, Augustine writes that he 'ran wild in the shadowy jungle of erotic adventures' and that 'Clouds of muddy carnal concupiscence filled the air; The bubbling impulses of puberty befogged and obscured my heart; I couldn't tell the difference between lust and love.' Augustine saw sin as a deprivation, the absence of God's good created order (for example, lust as the absence of love). Whilst some commentators see his personal sexual guilt as the source of much negativity towards sexuality in Christian thought, he saw true sex as the expression of the whole person – the integration of body, heart and soul in a committed and lifelong devotion. It was this love between husband and wife that reflected the love of Christ for his bride the Church. As Paul writes in Ephesians 5:25–7, 'Husbands love your wives, as Christ loved the church and gave himself up for her.'

Utilitarian perspectives

Utilitarianism emphasises sexual freedom in relationships between consenting adults. The consequences of pre-marital sex in terms of unwanted pregnancy or of extra-marital sex for marriages, particularly when the interests of children are to be considered, would call for responsible decision-making. Sex is a private matter for consenting adults and the law should not regulate the bedrooms of the nation. Cases of trafficking, exploitation, abuse or sexual violence are quite different and, on the grounds of Mill's Harm Principle, ought to be regulated by the courts and police. Health, honesty and liberty are concerns, but there is nothing intrinsically wrong with promiscuity or prostitution for Utilitarians. Rights and wrongs are judged instrumentally – on the consequences they bring about.

Kantian perspectives

Kant is concerned that when lust not friendship drives sex, people (particularly women) are objectified and seen as instrumentally, not intrinsically, valuable. Human nature becomes beastlike, possessed by lust and dehumanised – the woman becomes 'something not someone'. He writes that:

Because sexuality is not an inclination which one being has for another as such, but is an inclination for the sex of another, it is a principle of the degradation of human nature . . . That [the woman] is a human being is of no concern to the man; only her sex is the object of his desires. Human nature is thus subordinated. Hence it comes that all men and women do their best to make not their human nature but their sex more alluring and direct their activities and lusts entirely towards sex. Human nature is thereby sacrificed towards sex.

(Soble 2007, p. 282)

In both pornography and dehumanising sexual encounters, what is absent is the reason and Good Will that characterise human nature at its highest – 'love presupposes the same mutual esteem for the other's character' (letter to Maria Von Herbert, 1792, in George Sher, *Ethics: Essential Readings in Moral Theory*, Routledge, 2012, p. 378). There is also a contradiction of the will in treating others as a means to an end whilst wanting to be treated as an end in oneself. Add to this the exploitation and oppression that often goes with inequalities of power in a male-orientated consumer society, and Kant would question what kind of a commonwealth of ends we are bringing about.

Kant says that friendship is a rare thing like a black swan. The danger is that we retreat into a society of individual self-interest in which connections of friendship, family, community and society are eroded. Kant also condemns the arousal of sexual desire through fantasies rather than relationally between persons. A number of modern feminist writers have drawn on Kant's view about the objectification or commodification of women in their analysis of the dehumanising effect of pornography, in which non-relational desire is focused on a fantasy. The real person is reduced to a commodity to be traded. Yet, as Kant puts it, 'we are not for sale at any price . . . we possess an inalienable dignity which instils in us reverence for ourselves'. One aspect of this reverence is to respect the autonomy of the other person. Their subjective feelings, wishes and intentions are ignored when they are treated as objects.

Kant looked for principles which had the same certainty as the principles underlying Mathematics and Logic. Such principles are of universal application and to deny them is to be self-contradictory. Kant, therefore, tried to establish certain fundamental principles which must be held and could not be refuted without falling into the trap of inconsistency. The principle that we should act with rational consistency leads us to the Kantian maxim that we should at all times act in such a manner that we should will our action to be universal law. This is the principle of universifiability. If we apply this to the issue of adultery, we must conclude that Kant considers it unacceptable. If a man commits adultery, he must accept that it would be just as morally acceptable if his own wife had sex with another man. If he did not accept this, he would be being irrational, and going against the first formulation of the Categorical Imperative.

Kant taught that one form of the Categorical Imperative was that all persons should be respected as ends in themselves. This means that no person is merely the instrument for another's interests and no person may be used as such. Every person has to be regarded as being so valuable that they constitute an absolute moral claim against all others. This is an important concept for Kant, as all individual persons enjoy rights which give substance to their moral claims on others. This relates to adultery because adultery often begins when one person stops treating his/her partner as valuable and being a person in his/her own right, which leads to the first person wanting to begin a relationship with someone else.

Kant gave the example of promise-keeping to illustrate the importance of duty in his ethics. Promises, he said, only have value if people can assume that they will be kept. If I know that Ann will break her promise, there is no point in my acting as though she would keep it. It is a necessary function of the idea of 'promise-keeping' that they are actually kept. Otherwise there is no point in promising. In breaking a promise we are denying the social institution whose value we assert in making the promise. This entails us in a self-contradictory position, and is therefore immoral. When a husband marries his wife, he makes a promise to be faithful. In committing adultery, he breaks that promise and therefore fails in his duty to his wife. He is therefore being immoral in committing adultery.

Virtue Ethics perspectives

Virtue ethicists are not concerned with any rules about the rightness or wrongness of adultery. Rather, they look at the kind of personality traits that would influence a person to commit adultery. However, if it is true that adulterers can be said to have undesirable moral characteristics, this would be taken as an indication that adultery is a morally undesirable thing to do.

The kinds of question that a Virtue ethicist might ask could include the following:

- What kind of person commits adultery? Are they, for instance, honest, temperate, kind, etc.?
- What sorts of reasons do they give for the actions they choose?
- How do they assess their action?
- Do they understand themselves to be doing something moral or immoral with their choice?
- Why do adulterers choose to have sex with people other than their spouses?
- Are their motives/desires/reasons selfish or unselfish ones?
- Do they seem to speak of their reasons for their choice honestly or do they seem to be rationalising?
- What sort of life have they been leading prior to the action which they choose; is it a life which exhibits the characteristics we admire?

(See Janet E. Smith, 'Abortion and Moral Character,' at www.mycatholicfaith.org)

> **Exercise**
>
> Research some high-profile cases of adultery and analyse the causes and consequences for the people involved. Could anything have been done to avoid the consequences? Why did people commit adultery? Do you think they are guilty of moral wrong-doing?
>
> You might start your search with British government minister John Profumo, President Bill Clinton or Conservative MP Zac Goldsmith.

Discussion Questions

1. No form of sexual behaviour can be regarded as unacceptable, sinful, or deserving of censure unless it has demonstrable ill effects on the individual who practises it or on others.

(Alex Comfort, *Sex and Society*, Penguin, 1964, p. 15)

Do you agree?

2. Writing on Christian marriage, Tim Keller suggests that people approach sexual relationships in one of two ways:

(a) *A consumer or contractual mind-set – how can I trade my looks, wealth, intelligence, status for the best possible deal? What's in it for me?*

(b) *A covenantal mind-set – in making promises of lifelong faithfulness and monogamy, mutual service creates a trusting and nurturing environment for personal, emotional, moral and spiritual growth.*

Do you think that there is truth in this analysis, or is marriage a blend of both?

3. The Gillick case

In 1985, UK Law Lords decided that girls below the legal age of consent (sixteen) could be granted contraceptive advice by their doctors without necessarily obtaining the permission or knowledge of their parents. Consider some of the arguments that were made for and against this ruling and decide on whether or not you agree with them:

Against doctors giving advice or contraceptives without parental knowledge or consent	For doctors giving advice or contraceptives without parental knowledge or consent
Parents are the legal guardians of their daughter and know her best and have her best interests at heart. They ought to be consulted.	If a girl has the courage and responsibility to approach her GP for contraceptive advice, her doctor should see this as a sign of maturity.
Freely available contraceptives and advice on how to break the law in having underage sex are being legalised – this is contradictory.	Teenage pregnancy is a serious issue in the UK – denying access to teenagers who will fear the lack of confidentiality is short-sighted.
Freely available contraceptives encourage promiscuity and put young teenagers who are already under pressure to have sex at risk of Sexually Transmitted Infections (STIs), pregnancy and abusive relationships.	The consequences are all that matters. Underage sex will go on – doctors have a responsibility to do all they can to help teenagers make informed decisions.

FURTHER READING

Margaret Farley (2008) *Just Love: A Framework for Christian Sexual Ethics*. Bloomsbury Academic

Stanley Grenz (1998) *Sexual Ethics, A Biblical Perspective*. Westminster John Knox Press

Mark D. Jordan (2002) *The Ethics of Sex*. Wiley-Blackwell

Timothy Keller (2011) *The Meaning of Marriage*. Hodder and Stoughton

Neil Messer (2007) *Doing What Comes Naturally: Exploring Sexual Ethics*, Church Times Study Guides. SCM Press

Jonathan Rowe (2014) *Sexual Ethics Revision Guide*. Push Me Press

Peter Vardy (2013) *The Puzzle of Sex*. SCM Press

Michael Wilcockson (2001) *Access to Philosophy: Sex and Relationships*. Hodder Education

OCR Past Paper Questions

JANUARY 2010
'Some ethical theories are of more help than others when making decisions about
sexual issues.' Discuss.   *[35]*

JUNE 2010
To what extent are ethical theories helpful when considering the issues surrounding
homosexuality?   *[35]*

JANUARY 2011
'Natural Law is the most reliable approach when making decisions about pre-marital
sex.' Discuss.   *[35]*

JUNE 2011
To what extent is Virtue Ethics helpful when making decisions about extra-marital sex?   *[35]*

JANUARY 2013
'Religious approaches to sexual ethics are more helpful than secular approaches.'
Discuss.   *[35]*

Glossary

Absolute pacifism   War is always morally wrong and ending an innocent life is never morally justifiable

Absolutism   The view that certain moral standards are unchanging and universal and ought never to be violated, even if it may at times be difficult to agree upon what these are or if making exceptions would avoid suffering. Moral absolutists would agree, for example, that slavery and cannibalism did not become wrong at a certain point in history – they were always so. Divine Command and Kantian Ethics are generally taken to fit this mould.

Act Utilitarianism: This is Bentham's version of Utilitarianism, which operates by taking each situation on its own merits, wishing only to achieve the greatest good of the greatest number of people involved. There are no general rules, only the situation that applies to the individual.

Active euthanasia   Someone (e.g. a relative or a doctor) brings about another person's death for the second person's benefit

Advance directive   Also called a 'living will', in which a person states their wishes about dying before they become incapable of doing so

Anthropocentric   Human-centred. In such a viewpoint, non-human nature is instrumentally valuable insofar as it supports human survival, needs and interests. Humankind are intrinsically valuable and their interests prioritised.

Apparent goods   Real goods can often be mistaken for apparent goods like seeking pleasure as an end in itself. Rather than fulfilling our nature, apparent goods recede from us.

Arêtê   Virtue, or any good characteristic or excellence. *Arêtê* involves committed and purposeful training and practice usually under the tutelage of a master-practitioner.

Assisted suicide   A deliberate act that causes death, undertaken by one person with the primary intention of ending the life of another person, in order to relieve the second person's suffering.

Authoritarian conscience   Eric Fromm's term for the internalised voice of an external authority, something close to Freud's concept of the Super-Ego. This internal voice may be backed up by fear of punishment, or spurred on by admiration of an authority figure.

Biocentric   The view that consideration of the interests of all life on earth, rather than human interests in particular, should inform our environmental decisions. A political and ethical worldview which argues for the inherent value of all living things.

Biodiversity   The diversity of living organisms in a habitat or the world, e.g. the range of plants and animals in a national park. Some estimates suggest there are 12.5

million species globally, with particularly intense biodiversity in areas such as the Amazon rainforest.

Birth   The point at which a foetus becomes a baby

Cardinal virtues   These are the most important virtues. Plato and Aristotle, followed by many ancient philosophers, regarded temperance, wisdom, justice, prudence and courage as the most desirable character traits.

Categorical Imperative   this is Kant's test for knowing whether a proposed action is good or not. He discusses three main versions of the Categorical Imperative.

Church ethics: A Protestant view that links ethics with Christian doctrine, which makes it distinct from secular ethics.

Cloning   Making a group of genetically identical cells from a single cell.

Cognitivism   Moral judgements are not just feelings – they are making truth claims and so can be true or false (though it may be difficult to prove that the judgements of religion or relativism are true or false).

Conception   The beginning of life, when the sperm and egg join together.

Conscientia   Aquinas thinks that humans use their reason to make moral decisions. We have to train ourselves to recognise our conscience.

Consciousness   Awareness of self, a key component of personhood

Contraception   The deliberate use of devices or techniques aimed at preventing a woman from becoming pregnant as a result of sexual intercourse. Examples include the pill to prevent ovulation, intrauterine devices to stop implantation in the uterus and barrier methods such as the condom, or male/female sterilisation.

Deontological ethics   Deontological ethics are concerned with fulfilling one's duty (*'deon'* in Greek means 'duty'), to obey the moral law, as opposed to justifying an action in terms of motives or consequences. Duty presupposes a fixed and universal law, and the spirit of this approach is captured in the phrase 'Let justice be done though the heavens fall.'

Deontology   The idea, central to Kant's ethics, that there should be universally applicable rules, which are true without exception and not dependent upon the consequences of actions.

Divine Command Theory   The idea that morals derive from God (or the gods); there is no standard of moral behaviour that is independent of God.

Doctrine of Double Effect   Where a doctor acts with good intentions (e.g. giving a drug to help a patient's condition) but where bad consequences arise (the drug harms the patient).

Doctrine of the mean   When talking about the moral virtues, Aristotle says that the virtuous man establishes a 'mean' or middle point between deficiency and excess, e.g. courage is the mean between cowardice (deficiency) and foolhardiness (excess).

Duty   What every human must do if they are to act morally. Involves acting according to reason and the Categorical Imperative.

Egoism   The belief that individuals have a moral duty to optimise good consequences for themselves.

Embryo   The name given to the multiplying cells between 14 days and 8 weeks

Emotivism   The view that any moral claim (e.g. 'Abortion is murder!') is essentially an *emotional* plea on the part of the one who expresses it for others to share such disapproval or adopt this feeling.

Ensoulment In traditional Christian thought, the point at which a foetus gains a soul. According to Aquinas (based on Aristotle), this was 40 days for boys and 90 days for girls.

Ethical consumerism The deliberate choice to purchase certain goods or services rather than others based upon moral beliefs and values

Ethical hedonism The view that pleasure is intrinsically good and pain bad, so you ought to aim at maximising pleasure (note that this led the ancient Greek Epicurus to lead a life of moderation free of the highs and lows of excess).

Ethical Naturalism This approach defines 'good' in terms of some natural property of the world, e.g. pleasure, human flourishing. A subjective naturalist might argue that moral statements are true in terms of the attitudes society approves of. An objectivist naturalist might argue that what is good is what will promote human flourishing in harmony with the resources of the planet.

Eudaimonia The good life – flourishing, fulfilment and happiness in a holistic sense – the flourishing of any form of life aimed at actualising its full potential

Euthanasia Bringing about the death of a person in a painless and gentle way for their benefit. Sometimes called 'mercy killing'.

Euthyphro Dilemma From a dialogue between Socrates and Euthyphro related by Plato – does God command an action because it is right, or is it right because God commands it?

Externalities The consequences (negative or positive) of commercial and industrial activity for other parties (e.g. where true costs of production are dodged by the producer).

Extra-marital sex Sexual intercourse with someone other than one's spouse or marriage partner. Traditionally called 'adultery'.

Fair-trade A movement which seeks fair treatment for developing-world workers and producers in the supply chain. It seeks fair prices, living wages, safe conditions and rights for workers, together with greater transparency and justice in trade.

Foetus The developing organism from 8 weeks after conception onward.

Gaia Hypothesis James Lovelock's theory that the earth is a self-regulating biosphere with feedback loops to maintain balances and life systems. The revenge of Gaia against the industrial-scale pollution of humans is to turn to red-hot mode (the theme of Lovelock's 1996 book).

Gene therapy The use of genes to treat or prevent disease. In the future, this technique may allow doctors to treat a disorder by inserting a gene into a patient's cells instead of using drugs or surgery.

Genetic engineering The deliberate introduction of changes to the genetic structure of cells.

Geocentric In this kind of view, the earth's resources, organic and inorganic, are treated as a whole, and life systems (human/flora and fauna) are not privileged in a separate hierarchy. This is in opposition to an anthropocentric or biocentric view.

Globalisation The interconnectedness of global finance, markets, institutions, business, technology, culture, politics, law and environment.

GMO: Genetically Modified Organism Genes are altered in plants, bacteria or other substances to enhance the organism being changed. GMOs are widely used in scientific research.

Good Will   Kant's term for acting in accordance with the moral law and out of a motive of duty, rather than pleasure or to achieve a desired outcome. The Good Will is intrinsically good. Unlike other goods like pleasure, wealth, or health, the Good Will cannot be used for bad purposes, as the Good Will is good without exception, an honourable motive even if the consequences do not turn out as hoped.

Greenwashing   When companies seek good public relations by making trivial and low-cost eco-friendly changes to products, services and processes that are merely for show

Hard determinism The view that human beings do not have any free will because they are controlled by some external force. Humans cannot be held responsible for their actions.

Hedonic Calculus   This is also known as the Felicific Calculus. It refers to Bentham's quantitative method of determining what will provide the greatest good of the greatest number, and is therefore the moral thing to do. Its seven elements help an individual to add up the pros and cons of the possible consequences of an action.

Hedonism   The term comes from *'hedone'*, the Greek word for 'happiness'. Hedonism is an ancient school of thought, allegedly founded by Aristippus of Cyrene, a pupil of Socrates, which argues that happiness is the highest good. In most forms of hedonism, happiness is interpreted as 'pleasure'.

Heteronomy   Being subject to, or under the authority of, the 'law of the other', coming from outside of the rational will (autonomy) of a person. This might be from authority figures such as parents, teachers, the Church or societal codes, or it may be from appetites or desires that are not rationally willed.

Homosexuality   Attraction towards, desire for or sexual activity with a person of one's own sex.

Humanistic conscience   Fromm's term for a person's own voice, present in every human being, and independent of external sanctions and rewards. This voice is a person's true self, found by listening to and heeding one's deepest needs, desires and goals.

Informed consent   When an informed and competent person freely chooses to enter into an action after being made fully aware of the risks and benefits that may result from it.

Intellectual virtues   Aristotle listed five intellectual virtues: practical intelligence, scientific knowledge, intuition, wisdom and art or technical skill.

Intuitionism   The view that 'good' and 'evil' are objective but indefinable. Basic moral truths are either self-evident or perceived similarly to how our senses experience the physical world.

Involuntary euthanasia   A decision is made to end the life of a person, either without their knowledge or against their wishes

IVF: In-Vitro Fertilisation A medical process whereby eggs are removed from a woman's ovaries and mixed with sperm, and the fertilised eggs are implanted into the woman's womb. It is used for couples who have fertility problems.

Jus ad bellum Justice in resorting to war. The principles according to which war might legitimately be waged: Authority, Cause, Intention, Success, Proportionality, Resort.

Jus in bello Justice during war. The principles which apply during the waging of a war.

Jus post bellum Justice after war. The principles which apply after a war has been won.

Just War theory Principles for deciding whether a war is morally acceptable, developed by St Augustine and St Thomas Aquinas.

Libertarianism The view that humans have free will, unrestrained by any external force.

Medical abortion Abortion is achieved by taking a pill (mifepristone) and inserting a tablet (prostaglandin) into the vagina 36–48 hours later. No surgery is involved

Moral objectivism The opposite of subjective ethics, this view holds that moral statements are true independently of what people think or feel.

Moral realism The view that claims are true in respect of how they correspond to the real world. Moral realists hold that moral statements can in principle be verified or falsified – there is an objective reality to them. This may, for example, derive from God's created moral order or commands, but not all realists are theists.

Moral virtues Aristotle's definition is: a disposition to behave in the right manner and as a mean between extremes of deficiency and excess, which are vices

Natural abortion Commonly referred to as a 'miscarriage', this is where the body rejects the pregnancy, usually because there is something wrong with the developing foetus.

Natural Law An ancient belief that is enjoying a revival, in which the principles of human action are in line with nature and therefore are universally valid. Human flourishing entails identifying and living according to these Primary Precepts.

Naturalistic Fallacy Claiming that what is good is arrived at by identifying a natural property, e.g. pleasure. It is fallacious in the sense that the mere fact that something is natural does not mean that we ought to do it.

Nihilism In terms of ethics, Nihilists believe that objectivity is impossible. No moral truth claims exist, or if they do they're unknowable.

Non-cognitivism The view that moral judgements are not true or false as they do not make truth claims. Instead they express emotions, preferences, commands or attitudes.

Non-voluntary euthanasia A decision is made to end the life of a person who is not in a position to make that decision themselves

Objectivism For the objectivist, objects exist independently of a subject's perception of them. In the case of moral objectivism, the claim is that moral truths exist independently of culture or personal preferences.

Palliative care Caring for a person with an incurable disease so that they maintain some QoL and are not in pain in the final stage of their life

Passive euthanasia A person (usually a doctor) allows another person to die painlessly by withdrawing treatment, which indirectly brings about that person's death

Persistent Vegetative State (PVS)   Most of a person's brain functions are absent, but the body may still function (i.e. heartbeat, breathing)

Personhood   The distinguishing characteristics that make up an individual person

PGD: Pre-Implantation Genetic Diagnosis A treatment to assist some couples to have a child, whereby genetic material (DNA or chromosomes) that occurs within each cell is tested for a known genetic or chromosome abnormality, such as those linked with Sickle Cell Anaemia or Huntington's Disease

Phronēsis   Practical judgement or wisdom generally built up through experience and observation, and seen in judgements that find the mean or middle course between deficiency and excess

Physician aid in dying   A qualified doctor administers lethal medicine in order to assist a person who wishes to commit suicide

Physician-assisted suicide   A qualified doctor prescribes a drug which assists a person to take their own life

Potential   This relates to the ability of the foetus to become a human being

Predestination   A doctrine particularly linked with St Augustine and John Calvin that argues that some people are selected before their birth for salvation by God, while others are selected for damnation.

Pre-embryo (blastocyte)   The fertilised ovum, a group of multiplying cells between 5 and 14 days after conception

Preference Utilitarianism   This is the version of Utilitarianism proposed by Peter Singer. It aims to maximise the choices made or preferences shown by individuals. The interests of all sentient beings (not just humans) need to be taken into account when ethical decisions are made. It focuses on minimising pain rather than maximising happiness. The theory is sometimes known as Negative Utilitarianism.

Preferential option for the poor   A belief championed by liberation theologians like Gustavo Guttierez (originating in 1960s Latin America), in which God was seen as choosing 'the foolish things of the world to shame the wise and the weak things of this world to shame the strong', as a result of which, in faithfully reading the Bible as a text of liberation and justice, the Church should adopt God's preferential option for the poor. It should be active in political and economic systems to challenge injustice and oppression and create a fairer society.

Pre-marital sex   Sexual relations prior to marriage. Also traditionally termed 'fornication'.

Prescriptivism   Moral statements as commands or imperatives, as opposed to descriptions. Moral terms are used to guide action and prescribe what people are to do in similar situations. An attempt to move on from emotivism and treat ethical reasoning as rational rather than a form of emotional manipulation, it sticks to 'ought' statements that one lives with consistently.

Prima facie duty   W. D. Ross' attempt to clarify a difficulty with Kant's theory. When there is a conflict of duties, Ross suggests that they are put in order of importance.

Primary Precepts   Arrived at by observing the goals towards which human action tends to gravitate (e.g. life, knowledge, social goals)

Principle of Utility   A phrase first used by Jeremy Bentham in his *Introduction to*

the Principles and Morals of Legislation, to refer to the principle that should govern society and bring the greatest amount of happiness to the greatest number of people. Bentham was a social reformer and wished that all members of society could achieve as much happiness (and avoid as much pain) as possible during their lives. This is the fundamental idea behind Utilitarianism.

Proportionalism An attempted moderation of the absolutism of Natural Law theory extension of the Doctrine of Double Effect. Aquinas allowed for theft in extremes to stave off starvation. His Just War theory also allowed for killing as long as the intentions were good and a greater good was thereby brought about.

PVS Persistent Vegetative State: most of a person's brain functions are absent, but the body may still function (i.e. heartbeat, breathing)

Quality Adjusted Life Years (QALY) A method used by physicians to calculate the Quality of Life of a patient to estimate the number of valuable months or years a patient may live

Quality of Life (QoL) This is a key concept in the debates concerning abortion and euthanasia. In the abortion debate, it can help decide whether a foetus has a 'life' distinct from the mother, and in the euthanasia debate, it can help to focus the decision of whether someone's life has any value.

Quickening The moment at which the mother can first feel the foetus move, commonly at between 16 and 20 weeks of gestation

Reason The ability to work out correct ethical decisions, with which every human is born. This is a key concept in Kantian Ethics

Relative Pacifism Whether a war is morally justifiable has to be decided on the relative merits of the case, e.g. use of nuclear weapons would never be justified, but use of Just War theory may be justified

Relativism Moral relativism goes further than merely observing the disagreements among people and in society about ethics. It goes on to suggest that moral claims are true or false relative to the standpoint of a society, community or person that holds them.

Reproductive cloning Production of an embryo which is genetically identical to the donor to transfer into a uterus. This is currently illegal.

Rule Utilitarianism: This is (arguably) Mill's version of Utilitarianism. The greatest good of the greatest number is achieved when everyone follows laws and customs that aim to maximise the happiness of everyone, not just some individuals.

Sanctity of Life (SoL) The belief that human life is made in God's image and is therefore sacred in value and inviolable. It is a gift rather than a possession. Focused on human life, it places a uniformly high value on innocent life (though disagreements exist over when this begins) regardless of its quality.

Secondary Precepts These make Primary Precepts normative in terms of what ought to be done (e.g. provision of shelter, healthcare, protection for the vulnerable). Through practical knowledge, the primary goods come to be applied.

Sentience Having the ability of being aware

Situation Ethics A radical Christian-based Utilitarian moral theory, developed by Joseph Fletcher. The only absolute moral principle is to do 'the most loving thing in any situation'.

Soft determinism The view that human beings have limited free will but are to some extent controlled by external forces. Humans are partially responsible for their actions.

Stakeholders Parties such as customers, local communities, government, suppliers, employees, civil society and shareholders who are affected by business practice and therefore have an interest or stake in it, making business more democratic and accountable.

Stewardship A reading of Genesis 1:26 in which humankind being given 'dominion' to rule over nature is interpreted as people being God's vice-regents or stewards. Responsible and caring rule, rather than selfish exploitation, ought to be characteristic.

Subjectivism Subjectivists see morality in terms of personal preferences or tastes. They reject the idea that there are objective moral values that may be established by reason. They see moral values as subjective – as Hume saw it, human behaviour was more passional than rational.

Suicide A person takes his/her own life voluntarily and intentionally

Surgical abortion Abortion is achieved by suction methods (from the 7th to 15th week of pregnancy), or by putting surgical instruments into the womb and removing the foetus (later than 15 weeks)

Sustainability Taking the long-term view in managing present economic, social equity, and environmental interests without endangering those of future generations. The three 'r's (reduce, reuse, recycle) are at the heart of this kind of movement, pithily captured in the question 'What use is a saw mill without a forest?'

Synderesis According to Aquinas, this is our inner knowledge of and natural disposition towards doing good and avoiding evil – 'that good should be done and evil avoided' – a natural disposition of humans to understand the first principles of morality instinctively.

Teleological ethics *'Telos'* is the Greek word meaning 'goal' or 'end', and teleological ethics refers to moral statements based upon consequences. Actions are justified in terms of the favourable outcomes they result in.

Telos The goal or end purpose of anything. All of nature is seen in Aristotle's thought as directed towards a final end – as goal-orientated.

Theological virtues After the New Testament was written, the four ancient virtues became known as the cardinal virtues, while faith, hope and charity/love were referred to as the theological virtues. They were developed particularly by St Thomas Aquinas and became part of Natural Law theory.

Therapeutic abortion Where an abortion is carried out in order to protect the life or health of the mother, e.g. in the case of an ectopic pregnancy

Therapeutic cloning The cloning of an embryo in order to produce stem cells for therapeutic uses, such as research into serious genetic diseases

Triple bottom line In addition to the bottom line of *profit*, in 1994, John Elkington's SustainAbility consultancy suggested that successful businesses also have a *people* account (for social responsibility to stakeholders) and a *planet* account (for environmental responsibility).

Universal ethics: A Roman Catholic view that emphasises that the moral law is understood through reason and conscience. Linked to Natural Law theory.

Universalisability   Refers to Kant's first version of the Categorical Imperative: what would happen if everyone were to do what is proposed? If a maxim is universalisable, without contradiction, it is the moral thing to do.

Viability   When the foetus is considered physically capable of living outside the womb (often with medical assistance)

Voluntary euthanasia   A person states their wish to die and a doctor brings this about

Whistle-blower   A person with insider knowledge who reveals illegality or wrong-doing in an organisation or government. Often done in the public interest and at personal cost (e.g. loss of employment).

Zygote   The fertilised ovum when it is between 0 and 5 days old

Illustration Credits

Front cover, Dennis Brown

Chapter 1
p. 7, © Mark Coffey; p. 8, Library of Congress; p. 14, Wikipedia Commons; p. 15, Wikipedia Commons; p. 15, Wikipedia Commons

Chapter 2
p. 18, Wikipedia Commons; p. 19, Wikipedia Commons; p. 20, Wikipedia Commons; p. 22, Wikipedia Commons; p. 23, Wikipedia Commons; p. 24, Wikipedia Commons; p. 25, Wikipedia Commons; p. 31, Wikipedia Commons; p. 32, Pete Souza/Wikipedia Commons

Chapter 3
p. 36, Wikipedia Commons; p. 36, Wikipedia Commons; p. 38, Wikipedia Commons; p. 40, Wikipedia Commons; p. 44, MorgueFile Free Photo; p. 45, © Zach Brown/ Stickmenwithmartinis.com; p. 46, Wikipedia Commons; p. 47, Wikipedia Commons; p. 48, Wikipedia Commons; p. 53, Wikipedia Commons

Chapter 4
p. 57, Wikipedia Commons; p. 58, Wikipedia Commons artist unknown (The English School of Painting, c. 1715–1720); p. 58, Wikipedia Commons; p. 62, © Punch Magazine; p. 67, Wikipedia Commons, p. 67; © Zach Brown/Stickmenwithmartinis. com

Chapter 5
p. 77, Wikipedia Commons; p. 78, Wikipedia Commons; p. 79, Wikipedia Commons; p. 80, James Tissot/Wikipedia Commons; p. 81, Wikipedia Commons

Chapter 6
p. 102, Wikipedia Commons; p. 103, © Istock Images; p. 104, MorgueFile Free Photo; p. 111, ekem/Wikipedia Commons

Chapter 7
p. 118, Dignitas; p. 119, Wikipedia Commons; p. 126, Wikipedia Commons

Chapter 8
p. 139, © Nick Kim; p. 145, Wikipedia Commons; p. 150, Wikipedia Commons; p. 152, Wikipedia Commons; p. 155, Wikipedia Commons; p. 155, IstockPhoto; p. 156, IstockPhoto

Chapter 9
p. 160, Michael Leunig/leunig.com; p. 164, Wikipedia Commons; p. 165, Les Todd, Duke Photography, Wikipedia Commons; p. 166, Wikipedia Commons; p. 167, Wikipedia Commons; p. 169, Bundesarchiv Germany/Wikipedia; p. 171, Wikipedia Commons; p. 173, Wikipedia Commons; p. 174, Pharos/Wikipedia Commons; p. 176, Wikipedia Commons; p. 179, Flickr Policy Exchange; p. 181, Wikipedia Commons

Chapter 10
p. 190, Wikipedia Commons; p. 195, MorgueFile Free Photo; p. 195, Wikipedia Commons; p. 198, Wikipedia Commons

Chapter 11
p. 204, Java University/Wikipedia Commons; p. 206 Wikipedia Commons; p. 209, IstockPhoto, Wikipedia Commons; p. 220, Wikipedia Commons; p. 224, Wikipedia Commons; p. 230, Wikipedia Commons

Chapter 12
p. 233, © R.J. Romero/hipstaa; p. 234, Wikipedia Commons; p. 235, © Rex May/baloocartoons.com; p. 236, © Rex May/baloocartoons.com; p. 237, Wikipedia Commons; p. 240, Wikipedia Commons; p. 242, Wikipedia Commons; p. 243, Wikipedia Commons; p. 245, Wikipedia Commons

Chapter 13
p. 249, © Universal Pictures; p. 250, Wikipedia Commons; p. 252, Wikipedia Commons; p. 253, Wikipedia Commons; p. 254, Wikipedia Commons; p. 256, Wikipedia Commons; p. 259, Wikipedia Commons; p. 259, Wikipedia Commons; p. 260, Imperial War Museum/Wikipedia Commons; p. 263, © Mark Coffey; p. 271, Wikipedia Commons; p. 273, Wikipedia Commons

Chapter 14
p. 279, NASA/Wikipedia Commons; p. 281, Wikipedia Commons; p. 283, © Twentieth Century Fox; p. 284, Wikipedia Commons; p. 287, Wikipedia Commons; p. 289, Wikipedia Commons; p. 290, Wikipedia Commons; p. 293, Wikipedia Commons; p. 298, Matt Yohe/ Wikipedia Commons; p. 300, Twentieth Century Fox; p. 300, Twentieth Century Fox

Chapter 15
p. 307, Incorporated Television Company; p. 308, Wikipedia Commons; p. 312, Wikipedia Commons

Index